THE COMPLETE
ESTATE PLANNING
GUIDE

REVISED AND UPDATED

The
COMPLETE ESTATE PLANNING GUIDE

REVISED AND UPDATED

KATHLEEN ADAMS, CFP®

 NEW AMERICAN LIBRARY

New American Library
Published by New American Library, a division of
Penguin Group (USA) Inc., 375 Hudson Street,
New York, New York 10014, USA
Penguin Group (Canada), 10 Alcorn Avenue, Toronto,
Ontario M4V 3B2, Canada (a division of Pearson Penguin Canada Inc.)
Penguin Books Ltd., 80 Strand, London WC2R 0RL, England
Penguin Ireland, 25 St. Stephen's Green, Dublin 2,
Ireland (a division of Penguin Books Ltd.)
Penguin Group (Australia), 250 Camberwell Road, Camberwell, Victoria 3124,
Australia (a division of Pearson Australia Group Pty. Ltd.)
Penguin Books India Pvt. Ltd., 11 Community Centre, Panchsheel Park,
New Delhi - 110 017, India
Penguin Group (NZ), cnr Airborne and Rosedale Roads, Albany,
Auckland 1310, New Zealand (a division of Pearson New Zealand Ltd.)
Penguin Books (South Africa) (Pty.) Ltd., 24 Sturdee Avenue,
Rosebank, Johannesburg 2196, South Africa

Penguin Books Ltd., Registered Offices: 80 Strand, London WC2R 0RL, England

First published by New American Library, a division of Penguin Group (USA) Inc.

First Printing, February 2005
10   9   8   7   6   5   4   3   2   1

NEW AMERICAN LIBRARY and logo are trademarks of Penguin Group (USA) Inc.

LIBRARY OF CONGRESS CATALOGING-IN-PUBLICATION DATA:
Adams, Kathleen, 1943-
The complete estate planning guide / Kathleen Adams.—Rev. and updated.
p.   cm.
ISBN 0-451-21403-X (trade pbk.)
1. Estate planning—United States—Popular works.   2. Tax planning—United States—Popular works.
I. Title.
KF750.Z9A33 2005
332.024'016—dc22

Set in Adobe Garamond
Designed by Patrice Sheridan

Printed in the United States of America

PUBLISHER'S NOTE

This publication is designed to provide accurate and authoritative information in regard to the subject matter covered. It is sold with the understanding that the publisher is not engaged in rendering legal, accounting or other professional services. If you require legal advice or other expert assistance, you should seek the services of a competent professional.

To Robbie, who "wrote the book" on estate planning,
and at the age of 94 was still enjoying the estate he built—
while, like his father before him, breaking every rule in the book.

CONTENTS

Foreword   xiii

Preface to the Revised Edition   xvii

PART ONE: CREATING YOUR ESTATE   1

1. THE CURRENT DILEMMA:
   CREATING AN ESTATE IN TODAY'S WORLD   3
   The Statistics of Security • The Current Dilemma • Three Horns of the Dilemma • The Great Equalizer • Toward a Solution: For a Current Dilemma, Current Techniques of Planning • Needed: A Whispering Slave

2. GETTING STARTED   15
   The Dynamics of the Five Firsts: Home, Income, Disability Insurance, Savings Account, Life Insurance • To Resolve the Dynamics: Determination, Plus Objectives • Three People and Their Objectives • The Right and Wrong of It • Starting Point: Inventory Your Assets • Analyzing the Inventory: Your Estate Picture

3. LIFE INSURANCE:
   THE UNIVERSAL ESTATE BUILDER   23
   The Uses of Life Insurance • Types of Life Insurance •
   Insurance Riders • Modes of Settlement and Options •
   Dividends and What to Do about Them • Premiums and
   How to Finance Them • Insurance and the Income Tax •
   Insurance and the Estate Tax • How Much Insurance? •
   The Realistic Approach: Assessing Your Family's Needs

4. YOUR OCCUPATION AND ITS OPPORTUNITIES:
   THE COMPANY COMPENSATION AND
   EMPLOYEE BENEFIT PACKAGE   45
   The Contents of the Package • Profit Sharing: Qualified
   and Unqualified • Defined Benefit Pension Plans • 401(k)
   Plans • 403(b) Plans • Section 457 Nonqualified
   Deferred Compensation Plans • Savings and Thrift Plans •
   SIMPLE 401(k) Defined Contribution Plans • 401(k)
   Safe Harbor Plans • SIMPLE IRA • Simplified Pension
   Plans (SEPs) • Employee Stock Ownership Plans
   (ESOPs) • Nonqualified Deferred Compensation • Group
   Life Insurance • Group Medical, Health, and Accident
   Insurance • Group Disability Income Insurance •
   Individual Retirement Accounts (IRAs) and Roth IRAs •
   Summing Up

5. YOUR OCCUPATION AND ITS OPPORTUNITIES:
   SELECTIVE BARGAINING FOR THE EXECUTIVE   79
   The Executive's Goals • Bonuses: Cash, Stock, Deferred, or
   Restricted • Stock Options • Other Stock Plans •
   Deferred Compensation • 162 Executive Bonus Plans •
   Restricted Endorsement Benefit Arrangements • Long-Term
   Care Insurance as an Executive Benefit • The Estate Built
   from Bargaining

6. YOUR OCCUPATION AND ITS OPPORTUNITIES:
   SELF-HELP FOR THE SELF-EMPLOYED   99
   The Professional: Their Avenues to Security • The

Independent Businessperson • The Meaning of Double Taxation • Retirement Benefits for the Independent Businessperson • The Payoff

7. INVESTMENTS:
    MAKING YOUR CAPITAL WORK FOR YOU   117
    Surplus Capital: The Basis of Investments • Estate Planning Principles of Investment • Investments and Taxation • Types of Investments • Selecting a Mutual Fund • Qualified Tuition Programs: Section 529 Plans • Other Tax-Favored Ways to Pay for College • Investment Advice and Assistance

8. INVESTMENTS:
    PUTTING YOUR CAPITAL IN REAL ESTATE   150
    The First Real Estate Investment: The Home • Home Ownership: Individual • Home Ownership: The Cooperative Apartment • Home Ownership: The Condominium • Unimproved Real Estate • Improved Real Estate • Ownership: Sole or Participating? • Partnerships • The Syndicate • The Real Estate Corporation • Real Estate Investment Trusts (REITs) • Master Limited Partnerships • Mortgage-Backed Securities • A Special Consideration: Where to Get Advice • Looking Ahead

9. THE DAY THE WORK STOPS:
    DISABILITY AND RETIREMENT   164
    Disability • Retirement • A Last Word on Retirement: Deciding Where to Live

10. LONG-TERM CARE:
    THE RETIREMENT BUDGET BUSTER   182
    The Need for Long-Term Care • How Do You Cover the Costs of Long-Term Care Out of Pocket? • How Do Health Insurance, Medicare, and Medicare Supplemental Insurance Cover Long-Term Care? • How Does Long-Term Care Insurance Cover the Costs of Care? • A Frequent Financial

*Planning Tool • Future Needs for Long-Term Care: Is
Long-Term Care Coverage Here to Stay? Yes, and Congress
Thinks So, Too. • What Is a Long-Term Care Need?
What Sort of Care Does It Involve? • Where Can You Get
Long-Term Care Insurance? • What Long-Term Care
Insurance Benefits Are Available? What Should You Look for
in a Policy? • How Do You Select Benefits to Include in a
Policy? • How Do You Qualify to Receive Benefits Once You
Are Covered? • When Should You Purchase Long-Term
Care Insurance? • Making It Personal: Getting Insurance
Quotes • How Do You Make a Final Decision When
Purchasing a Policy?*

**PART TWO: CONSERVING AND
TRANSFERRING YOUR ESTATE   205**

11.   ESTATE TRANSFERENCE:
      THE PROBLEM AND THE GOALS   207
      *Estate Conservation • The Problem of Erosion • Analyzing
      Your Objectives • Planning for Your Beneficiaries •
      Secondary Objectives • Where to Begin*

12.   THE UNIFIED ESTATE AND GIFT TAX AND
      HOW IT WORKS   213
      *Questions and Answers on the Gift Tax • Should I Make
      Gifts and How Much Should I Give? • What Does the Gift
      Tax Tax? • How Is the Value of a Gift Determined? • How
      Does the Annual Exclusion Work? • How Are Gifts Made
      Before 1977 Treated? • When Must a Gift Tax Return Be
      Filed? • What About Annual Gifts That May Increase in
      Value? • What About Gifts Made Within Three Years of
      Death? • Can Husband-Wife Gift-Splitting Be Used for All
      Gifts? • Are Transfers by Sale Ever Taxed as Gifts? • Are
      Gifts in Trust Subject to the Gift Tax? • What About Joint
      Ownership of Property? • What About Gifts Made During
      Life but Not Payable Until the Death of the Donor? • Is
      There a State Gift Tax as Well as a Federal One?*

13. GIVING DURING YOUR LIFETIME:
THE BENEFITS OF FAMILY OWNERSHIP
OF PROPERTY   224
*The Personal Side • The Economic Side • What to Give
and How to Give It • Other Types of Transfers: Sales, Sales
and Leasebacks, Annuities • Gifts to Minors: A Special
Problem • Family Planning • Family Communication*

14. USING TRUSTS TO TRANSFER YOUR ESTATE   238
*Living Trusts • What Is a Trust? • The Revocable Living
Trust Agreement • Qualified Terminal Interest Property
Trusts (QTIPs) • The Generation-Skipping Transfer Tax •
The Irrevocable Trust • Trusts with Grantor Retained
Interests • Accumulation Trusts • Life Insurance Trusts •
The Small Trust • Protecting Your Beneficiaries • A
Special Device: The Sprinkling Trust • Guaranteeing
Privacy • Previewing the After-Death Estate*

15. WHY EVERYONE NEEDS A WILL   263
*The State of Intestacy • With a Will There's a Way •
Women and Wills • Wills and Joint Property • Beware of
Joint and Mutual Wills • Don't Procrastinate*

16. AN OUNCE OF PREVENTION:
MEETING THE PROBLEM OF TAX EROSION   275
*What Are the Taxes? • What the Estate Tax Taxes •
Deductions • The Federal Unified Credit • First Step in
Tax Planning: The Dry Run • Second Step in Tax
Planning: Reducing Taxes • The Need for Tax Planning*

17. ASSESSING YOUR ESTATE:
WHAT TO LEAVE AND HOW TO LEAVE IT   291
*The "Distributable" Estate • Establishing Liquidity •
Reviewing Your Beneficiaries • Freedom of Disposition •
Previewing Your Transfers • The Final Picture*

18.   IT PAYS TO BE CHARITABLE   309
*What Is Charity? • The Timing of Your Gift • Lifetime
Giving: The Income Tax Approach • Charity After Death:
Helping to Conserve the Estate • Using a Charitable
Trust: The Charitable Remainder Trust • The Charitable
Lead Trust • The Charitable Foundation and the Family
Business • Charitable Gifts Through Insurance • Charity:
Which Way?*

19.   WHAT TO DO WITH YOUR BUSINESS:
THE SOLE PROPRIETORSHIP, THE FAMILY
ENTERPRISE, THE PART OWNERSHIP   326
*The Sole Proprietor • The Head of the Family Enterprise •
The Part Owner • Continuation for the Family •
Management and the Family Enterprise • Economic
Cushions • Liquidity and Taxes • Estate Tax Exclusion for
"Qualified Family-Owned Businesses" • Continuation and
Your Will or Living Trust • Sale at Death • Lifetime
Transfers: Sales and Gifts • Going Public • How to Value
Your Business • Keep It Workable*

20.   CHOOSING YOUR ESTATE MANAGERS   348
*The Executor • The Trustee • The Guardian • Choosing
Your Fiduciaries: How Many? • Choosing Your Fiduciaries:
Who? • Fiduciary Powers • Commissions: Fiduciary
Compensation • Finally*

21.   A LAST WORD ON ESTATE PLANNING:
DON'T DO IT ALL YOURSELF   360
*The Attorney • The Accountant • The Life Insurance
Underwriter • The Bank or Trust Officer • The
Investment Advisor • The Estate Planning Team*

Appendix   367

Index   435

FOREWORD

This book is about something that almost everyone has or wants to have: an estate.

The word is perhaps an unfortunate one, for it fails to indicate the universality of the subject. It summons up images of landed gentry, of vast fortunes or great property holdings. It is commonly associated with death; a man's estate is what he leaves behind him.

An estate is all of these things, certainly, but it is also much more and much less. The family savings account, a house, an insurance policy, the benefits from a job, even the monthly payments to a widow from Social Security—these are part of an estate as well. In fact, if you own any capital at all, you have an estate. Everyone wants a large estate because having one means financial security—security for one's self and one's family during life and the family after one's death.

How to accumulate capital, how to build an estate, how to increase it, how to keep it, how to enjoy it, and how to pass it on—this is estate planning, something we do all our lives. When you buy stocks, change jobs, start a business or sell one, pick a street to live on, give money away, you are planning your estate, whether you realize it or not.

Unfortunately, most people don't really *plan* their estate. Or at best, they do it spasmodically, when and if the spirit moves them—now writing a will, now making an investment, now buying an insurance policy. One action bears little relation to the other. The result is a crazy quilt; it lacks a visible and orderly pattern. Opportunities are lost, capital is dissipated and the goal of the plan—family security—is threatened.

Thus, the purpose of this book is to set forth the principles of estate planning, to point out how they can be applied, and, finally, to emphasize the very real and sizable gains to be had from the estate plan that is conscious and continuous as opposed to the one that is casual and makeshift.

We can think of no area where this approach is more meaningful than that of tax planning. Our government not only allows but, indeed, has consciously *created* opportunities for lessening the impact of taxation. It is up to the planner, however, to use these opportunities in every aspect and at every stage of his estate planning.

On this question one of the great jurists of our country, Judge Learned Hand, wrote: "Anyone may so arrange his affairs that his taxes shall be as low as possible; he is not bound to choose that pattern which will best pay the Treasury; there is not even a patriotic duty to increase one's taxes."

This does not mean that the government should be considered an adversary to be defeated by manipulation, subterfuge, or clever tax tricks. The well-planned use of available tax shelters makes this type of tax thinking both unwise and unnecessary.

This is what we hope the reader will gain from the extensive treatment of taxes that every chapter contains—not a series of gimmicks but an explanation of numerous clear-cut and acceptable examples of when, where, and how to save taxes at each point in the estate plan.

This book is not a technical treatise on estate planning—that would take volumes and would be for the use of experts. Look at it, rather, as a map—a contour map which reproduces the estate-planning landscape in broad perspective. All the main outlines are there, the avenues laid out, the guideposts indicated.

There is something in this book for nearly everybody: for the person of wealth, for the corporate executive or professional, for someone who is about to retire, and for the person who is just beginning his working life; for the independent businessperson and for the possessor of an inherited fortune. The problems of each are different. For all of them there are suggestions and directions on how to evolve and develop their own individual estate plans.

No one should sit down with this book and plan to read it straight through. A young person at the start of a career will probably want to read the first part thoroughly, but the established professional who already has an estate can skip this entire section if he wants to, and concentrate on the latter part. A corporate executive isn't going to be interested in the parts that deal with the independent businessperson or professional. They, in turn, will find large sections of the book which do not bear on their problems.

Then, too, the reader may find that some parts of the book have meaning for him today; others will take on greater importance five, ten, fifteen years from now. It is our hope that readers will use the book not only for current information, but as a reference to principles which they can call on repeatedly during various stages of their lives and careers.

There is one element of the book that is meant for every reader, the "Estate Planning Worksheets," which are in the Appendix and are an important part of the book. They are designed to give you your estate picture at a glance. Used properly they can give you the information you will need to do your planning.

Don't just fill out the Worksheets, use them once, and then forget them. You must keep them up-to-date, just as you must keep your entire plan up-to-date. For estate planning is like life itself—continuous, changing, dynamic. The person who seriously sets about an estate planning program can never say the job is done.

The organization of the book is somewhat unorthodox, since it separates estate planning into two distinct parts—creation and transfer—and gives equal stress to both these aspects of estate planning. The more usual pattern is to give estate transfer the primary emphasis, relegating estate creation to a lesser, subsidiary role.

Our deviation from this pattern is due to the thesis of this book: family financial security. It is not enough just to have an estate to pass on; it must obviously be an estate of sufficient size for security and enjoyment during one's lifetime, and so that, when transferred, it will truly provide security to survivors. Thus, the emphasis on estate building.

In addition, we have treated the two aspects separately because the problems they deal with, while interrelated, are separate. They affect different people in different ways and are made clearer by this somewhat arbitrary divorcement.

Out of it all, we hope that you will develop your own philosophy of estate planning. It is up to you to do this, based on your personal evaluation of the long-range economic trends of our society. We have tried to suggest some of these directions in the book. It is obvious, for example, that we are now, and have been for some time, in a period of lower inflation. However, any long-range planning you do must still consider the effect of a continuing and possibly accelerating inflation. Times can change; we all know that. So can laws, especially tax laws. Hence the need for periodic reevaluations to adapt your plan to changing times and opportunities.

And finally, we want to say that this book has been more than an individual effort, and is, we hope, the better for that. To Dorothea Garber Cracas, we are indebted for bringing her practiced legal abilities to the meticulous research and elaboration of its material. Without her dedication to the project, it is doubtful that the book would have been begun or could have been finished. We owe a special debt of gratitude to Madelon Bedell, public relations consultant and former member of the editorial staff of *Fortune Magazine*, who contributed her literary skills to the writing and organization of the book. Whatever felicity of style it contains is due to her.

Kathleen Adams
Robert Brosterman

Authors' note: The material in this book applies equally to men and women. If the personal pronouns *he* and *his* are used most frequently it is because *he or she* and *his or hers* is often awkward.

PREFACE TO THE REVISED

EDITION

This paperback edition includes all the material from the original hard-cover book, but has been extensively revised to keep abreast of changes in laws and taxation in the forty years since it was first published. The second edition takes into account the many changes brought about by the Economic Growth and Tax Relief Reconciliation Act of 2001 (EGTRRA 2001). It also contains revisions related to changes in our way of life, recent dramatic events in investment markets, economic changes and world events.

In setting down in print a book about estate planning, an author must contend with the fact that the law is ever-evolving. The basic principles of and reasons for estate planning, however, remain the same. The need for a will and trusts and the elements in their planning have not changed since this book first went to press; nor has there been a change in the need to build an estate toward retirement, for protection in case of disability, or for family security on the death of a breadwinner.

We all know that building an estate and attaining estate objectives are often frustrated by tax erosion. In this respect, EGTRRA 2001 has imposed new and unusual pressures on the best-laid estate plans. The fact that it contains provisions for gradually providing tax relief to the end of

2010, then rescinds them all, makes long-term planning a challenge. Planners will need to seize certain opportunities and lock them in before EGTRRA "sunsets" after December 31, 2010. After that time, estate plans will need to be reviewed to be sure they comply with previous laws. Meanwhile new tax laws will come; although possibly meant to simplify tax planning, they are likely to complicate it further. In these circumstances, a current review of your existing plan is required and continuing attention should be given to the way interpretations of the existing laws, and the enactment of new laws, will affect your estate and family planning.

As never before, you will need expert advice to lead you through the tax maze to the attainment of your objectives. This book can help you to understand your tax and estate planning problems and how and where to seek advice and solutions.

Some advantages of the recent tax laws lie in more favorable tax treatment for the charitable donation of appreciated assets; lower long-term capital gains and dividend rates; the $500,000 exclusion of gain on sale of a principal residence if married, filing jointly ($250,000 if single); a graduated increase in the estate tax exemption from $1,500,000 in 2004–5 to $2,000,000 in 2006–8, $3,500,000 in 2009, no estate tax in 2010, then a return to $1,000,000 in 2011; qualified college tuition programs under Section 529 of the tax code; a higher $2,000 contribution level for the Coverdell Education Savings Account (formerly the Education IRA) for children under age 18 and greater access to IRA funds for higher education expenses; and increased generation-skipping exemptions through 2009, then repeal for 2010, then back to $1,000,000 in 2011 with indexing for inflation.

Despite the tax relief provisions made in 2001, there is still a need to focus on personal savings for retirement and on cost-effective estate planning. Using qualified retirement plans, IRAs, tax-deferred annuities, cash-value life insurance, and charitable donation strategies for retirement savings can provide tax leverage. Moving assets you don't need out of your estate while you are still alive and providing for the cost-effective payment of estate taxes with funds outside your own estate will minimize the impact of estate taxes.

Of special interest for all taxpayers are the income tax rates. As of January 1, 2004, they are as follows: For single taxpayers, they are 10% on income up to $7,150; 15% on income between $7,151 and $29,050; 25% on income from $29,051 to $70,350; 28% on income between

$70,351 and $146,750; 33% on income between $146,751 and $319,100; and 35% on incomes over $319,100.

Taxpayers filing joint returns pay 10% on income up to $14,300; 15% on income between $14,301 and $58,100; 25% on income between $58,101 and $117,250; 28% on income between $117,251 and $178,650; 33% on income between $178,651 and $319,100; and 35% on income over $319,100.

Trusts and estates are subject to a lowered top rate of 35% on taxable income over $9,550.

Capital gains and dividends now receive more favorable taxation at 15% for those in tax brackets of 25% or higher, and 5% for those in the 10 or 15% tax brackets.

For more details on the 2004 income tax and estate tax rates, see pages 367–370 of the Appendix.

In the considerable task of creating this second edition, I gratefully acknowledge Donald Harrington, whose skilled reading of and comment on the material helped to assure its clarity.

Kathleen Adams
June 2004

Part One

CREATING YOUR ESTATE

The Current Dilemma: Creating an Estate in Today's World

Does security have a price tag?

And if so, what is the amount? How much money does it take in today's world to meet personal and family needs, now and in the event of a person's death, his retirement, or his disability?

Is the $60,000-a-year person secure? Or should the figure be put at $90,000, perhaps $150,000? If married, should both spouses expect to work to provide security? Somewhere in the income structure, the security threshold must exist, for surely the $250,000-a-year person is secure, rich even. Otherwise, what is the point of success?

We have had this question posed to us innumerable times over the years. Sometimes it is asked in casual conversation, but just as frequently it comes up in discussions with clients. It is a haunting issue of our times, a problem that occupies the thinking of nearly every successful person and every struggling person, especially in times when job security is not a given, and multiple careers in a lifetime are real possibilities. Recently, the financial security question was asked by four different people in various stages of successful careers.

Let's take a look at them. They are all real people, incidentally, clients or friends whom we'll call by their generic rather than their individual names. In so doing, our purpose is more than disguise; it is also to underline the universality of their situation. One of them might be you, and if not you, surely someone you know.

Mr. Junior Executive: A Person with Great Expectations

He is our $60,000-a-year person. Just past thirty years old, a young executive in a small but growing advertising agency, Mr. Junior Executive is talented, ambitious, and energetic. In the manner of his profession, he may shift from one agency to another, but he expects to at least double his income in five years.

Junior Executive's financial situation is a bit tangled. He and his wife just had a second child. To give his family more room and a better environment, he recently gave up their four-room apartment in the city and bought a modest house in the suburbs. Price $215,000, $40,000 down. The house and the inevitable purchases that accompany it—furniture, automobile, appliances, garden equipment—have taken all of Junior Executive's savings and more. His wife has recently gone back to work to help make the added purchases and improvements to their home. She earns $35,000 per year as an administrative assistant in an office. They are in credit card debt to the tune of $15,000. If Junior Executive should die now, all that he would have to leave his family would be the house (with only a few hundred dollars of the mortgage paid off), plus $165,000 worth of personal and group life insurance—a net liquid, after final expenses and paying off their credit cards, of about $140,000; counting the equity in their house, $180,000. But then, at his age, the chances of an untimely death are unlikely. Or so he reasons.

There is also his occupation. It has not escaped Junior Executive's attention that the only people in his office who are over 50 are the owners of the company. Advertising and the communications field in general are a young person's business. Junior Executive realizes that he has to make it within the next twenty years or face an uncertain future. But he is confident of his ability to succeed, and on the whole, this confidence overrides any anxiety he might have about his security—present and future. His wife's earning capacity gives them something to fall back on, but not enough to cover the family's needs, and they would both prefer that she stay home to raise the children—an important goal for each of them.

Mr. Corporate Executive: Expectations Realized

Mr. Corporate Executive is a true successor to Mr. Junior Executive. He might well be the same man, fifteen years later. At 45 years old he is making $150,000 a year. There are some differences between them, however. Corporate Executive is an organization man, a plant manager with a big corporation. He feels some measure of job security and a sense of where his career in the organization can go. The company for which he has worked for twenty years is well established and has better corporate fringe benefits than the design firm where Junior Executive works. He is less worried about getting fired or shifting jobs, since his leadership abilities have directly contributed to the success of the business. He has become a key person in the ongoing profitability of the company. Barring a substantial turn of fortune, his position feels safe. He also banks on the security of the better corporate fringe benefits to deal with death or disability and for a secure retirement.

Corporate Executive is a suburban home owner, too, but on a higher status level. His house is located in a more exclusive section of town. It has grown to a value of $380,000—mortgage $250,000. He owns two cars—a new minivan which his wife uses and a three-year-old European car that he drives to and from work every day.

He has more expenses than Junior Executive. There is a son in college, a daughter who will be entering next year. The two younger children are in public school, but their music and dancing lessons, plus their summer camp, cost about $12,000 per year.

Assets? The house, of course, $15,000 in an equity index mutual fund, about the same in his checking account, stocks worth $40,500 at the current market value, $200,000 in personal and group life insurance, pension and profit sharing in his company of about $175,000.

Less debts and other estate expenses, Corporate Executive's estate will amount to about $582,000.

Ms. Professional: Nonorganization Woman

She is a successful physician who works outside health insurance networks, is only a year or so older than Mr. Corporate Executive, but at a higher income level. Her yearly net earnings amount to $300,000. Her husband teaches at a nearby college and makes $60,000 a year.

Ms. Professional's scale of living is correspondingly higher than

Corporate Executive. She and her husband have a $550,000 house; they belong to a country club; they entertain frequently; she drives an SUV, her husband a sports car; and they have a twenty-four-foot sailing sloop. For her own part, she could do without some of these things, but she believes her status in her community—and by implication her future success in her profession—demands a display of this sort of affluence.

Unlike Corporate Executive, Professional has none of the benefits of corporate paternalism, no pension plan, no profit sharing. She belatedly started a self-employed retirement plan last year and has $20,000 to her credit. This plus $30,000 of group insurance through her medical society, $200,000 of personal insurance, $50,000 in securities, the $250,000 equity in her house, and $60,000 equity in the cars and the boat make up her estate.

Her debts amount to $55,000, which she borrowed last year to meet some pressing bills. It all adds up to a net of about $600,000 assuming final expenses and debts. This is the amount that would be left for her husband and her two teenage children if she died.

Ms. Professional, a heart specialist, knows all too well that she is reaching a dangerous age. One statistic on fatalities among doctors sticks in her mind: the death rate of physicians in the 55 to 70 age bracket is 15 percent higher than that of the general population. She also realizes that she cannot keep on working at her present pace. She doesn't dare think that if she were disabled, there would only be invested assets plus social security to support the family for the rest of her life. She and her husband have been depending upon her income to fund college costs for their children when the time comes.

These thoughts occupy Professional's mind at night when she should be getting her sleep, and that is why her blood pressure goes up and she gets irritable when she reads about "money-grubbing doctors."

Mr. and Mrs. Successful: The American Dream Personified

At 55, Mr. and Mrs. Successful are the couple who have everything: jobs as executives in one of the country's largest corporations, which pay them a combined $450,000 per year, two homes—a house in the country and an apartment in the city—a part-time gardener and a full-time cook-housekeeper. They belong to a country club and a club in the city. Their two teenagers, 15 and 17, attend boarding school and are bound for private colleges.

The Successfuls are constantly on the go, partly because they want to be and partly because they have to be. They have practically no leisure time. All their pleasures are cast in the framework of business. He plays golf with business contacts three times a week, not because he wants to, but because he finds it is good business. Several times a year she goes to conventions where she eats too much and stays up too late. Her husband goes with her on these junkets and she accompanies him out to dinner when he entertains his business prospects, or on weekends at the beach spent with other business contacts.

It's not only that this life is wearing; it also costs them money. The company pays for some of these expenses, but not all. It doesn't pay a cent of the $25,000 a year she spends on the clothes she must have to fill her proper role as an executive. Nor does it pay for marginal business entertainment, the two cars, or for many of their club expenses, not to mention the largesse they must display during the holidays or the many "little extras" that add up to $20,000 a year.

By any ordinary standards, the Successfuls are secure. Let's see how secure. There is $50,000 of ordinary life insurance and $200,000 of group insurance each, a total of $500,000. Their stock options are now worth $100,000 and their estate could get $50,000 out of them if they died. The house is worth $425,000, but there is a mortgage of $200,000. (The apartment is a rented one.)

There is $150,000 they have paid into the retirement plans. His securities are worth $23,000. Add it all up, count in $50,000, the value of their personal property, the $5,000 in their checking account, and it comes to a nice-sounding sum of $933,000.

Now, subtract their debts of $45,000 (the Successfuls have them too; like many people in their economic bracket, they have to borrow at income tax time), their funeral and estate administration expenses, and taxes. Total net estate of the Successfuls: $720,000. About $653,000 would go to the surviving spouse.

THE STATISTICS OF SECURITY

So far we have spoken only of the total estate each person will leave if he dies now. This total sum represents the capital they have created. Some of these estates, especially the Successfuls', seem impressive: $720,000 is quite a large sum. Now let's analyze this capital (assuming all of it can be productively invested) in terms of the income it will produce for their families. This, after all, is the true measure of security.

Assuming an income after taxes of 5 percent on investments, Junior Executive's family will collect about $9,000 per year; Corporate Executive's family, about $29,125; Professional's husband and children will have $30,000; the Successfuls' survivors, should both of them die, will receive about $36,000. This assumes they liquidate houses and retirement plans and do not spend down the principal. In addition, all of the families qualify for social security in varying amounts, at varying times, depending on the ages of the surviving spouse and children. The *most* it will ever be for any of them, however, is $18,324 per year for survivors with children under age 16 (possibly partially taxable) for differing periods and at different times, as we shall later see.

Will they be secure?

According to the Bureau of Labor Statistics, it takes an income of $43,000–$52,000 per year to support a family of four on a moderate level in most urban areas. This is more than the estates of Junior Executive, Corporate Executive, Professional and the Successfuls will provide. Yet this sum isn't really enough to supply what most of us consider to be "necessities" for our families. There is no room in it for college educations, for advantages that will enrich the lives of our children, for emergencies, not even for the kind of food, shelter, and environment that we consider healthy. It represents survival only. Is that the fruit of success today?

If these people are in a paradoxical position, they are not alone. Many people with careers are with them, not only in financial insecurity, but also in levels of net financial affluence. That is what makes the whole picture so challenging. Things are good for them, their incomes have steadily risen. Double jobs and working spouses have contributed to increases for families able to sustain ongoing employment. Median family income is more than double that of fifteen years ago. Working wives contribute about 40 percent to the total of their families' incomes. In addition there are approximately ten million single and widowed women who work to support themselves and their families. They are faced with the same problems as their male counterparts in building an estate and creating security for themselves and their families.

Now look at the other side of the picture. Consumer debt had grown from $685 billion in 1985 to $9 trillion in 2003. In the housing area, total mortgage debt rose from $47.4 billion in 1985 to $6.8 trillion in 2003. This has been especially encouraged by very low interest rates and inflated values in the fair market price of homes in several areas of the country. In an era when retirement plans have become common, families whose head is 65 or older show an average income of $22,200.

In short, though it is possible to make or get money now, at the same time it has never been more difficult to keep it. Recent job losses in the manufacturing sector of the economy have added to the problem, causing many families to drain their savings while looking for alternative employment. Energy costs have been rising; investments and interest-bearing accounts and securities have been paying low yields, making it difficult to make ends meet for many people.

THE CURRENT DILEMMA

Most of these people—the Junior Executives, the Corporate Executives, the Professionals, and the Successfuls and all their counterparts—are not careless spendthrifts or hedonists by nature, as some would have it. Their trouble is simple to define, but not so simple to solve. Despite their relatively high earnings, they have been unable to accumulate capital which might be expected from such earnings. Capital, not earnings, is what produces security. *Earning power diminishes or ceases with death, disability, or retirement.* Only a large amount of capital has the ability to produce a sufficient income in these instances. This is the missing element in the lives of these people, and that is why none of them have been able to establish security for themselves and their families.

This is the current dilemma. It is a dilemma composed of three horns so strong and tenacious that most members of our society have been unable to escape their clutches.

THREE HORNS OF THE DILEMMA

The First Horn: The High Cost of Living

Everybody talks about it. We all know it. Money doesn't go as far these days as it used to. Your parents fed a family of four on $20 a week, and there were meat and potatoes, not to mention dessert, on the table every day. It costs at least eight times that amount to buy food for your family.

The word is inflation. Measured by its arithmetic, today's salaries are worth a good deal less than they appear to be. The cost of living has more than tripled since 1960, reducing the value of the dollar to less than thirty cents. Today an after-tax income of $34,000 is worth $7,500 in the purchasing power of the 1960 dollar.

The Second Horn: The High Cost of Living High

But, although it is true that the high cost of living reduces the effect of affluence, it doesn't cancel it out. No equalizing process is involved here. Inflation notwithstanding, the nation is still far better off than it used to be. The rise in median family income since 1960 has surpassed the rise in the cost of living by 50 percent.

The trouble goes deeper. It's not so much the cost of living; it's the high cost of living high. The meals your spouse serves not only cost more; they are composed of richer, more varied fare. Your parents owned one car and thought themselves well off. You need two to supply the needs of your family. You went to college; your daughter feels she needs both a bachelor's and an advanced degree to succeed in her profession. TVs, cable service, cell phones, computers, vacations for the family are considered necessities even in low income groups. Going up in the economic scale, the same applies to the private club, the second house, and private school for children.

In higher echelons, the definition of necessities becomes even broader. It embraces luxury travel, the pleasure yacht, the wardrobes, the large-scale entertainment, the sumptuous homes. Gross materialism? Perhaps, but if so, such materialism is the very fabric of society, particularly the society of success. In large measure, an open display of affluence is expected of the successful person. Some of it, although not all, is unavoidable if one is to continue the climb upward in the economic strata. It takes determination and willpower to separate the true demand, the true necessity of displaying affluence from its simulated counterpart, the social and commercial pressure to spend.

The Third Horn: High Taxation

If it costs an individual more to live today, exactly the same applies to society as a whole; or, in more precise terms, to the government that administers, sustains, and protects the economic life of the people. Thus the third horn, and one we all know and talk about too, the inevitable accompaniment of the successful life. In a word, taxes.

Spell out its implications in figures, and the present-day tax impact on capital and earning power is clear. In 1939, a married man with two children earning a salary of $25,000 paid out about $1,700 in income taxes. In 2003 a person on the same salary will pay some $3,750 in taxes. Do you want to earn a net of $100,000? Then you must gross at least $128,000.

This is what economists call the "tax squeeze." The phrase is apt. A person's earnings, his profits or his inheritance are caught in the grip of a vise; the excess is squeezed out. What is left may be enough for support, but it often leaves precious little for security. Security, if you remember, is based on capital, and this is what taxes make it so difficult to accumulate. The problem is the same for nearly all the stages of success in society; for the salaried junior or top person; for the businessperson; even in some degree, for the person of fortune.

The Great Equalizer

Here, then, the three horns. There is no getting around them. Like the mythical ones of old, they are encountered by everyone who charts a course through the seas of our world today. Together, they form a great equalizer which is at the heart of the current problem of estate creation.

To the woman who is earning $400 per week, hard put to make ends meet even on a day-to-day basis, an income of $50,000 or $100,000 seems like unbelievable wealth. She cannot believe there are any financial problems for the possessor of such an income. What she does not realize is that the dilemma for these incomes—widely separated though they are—is essentially the same. That is what makes the accumulation of wealth just as knotty a problem for the Joneses as for those who want to keep up with them.

Toward a Solution:
For a Current Dilemma,
Current Techniques of Planning

Does all this mean that the situation is hopeless? Obviously not, or we would not be writing this book and you would not be reading it.

Certainly, some people have found the solution. If we all know cases like our "typical four," so also do we know their opposites, persons who have been able to create estates that provide security for themselves and their families despite the economic stresses of their time. They are many in number, and they are not limited to any one group. They are found in all strata, all situations, and all ages. The "secret" of their success is no secret but a matter of common sense; they have dealt with the dilemma on its own terms.

Remember that this is a current dilemma, one that did not exist until recent decades. So, dealing with it on its own terms means the use of *current* methods of estate building, methods that take into account the problems of both high living costs and tax erosion.

Classic estate planning was limited, based on two prime principles: thrift and sound investment. These still apply; they are still at the heart of estate creation, as you will see in the course of this book. But other elements, just as organic to the successful estate plan, have been grafted onto them.

One such element is surely at the core: tax relief. The old techniques paid only peripheral attention to taxes. They did not constitute a major block to capital accumulation in former days. But today, as we have seen, our economy is tax saturated with complex and ever-changing tax laws, and no estate plan is worth its effort, unless it, in turn, is saturated with tax *relief.* For, although current tax law schedules estate taxes to disappear in the year 2010, they are scheduled to return to 2001 rates in 2011 (more about this in chapter 12).

The guideposts which point the way to tax relief are contained in the tax laws themselves, in the numerous preferential openings these provide for tax-favored methods of capital accumulation. We call these openings tax shelters. And shelters they truly are, places of refuge from the heavy downpour of both estate and income taxes. In essence, the term "tax shelter" refers to various ways and means of making investments, transfers, and compensation arrangements that result in profits or accumulations from which some of the burden of tax erosion has been lifted or deferred. You will be reading about numbers of them in the following chapters. Tax shelters run like a thread through the maze of estate-creation techniques.

A second element is equally important, equally integral to the contemporary estate plan. Properly speaking it is not a technique but an opportunity: the opportunity for capital accumulation that lies in a person's own occupation.

The catch-all term for it is "fringe benefits," the variety of plans offered by many employers to their employees as additional compensation above and beyond their salaries: the profit-sharing, pension, and savings plans, the deferred compensation arrangements, the group medical and life insurance contracts, long-term care insurance, all the extras that are tacked onto a person's salary and which can—although he may not be aware of it—form the basis of a lifetime estate building plan.

Fringe benefits have been part of the corporate way of life for many years, but they came of age during World War II and have continued to expand during the ensuing decades. By now the term "fringe" is really a misnomer. Depending on the individual and the company that employs him, they are no longer the frosting on the cake, but the cake itself—so far as estate creation goes.

This is true for three reasons: first, they operate as a sort of semi-compulsory savings plan. Unlike regular salary compensation they are usually deferred and held in reserve for a number of years. This aspect has obvious importance to the planner, who is bedeviled by the pressures of our times to spend whatever monies he has on hand. Second, they are ordinarily invested for the benefit of the employee, thus providing him with a built-in investment program. And third, most of them are tax-sheltered. All in all, quite a package.

Moreover, fringe benefits are not limited to the employees of corporations. In recent years, professionals and independents of all types have sought and won the right to acquire them. An increasing portion of the United States working force is being swept under the protection of their benevolent umbrella.

They are not there simply for the taking, however. They vary widely from company to company, and in many of the smaller businesses they scarcely exist at all. In the case of high fringe benefits for high-echelon executives they must be bargained for. In all cases, they have to be sought after, pursued, and actively incorporated into an overall program. It takes individual planning and, above all, individual initiative to bring to life their great potentiality as estate builders.

NEEDED: A WHISPERING SLAVE

We have talked a good deal about the obstacles in the path of estate creation. But so far we have not mentioned the final and most important one. It has nothing or little to do with taxes or the cost of living, nor with the conditions of society nor the economy. It goes deeper. It is a condition of human nature, called default.

It is easy to define default, harder to cure it. In terms of estate planning, it means a failure to take advantage of the opportunities that exist for estate building; failure to meet one's responsibilities as head of the household and guardian of the family; failure to provide security. It is a failure exemplified by the plight of Young Executive, Corporate Executive, Professional, and the Successfuls and all their counterparts in working men and women everywhere.

All manner of reasons can be put forth for default. The estate planning picture is complicated. It requires energy and zeal for the average person to find out whom to go to for help, or what to do. Successful people lead busy lives. It's hard enough for them to meet the demands of the day, let alone those of the distant future.

True enough, but we suspect that the real cause for default goes deeper. It is simply the all-too-human reluctance to accept the inevitability of age and retirement. Or, even beyond that, the inevitability of death. "No young man," said Hazlitt, "thinks that he will ever die." The fact is that few of us—young or middle-aged, men or women—face up to the prospect of either age or death.

The Romans had a way to handle this problem. Theirs was an age of heroes and the heroes tended sometimes to forget that they, too, were mortal. To remind themselves of this unpleasant fact they retained a "whispering slave." His function? To follow the hero through the streets as he rode in triumph and whisper in his ear the truth that all men, even he, must someday die.

The affluent hero and heroine of today could use a whispering slave. Sometimes, it is true, the slave does appear and issue his warning: to the person who has a serious but nonfatal heart attack, or to the person who sees his friend's unprepared widow forced to go to work.

But do we really need such drastic warnings to force us to attack the problem of default? We refuse to believe it.

The means to build and pass on a sound estate are within the reach of nearly every executive, professional, employee and businessperson today. They are not limited to the already successful but can be used by the would-be successful as well—by the young and old alike. The main thing is to get started, for if it is never too late to begin building an estate, it is also never too soon.

CHAPTER 2

GETTING STARTED

Estate planning has sometimes been called social work among the rich. It is also described as a means of passing from this world into the next without passing through the Internal Revenue Service.

These wry statements are more notable for their nice grasp of the comic than for their accuracy of definition. In reality, estate planning is not limited to the rich but encompasses a broad group of society. Nor is its sole concern the reduction of the tax impact. Indeed, one of its basic precepts is that family security must never be sacrificed for tax advantages.

What is estate planning then? We would define it in this manner: *the creation, conservation, and utilization of family resources to obtain the maximum support and security for the family during the lifetime and after the death of the planner.* In less formidable terms, it means making the most of what you have or can develop.

Estate planning has both long-term and short-term objectives. Its short-term goals are current support, providing for the needs of each of the family now, while the head of the household is actively employed. At the same time, the long-term goals have to be considered, providing for the same needs of the same people if and when the planner becomes *disabled, retires,* or *dies.* There are many qualitative issues as well, encompassing family values, the differing needs and capabilities of various family members and attachments to charitable needs of the world around you.

Do you want to get started on your estate planning program? Then you must mesh both the short- and long-term goals together, and you must not neglect one for the other. You must actively plan for both present and future.

All this sounds rather elementary and, philosophically speaking, it is. But when the philosophy is put into action, deep-seated problems appear. The trouble is that the achievement of the current objectives is likely to interfere with and sometimes—in fact often—prevents the realization of the long-term goals.

THE DYNAMICS OF THE FIVE FIRSTS: HOME, INCOME, DISABILITY INSURANCE, SAVINGS ACCOUNT, LIFE INSURANCE

Let's look at the problem of current support and security. When does a family have such security and when doesn't it? A time-honored definition says that it starts with the establishment of five elements: a *home*, that is, a place to live; an annual *income*, usually secured by a job (often two, in dual income families); *disability insurance* to protect earned income from a prolonged illness or recovery from injury; a *savings account*, a reserve fund which can be drawn on in case of emergency; and finally *life insurance*, a source of future income if the planner should die.

The manner in which you set about achieving these goals, however, involves far-reaching decisions which are going to affect your long-term objectives. Two of the five, your income and your home, have ramifications which go deeper than their surface definitions. Not only do they help establish an estate; they also establish a standard of living. This latter aspect usually operates to prevent or impede further estate building. The simple decision of selecting a home, for example, sets in motion complicated problems of estate creation. So too with the requirements of "living up to one's career or income position."

We can illustrate these dynamics with a concrete example. A young friend of ours just bought a home. He is 35 years old and, for his age, not just successful but extremely successful. He's a salesman; clever, ambitious, and energetic. His income is presently $200,000 and he has every reason to believe that it will go much higher in the future.

He bought the home to take care of the needs of his family—a wife and three children. It is large and expensive. He can afford the initial purchase price—that is not the question. The question is, can he afford to maintain the standard of living that residence in this house, in this section of town, with these neighbors, will demand? He will need to hire domestic help; he will have to entertain and be entertained in a fairly luxurious style; he will acquire expensive tastes and so will his wife and children. The satisfaction of these tastes will soon appear to be necessities and he will work harder and earn more money to meet them. But will he build an estate?

To Resolve the Dynamics: Determination, Plus Objectives

So far, our young friend has not come to grips with his problem. For two reasons:

First—he has not yet acquired the *determination* to build an estate. By determination, we mean the conscious and active desire to make estate building an integral part of his financial planning—from now until the day he dies. Without this determination, it is almost impossible to build an estate; with it, the way is opened up. It is the foundation of the estate plan, the catalytic ingredient which sets the rest of the process in motion.

Second—and as a result of his lack of determination—our young friend has not yet made a conscious evaluation of his estate planning objectives. Without such objectives, an estate plan lacks direction; it is like sending a ship to sea without a rudder.

Three People and Their Objectives

Here are three people we know. Examine for a moment their attitudes toward this problem of determining objectives.

The first is a doctor, just finishing her residency, married, no children yet. She has a clear idea of exactly how much money she can earn from her specialty, pediatric surgery. She has selected the locale where she will set up practice, made a rough estimate of her yearly earnings and expenses for the next five years. She has already started an insurance and investment program. All this done with some definite goals in mind. She and her husband, a sales manager, want to create an estate of about $1 million before they are 45, and think they can do it.

The second is a patent attorney, age 63, very successful. His income is substantial and has been for years. He has the usual accoutrements that go with success; he and his family live extremely well. He has saved very little, has no insurance or investment plan, has never really thought about where he is going, financially speaking, or why. In a vague way he knows he's going to have to work till the day he dies. But what about his family's security after that? He has for some years past resolved to do something about hedging against the possibility of his disability or death. But he has never really made a determination of what he wanted to do or how to do it—and certainly has never taken the first small steps in translating his wavering resolution into action.

The third is a businessman, married, three children. He is a real loner. He operates his export-import office without benefit of even a secretary. Some years he brings in a good deal, as much as $150,000 or $200,000. In others he earns only $50,000. He has no savings; he makes no investments; all he has in the way of an estate is a small insurance policy. When he has money he lives high. When he doesn't he hauls in his belt and lives off his much reduced income. He is a nonconformist, who is not interested in security for either himself or his family. He believes that such considerations hamper his freedom and restrict his life. He is confident of his ability to produce enough income to support the family and educate his children. Beyond that, they must take their chances as he did.

Which of these three have determined their estate planning objectives?

Obviously, our first person, the young doctor, is the very model of an estate planner. She knows exactly where she is going and what she wants and is taking measures to achieve these goals. But you will probably be surprised when we tell you that the last person has also determined *his* estate planning objectives. They are far from orthodox and we do not recommend them. But nevertheless they are the product of a rational decision; they represent a life plan at which he has arrived *consciously*.

It is our middle man who is in trouble. He is the only one who has not determined his objectives and therefore has no estate plan. He is a procrastinator. So much so that he hasn't even thought seriously about what he wants, let alone how to get it.

THE RIGHT AND WRONG OF IT

There is no "right" or "wrong" set of objectives, you see; they must be personally determined by each individual, and one set is as good as another. (Although it should be said that our export-import loner's family may not agree that his "plan" is a good one.) The point, however, is to have objectives. What income do you want your spouse to have available if you should die? How much will he or she and the children need? What will you need for the support of yourself, your spouse and your family, when you retire, or if you should become disabled?

The answers to these questions will determine your objectives. They require a good deal of thinking through. You will have to evaluate the needs of each member of the family, not forgetting any support obligations you may have for relatives outside your immediate family. You must make lifetime decisions about such things as the standard of living you expect yourself and your family to maintain. Do you want your children to go to college? To graduate school? And if so, do you plan to pay the full cost of this education or will you expect your children to help by working or getting scholarship aid?

Do you want to give them further security by leaving them an inheritance? By transferring part of your estate to them while you are still alive? Or do you think it better to send them out in the world to make their own way?

Each person's answer to these questions will be different. In addition, they will vary according to the individual's age and station in life. The determination of objectives is—as are all parts of estate planning—both flexible and continuous. It will change as you change.

But for the younger person, one thing is sure. Whether his objectives are modest or grandiose, he will need to scrutinize his current standard of living most carefully. In all probability it will have to be more modest than he might wish, for he must begin, now and not later, to set aside part of his income for capital accumulation, if he is to achieve those objectives. Therefore, he must ask himself at every juncture where a rise in the standard of living is indicated: Is this necessary? Does my job really require more expensive living? Can I afford it and still continue my estate-creation program?

It is easier to make such decisions before rather than after the upward step has been taken on the status escalator. Tastes once acquired are not easily abandoned. Few prospects in life are more agonizing to contemplate than the reversal of a standard of living, once it has become a habit.

STARTING POINT: INVENTORY YOUR ASSETS

So far we have only talked about the philosophy behind getting started—the frame of mind, the strength of character, and the objectives. Let us assume that you do possess the determination and you have established objectives. Where do you go from here?

You begin by taking stock. This is the first and absolutely essential step. Before you explore all the estate-creation opportunities open to you, you must know what you have to start with.

What is the value of your estate in terms of providing security for your family right now? This isn't determined by a mere listing of assets (although this must be done). The market value of assets alone is not a measure of their security value. After all, some assets might not be liquidated to produce income (such as a home). To determine the security potential of your available capital, you must determine how much annual income it will produce. When you know what this is, then you have a true idea of the ability of your estate to provide security for you and your family in the three situations: retirement, disability, and death.

A word here about the significance of capital. We say that capital should never be encroached on, for the moment it is, it loses a portion of its income-producing capacity. A rule of thumb says it should last the lifetime of the individual as well as that of his surviving spouse. For a person of 45 years with a spouse 5 years younger, that would mean about 41 years. Sometimes, of course, the principal of an estate will not be large enough to produce a sufficient annual income to meet a family's needs, and so principal will have to be used. How long, then, will the principal last? What if the estate owner and his spouse live long past their life expectancies? These days, ninety years or more is not an unusual life span. The need for support and financial independence must be projected on the basis of the possibility of such a long life. What happens, for instance, if capital is exhausted at some point and the widow lives on for an additional ten, maybe twenty years?

An estate owner should try to plan so that this situation never arises. The production of income and the inviolability of capital as long as possible are, in other words, prime objectives of estate planning.

All estate planning begins with an estimate of income potential. You should make this estimate whether your estate is large or small, whether you are going to leave your family a fortune, or merely a sum to ensure their security. It is something you can do for yourself, without calling on any expert advice.

In the Appendix of this book for your use are "Estate Planning Work-sheets." Used properly, they will provide you with an immediate and continuing record of all your assets and the important facts about them from an income-producing point of view. The record, when completed, will show you at a glance whether your estate can meet your objectives.

You will have to do a number of calculations to use the Worksheets; not difficult, only time-consuming.

Begin by making a list of all your properties. Include everything you own or have a right in: securities; real estate holdings; business interests; corporate benefits, such as pension plans, stock options, and group insurance; personal insurance and annuities; personal property; even such things as veterans' benefits and social security.

Now determine the prospective income from each of these in three instances: death, retirement, disability. Use as a basis for figuring income a standard estimate of 5 percent annual return after taxes on invested capital. (This standard will be used throughout this book. It may not be valid for particular types of investments, but it is useful as an overall guide.)

There will also be administration costs and estate taxes, plus income tax on retirement plan assets to be subtracted from the value of the after-death estate to determine how much property will be left to the surviving family.

ANALYZING THE INVENTORY:
YOUR ESTATE PICTURE

With your inventory completed, how does the picture look? How much security have you assured for your family?

You may be shocked by what you see. The unplanned estate rarely presents a balanced picture. Usually, there are great holes left—especially in the retirement and disability columns. Estates that appear to be small can turn out to be quite productive in providing income and vice versa. We know of the estates of two people, both of which had been described as worth $500,000. After the assessment was completed, it turned out that one of them—being largely invested in securities returning 7 percent—had an income potential of $35,000. The other turned out to be comprised of a $250,000 home, a thirty-foot cruiser, and a locked-in minority interest in a closely held corporation that paid no dividends. Annual income potential: zero.

The first part of this book will show you how to fill in the gaps. Numerous paths of estate creation will be analyzed. The many uses of insurance will be explored, the occupational opportunities clarified, the special problems of retirement and disability treated, principles of investment outlined, retirement asset protection discussed.

The second part deals with the problems and opportunites of estate transfer, a progression of investment strategies explained, and the methods of distributing your capital both during your life and after death, so that it can be conserved and best used for the benefit of your family.

Don't think you have to read the entire book through from beginning to end. Glance through it, read the sections that interest you most, or have the most bearing on your own problems. Get an idea of what each chapter contains so that you will know when and how to refer to the specific information it covers. This will give you a broad picture of your own estate-planning problems and supply a frame of reference for utilizing the Worksheets. The Worksheets will help you analyze your estate. You should begin filling them in at this point, using the body of the book as a guide and aid. A careful reading of the book is the last step. It should help you in formulating your plans and finding the ways and means of improving your estate picture. It should also give you ideas for constructive and proactive ways to use your advisors, such as your accountant, attorney, and financial planner to help you achieve your goals.

We begin with the "universal" estate builder: life insurance.

LIFE INSURANCE:
THE UNIVERSAL
ESTATE BUILDER

John Doe is a fortunate young man. At age 28 he already has three of the necessary requisites for building an estate: *ability* (he is intelligent, hard-working, competent); *opportunity* (he has a good job with a corporation that could eventually provide him with a number of estate-building sources); and *determination* (he has even established an estate-creation program and has the will and strength of character to carry it through). All he needs now is *time*: the time to use his ability, opportunities, and determination to create his estate.

In the usual course of things, John will get that time. He is quite healthy, stays fit and will probably live to a ripe old age. If he uses his ability and opportunities well, regardless of possible changes in employers over the years, and continues to maintain his determination, he can accumulate the estate he desires.

But what about his estate position right now? Suppose he were to die prematurely. Where's the estate going to come from if the time is lacking?

Like many things in life, the time is for sale. It can be bought for an initial payment of as low as $200 to create an instant estate worth $100,000.

Quite simply, his answer is life insurance, for life insurance buys time; it is the only investment that does. This is its basic function; it is what makes it the "universal" estate creator and the first outside investment family bread earners should make.

The ordinary John or Jane goes ahead and makes that investment. Not being an insurance expert, they probably never do get around to reading the fine print in their policies. They have only a vague idea of such things as dividend options, investment versus risk, the taxability of insurance, modes of settlement, and the like. They are aware of the amount of yearly premiums they pay, the face value of their policies, and not much else. Yet the fact is that life insurance often represents the largest single continuing investment that the average person makes during the course of a life.

Beyond this, life insurance is, of all estate-building tools, the most flexible. Although its first and most important function is to create an instant estate, it has other uses and other ramifications, which make it of interest to the owner of the large estate as well as the small, to individuals and companies alike, to business owners as well as employees.

THE USES OF LIFE INSURANCE

It *indemnifies*, that is to say, it replaces a financial loss caused by the death of an individual, and instantly creates an estate that otherwise would take years of earnings and savings to accomplish. It is a *funding* device, used to supply monies for business and estate settlement purposes. And finally, it is an *investment*, providing an opportunity for saving with tax-deferred capital accumulation, which is especially attractive in today's volatile investment and restrictive tax climate.

Indemnification

- *Mr. A is a young man with a family.* Good job, good future—but no estate as yet. Since his children are young, he needs somehow to ensure their security if he should die and leave his family without a source of income. He figures that $1,000,000 would suffice to at least take care of his family until the youngest child reaches 21. He buys a life insurance policy in this amount and breathes easy. He has partially indemnified his family against his loss. He adds a rider to waive his premium should he become disabled and unable to earn a living to be sure his policy would stay in force, even if he couldn't work.

- *Ms. B is the president of Successful Enterprises, Inc.* She has been the prime organizer and motivating force behind the success of her company. Her death would represent a profound loss to the firm if she were to die at this point in its development. Nothing could make up for the loss of her personal contribution, that is true. But life insurance could soften the blow considerably by indemnifying the company for the financial losses.

- *Mr. C and his wife have built their dream house.* The mortgage payments are rather high, but he'll have it paid in full by the time he's 52—if he lives that long. He's afraid that his wife wouldn't be able to keep up the payments if he died prematurely. So he buys mortgage insurance. If he dies before the mortgage is paid off, the insurance takes care of it.

Remember, too, that in each of these cases, as well as in most others, the liquidity of life insurance is of great importance. The typical beneficiaries of insurance—widows, estates, and independent businesses—are usually in great need of ready cash. In most instances, insurance proceeds are transferred income-tax-free without delay or administration costs.

Funding

- *Ms. D and her closest friend are the sole stockholders in a small corporation.* Each of them wants to be sure that she would have complete control if the other one died, so they enter into a stockholder's buy-sell agreement providing for this. But neither of them, nor the corporation, has enough money to buy out the other's interest at her death, especially since the business has grown in value way beyond their original investment.

  They use life insurance to provide funding in the following way: Each takes out insurance on the other's life, equal in value to a half interest in the corporation. If one of them dies, the necessary cash is immediately available to carry out the agreement and buy the deceased's half of the business at its current value. This establishes a new, higher cost basis for the newly purchased half of the business. They could accomplish the same goal by having the corporation insure both of them. Then the corporation would redeem the dead partner's stock, using the insurance money to pay for it. However, no new cost basis would be established. Should the survivor then sell the business, the first approach would result in capital gains tax on only the survivor's own original half of the business; a 50 percent reduction in tax. The corporate-owned insurance would result in capital gains tax on both halves of the business. In this case, not only having life insurance, but attending to its ownership makes a significant difference.

- *Mr. E is the sole owner of a $3-million-dollar corporation.* He wants to be sure that his company will continue after his death for the benefit of his family, but he knows there will be a heavy demand for cash in the period immediately following his death. It will be needed by the company to redeem stock so that his estate has liquidity to pay estate taxes. It may also be required to pay off creditors, to hire key people to replace him, and to maintain the business community's confidence in the firm.

  Life insurance can supply his company with this money. The company can take out what is known as a "key man policy" on E's life and pay the premiums out of its surplus. When E dies, the proceeds will be available, tax-free, to help the business through the many difficulties that lie ahead.

- *People in her community say that Ms. F is rich.* They are right. When she dies, she will leave her family an estate worth $3 million. Having no surviving spouse, there is no marital deduction available to Ms. F's estate. Half her estate, less the $1,500,000 equivalent exemption that everyone is entitled to (in 2004–5), will be subject to the estate tax. The trouble is that none of her assets are liquid. Where, then, is the cash going to come from to pay the $767,400 in taxes and administration expenses?

  Insurance is the answer. It will be immediately available on her death to use for this purpose. If it is owned by her children, or an irrevocable life insurance trust, the death proceeds will not be a part of her taxable estate. This means that the other assets in her estate can be passed on whole, undiluted by losses that usually accompany a forced liquidation.

- *Mr. G is a man with a number of business interests.* In some years he has heavy debts. He is afraid that if he died in one of these bad years his creditors might wipe out his entire estate. To forestall such a disastrous event, he carries insurance sufficient to meet all these obligations.

Insurance as Investment

- *Ms. H earns $50,000 a year and can't save a dime.* She makes periodic resolutions to do something about savings, but as soon as she accumulates a little money for the family, she finds something to spend it on. A strong-intentioned but weak-willed planner, she finally solves her problem by buying an insurance policy with a death benefit sufficient to provide support for her family. She pays her premiums on a regular schedule, just like her mortgage payments, with not too much strain, as part of the family budget. *The cash value of her insurance is her savings, and if she doesn't have time to complete her savings plan for her family, the death proceeds will complete it for her. It is a savings plan that is semi-compulsory, and therefore more likely to be continued.*

- *Mr. I is a child of the depression years* who saw a family fortune disappear in a few days, then saw it again in 2000–3. This traumatic experience has turned him into an ultraconservative investor. For years he has been sacrificing capital appreciation and high rates of return for safety. Now he wants to branch out into investment fields which offer more opportunity for capital appreciation, but he is still too conditioned by his "safety-first" code to give up his fixed-return investments (even though they provide a very low yield).

  He doesn't have to. If he substitutes insurance for some of his fixed investments, he can free a large part of his assets for well-diversified equity investments, in the knowledge that his family will be taken care of if he dies before accumulating his estate. *Not many investments are as risk-proof as insurance death benefits. They offer a fixed amount which the purchaser specifies in advance, and are not subject to change because of business conditions, economic factors, or other circumstances beyond the control of the policyholder.*

- *Ms. J makes a good deal of money.* Her salary and other income put her in a 35 percent tax bracket. When she makes her investment plan, she realizes that she has to either find an investment that earns 7.7 percent (in order to realize an after-tax income of 5 percent) or buy tax-free bonds yielding at least 5 percent. The first is sometimes hard to come by. If she takes the second course, unless she purchases bonds through a tax-exempt fund, she may not attain the level of diversification she should have. Also, whether she invests through a fund or directly, she may realize capital losses if general interest rates subsequently shift upward or the underlying state or municipality suffers a drop in its credit rating.

She could get both yield and liquidity, however, if she substituted insurance for some of the low-yield investments she now owns. The cash value of her insurance, after figuring her insurance cost, could grow at an accumulating yearly rate of 5 percent (subject to rise as interest rates rise), or more if she uses her cash values as an investment medium for capital growth (say, in a variable universal life policy). She pays no income taxes on this growth while it is being earned, and the likelihood is that she never will. At retirement, she will have accumulated a cash value to supplement her income needs. She could take out the amount she put in tax-free, borrow the rest, or convert the entire cash value to an income-paying annuity for the rest of her life.

Thus, the nature of insurance as an estate planning tool:

- A source of capital accumulation.
- Supplies money that instantly explodes in value upon your death.
- Creates an immediate estate.
- Can pay for itself when you are disabled.
- Builds a cash value available for borrowing.
- Can provide tax-free borrowed income at retirement, or . . .
- Can be converted at retirement to a favorable annuity program.
- Can pass to heirs as income and is often estate-tax-free.

TYPES OF LIFE INSURANCE

Today, there are many types of life insurance policies to meet a variety of insurance needs and many investment objectives. As only one element in the estate plan, the insurance program must be tailored to the needs of each individual estate. Basically, however, you will have a choice among several principal types.

Term Insurance

The chief thing to keep in mind about term insurance is that it is *temporary* insurance, which exists for a given period of time—such as five, ten, twenty, in some cases thirty years. You pay a fixed amount in premiums for the period of its term. If you don't die in that period, the policy expires and protection ends. Most term policies, however, give the holder an option to renew. On each renewal, the premium rises, and usually the renewal option ceases at age 65 or 70. Term can usually be converted, however, at any time to permanent insurance with no physical examination required, generally up to age 65.

Term insurance requires the smallest outlay of cash. A man, age 35, could carry $100,000 of five-year term at a net premium of only $300 per year. He'd have to pay a net of $1,148 for the same amount of whole life insurance.

But in the long run, term is not inexpensive. It's costly. The premium keeps rising with every renewal. Over a period of years, your total net costs for term will exceed the total net cost (your net premium less cash value) of permanent insurance.

Remember, too, that since most term policies cut off at age 70 or 80, they cannot give either continuous or permanent coverage to a person with a normal life expectancy.

Should you buy term or not?

If you are a young person, married, and about to buy basic insurance, term insurance is not the long-term answer. You need permanent coverage until you die, at the lowest net cost. Why? Well, take the case of Mrs. Widow, age 78, at the other end of life. Her husband had carried twenty-year level-premium term life insurance for $500,000. He died fifteen years after it had passed its twenty-year mark. It was too expensive to renew, and after all, they had bought it to cover the family's needs until the children were through school. Unfortunately, retirement savings were inadequate, and Mrs. Widow has had to sell their home, hoping she can manage to live off the net sale proceeds until she dies.

But what do you do if you can't afford the premiums for permanent insurance? The best solution is to buy part term and part permanent, converting your term to permanent as your income rises. In other words, it's better to supplement permanent insurance with term than to carry no permanent insurance at all. There are also policies that blend term insurance with whole life. Over time, dividends replace the term insurance with whole life.

There are many situations, however, when term insurance is a useful solution. It's usually the best answer when there is a need for immediate protection for a limited period of time or for a particular purpose. This is the case with term mortgage insurance, which Mr. C bought to make sure his wife would never have to sacrifice their dream house.

So, too, with many business and investment situations. Take the case of an inventor seeking financial backing. He has a new product with great potential, but it will take several years to get it ready for the market. Investors, while interested, are cautious about advancing money. What will happen if the inventor dies before the product is ready? The solution: They take out term insurance on the inventor's life and thus protect themselves against the loss of their investment, at the lowest cash outlay, in the event of his premature death.

Whole Life Insurance

Whole life is permanent insurance. It differs from term in that it will pay off at any time the insured dies, rather than within a specified period. It embraces two different types of insurance plans: ordinary life and limited payment life. These differ mainly in the length of time premium payments are to be made.

Ordinary Whole Life

Under this type of contract, for a set premium payable for the whole of the insured's life, the policyholder gets permanent coverage. Ordinary whole life can function as part of an investment program and savings account. We saw some examples of how this works in the case of Ms. H, Mr. I, and Ms. J. Let's now take a look at the principles which underlie this aspect of ordinary whole life.

When you buy ordinary whole life, both your policy and your premium payments are divided into two parts: risk protection and investment. The risk part represents term insurance. The investment part forms the cash value of your policy.

At the beginning of your policy much of your premium goes toward risk and the "loading cost" of putting the policy in force. Gradually, however, the cash value rises, the risk cost decreases, and a larger share of the premium is consequently added to the cash value. At the same time, the cash value has a built-in annual earning factor. This results in a continuous build-up of the cash value of your policy. If dividends are paid (such as with mutual insurance companies), they can add to the cash value, and may even build to the point where they could be used to pay the premium for the policyholder. How does all this affect an investment or savings plan?

If you have bought your insurance at age 35, for instance, in about seventeen years the yearly increase in the cash value (including dividends) of your policy will exceed your annual premium. In one company, for every dollar of premium paid in the twelfth year, $1.12 is credited to the cash value and dividends. This is in addition to the fact that the term insurance part of the policy is being paid for. The build-up of dividends and cash value may make it possible to cease paying premiums after a period of years.

The cash value gives you a liquid asset. It is always available for borrowing—sometimes in periods when no other source is available. We know of at least one person who was saved from financial ruin through the cash value of an insurance policy. He had overextended himself in the stock market in 2000, and was called for margin. He was able to meet the call by borrowing the cash value out of his insurance policies for a limited period of time and so saved his stock interests, and rode the slump through, on into the rise that providentially followed it later.

Cash value should also be considered as a potential source of investment capital. When and if your insurance needs stop, you can terminate your policy, walk away with the cash value, and use it to make other investments—or conversely, you can use it to buy other forms of insurance or an annuity.

The build-up of the cash value is free of income taxes during the existence of the policy. This tax-sheltered treatment turns insurance into an attractive investment. Depending on your tax bracket, you would have to earn a very favorable rate of return before taxes on your other investments in order to equal your tax-free build-up of cash value in your life insurance policy.

Let us look at the investment return on cash value life insurance. Assume you are 35 years old and need $50,000 of insurance coverage. At this age, you will pay out a total of $12,980 in premiums over a period of twenty years on an ordinary whole life policy.

At the end of the twenty years, the build-up of the cash value plus the dividends will amount to about $17,247—a gain of $4,267.

If you terminate a policy and take the cash value at some point in the future, you pay an income tax only on the amount you get back which exceeds the total amount of premiums you have paid less dividends you received; in this case, if it were after twenty years it would be $4,267 and, between what you paid in premiums and received in dividends, no tax would be due.

Universal Life and Variable Universal Life

Universal life and variable universal life are basically an investment program tied to a term insurance contract. For income tax purposes it qualifies as life insurance and as such enjoys its tax advantages. It differs from most other forms of insurance in that once the initial premium is paid (in any amount necessary to pay the costs of establishing the policy, paying the term insurance rate, and setting up a cash value account), annual *fixed* premiums are no longer required. Premiums can be flexible; one initial large lump sum; large premiums in the first few years of the policy, then none thereafter. The policyholder may invest as much as and whenever he wishes into the cash value account within certain tax restrictions (lest it becomes a modified endowment contract. See page 34). The annual term cost will be taken out of this account as long as it has a sufficient balance—it is the "bank account" for the policy's costs of insurance. If variable universal life is used, the cash value account may be invested in specified types of investment programs and may be transferred from one type to another at the election of the policyholder. The accumulation of earnings in the cash value account is tax-deferred. The death benefit can amount to the term insurance in force plus the value of the cash value account, or just the death benefit alone, and will be received tax-free by the beneficiary. Some insurance companies have a third option that requires larger premiums, but pays a death benefit that is equal to the death benefit *and* all the premiums paid. (Useful for split dollar arrangements, or for returning the cost of insurance to an estate or a business.)

A new type of variable universal life provides even greater death benefit security and access to cash values. It provides a guaranteed component that allows the policyholder to select a period of time during which the death benefit will be guaranteed; this can be lifetime or a specified period. It has a special death benefit option that allows premium amounts not needed for the guaranteed portion of the costs to be invested in separate accounts that are not burdened by insurance costs. This type of policy typically offers a broad menu of mutual fund-like separate accounts in various asset classes with varying levels of risk/return potential. These policies have a very favorable feature: The cash values grow tax-deferred as with other policies, but the amount of the cash value available for tax-free withdrawals is composed of *both* the values in the separate account *and* the cash value of the guaranteed account. This gives the policy owner a higher cost basis in the cash value represented by the separate accounts, and can be very beneficial for retirement supplement purposes.

Limited Payment Life

This is like ordinary whole life, except that the period of premium payments is limited to a certain number of years, such as ten or twenty years, or until you reach a certain age, such as 65. After that your policy is paid up and remains in force for the full face amount. You need make no further premium payments.

Premiums for limited payment life are, of course, higher than those for an equal face amount of ordinary whole life because the period of premium payment is shorter. At the same time the cash value increases at a much greater rate. The high cash value makes it an attractive investment for those who want to use their insurance to provide a retirement income. Limited payment is also a good type of insurance for a person who has a high income in early years which may go down as he gets older. Professional athletes, artists, and entertainers might consider it.

Paid-up Life

Another form of permanent insurance, it is similar to limited payment life except that here the entire premium is paid in one installment.

An ordinary or limited payment life policy can be converted to a paid-up policy for a reduced face amount. This amount will be determined by the cash values which are in the existing policy. The cash value is used as a single premium, based on the age of the insured at the time the conversion is made.

Retirement Annuity

In a sense, this represents the opposite of life insurance. With life insurance, the company that insures you is risking its money against the possibility that you may die before the age at which the actuarial tables say you will.

With annuity policies, the risk is still based on the actuarial tables—but here the company takes the risk that you will live *beyond* your life expectancy. It pays you a fixed sum for the rest of your life—an annuity. The annuity payment consists of the installment return on your investment as well as an interest return on it. You might say that annuities are really "life" insurance, and what we call life insurance is actually "death" insurance.

This possibility—that you may live to retirement, and perhaps many years beyond your life expectancy—is one that every planner must take into consideration. Life spans are increasing today. Life expectancies represent only an average; it is not uncommon for a person to live to a great age; 80, 90, 95 even. There may be twenty to thirty years of retirement for which income has to be found. The value of the annuity income is that you can never outlive the payments of principal and interest which it provides. No matter how long you live, the payments continue; this is something that no other form of investment can offer.

Chapter 9 takes up the problems of retirement more fully. We deal with the annuity policy here, however, because it is frequently combined with a life insurance element. The *retirement income policy* is basically an annuity policy that includes decreasing term insurance. Thus, if you die before your retirement, the policy pays off to your beneficiaries. If you live to retirement, it pays off to you. The term insurance part is less expensive than ordinary term because, like a rider, it is part of a combined policy.

Single Premium Life

This policy contains many of the features of term, variable, universal, and paid-up life insurance. For the payment of a lump sum, the policyholder receives life insurance coverage in a greater amount than his premium. He has two investment options. He may elect to have the cash value invested at a fixed return that will vary with the change in general interest rates. In this case the insurance company will guarantee the principal. Alternatively, he may elect a variable investment plan similar to those of the variable and universal programs. The death benefit will vary according to the amount of the underlying insurance and the cash value at the time of death, and may be received by beneficiaries free of tax as a distribution of life insurance death proceeds.

Since the tax law changes that took effect after June 21, 1988, this form of life insurance has lost some of its tax advantages. Although build-up of the cash value from fixed returns or variable investments within the policy is still tax-deferred, borrowing from the policy is no longer tax free as it was in the past. Loading the policy up front with a lump-sum premium creates what is now called a "modified endowment contract." Withdrawals or loans from such contracts during the lifetime of the policyholder are taxed first as ordinary income to the extent that there is a gain, then as a return of the policyholder's investment in the contract. Additionally, unless such distributions are taken after age 59½, disability or annuitization, a 10 percent penalty tax is applied.

Second-to-Die Life Insurance

Second to die, or survivorship, life insurance offers a low-cost way to preserve both business assets and estates. As an estate-planning tool, it works hand in glove with the unlimited estate tax marital deduction. It is a single policy insuring two lives and pays off at the second death only, just when estate taxes create the need for cash. Because the face value of the policy isn't paid until the second death, the premiums are lower than two separate policies. After the first death, with whole life policies of some dividend-paying mutual insurance companies, the dividends and cash value increase and the death benefit goes up, an advantage to estates appreciating in value. Some policies offer the option of combining whole life with term life insurance to reduce premium costs. Second-to-die universal life and variable universal life policies can also be used, providing the same premium flexibility as their single life counterparts.

Whole Life with Supplemental Term Life Insurance

A hybrid policy composed of whole life and term insurance can be used to create a level death benefit, while keeping premium costs down. Insurance companies that pay dividends to policyholders can use the dividends to create a combination of one-year term insurance and paid-up additions of whole life insurance. Each year dividends are used to purchase more and more whole life, until the term insurance is gradually replaced, and the policy is 100 percent whole life. If ongoing dividends are sufficient, the policy may reach a point in time when the policy can pay its own premium for you.

INSURANCE RIDERS

For additional premiums most policies will include riders—provisions attached to the basic contract which give the policyholder extra benefits or options. Some of these are so common that they are automatically inserted in the policy, and the premium is quoted as part of the whole policy.

Double Indemnity

A famous novel and movie turned this rider into a household word. If you have a double indemnity rider your beneficiaries will get double the face value of the policy should you die in an accident. Some policies triple the amount if the accident occurs while you are traveling in a common carrier.

Is it worth buying? We'd say it's a matter of personal choice. The chances are statistically small that you will die as the result of an accident; on the other hand, the extra premium cost is modest and the returns are large.

Disability Waiver

For a small extra premium, your policy may include a waiver of premiums in the event of disability before 60 or 65 years of age (depending upon the company). This is an extremely important rider, and one that we advise you to consider most seriously. Here's what it provides:

If you become totally and permanently disabled, the company will pay your premiums for you. At the same time, all the provisions of the insurance contract remain effective. Generally this covers only disability which lasts longer than six months. But the waiver is retroactive to the beginning of the disability period.

The waiver is obviously a great protection against a loss of security in a time of emergency. But it is also a moneymaking machine. During the period it operates, the cash value keeps increasing, and so may be borrowed against if extra cash is needed, or withdrawn, if you want to terminate the policy later. If you have a term policy, you may even be able to convert it to a permanent policy such as whole life or universal life insurance during the time you are disabled and using the waiver. If the rider allows for it, the insurance company will pay the new premiums—an incredible advantage if you are permanently disabled. If you are only temporarily disabled, be sure you will be in a position to pay the new, higher premium once you return to work.

Insurability Protection

This is a useful type of rider for the young family provider. It gives the insured the right to buy additional insurance of specified amounts at certain ages, usually up to age 40, without further physical examination. This is a good deal: the additional premiums are low and your insurability is guaranteed, even if you become ill or disabled. Also, if you have the waiver of premium rider, you can exercise this rider during your disability and the insurance company will pay this additional premium during your disability—an advantage worth having.

MODES OF SETTLEMENT AND OPTIONS

This phrase refers to the ways and means available to you and your beneficiaries for payout of the policy proceeds. A number of alternatives are available.

1. *Lump Sum Payout.* Your beneficiaries get the whole face value at once. They may also have the right reserved to select other options, however.

2. *Interest Option.* The proceeds are left with the company, which pays a guaranteed rate of interest. The interest is taxable to the beneficiary as ordinary income. This option is used when the policyholder wants to prevent his beneficiary from dissipating the insurance fund. It can also include a "spendthrift clause," which protects the insurance from the beneficiary's creditors.

   It's better, however, not to use this option too rigidly. Unless you specify that the beneficiary has the right to withdraw part or all of the principal, or elect other options, the insurance proceeds are not available for emergencies.

3. *Fixed Period Option.* Proceeds are paid out in equal installments over a specified number of years. The installments are made up of payments from principal (i.e., the insurance proceeds) and interest.

4. *Fixed Amount Option.* Installments are paid out in fixed amounts until the proceeds are exhausted.

5. *Life Income Option.* This is like an annuity in that the company agrees to make periodic payments during the life of the beneficiary. How much these payments amount to depends, of course, on the amount of the insurance proceeds and the life expectancy of the beneficiary. Its great advantage is that it provides larger annuity payments than a new annuity policy purchased with an equal sum of money.

What about Settlement Options?

Which one is best? There's no pat answer. They have to be carefully considered and fitted to the individual case. Very often they are simply too rigid. The payment should be made a flexible matter, depending on the particular situation at the particular time.

This can be provided by using the interest option with the right of the beneficiary to withdraw principal on an unlimited basis or in installments at stated intervals.

Flexibility can also be obtained by having the insurance proceeds paid into a trust. The trust proceeds can be invested by the trustees (people with investment experience—possibly a corporate trustee) and then paid out to the beneficiaries on the basis of their changing needs. Thus, the insured does not have to make a rigid arrangement which may not meet his family's needs after he is gone. He has substituted personal representatives for himself who will make new dispositions as changed circumstances require. Insurance trusts are dealt with in greater detail in Chapter 14.

DIVIDENDS AND WHAT TO DO ABOUT THEM

If your policy is issued by a mutual company or as a special policy by a stock company, you will receive annual dividends. You have several choices in their use. Which one you select is of importance in your estate picture.

1. You can take your dividends in cash. Since a dividend is considered a return of a part of the premium, there is no income tax on the dividend receipt until they exceed the premiums paid.
2. You can apply them to your premium payments, thus reducing your annual payments to the company.
3. You can leave them to accumulate with the company, and receive in return a guaranteed rate of interest on them. This interest rate is often increased because of increased company earnings. The accrued interest is taxable, and must be reported annually, whether or not you withdraw it. You may withdraw it at any time (at which point you would owe tax), or leave it as a savings account.
4. You can buy additional paid-up insurance with your dividends. This is an attractive option; the insurance is at "pure cost"

(meaning there is no overhead or "loading" charge); therefore, it is cheaper than insurance purchased in the ordinary way. The additional insurance will have a cash value like any other type of permanent insurance and often this cash value may be used to pay the premium on the policy, or it may be used to purchase additional paid-up insurance.

5. You can use a portion of your dividends to automatically buy each year one-year term insurance equal to the cash value of the policy. No physical examination is required for this purchase.

    This option is called the "fifth dividend option." If you use it, you are purchasing additional protection at "pure" insurance rates.

The fifth dividend option is important. It cancels out one of the major objections to life insurance as an investment: The fact that the owner becomes a "coinsurer" with the insurance company on the policy.

How does this happen? Ordinarily, as the policy continues in force the cash value grows; the death value, however, remains the same. When the death claim is finally paid, the company is in effect returning the cash value (which belonged to the insured anyway) plus the balance of the face value. This balance is the only amount which really represents the insurance risk. But when the fifth dividend option is used, the company must pay at risk, over and above the cash value, the full face value of the policy at most ages.

In addition, the fifth dividend option has a number of uses in helping to *finance* a policy—which is a subject in itself.

PREMIUMS AND HOW TO FINANCE THEM

Up to now, we have been speaking about the purchase of insurance by the regular payment of premiums out of pocket.

An alternative is to obtain a loan or to open a line of credit secured by your residence to pay premiums. Interest on loans secured by your residence will be fully deductible up to the cost of the home plus improvements.

The cost of obtaining such a loan, commonly referred to as a "home equity loan," varies with the lending institution. Closing costs include an appraisal fee, title fees, and recording fees, and may range from $500 to $900, although some banks have waived these closing costs. Several lending institutions will issue special loans for the payment of life insurance premiums, and have the cash value and death benefits pledged as collateral to repay the loan. This can be especially helpful when large premiums are needed for protecting a large estate, or providing for the buyout of a valuable business upon the death of the owner.

Split-dollar financing has been commonly used between relatives (or between employers and employees) in the past. For families it is a way of dividing the ownership and rights in a cash value life insurance policy between two family members, and allows one family member to provide the premiums for a policy owned by another without it being a gift. The payer retains rights to have their premium payments returned from the policy's cash value or death benefit. Under such an arrangement, a father, as an example, might pay premiums on a policy insuring his son-in-law, so as to ensure his daughter's support if her husband dies prematurely. Since his son-in-law may not be able to afford costly life insurance premium payments, the solution is to enter into a split-dollar arrangement with him and still get a fair return on any money he invests.

Thus Mr. Jones, age 45, enters into a split-dollar arrangement with his father-in-law, Mr. Smith, in which Jones takes out $500,000 of insurance on his own life. Jones owns the policy and has the right to name his wife or children as beneficiaries of the death proceeds in excess of the policy's cash values. Smith pays the annual premium of $10,205. By the end of the first year, the cash values could equal nearly 90 percent of the annual premiums paid by Smith and his investment in the policy will be protected by collaterally assigning the cash value and the death benefit to return the premiums paid by Smith during Jones's life, or upon his death.

Upon Jones's death, the policy would return the premiums paid by Smith to him. Smith's daughter, Jones's wife, will receive the balance of the death proceeds. If Smith and Jones want to assure that Jones's wife receives the full $500,000 of death benefit, they could purchase a higher death benefit to achieve that goal.

This was a very effective way of financing a family insurance program in cases where an individual has limited capital or income but at the same time has need for a large amount of insurance. However, as of January 1, 2004, new tax rules went into effect. They focus on the very issues of who owns the policy and who pays the premium. Where policies are owned by the insured, the premiums paid by another will be treated as loans. The owner will owe interest payments to the person lending the premiums. These interest payments are not deductible by the owner, and are taxable to the premium payer. Where the payer owns the policy, the insured would be taxed on any portion of the cash value to which they have access. Split-dollar insurance has often been used by corporations and their stockholders or key people. The new tax treatment of these arrangements has now altered many of the tax advantages that existed, calling for new planning considerations. More about this in Chapter 5.

INSURANCE AND THE INCOME TAX

Insurance death proceeds are specifically exempted by law from income tax liability whether they are paid to an individual, an estate, or a corporation.

There is one major exception to the rule, however, and that is where a policy is sold or transferred for "valuable consideration." In such a case income taxes are payable on the part of the death proceeds which exceed the new owner's cost.

Thus, if a $25,000 policy is sold for its cash value of $5,000 and the new owner later pays a total of $5,000 in premiums, she will have to pay a tax on $15,000 when she receives the death benefits of the policy. This is considered to be ordinary income and will be added to her other income for tax purposes.

This tax treatment holds even though a policy is sold to the insured's spouse. When transferring a policy to a member of the family, you must be certain that it is done as a gift and that nothing of value is paid for it.

Exceptions are made to the so-called "transfer for value" rule in the case of transfers to a corporation where the insured is a stockholder or officer, to the insured's partner or partnership, or to the insured himself. In these cases, even though consideration is paid for the policies, the death benefits are not subject to the income tax.

INSURANCE AND THE ESTATE TAX

There is a prevalent notion that insurance isn't subject to the estate tax. This isn't necessarily true. If it is payable to your estate or if you retain ownership of the policy, the death proceeds are going to be *included* in your taxable estate. This definition of ownership includes what the law calls "incidents of ownership" such as the right to surrender or to pledge the policy, the right to borrow on it or assign it, and the right to change the beneficiary.

One way to remove insurance from your taxable estate is to relinquish all rights in it by assigning the policy to someone else. However, there might be a gift tax imposed upon such an assignment. Still, only the cash value of the policy and the unearned and subsequent premiums paid by you are subject to this tax, not the face value of the policy. The gift tax can be avoided or reduced. By virtue of the unlimited marital deduction, there is no gift tax payable on an insurance policy assigned to your husband or wife, nor any estate tax on the proceeds of insurance which are paid to your spouse.

The gift tax annual exclusion of $11,000 ($22,000 if your spouse consents to the gift) means that a tax-free transfer can be made of a policy with a cash value of up to that amount and of subsequent premium payments of no more than the amount of the annual exclusions. However, if death occurs within three years of the transfer, the proceeds of the policy will be subject to estate taxes.

But are you sure you want to make such an irrevocable assignment? Are you certain you will never need to borrow on the cash value? Never want to change your beneficiary? Better look before you leap, because here as elsewhere in estate planning, family security and your own needs should not be sacrificed to save taxes.

Additional point: If a man transfers his policy to a wife with a separate estate (such as in a second marriage) and she dies before he does, the cash value of the policy is taxable in her estate. Unless his wife's estate is substantial this won't create a tax problem. But if it is large, there is not only this problem to consider, but also the fact that, if she survives him, the entire proceeds will go to her. Then, when she dies they will be part of her taxable estate.

In such cases, you should consider other forms of ownership. It may be worthwhile to have other members of the family own and be beneficiaries of the policies; or it may make more sense to assign the policy to an irrevocable trust, with income and part of the principal payable to your spouse or children according to their needs, and the remainder of the principal to your children after your spouse dies. Some taxable gift may be involved depending upon the cash value of the policies, the amount of the subsequent premiums paid by you, and whether or not the trust qualifies for the use of the $11,000 annual exclusion. The proceeds, however, will be exempt from taxation in both your estate and that of your spouse.

How Much Insurance?

This is, after all, the most perplexing question for most people, and one that is not answered by all this talk about options, modes of settlement, types of insurance and financing, regardless of their importance.

But no one, except you, can really answer that question for you. Let us show you why.

Ideally, you might consider life insurance as being like other types of insurance. It should be used to replace an asset—something that has been lost, destroyed, or stolen. In the case of life insurance, the asset is your economic value to your family in the event that you die.

How do you assess the economic value of a human being? Suppose that you are 40 years old and are now earning $50,000. Realistically assessing your future, you decide that your future earnings will look like this:

$50,000 per year for 10 years..$500,000
$55,000 per year for 10 years......................................$550,000
$60,000 per year for 5 years..$300,000
          (to age 65)
$40,000 per year for life—as
          retirement income—
          life expectancy of
          15 years $600,000
Total economic value...$1,950,000

Theoretically, you should then take out insurance coverage for nearly two million dollars. But, of course, you can neither afford nor would you want to do that. Unfortunately, the economic value of a human being just doesn't operate as a practical measuring rod.

Let's try another "ideal" way of determining how much insurance you should have. A time-honored principle says that the face value of your insurance policy should equal four or five times your current earnings.

Here's Mary Smith then, on the first rung of the success ladder and earning $55,000 per year. The rule says she would need only $275,000 of insurance. But this amount wouldn't begin to provide even minimum support for her two small children.

Take another case, Bob Brown, an upper-echelon executive earning

$90,000 a year. The "rule" tells him he needs $450,000 worth of insurance. But Bob has a wife with a large estate and a number of family trusts that have amply provided for the future welfare of his descendants. For support purposes Bob doesn't need any insurance at all (although he may need it for other purposes), regardless of the rule.

THE REALISTIC APPROACH: ASSESSING YOUR FAMILY'S NEEDS

The only realistic way we know of to arrive at a proper figure for life insurance coverage is to assess it in terms of your family's needs—now and in the future. How much income will they need for adequate support if you die? Your "Estate Planning Worksheets" will give you an approximation of how much they can expect. The difference between the income expected and the income needed is your deficiency. The amount and type of insurance you select should be adequate to make up that deficiency.

In determining that "income needed" figure, bear in mind that your estate will be depleted by taxes, funeral and administration expenses, and the payment of debts, including possible final medical bills and income taxes. Remember, too, that income needs will vary. The earning capacity of your spouse can help take up part of the shortfall. Your spouse will need more income while your children are young. Their educational costs will rise sharply when they reach college age. Your spouse may have large medical expenses in later years. All these factors have to be considered.

We realize that women like Mary Smith, just beginning their careers with small salaries, large responsibilities, and no estate, can't afford to buy the amount of insurance they need. But they can make a start by providing at least enough to tide their family over for a period of years and then add to it later, just as they are adding to the rest of their estate.

Moreover, if they begin their insurance program at a young age, the cost will be less. Letting time go by also means risking the possibility of becoming uninsurable due to health conditions that may change.

And when you come to select the type of insurance and decide on its amount, don't be misled by the idea that the "best kind of insurance is the cheapest." With insurance, as with every kind of purchase, you get no more and no less than what you pay for. The best kind of insurance is the kind which is tailored to your own specific needs, tailored to whether you want it in force for a limited time, or as long as you live, and is issued by an insurance company of great financial strength.

꩜

Your Occupation and

Its Opportunities: The

Company Compensation and

Employee Benefit Package

The time is the present, a fine evening in the spring. Mr. Young Executive, 35 years old, $115,000-a-year man, and employee of Corporation Americana, bounds up the walk to his house, throws open the doors, and announces the glad tidings.

He has just been given a $5,000 raise. If things continue the way they are going, it won't be long before he clinches that $130,000-a-year spot he has his eye on. Already he has big plans for using the $5,000. Here is the extra cash he needs to do some investing in the market. At last, he has the opportunity to build up some capital. Mentally, he savors the prospect of $5,000 growing to $10,000 to $20,000, and more. The taste is sweet.

Push the clock ahead to April of the following year and look in on Young Executive again. The season is the same but not the weather. It is raining, an appropriate setting for his mood, which is considerably gloomier than it was twelve months ago. Young Executive is hard at work, filling out his income tax return. As he works, some unpleasant facts begin to dawn on him. The $5,000 raise wasn't really worth $5,000. It upped his income taxes from $28,750 to $33,600, leaving only $150 of additional spendable income.

"Spendable" is a fitting description, too, because he hasn't invested a cent of it. What's more, he doesn't exactly know where the $150 has gone. It has apparently been dropped, along with the rest of his salary, into that bottomless pit labeled "family needs." On the whole, his position hasn't changed a bit. He has more possessions perhaps, but that priceless one, security, seems as far away as ever.

It takes only a little figuring for Young Executive to calculate that when he reaches the $130,000-a-year salary he is aiming at, he may well find himself in exactly the same straits. The increase won't really represent $10,000 but only $7,200 after taxes. He wonders if it will be just as easy to spend that amount, and knows in his heart that indeed it will (the car that needs replacing, the roof that needs to be redone . . .).

But our hero need not despair. The picture he is painting for himself is only half completed. He has faithfully depicted the darker aspect of estate creation—the fact that salary increases alone do not very often result in capital accumulation—but he has neglected the sunnier side. The opportunities he seeks for building capital lie within his reach—within his occupation, his own employer.

At Corporation Americana Mr. Young Executive receives not only a salary, but a set of "fringe benefits" as well: the various plans, arrangements, and contracts which his company provides to give him and his family greater security against old age, illness, disability, and finally death. This is the "employer compensation package" available in one form or another to nearly every company employee in the country.

The package had its origins in the incentive theory of labor compensation. The idea was to offer the employees something extra in return for extra effort. Much of that character has been lost today; employees and companies alike now look on the package as part of the standard and expected compensation. It became private enterprise's own form of "cradle to the grave security." Cradle to grave careers with the same company are more rare than common these days, but the fringe benefits in some form are a given. In fact, for employees whose talents are key to the profitability of the company, the total company compensation package and its "golden handcuff" executive benefits have become a way to attract and keep these valuable people. (But more about that in the next chapter.)

However, in the age of corporate downsizing and mergers and acquisitions, it is important for Young Executive to understand not only how to make the best use of his current compensation package and its fringe benefits, but which benefits he would take with him if he left, and which he would need to replace in a position with a new company.

If Young Executive examines the typical employee benefit package carefully, he will discover that it will help him overcome the two major obstacles to capital accumulation he faces: the erosive effect of taxation and his inability to save out of salary alone. As such, it offers him one of the most valuable opportunities for estate creation he is likely to meet during his life.

How so? Because of two unique features that the employee benefit package has, but the individual salary does not: favored tax treatment and favored investment prospects.

Thus, with the tax treatment:

1. Some benefits are entirely tax-free when received; with others, taxation is deferred.
2. Some benefits may be taxed when received at a 15 percent rate or other preferential rates rather than at regular income tax rates.
3. Others can be made to pass at death free of estate taxes.

And with investment:

1. Investment is made for the employee with untaxed dollars. This means there is more money available to be invested for him than if he were to use his own after-tax dollars.
2. Since income and capital gains on these package investments accumulate tax-deferred, the funds build up faster.
3. The individual invests as part of a group, not by himself. Hence, wider and more diversified investments are made.
4. The funds are handled by professional management.
5. The individual is provided with an enforced savings plan.
6. And finally, under certain plans, windfall benefits can result for the remaining employees when departing employees forfeit part or all of their unvested shares in the fund.

THE CONTENTS OF THE PACKAGE

The employee benefit package varies from company to company. Some companies offer a very full package indeed; with others, the pickings are slimmer. Some companies give the benefits across the board to all employees. Others limit some or all of them to particular groups, categories, or departments. Some of the plans contain much greater estate-creation opportunities than others. What has changed most over time is that employ-ers are shifting the ever-accelerating costs of company benefits to employees in the form of retirement plans to which employees must contribute, and higher health plan deductibles with premium costs often shared by employees. If you are employed by a company, it really pays to know how their benefit package works and how to use it to your greatest advantage.

At this point, however, let us explore the contents in a more general way, looking for the types of benefits provided by the various plans.

PROFIT SHARING: QUALIFIED AND UNQUALIFIED

Profit sharing has become a common practice for companies. It appeals to the union member and clerical worker as well as to the executive. Basically, it is an arrangement whereby a percentage of a company's profits go into a profit-sharing kitty, and the actual amounts can vary from year to year—quite helpful for businesses with uneven profits.

Profit-sharing plans hark back to the incentive philosophy because they tie the employee's financial gains to those of the company. In a good year the return to an employee may be great. The profit-sharing benefits received by executives have equaled, even exceeded, their salaries in high sales years.

The important consideration for estate-creation purposes is whether a plan is "qualified" or not. The adjective "qualified" refers to tax treatment. Qualified plans meet certain requirements of the tax laws and therefore get favored tax treatment, i.e., a deferral of taxation to the employee recipient. Unqualified ones do not.

Unqualified profit-sharing plans usually provide for the profit-sharing fund to be paid out at the end of a period, say, monthly or yearly. The share, when the employee becomes entitled to it, represents additional compensation to him and is taxable as ordinary income in the same way as his salary. The company can take its tax deduction for its contribution into the fund in the years in which they are taxed to the employees. Companies can favor certain employees or categories of employees over others, using shared profits as ways to reward valuable employees. Profits may also be shared with all employees as a way of encouraging all employees to further the profitability of the company.

Qualified profit-sharing plans have tax advantages for both employer and employee. They allow the corporation to get an immediate tax deduction. They defer or postpone taxation for the employee, and give him further tax benefits.

Such plans are formalized in writing. They may contain a formula for allocating contributions and for distributing funds after a fixed number of years, at a certain age, or upon a certain event, such as retirement, disability, medical expenses or termination of employment. The qualified plan is not allowed to discriminate in favor of any employees within the group. As pointed out above, the same does not hold for the unqualified plans, many of which discriminate in favor of the higher-paid executive.

Employer Contributions: The profit-sharing fund in a qualified plan is set up in the form of a trust. The company pays into this trust a discretionary or formulated share of its profits (limited to the lesser of 100 percent of each participating employee's compensation or a maximum of $41,000 in 2004). How these contributions are allocated to employees will be based on a formula that can relate to the amount of your compensation, and possibly age and years of service.

Employee Contributions: Some plans allow the employee to make investments using after-tax dollars. The investment opportunities here are attractive. Even when the contribution is made with after-tax dollars, the build-up of the fund is tax-deferred; the part of the income and capital gains which otherwise is taxed away remains in the fund for further investment. In addition, the employee gets the advantage of an enforced savings account and professional management of his own funds as part of a group investment.

Tax Issues for the Employer: The company gets a deduction for the share of its profits which are contributed to the profit-sharing trust.

Tax Issues for the Employee: The employee pays no tax on the amount contributed to his account at this time, regardless of whether his interest is forfeitable or nonforfeitable. The full untaxed amount is invested by the trustee. These contributions may be pooled, or may allow employees to direct the contributions made on their behalf. Taxes for the employee enter the picture when withdrawals are made.

Some plans allow you to withdraw part of your share of the funds while you are still employed, for reasons such as hardships. This is taxed as ordinary income, and incurs a 10 percent penalty tax if withdrawn prior to age 59½, unless you have contributed after-tax dollars to the funds. In that case, if the withdrawals do not exceed your contribution, there is no tax.

If your employment ends and the profit-sharing fund (plus *any other* qualified plans your employer has in place, such as a 401(k), a defined benefit pension plan) is paid out to you *within one taxable year*, here is the way the "lump sum distribution" you receive will be treated (but it must include full distributions from *all* the employer's qualified plans):

1. Your own after-tax contributions come back to you tax-free.
2. If you reached age 50 before 1986 (born pre-1936), the taxable portion attributable to your participation in the plan before 1974 can be taxed, at your option, at a flat 20 percent rate or with the benefit of a ten-year income averaging rule under 1986 rates.
3. The taxable portion attributable to post-1975 participation is subject to the above averaging rules if you were a participant for at least five years.
4. If you received stock of your corporation as part of the distribution, the unrealized appreciation on that stock is not included in the taxable amount. It is not taxed until you sell the stock.
5. Until December 31, 1999, if you had not attained age 50 prior to 1986, favorable lump sum treatment was limited to a one-time election of five-year averaging after you have reached age 59½. After 1999, this option was no longer available.
6. If none of the above apply to you, then the entire lump sum distribution would be included in your taxable income for the year in which you receive it. Such a spike in your taxable income could push your adjusted gross income so high that you would be in a higher tax bracket. This could cause you to be phased out of personal exemptions and itemized deductions.
7. *Better yet*—if you were born after 1935—consider rolling over your lump sum into an IRA. It is possible to defer taxes on a lump sum distribution if, as you retire or depart, you transfer the distribution (less your own contribution) into an Individual Retirement Account. Until you draw out money from the IRA, earnings within your fund will accumulate tax-free. You can begin drawing from your IRA at age 59½, or take earlier distributions prior to 59½ that are part of a series of substantially equal

periodic payments made at least annually for your life or a joint life expectancy or joint lives of yourself and a designated beneficiary. You could also wait until age 70½, at which point some form of annuitized payments could be elected. Funds drawn from IRAs are taxed to the recipient. Premature withdrawals prior to age 59½ that do not meet the above conditions (except for death or disability) result in a nondeductible 10 percent penalty tax on top of ordinary income tax and possible 20 percent tax withholding. See information on this and other uses of the IRA later in this chapter.

Some people prefer to take out their benefits in installments over a period of years. In this case, the payments are taxed when received. Even though capital gains treatment has been eliminated and the top tax bracket is now 35 percent, there is some likelihood that you will pay lower taxes when you reach retirement age.

Suppose you die before you retire. If your beneficiary takes the proceeds in installments, he would have the same income tax treatment you would have had, but gains would be measured from the value of the underlying investments when *he* inherited them, rather than the original price *you* paid for them. If the proceeds are transferred to a beneficiary account in a lump sum, your beneficiary may spread the payout of funds, and thus their taxability, over their life expectancy.

Forfeitures: Ordinarily your interest in an *employer's contributions* to a qualified plan is forfeitable at the start. Plans must provide for gradual "vesting"—i.e., a certain percent becomes nonforfeitable, vested to you, from time to time.

One plan might allow for vesting to begin three years after you begin work, and to continue at the rate of 20 percent per year. By the end of seven years, the vesting would reach 100 percent and your interest would become entirely nonforfeitable, i.e., you would be fully vested in the contributed funds. Another might not vest for five years of service at all, but then give you nonforfeitable rights to 100 percent of your accrued benefit. That way, vesting would reach the 100 percent mark within only five years. For employer matching contributions, such as to a 401(k), vesting occurs at 100 percent only after three years. Most plans provide that if you leave or die before your share is fully vested you forfeit the nonvested portion of your account.

Fringe Benefits: Profit-sharing plans can encompass other fringe benefits within themselves. Some plans make provisions for layoff payments, and permit the employee to borrow from the fund. In addition, funds from a qualified profit-sharing or pension trust may be used to buy life insurance for the employee. This is a way to supplement your personal insurance at little cost to you. It is true that the term part of the premium is considered part of your taxable income. However, this usually amounts to only a fraction of the total premium, and the actual tax is, ordinarily, nominal.

If you resign, you can take the policy with you (buying it from the trustee, if it hasn't vested), and continue to pay the premiums without having to pass a further physical examination, and at the rates which were in effect when the policy was first issued. If you retire, you can take the cash value or elect to have a lifetime annuity.

It is often advantageous to fund life insurance through a profit-sharing plan. Take the case of a 40-year-old executive who is in the 28 percent tax bracket. If he were to take out an ordinary life insurance policy for $100,000, he would have to pay about $1,500 in premiums every year. To pay those premiums, he has to earn $2,100 before taxes. But if the profit-sharing trust takes out the insurance instead, then this $1,500 (less a small income tax on the term rate) is available to him for other investments. If he dies before retirement, the death benefit helps to pre-fund the retirement dollars needed for his spouse's retirement security.

THE END RESULT: How does qualified profit sharing work out in actual dollars?

Here is Ms. Young Executive, age 35. If she had received a salary increase of $3,500 she would have about $2,625 left after taxes (25 percent bracket). Assuming that she invested this amount each year at 6 percent compound interest after income taxes, she would have $219,979 available to her at age 65. On the other hand, if instead of taking the increased salary, she had the $3,500 credited to her in qualified profit-sharing and pension plans and invested at 7.5 percent percent pretax she would receive a distribution of $389,040 at retirement—an increase of $169,061. However, the $389,040 is subject to taxation when received.

A drawback, but sometimes also an advantage, to profit sharing as an estate builder is that the ultimate distribution is subject to two variables. Obviously, if the company does not earn sufficient profits it will not make its annual contribution to the profit-sharing fund. Also, if the investments in the fund lose their original invested values, the overall value of the fund will be decreased. This will, of course, depend upon the type and success of the fund's investments. If they are fixed-return or insured, there is a reduced problem of capital loss. On the other hand, if the fund invests in equities, the amount to be distributed to the participants will be in direct proportion to the increase or decrease of their values. Some profit-sharing funds have had phenomenal success. We can think of several which had doubled and tripled as a result of the increase in the market value of the securities they held. The plunge in stock values between the spring of 2000 and 2003 took its toll on values, though a good portion has been recovered as of this writing in 2004.

As we know, a participant will receive at his retirement his share of the value of the fund on that date. What happens then if at this time there is a temporary drop in the value of the fund?

Consider the case of two persons who worked for the same company at the same salary. We'll call them Mr. X and Ms. Y. Both were due for retirement at the same time. Mr. X retired on the due date, February 28, 2000, and took out $200,000 from the profit-sharing fund; Ms. Y was asked if she would stay on for another year, and did. This action proved to be disastrous for her, because the market proceeded to drop. The value of the fund's securities shrank and the value of her share on her retirement date was correspondingly reduced from $200,000 to less than $135,000. Or in other words, profit sharing can seem to promise, but it cannot guarantee you, a fixed sum on retirement. Ms. Y then needed to consider at least another two years of work and waiting before daring to draw income from her retirement funds. Things could have been worse if her health required her to discontinue work sooner.

A flexible feature of profit-sharing plans is their portability. Should you leave the company prior to retirement, your vested portion of the funds contributed can generally be transferred to the retirement plan of a new employer, or to a Rollover IRA that you control. Still, between uneven employer contributions and the ups and downs of investment performance, there is no guarantee of a profit-sharing plan's future ability to produce income when you are ready to retire. Having a well-diversified portfolio can help even out volatility, but more about that in Chapter 7.

DEFINED BENEFIT PENSION PLANS

A defined benefit pension plan, on the other hand, can make such a guarantee. The amount you get when you retire doesn't depend on profits or vary with business conditions, but can be actuarially determined. An employee might prefer a company that offers the security of a pension plan to one which has a profit-sharing plan. Some companies provide both, but they are fewer in number. In fact, the number of companies that offer defined benefit pension plans has shrunk vastly over the last two decades.

Most pension plans are qualified. As such they get the same type of tax-favored treatment as the qualified profit-sharing plan. There are tax-free accumulations and tax advantages on payout, which in this case is retirement. If the employee contributes to the plan himself, he gets favored tax treatment on the income earned on his own contributions. But, unlike the qualified profit-sharing plan, pension funds cannot be used for layoff, sickness, accident, or medical expenses.

Benefits. Usually, the income you get from a pension plan is determined by your salary, your age, your length of service, your social security, or a combination of these factors. There is usually a regular increase in benefits over the course of employment so that the longer you work, the greater your benefits. In one company, these ranged from $30,000 a year for a person at the $100,000 salary level who has worked for fifteen years prior to retirement, to $50,000 for the person at the $100,000 level who worked for twenty-five years.

You can sometimes elect to have the pension paid out to you on your retirement in a lump sum rather than in installments. The plan must also provide for an optional selection of a joint and survivor annuity to ensure income for you during your life and for your spouse if she survives you. To maximize payouts, you can elect income during your life only and replace income lost to your survivor after your death with life insurance in an amount that can generate income for their remaining life. This is referred to as *pension maximization*.

As of 2004, the maximum annual benefit that can be received from a defined benefit plan is the *lesser* of 100 percent of the average compensation earned during the highest three years of consecutive employment or $165,000. This is indexed for inflation in increments of $5,000.

What About Inflation? Inflation can greatly reduce the value of a pension. The person who, twenty-five years ago, looked forward to getting $480 per month on retirement finds, when the great day arrives and his 3 percent cost of living provision is applied, that the resulting $1,005 per month is hardly enough to support him and his wife.

Some companies recognize the effect of inflation and make provisions for it. In others, the fund is divided into two parts. One part is in fixed investments or is insured to provide a guaranteed pension; the other is in equity investments. The latter is intended to act as a hedge against inflation. Still other companies increase and decrease the amount of pension payments with the rise and fall of the cost of living, somewhat like the escalator provisions of union contracts, or a minimum 3 percent.

If your employer offers a defined benefit plan, it is very important that you understand the projected benefit you will receive, and at what age or ages you can receive it. Annually you will receive a statement showing these projected benefits. For your own financial planning purposes, it is important to save these statements to gauge how closely you are on track for your own retirement income goals.

Fully Insured Defined Benefit Plans, 412(i) Plans. Some defined benefit plans are funded entirely with annuity and life insurance contracts. For the employer, these plans provide greater funding simplicity than the traditional pension. There are strict rules for such plans, but because employer contributions are based on the scheduled payments needed to fund these contracts, employers can provide level funding amounts each year without having to use the annual services of an actuary to determine what they must contribute.

For the employee, these plans can allow for higher funding levels, since employer contributions are based on low, scheduled premiums and annuity contributions. These plans are especially beneficial to employees and company owners who are nearing their retirement age, when higher contributions are needed to hit the targeted benefit by a specified, approaching age. The cash values can become substantial, helping to support benefit payouts at retirement.

What If You Leave or Die Before Retirement? Ordinarily, if you leave before you retire you will get back from the pension fund only what you have contributed to it, plus a small interest return. The purpose of the pension fund, after all, is retirement security.

If you die before retirement, your beneficiaries may get little else than your contribution. Some plans, however, like profit-sharing plans, defined benefit plans and the 412(i) plan described above, allow the pension trust to purchase a limited amount of insurance on the employee's life, so that your family will receive some benefit if you die prematurely. This added security for a family makes defined benefit plans that purchase life insurance particularly advantageous.

401(K) PLANS

Under a cash or deferred plan (commonly referred to as a "401(k) plan") you may elect to have your employer make contributions to the plan, deferred from your salary, that will not be included in your gross income for the year. The advantage of such a plan is the deferral of income tax to the year in which the distribution from the plan is made (generally at retirement).

The deferred arrangement often takes the form of a salary reduction agreement. In addition, your employer may make matching contributions that are based upon a percentage of your total elective contributions. A common example might be an employer match of fifty cents on the dollar for up to 6 percent of your compensation.

Your annual elective deferral contributions to a 401(k) plan were originally limited to a specific percentage of salary (10 percent) and a maximum dollar amount ($7,000). Inflation adjustments on this amount began in 1988. The contribution limit for 2004 is $13,000 ($16,000 if you are age 50 or older and want to take advantage of catch-up provisions), *and* the limitation on the percentage of salary that can be deferred has now been removed.

As of 2002, you can defer 100 percent of compensation or $13,000, whichever is less.

Scheduled increases in this dollar amount are as follows:

401(K) ANNUAL ELECTIVE DEFERRAL LIMITS
(NOT TO EXCEED 100% OF COMPENSATION)

Years	Dollar Limits Under Age 50	Dollar Limits, Including Catch-up Provisions for Those Age 50 & Older
2005	$14,000	$18,000
2006 & After	$15,000 (indexed)	$20,000 (indexed)

One year's employment may also be required before you are eligible to participate in the plan. Once eligible, this is one of the better investments for retirement you could make. The deferral of income, the employer matching contributions, and the deferral of tax on the growth of underlying investments help to accelerate your retirement savings.

Withdrawing Funds Prior to Retirement: This is money meant to provide you with financial security when you retire. It has the advantage of growing and compounding tax-deferred to help you build a larger retirement nest egg. The best strategy is to not tap funds within a qualified retirement plan until you are ready to cease work. Nonetheless, some retirement plans allow you to withdraw part of your share of the funds while you are still employed. These opportunities are in the form of loans or hardship withdrawals.

Loans: Generally, you are allowed to borrow as much as half your vested balance, but with a cap of $50,000. You are expected to pay back the loan over a five-year period, making payments of principal and interest. The interest is charged at a going market rate, generally prime plus one to two percentage points. If your purpose for the loan is a down payment on your primary residence, you can extend the payback period beyond the five years. Getting the loan can generally be quite easy and fast, requiring a phone call or an online, downloaded form to make the request. Within a few days, a check is sent to your address on record.

Hardship Withdrawals: It is difficult to actually withdraw money from a 401(k) while still working for the sponsoring employer, but under certain circumstances it can be done. It should be said again that taking these withdrawals jeopardizes your ability to save adequately for retirement for three reasons: 1. It lowers the amount of retirement savings that is compounding for your future; 2. The money withdrawn is subject to ordinary income tax (as high as 35 percent in 2004), *and* is subject to a 10 percent federal penalty for a withdrawal that occurs prior to age 59½. Allowable reasons for hardship withdrawals include:

- Paying medical expenses
- Covering the down payment, or avoiding eviction, or avoiding foreclosure on your personal residence

- Paying for college tuition
- Covering funeral expenses for a family member

As with profit-sharing plans, the funds in a 401(k) are portable if you leave the company. Your own contributions and your vesting in employer contributions are yours to transfer to a retirement plan associated with your new employer, or to a Rollover IRA.

403(B) PLANS

If your employer is a charitable, religious, or scientific organization; a public school or college; or a nonprofit hospital, you may have a 403(b) retirement plan available to you. These plans allow you to defer income up to $13,000 in 2004. Alternatively, if a lower contribution results, you could defer 100 percent of compensation (up to $41,000 if made collectively to more than one 403(b) plan). The plans also have catch-up provisions for those over the age of 50 or with 15-plus years of service, allowing the deferral of an additional $3,000 in 2004. Employers may make contributions as well, and as with your own deferrals, they will be made with before-tax money.

Contributions are generally made to mutual funds or a tax-sheltered annuity, which may be a fixed annuity or one with subaccounts similar to mutual funds, allowing you to have a diversified portfolio of investments. If you leave and go to another qualifying employer, your annuity or mutual fund investments can be transferred to that plan. Your contributions can then continue.

If you leave a qualifying employer and go to work at a nonqualifying employer, you can roll over your 403(b) balance tax-free to an IRA, a 401(k), or a 457 Government Plan.

Withdrawing Funds Prior to Retirement: If you take money out of a 403(b) Plan prior to the age of 59½, the money distributed to you will be subject to ordinary income tax, plus a 10 percent penalty.

Exceptions: There are exceptions to this that allow you to avoid the penalty. For instance, if you are separated from your employment after reaching the age of 55 and take distributions as substantially equal periodic payments, or if you become disabled, die, or are required to make payments to an ex-spouse due to divorce (a qualified domestic relations order), or if you use the withdrawals to pay for medical expenses that exceed 7.5 percent of your adjusted gross income.

Loans: Generally, you are allowed to borrow as much as half your vested balance, but with a cap of $50,000. You are expected to pay back the loan over a five-year period, making payments of principal and interest. The interest is charged at a going market rate, generally prime plus one to two percentage points. If your purpose for the loan is a down payment on your primary residence, you can extend the payback period beyond the five years. Getting the loan can generally be quite easy and fast, requiring a phone call or downloaded form to make the request. Within a few days, a check is then sent to your address on record.

Distributions at Retirement: You must begin to take money out of a 403(b) Plan the later of April 1st of the year following the year you retire or of the year following the year you reach age 70. If you are using an annuity as your payout vehicle, you will typically have payment choices that are 1) for your lifetime (maximum income), 2) for the joint lives of you and your named beneficiary, or 3) for a certain period of time (but not longer than your life expectancy).

SECTION 457 NONQUALIFIED DEFERRED COMPENSATION PLANS

Employees of state and local governments and their agencies and employees of tax-exempt organizations also have the opportunity to defer income and have underlying investments that can grow tax-deferred until retirement. These appear on the list of employee benefits as Section 457 Plans.

Governmental plans are held in trust, an annuity contract or a custodial account. The deferrals made by employees are held for the sole benefit of the plan participants and the beneficiaries they name. By contrast, 457 plans established by tax-exempt organizations that are not part of a governmental body hold the deferred income and the underlying investment assets as property of the employer sponsoring the plan. As such, these assets are unsecured and remain subject to creditors' claims. Nonetheless, such plans provide the opportunity to build an estate by deferring tax on a portion of income and allowing it to grow tax-deferred until retirement.

As with other retirement plans, there are limits on the amount of compensation that can be deferred. Currently, the limits are as follows:

SECTION 457 PLAN ANNUAL ELECTIVE DEFERRAL LIMITS (NOT TO EXCEED 100% OF COMPENSATION—AND INCLUSIVE OF NONELECTIVE EMPLOYER CONTRIBUTIONS) ADDITIONAL DOLLAR LIMITS

Years	Dollar Limits Under Age 50	For Catch-up Provisions for Those Age 50 & Older
2005	$14,000	$4,000
2006 & After	$15,000 (indexed in $500 increments)	$5,000 (indexed)

Section 457 Plans may also be rolled over to IRA accounts under the same rules as those for qualified retirement plans. If an employee stays in a Section 457 Plan until retirement age, he will be required to begin taking distributions by the "required beginning date" of April 1 of the calendar year following the later of the year in which he attains the age of 70½ or the year in which he retires.

SAVINGS AND THRIFT PLANS

A precursor to the 401(k) plan, savings and thrift plans offer more than their name implies. They are a valuable means of capital accumulation and growth because they can qualify for favored tax treatment and because the employer contributes as well as the employee.

Thrift savings plans operate in this manner: You put into the plan a certain amount—say, up to 10 percent of your salary. The corporation then matches your contribution in a fixed proportion and, in some cases, as much as dollar for dollar. Your contribution is made with after-tax dollars, while your employer's are a pretax contribution. These plans have the same tax-deferred accumulation benefits as qualified pension and profit-sharing plans.

Plans vary as to time of vesting. If you withdraw from the fund before time of vesting, then you forfeit the nonvested portion (but not your own contributions and the fixed interest return on them).

As with profit-sharing and pension plans, savings plans often include other features within the plan, such as stock purchase or profit sharing. You may also be able to select the type of investment you want, including life insurance.

The portability factor is the same as that of a 401(k) should you leave the company prior to retirement.

SIMPLE 401(K) DEFINED CONTRIBUTION PLANS

For companies with 100 or fewer employees (who earned at least $5,000 in the preceding year) and *no other retirement plans*, a SIMPLE savings incentive match plan for employers can be established. As the name would suggest, this plan is less expensive and more simple to establish and administer than the other qualified retirement plans we have just described. Employees may defer a specified percentage of compensation, not to exceed 100 percent or a limited dollar amount of their compensation, and employers are generally required to make a 2 to 3 percent matching contribution for all who participate. Following are the maximum deferral amounts for 2005 and 2006:

MAXIMUM DOLLAR DEFERRALS FOR SIMPLE PLANS (NOT TO EXCEED 100% OF COMPENSATION)

Years	Dollar Limits Under Age 50	Dollar Limits, Including Catch-up Provisions for Those Age 50 & Older
2005	$10,000	$12,000
2006 and later	$10,000 (indexed)	$12,500 (indexed)

401(K) SAFE HARBOR PLANS

Unlike the SIMPLE 401(k) above, 401(k) safe harbor plan designs can be used by companies of *any* size. Also unlike SIMPLE 401(k)s, safe harbor plans will allow the employer to establish more than one qualified retirement plan for you as an employee.

Safe harbor plans have the added advantage of allowing for higher salary deferrals than SIMPLE 401(k) plans. The maximum salary deferral limits for 401(k) safe harbor plans are the same as for regular 401(k) plans as listed above under that heading. This leads to yet another of their advantages for companies with a group of *highly compensated employees*. Safe harbor plans can provide greater flexibility for the highly compensated employees of a company with regard to the amount of salary they can defer from their own pay. Note: An employee is highly compensated if he (1) was at least a 5 percent owner during the previous year, or (2) was paid more than $90,000 (in 2004, indexed for inflation) by the employer during the previous year *and* during that same previous year was in the group receiving the top 20 percent of pay, if . . . the employer decides to apply this provision.

The added flexibility applies under strict conditions and works as follows: Certain minimum matches to *non-highly compensated employee* salary deferrals need to be made. This is either a $1 match for every $1 an employee deferred up to 3 percent of pay, plus a 50 cent match per $1 on the next 2 percent of pay, *or,* when an employee makes no deferred contribution from their own pay, the employer contributes 3 percent of that employee's pay. These employer contributions are immediately 100 percent vested. If these *safe harbor* requirements are met, then the highly compensated employees may make up to the maximum salary deferrals allowed from their own pay without having to conduct what is called a *nondiscrimination test*. Without trying to be overly technical, such tests require a certain parity between the percentage of pay highly compensated employees defer, and the percentage of pay other employees defer from their own pay.

SIMPLE IRA

This is another type of qualified plan designed for use by small businesses. The definition of an "eligible business" is the same as that for SIMPLE 401(k)s above. The letters in SIMPLE stand for "Savings Incentive Match Plan for Employees." Employees make contributions under a "qualified salary reduction arrangement." This is a written agreement between the eligible employer and the employees who are eligible to participate. Employees are eligible to participate if they earned at least $5,000 during any of the preceding two years and are expected to earn at least

$5,000 in the current year. (Employers may lower this threshold, but may not raise it.)

Employee Deferrals: Under this plan, employees may elect to receive payments from their employer in cash, or make *tax-deferred contributions* to the SIMPLE IRA. The contribution is expressed as a percentage of their compensation, or a dollar figure that has the same limits as those for the SIMPLE 401(k) listed above. *Catch-up contributions* may also be made as above. Each year an employee is given a sixty-day period prior to the start of the plan year to decide whether to participate that year, and whether to change their deferral amount or percentage.

Employer Contributions: Employers may elect to make *matching contributions* on a dollar-for-dollar basis for up to 3 percent of the employees' compensation (could be as low as 1 percent not more than two out of five years), *or . . .* they can elect to make *nonelective contributions* of 2 percent of an employee's compensation. This would be subject to the compensation limit of $205,000 in 2004, so the largest nonelective contribution would be $4,100. If an employer decides to make nonelective contributions, he must notify eligible employees within some reasonable amount of time prior to the sixty-day election period they have for deciding to participate in the plan.

Premature Distributions—A Special Note: Employees should be made aware that within the first two years of participating in the plan, SIMPLE IRAs have a larger, 25 percent penalty for withdrawals made by someone younger than 59½. After the two years, early withdrawal penalties are 10 percent, the same as for premature withdrawals on other qualified plans.

SIMPLIFIED PENSION PLANS (SEPs)

Your employer can set up a simplified pension plan, which must be nondiscriminatory, and contribute up to $41,000 or 25 percent of your compensation, whichever is less, to your IRA. If your employer contributes less than the IRA limit ($3,000), you may contribute and deduct the difference, subject to the IRA phase-out rule for active participants in an employer retirement plan (see "Traditional IRAs," page 71). You can participate in other qualified retirement plans and also be included in a simplified pension plan. This can be an excellent alternative for a self-employed person. If you are self-employed, your contribution will be based on your net business income up to 25 percent percent of $205,000, or $41,000 in 2004, whichever is less. Actually, for sole proprietors and partnerships the limit for the business owners is effectively 20 percent, since contributions are calculated after self-employment taxes. More about this in Chapter 6.

EMPLOYEE STOCK OWNERSHIP PLANS (ESOPS)

Some employers like the idea of giving employees an incentive to make the company grow in value. They do so by establishing retirement savings accounts (usually funded by the employer) that invest in the company's own stock. Of course, you wouldn't want this to be your only retirement nest egg, since you're tied to the success (or failure) of one company. Recent corporate scandals have become cautionary tales about relying too heavily on the growth of an employer's company to fund retirement. Still, in well-run companies with tangible promise, they can create incentives for good teamwork and allow employees, as part owners of a company, to share in the fruits of their own efforts. The name of the game is to diversify at your earliest opportunity.

Take the case of Corporation Americana's senior executive, Mr. Mature. Over the years he's accumulated a great deal of Americana's stock in the ESOP and has enjoyed watching the company's value rise. Nonetheless, at age 55, he is relieved to know that by law Americana must allow him to sell up to 25 percent of its stock. Americana's stock is not publicly traded, so the company is buying it back from him. In another five years, Mr. Mature will be able to sell up to half his stock and put it into more diversified investments.

The ESOP must begin distributions to the retiree during the plan year following the retirement year. Distributions may be taken in a lump sum or in substantially equal payments (no less than annually) over no longer than five years and may be made in stock or cash. Distributions are taxable at ordinary income tax rates, and subject to a 10 percent penalty if taken prior to age 59½ (or age 55 if you have terminated employment, for reasons such as disability).

Money from an ESOP can be rolled over to a Rollover IRA or a successor employer's qualified retirement plan. Such rollovers are available for distributions of stock or cash over periods of less than ten years.

This benefit may not be as portable should you leave the company prior to retirement. The company has up to the sixth plan year after the plan year in which you leave to make distributions. If the ESOP used a loan to purchase shares of stock, the distribution can be delayed until the plan year in which the ESOP loan is paid in full.

Nonqualified Deferred Compensation

Restrictions in the tax laws limit the amount of money that can be contributed to the qualified retirement plans of highly paid employees. Companies that want to reward and keep key employees can enhance retirement funds by creating deferred compensation plans for them. Employers can pick and choose specific employees and executives to reward in this way, and are not required to offer these plans to all employees. The employee agrees in advance to have a portion of his earnings set aside, thus not taking receipt of the taxable income for now, or the employer actually sets aside an addition to the employee's regular salary. The company retains the funds as *corporate* assets (not the employee's), and may or may not create specific investment accounts such as mutual funds, annuities, cash value life insurance or other investments earmarked for eventual return to the employee at retirement.

The employer does not receive a deduction for these contributions until the year they are received by the employee/executive. A popular funding vehicle is life insurance that accumulates some form of cash value and which can be used to meet the employer's obligation to furnish an income stream to the executive's heirs if death occurs before retirement. Often tax-free municipal bond mutual funds are used as well.

An executive would do well to seek participation in such a plan if the company is a well-run, stable, profitable one, expected to be in business for a long time to come. Both principal and investment earnings are tax-deferred, and amounts contributed are in excess of what qualified retirement plans allow, thus accelerating savings toward retirement. At retirement, the proceeds can be withdrawn all at once (likely a big tax bite), or taken over a period of time to spread the tax burden.

What allows this to be a *tax-deferred* plan for the employee is that the funds set aside are subject to forfeiture if the employee leaves the company or retires prior to a specified age or number of years. These plans are meant to be both a reward and a "golden handcuff" that provide an incentive for the employee/executive to remain with the company until at least the agreed-upon age or term of years has been reached.

A word of caution: A participant in such plans becomes a creditor of the company. In the event of its bankruptcy, the employee must wait along with all other general creditors to receive a portion of the remaining assets. For this reason alone, deferred compensation plans are not generally advisable for start-up companies or highly cyclical businesses whose futures are uncertain. As to portability should you leave the company prior to retirement, the forfeiture provisions built into the plan will generally eliminate your ability to take these assets with you.

GROUP LIFE INSURANCE

This can be a valuable supplement to personal insurance. It is purchased on a group basis by the employer from an insurance company. The employer pays a part of the premium; sometimes he pays the whole thing. His contributions are tax-deductible. The employee's contribution, if any, comes out of after-tax earnings.

The cost of group premiums is averaged out, based on the overall costs for a number of people, whose ages can vary from, say, 25 to 65.

If the employee is required to pay part of the premium, he should always compare the cost of his contribution with the premium price he would be paying for the same amount of individual insurance. If the group price is less, then obviously he has a good buy. But if it is more—and it can be for a younger person—then it may not pay for him to enter the group plan.

Term Insurance. This is the usual form of group insurance. It is issued annually and remains in force as long as the employer chooses. In most states, when you retire, you must have the right to convert the term policy to an individual ordinary life policy, without a physical examination. Don't overlook this right. It is a valuable one.

Be aware, though, that if you leave the company due to a severance, most companies' term life insurance benefits do not include conversion rights, so you would lose the coverage.

The employer's cost is tax-deductible. The employee, in turn, pays no tax on the part of the premium which the employer pays up to $50,000 of coverage. If the employer pays for more than $50,000 then the premium for the excess is taxable to the employee according to a Treasury table which is based on the employee's attained age.

This means that the employee is really receiving income, to the extent of the employer's contribution, in that he gets insurance, at no cost or at a cost below what he would have to pay for it himself.

Like individual term insurance, group term offers only temporary protection, but at ages over 40, even though the employee contributes, it is so inexpensive it usually makes a worthwhile benefit.

Cash Value Life Insurance. Some employee benefit packages also offer opportunities to purchase life insurance that builds a cash value that could be used to supplement retirement income, may reach a point in time where it pays for its own premium, and can be left in force to provide a death benefit to heirs no matter how long you live. Under some circumstances policies are offered with "guaranteed issue." This is especially valuable if you have a health condition that makes you otherwise uninsurable.

GROUP MEDICAL, HEALTH, AND ACCIDENT INSURANCE

These types of insurance are common. They can include hospitalization, medical and dental care, surgical benefits, maternity care, and beyond this, major medical insurance, for the individual and his family.

Employee benefit plans that require part payment by the employee should be examined carefully to see if they provide worthwhile benefits for the employee at comparatively low cost.

In general, however, this type of insurance carries the same advantage as many other employee insurance plans; being group rather than individual, it is usually cheaper than the individual policy and does not require a physical examination.

Moreover, it can either be fully paid for by the employer (to whom it is a tax-deductible expense) or partly paid for by him and contributed to by the employee.

The inclusion of these types of insurance coverage in the compensation package can be of substantial value to the employee. If the benefits were not available through his company, he would have to arrange for them on his own. To the extent the cost is borne by his employer, it does not have to be paid for by him. The savings he thus enjoys are therefore equivalent to a tax-free raise in pay. These days, it is rare for employers to pay for more than the employee's premium on health insurance. With the costs of health insurance rising, some employers pay only part of the employee's premium. It is common for employees to pay the cost of insuring spouses and children under the company's insurance plan.

A Tax Saving Opportunity: Cafeteria Plans: Fortunately, these out-of-pocket costs can be paid for with pretax dollars if the employer offers a Section 125 Cafeteria Plan. Depending on the plan, premiums, deductibles and co-payments can be set aside at the beginning of the year to be paid out of pretax salary dollars. Employees who are offered such plans would do well to seize the opportunity to take advantage of this tax savings.

Cafeteria plans may also be known as *premium-only plans* or *flexible spending plans*, depending on their complexity. Simple plans, known as premium-only plans, allow employees to use before-tax dollars for plan contributions such as their share of medical plan premiums. Flexible spending plans allow employees to select from a "menu" of benefits. They can choose those most meaningful to their needs and pay for them with before-tax dollars. These include such choices as dependent care expenses, insurance deductibles, coinsurance payments and eye care (exams, glasses).

Health Spending Accounts (HSAs): Starting January 1, 2004, a tax-advantaged way to pay for health insurance deductibles and premiums has been introduced. It established Health Spending Accounts (HSAs) that were created as part of the Medicare Prescription & Modernization Act in 2003. They offer employers, the self-employed and individuals the opportunity to purchase *high deductible health plans* (lower premiums for all concerned) and allow the insured to establish a Health Savings Account in which they can save and invest 100 percent of the plan's annual deductible up to $5,150 for a family. (For a single person it is up to $2,600.) Employer matches to these accounts are also allowed, but the combined contributions cannot exceed the maximums allowed. Money in HSAs can be distributed tax-free for "qualified medical expenses" that are not covered by the health plan (deductibles, co-pays, excess fees). They can also be used to reimburse the insured for premiums paid on qualified long-term care insurance policies. The health insurance plans that qualify for this program must have at least a $2,000 annual deductible and annual out-of-pocket expenses of no more than $10,000 for families. For individuals the deductible must be at least $1,000 with out-of-pocket expenses of no more than $5,000. Premiums are fully deductible for employees. Contributions made by employers are not included in the employee's income, nor are they subject to social security taxes. If some funds in the HSAs remain unused during any given year, they can be left to accumulate tax-free until needed in subsequent years, or may be withdrawn tax-free due to a disability, death or upon reaching the age for Medicare eligibility. A beneficiary can be named for HSAs in the event of the death of the account holder. If a spouse, it passes tax-free. If a nonspouse, the account is included in their taxable income for the year.

GROUP DISABILITY INCOME INSURANCE

Many employers offer group disability plans. Frequently, the premiums are paid by the employer, but some employers require that employees share the cost. Typical plans have benefits for short-term disability, such as six months, with specified weekly benefits. For disabilities that extend beyond six months, a long-term disability plan provides a second period of benefits. Typical plans might pay out 60 percent of salary to a maximum monthly benefit of $5,000 (or $10,000 for higher paid employees). Many of these plans do not cover income you receive from bonuses or commissions.

Supplemental Plans: If you run the numbers, group plans only take you so far. You may need to purchase an individually owned disability insurance policy to raise the income you would receive during a disability to a level that would sustain your household. This will help you avoid spending down savings during a prolonged illness or recovery from an injury. This is even more critical if you and your family have become accustomed to living on bonuses and/or commissions that are not replaced by your employer's group plan.

Take the example of Ms. Top, a 32-year-old high-performing salesperson at a computer company. She earns a salary of $90,000, but brings in additional income from commissions of $100,000. In addition, she routinely receives a bonus of $30,000 from the company. Her employer has a group disability plan in place. It covers 60 percent of salary (not her commissions or the bonus income) up to a monthly benefit cap of $5,000.

Let's see what happens to Ms. Top if she suffers from a long-term disability with only the group plan versus the group plan *and* a supplemental disability insurance policy. An important note: her employer pays the premium for her group plan. This means the monthly income benefit she receives when disabled is *taxable* income.

DISABILITY BENEFITS COMPARED:
GROUP BENEFITS ONLY, VERSUS ADDING
SUPPLEMENTAL INDIVIDUALLY OWNED COVERAGE

	Monthly Income While Disabled, Group Plan	Monthly Income While Disabled, Group Plan & Supplemental Coverage
Salary of $90,000	$4,500, taxable $3,375 after tax	$4,500, taxable $3,375 after tax
Commissions & Bonus of $130,000	$0	$6,400 tax-free
After-Tax Income: $3,375		After-Tax Income: $9,775

If Ms. Top is like most employees, she is aware that her employer's benefit package includes a group disability insurance plan, *and* like most employees, she has never run the numbers to see what it would actually pay her.

Another problem would occur should she decide to leave the current company. Her group disability coverage ends when she terminates her employment there. If she purchased individually owned disability coverage, it would be hers to keep. Discounts on her premiums may be available if several of her fellow employees decide to purchase this additional coverage from the same insurance company and have their premiums deducted directly from pay. The coverage and the premium discounts would remain in place regardless of where she works in the future.

INDIVIDUAL RETIREMENT ACCOUNTS (IRAS)
AND ROTH IRAS

With fewer employers offering defined benefit pension plans, it has become more important than ever to be responsible for the accumulation of our own retirement funds. For this reason, we mention IRAs within this chapter as a reminder of the need to take personal responsibility for securing retirement funds. Plans such as 401(k)s allow us to defer portions of our earned income. In addition, there are opportunities for using various

IRA accounts to increase retirement savings on a tax-deferred basis. Each has different provisions and limitations, so let's review them.

Traditional IRAs: Let's face it: The government would love it if we all saved enough to supply ourselves with adequate income for retirement. That was the reason the Individual Retirement Account (IRA) was made available originally—to encourage savings by offering the carrot of tax-deferred contributions and their growth. Subsequent law changes have cut back on the number of Americans eligible for making deductible contributions. However, the Economic Growth and Tax Relief Reconciliation Act of 2001 (EGTRRA) increased the maximum annual IRA contributions, allows catch-up provisions for those age 50 and over, and creates indexing for inflation as follows:

IRA CONTRIBUTION LIMITS

Year	Regular IRA Contributions	Catch-up Provisions for Those Age 50 and Older
2004	$3,000	$500
2005	$4,000	$500
2006	$4,000	$1,000
2007	$4,000	$1,000
2008 and later	$5,000 (indexed for inflation in $500 increments)	$1,000

Your ability to deduct IRA contributions remains limited. It is phased out if you participate in an employer-sponsored plan on the following scale:

IRA DEDUCTION PHASE OUTS FOR PARTICIPANTS IN EMPLOYER-SPONSORED RETIREMENT PLANS

Year	Singles & Heads of Households		Married Filing Jointly	
	100%	0%	100%	0%
2004	$45,000	$55,000	$65,000	$75,000
2005	$50,000	$60,000	$70,000	$80,000

Year	Singles & Heads of Households		Married Filing Jointly	
	100%	0%	100%	0%
2006	$50,000	$60,000	$75,000	$85,000
2007 and later	$50,000	$60,000	$80,000	$100,000

Nondeductible contributions to a traditional IRA can still be made. Their earnings will compound tax-deferred. After age 59½, withdrawals will be taxed on the growth portion only.

Spousal IRAs: Someone with earned income from employment and a nonworking spouse, or a spouse with less compensation, can make a deductible $3,000 contribution ($3,500 if age 50 or older) to a Spousal IRA if they file a joint return. If the working spouse or more highly compensated spouse participates in a qualified retirement plan, the amount that can be deducted from taxable income may be phased out by the same income limits as for traditional IRAs shown above.

IRA Early Withdrawal Penalties: In general, if you make withdrawals from an IRA prior to the age of 59½ you will incur a 10 percent penalty on top of paying ordinary income tax. However, there are circumstances under which early withdrawals can be taken and only the ordinary income tax paid.

No 10 percent penalty will apply on early withdrawals from IRAs if they are used for the benefit of your children, grandchildren, yourself or your spouse, and are used for:

- *Qualified higher education expenses* (tuition, fees, books, supplies, and equipment) required for the enrollment or attendance of a student at an "eligible educational institution." There is even a limited allowance for room and board.
- *First-time home buyers:* limited to a lifetime maximum of $10,000. The home buyer can be the IRA owner, a spouse, a child, grandchild or other descendant of the account owner or the owner's spouse.
- *A series of substantially equal payments:* made for the life or life expectancy of the account owner, or the joint lives or joint life expectancy of the account owner and his designated beneficiary.

- *Medical expenses in excess of 7.5 percent of adjusted gross income.*
- *Health insurance premiums paid by unemployed individuals.* This is only allowable if the account owner has received unemployment compensation for at least twelve weeks in the year funds are withdrawn, or in the year following the receipt of unemployment compensation.
- *Distributions taken due to a disability.*
- *Distributions made to a beneficiary, or the account owner's estate after death.*

This new opportunity began in 1998, and should help parents and grandparents fund a child's college expenses and first-time home-buying expenses. However, before making such a withdrawal, you should check to see if your retirement plan at work has a tax-free loan provision. It could be more advantageous in some cases. If your qualified plan has no loan provision, and you are in a position to do so, you may want to consider a rollover of your money from that retirement plan to an IRA, then withdraw the money without the 10 percent penalty. Of course, you will still owe ordinary income tax on such withdrawals.

Nondeductible, Tax-Deferred IRA: Many individuals and married couples have incomes that place them above the deductible line on IRA contributions. They can still make nondeductible contributions to IRAs and growth is tax-deferred until withdrawn at retirement after age 59½, when it is taxed as ordinary income.

When Must You Withdraw from an IRA, a SIMPLE IRA, or a SEP IRA?: Funds in an IRA, a SIMPLE IRA or a SEP IRA cannot be left to accumulate indefinitely. The shelter of tax deferral does not go on for a lifetime. This impacts you, your spouse or a non-spouse beneficiary in various ways. Let's look at each of these.

An IRA That You Own: You must begin taking distributions from an IRA account by April 1 of the year following the year in which you turn 70½. This is referred to as the Required Beginning Date. The amount of the minimum distribution you must take is referred to as the Required Minimum Distribution and is based on life expectancy tables. Regulations released in April 2002 simplified the way distributions are calculated and use a Uniform Lifetime Table that takes into account the longer lives people now live. The basis for your distribution amount is the value of your IRA on December 31 of the year in which you turned 70½ divided by your life expectancy. After your first distribution, which can be delayed until April 1 of the following year, you must take distributions by December 31 of each year thereafter. This could mean taking two distributions the first year after you turn 70½ if you used the April 1 deadline. If you fail to take distributions, there is a 50 percent tax penalty due on undistributed required amounts. After all, IRAs are meant to help you accumulate funds for retirement, and are not meant to be endless estate builders. Keep in mind, too, that you can, at that age, take out any amount you wish. Just be aware of the tax on tax-deferred contributions and account appreciation.

It should be noted that surviving spouses who were sole beneficiaries of a spouse's IRA may treat the Spousal Rollover IRA as their own IRA.

Multiple IRAs: If you have more than one IRA, the Required Minimum Distribution amounts will be calculated on the basis of the total account balances of all IRAs you own. The actual withdrawals can come from any one of them, using a liquidation order that best suits the nature of the investments in each account.

Beneficiary IRA Accounts: If you are the nonspouse beneficiary of an IRA, special rules apply as to how you can spread out the receipt of these taxable dollars over time. If you want to avoid the tax consequences of taking distribution of a large taxable sum in one year, these are worth considering.

The Account Owner Died Before *Their Required Beginning Date:* This affords you two choices:

- *The Five Year Rule:* You must take receipt of the entire amount by the end of the fifth year after the death of the original owner.
- *Life Expectancy Rule:* You must begin taking distributions by the end of the calendar year immediately following the year in which the death of the original owner occurred. The payments can be spread over your life expectancy as of your birthday in the year that follows the year of the original owner's death.

The Account Owner Died After *Their Required Beginning Date:* Here you also have two choices. Generally this will be the longer of the two circumstances below:

- *Remaining Life Expectancy of the Original Owner:* If the owner had begun to take distributions based on his own life expectancy, the remaining balance is distributed to you using at least the annual amounts the owner would have received.

- *Life Expectancy of the Beneficiary:* You could elect to spread the distributions over your own life expectancy

The Roth IRA: The Roth IRA, a tax-deferred nondeductible IRA, allows both individuals with income from employment and spouses to make nondeductible $3,000 contributions each year to a Roth IRA ($3,500 if age 50 or older.) There is still an income threshold where you can be phased out of this opportunity, but it's higher than for traditional IRAs. It begins at $150,000 for married couples filing jointly, and at $95,000 for singles, but if used properly, there is never any income tax on withdrawals.

Here's how it works:

1. You can make up to a $3,000 ($3,500 if age 50+) annual contribution. It will be reduced by any contributions you are making to a deductible IRA.
2. You can forever avoid income tax and 10 percent penalties when withdrawing funds if you meet the following conditions:
   - You wait five years after making your first contribution, *and*
   - You make your withdrawals after age 59½, *or*
   - You use the funds to buy a first home for yourself or a family member (such as a child or grandchild), *or*
   - You make withdrawals due to long-term unemployment, *or*
   - Withdrawals are due to your disability or death.
   Note: Be aware that if your withdrawal from a Roth IRA does not satisfy these requirements, it will be subject to income tax, and if you are under age 59½, to the 10 percent penalty as well.

Conversion of a Traditional IRA, a SEP or a SIMPLE IRA to a Roth IRA: Are you beginning to wish that your traditional IRA were a Roth IRA? Well, if your adjusted gross income is less than $100,000, you can convert your traditional IRA, your Simplified Employee Pension account, or your SIMPLE IRA (if these are held at least two years) to a Roth IRA. First you pay the income tax owed on the IRA, SEP or SIMPLE IRA. No 10 percent penalty tax will apply. From that point on, any growth in your investments within the Roth IRA will be income-tax-free as long as you leave the funds in the account at least five years and are over age 59½ when you withdraw them.

Before making such a conversion, be sure you calculate what your income tax bill will be. We suggest discussing it with your tax advisor to be sure you will come out ahead. Such conversions are likely to work best if you still have many years before retirement, so that the income tax paid at conversion is made up by tax-deferred accumulations and tax-free distributions after 59½.

Roth IRAs—No Mandatory Distributions—for Life!: Traditional IRAs will still be subject to mandatory minimum withdrawals when you reach age 70½. These begin no later than April 1 of the year after you turn 70½. Of course, these withdrawal amounts are subject to ordinary income tax.

The Roth IRA: Roth IRAs have no minimum distribution requirements during your lifetime. You can use them as a tax-free investment account in which capital gains, interest, and dividends are never subject to income tax as long as funds are left in the Roth IRA for the required five years and not withdrawn before age 59½.

One tax advisor we know has suggested to clients over age 70½ that they take the taxable mandatory distributions from their existing IRAs and roll over these payouts into a Roth IRA (if their adjusted gross income is less than $100,000). Then they can allow their Roth IRA to grow tax-free for a selected period of time, or for the rest of their lives. At death, Roth IRAs must be distributed to the named beneficiary, but with no income tax due. (Of course, the Roth IRA is still part of your estate, so any applicable estate tax would be due.)

The Roth IRA can be very helpful to families who wish to build funds that will enable them to not only supplement retirement income, but also to have the flexibility to provide tax-advantaged funds to help children purchase a first home.

Timing withdrawals from a Roth IRA properly will give you the greatest tax advantages, but if you need to make withdrawals prior to age 59½ and have not met other qualifications, you can still withdraw your *contributions* on a tax-free basis. After all, they were made with your after-tax dollars.

There are a wide variety of IRA investment vehicles. They include trust and custody accounts which can be invested in securities, mutual funds, and savings accounts. You may also purchase endowment contracts, retirement annuities, and federal retirement bonds.

Rollover IRAs. Individual Retirement Accounts offer other benefits. They can provide tax-free portability for an employee receiving a lump sum distribution from a qualified benefit plan or termination of the plan when leaving or retiring from a job. As long as you transfer the lump sum distribution into a proper IRA vehicle without taking receipt of the funds, you can defer its taxability. If you take a direct receipt of the funds and then deposit them into an eligible plan within sixty days, the payer of the distribution must withhold 20 percent of the amount. This 20 percent withheld will not be excluded from your taxable income unless you contribute an equivalent amount to your new plan within sixty days. The fund can be switched between different types of IRA investments, and even back to a new qualified retirement plan in which you may later participate. One valuable IRA provision permits a lump sum distribution payable to a surviving spouse to be rolled over into a "spousal" IRA. No income tax liability accrues until, and to the extent that, the IRA pays out to the surviving spouse. The funds in this account, however, cannot be later rolled over into a qualified retirement plan in which the surviving spouse participates.

One development that may allow an employee to forestall transferring retirement plan assets into a Rollover IRA is the Economic Growth and Tax Relief Reconciliation Act of 2001 (EGTRRA) which took effect on January 1, 2002. It allows for greater portability from one retirement plan to another when someone changes jobs. Thus, if the new employer's plan allows for such transfers, a new employee can move funds from a previous retirement plan to the one provided by his new employer. Retirement funds can then be consolidated and easier to manage. These exchanges can now be between such plans as 403(b), Governmental 457 Plans, SIMPLEs, SEPs, Traditional IRAs, Money Purchase Plans and Profit Sharing/401(k) Plans. Even after-tax employee contributions can be transferred to an IRA or a qualified retirement plan with a new employer. When you change jobs, it is important to ask if such consolidation is allowed in the new plan.

This provision within EGTRRA may or may not expire with the sunset provision it has after 2010. Nonetheless, its existence for now means that the Rollover IRA to which an employee may transfer retirement plan funds will potentially be quite large at retirement age. This creates an estate planning issue many families fail to consider. Sizable Rollover IRAs can pose tax problems when trying to transfer your estate to your family. Both income tax and estate transfer taxes can diminish the net amount received by heirs significantly. We know of many families who purchase life insurance to replace the amount lost to taxes, so that heirs receive the full value of what they worked so hard to accumulate over a lifetime out of earned income. We suggest consulting an attorney with tax-planning expertise to assist you in developing a plan that fits your needs and priorities.

Summing Up

The young executives of this world, and regular employees in the lower- and middle-income brackets, usually have no opportunity to bargain with their employers for special benefits. They are either available to them or not, as part of the overall company employee benefit program.

This does not mean that even the middle-echelon employee has no control over his compensation benefits. They vary from company to company, depend partly on the size of the company, and what one company doesn't offer, another will. From the estate planning point of view, they should be evaluated as carefully as the salary offered, the opportunities for advancement, and all the other things that make a job offer an attractive one. This is especially true in a climate of corporate mergers and downsizing, as well as with smaller, growing companies. Our young executive may find himself at more than one company during his career and should become astute at making optimum use of what each company's benefit package has to offer.

When negotiating for employment the executive should seek out the company whose benefit plans will provide his family with the most comprehensive security. What is involved is often more than a difference in immediate income; it may be the difference between an eventual estate and no estate at all.

Moreover, the compensation package is only the base, not the sum total of the occupational opportunities offered by a company's employment for estate creation. If a young executive stays with Americana and becomes one of its key players, avenues will open for him to negotiate *individual* corporate benefits, tailored to his needs and producing capital accumulation far beyond those offered by the basic package.

Let's turn the clock ahead and move on to the second act in the career of a young executive.

❧

YOUR OCCUPATION AND
ITS OPPORTUNITIES: SELECTIVE
BARGAINING FOR THE EXECUTIVE

The season and setting are the same, a fine spring evening outside the door of Mr. Young Executive's house. The time is different, however, and so is Young Executive. He is fifteen years older and fifteen years wiser. His salary is now $180,000 a year.

The main change in Young Executive, however, is that his name is different. In corporate circles he is known as Mr. Key Executive, a person whose business acumen and devotion to his company make him a valued asset. As Mr. Key, he is no longer merely a hired man. He has become a valued partner in the corporation, in spirit if not in fact. He is a decision maker, a planner, and a member of the corporate management team, performing many of the functions that the old-time individual business owner used to perform.

Corporation Americana wants to hang on to its Mr. Key. He is one of the important people on the team that makes the profits. They would like to build a fence around him, if that were possible, to keep him from straying down the street to a competitor.

By a not-so-odd coincidence, this is exactly what Mr. Key is thinking of doing on this very spring evening. He is returning from a most interesting meeting with a person known in the higher-echelon circles he frequents as a headhunter, a person who specializes in finding top executives for her corporate clients. The most likely place to find such top executives is in *other* corporations.

This particular "headhunter" has just "found" Mr. Key. The client in question is Corporation GlobalBiz: powerful, big and successful, just like Mr. Key's own Corporation Americana. Mr. Key got the idea, although no precise terms were discussed, that there would most certainly be a substantial salary hike for him, plus certain other unnamed benefits that they could "work out" if Mr. Key were interested.

He doesn't realize it, but the advent of the headhunter, her offer, and all that it implies, has just opened the door to a fruitful estate-building opportunity for him.

Mr. Key is now in a bargaining position. Both companies want him, and are willing to negotiate with him for additional benefits that will secure his services and his loyalties. Most corporations regard these additional benefits as inducements and incentives for key employees. They realize that people like Mr. Key are hard to come by, that they devote all their time and energy to their work, often to the neglect of their own financial problems. They know that they must help Mr. Key make up for that neglect by offering special opportunities to ensure the financial security of Mr. Key and his family. They know an unworried executive can concentrate on the company's needs instead of diverting his time and attention to his own financial concerns.

These additional benefits, if Mr. Key bargains well and wisely for them, will provide him with a custom-made program of capital accumulation that can be keyed to the rest of his estate plan and to his regular compensation package. Its long-range benefits may be worth far more than a mere salary raise.

The companies will make offers, undoubtedly. But if Mr. Key is to drive a good bargain, he must not only listen to offers; he should also make proposals of his own. To do that, he needs to analyze two important factors: his own needs and the range of possible benefits open to him.

THE EXECUTIVE'S GOALS

We know them in a general fashion: some form of tax-sheltered compensation; an opportunity to invest in the company and so accumulate money via the capital gains route; help in purchasing family benefits with before-tax dollars at no or little cost to him. All of those are available in some form or another, as we shall shortly see.

Before he puts together his package of proposals, however, the executive must make an important decision. How much is he willing to sacrifice (if need be) in the form of salary to attain them?

The high-salaried married executive will be taxed at a 35 percent rate. If Mr. Key were given a raise from $180,000 to $200,000, only $13,000 of that raise would be left to him after taxes.

This isn't the whole story, however. In reality, there are also intangible benefits to a salary raise. Since many package benefits are based on salary levels, these usually go up in value, along with the increase of the salary.

The intangibles are more difficult to assess, but just as meaningful. How important to Mr. Key is the status which $200,000 would give him within his company and industry? This is not a flippant question; future opportunities, advancements and offers may be contingent on this status-salary position. And what about his own immediate needs and desires? Will they be satisfied with the substitution of fringe benefits for a salary increase?

And finally, as Mr. Key weighs GlobalBiz against Americana, he must take into account the effect on his estate of the loss of the nonvested parts of the Americana compensation package, if he makes the change. What will GlobalBiz do to replace this loss?

He must analyze all these factors and come up with a balanced proposal—a package that he has fashioned out of his own and his family's needs, a package built out of benefits and salary that will work continuously to build his estate and secure the independence of his family when he dies, or ensure his support if he retires or becomes disabled.

What is the range of corporate benefits possibly available? There are a number. They vary from simple bonuses to highly complicated plans for deferring compensation. He needs to know them all so as to select for his proposal package those that would best develop and supplement his estate plan. At the same time he should keep his negotiating partner in mind—the corporation. How will these arrangements affect it? Are there mutual advantages to be obtained, and if so, what are they?

Our particular Mr. Key, incidentally, isn't the only executive in his corporation who should consider these proposals. They apply equally to other key players who are not considering a change, but who do want a custom-made set of benefits from their company.

BONUSES:
CASH, STOCK, DEFERRED, OR RESTRICTED

Individual bonus arrangements are commonplace today. They suit the company that doesn't want to commit itself to a high salary or whose by-laws do not permit it to pay salaries above a certain level. The president of a company who gets $400,000 a year in salary and $200,000 in bonuses is no longer an unusual figure on the corporate scene. Neither is the lower-echelon executive whose $90,000 per year compensation is made up of $60,000 salary plus $30,000 bonus.

There are many ways in which bonuses can be dispensed. If you are thinking of negotiating a bonus arrangement, you should be sure that you know which kind you want.

Cash-and-Carry Bonuses

This is the simplest type. Generally, it is given annually, and is based on the company's profit or the executive's productivity. There may or may not be a written agreement between the executive and the company. Cash bonuses are taxable in the year they are received. They are thus not true estate builders but more like a salary raise; they provide additional spendable income, theoretically available for investment.

Stock Bonuses

A stock bonus gives an executive a personal stake in the future appreciation of the market value of his company's stock and thus is often a greater incentive to him. It also has an advantage over other stock plans in that the executive doesn't have to pay out any money for his investment.

A word of caution about stock bonuses: they are taxable income, so it's wise to arrange for a partial payment in cash to pay the tax.

A further word of caution: The accounting scandals of the early 2000s create a cautionary tale about staking one's future on the fortunes of any one company. The executive would do well to attach his goals for a secure retirement to a diversified portfolio of investments in qualified retirement plans and personal investments and savings. Any financial rewards that *do* materialize from appreciated company stock should come as windfalls that may allow for an earlier or more comfortable retirement than had been envisioned. This possible frosting on the cake still provides a tantalizing incentive for the executive to lend his talents to the future growth of the corporation, but should not be at the core of fundamental retirement planning.

Deferred Bonuses

One way to overcome the tax impact on a lump sum bonus is to arrange to have your bonus paid out on the installment plan. This is a particularly good idea if the bonuses are tied to profits and so are liable to be high in some years, low in others.

Will the corporation agree to defer bonus payments? The only reason for objection is that it cannot take its tax deduction until the bonus is paid out. But this objection is offset by the fact that the corporation gets the use of the bonus monies until the payout time arrives.

The government will not consider a bonus deferred, however, if the recipient can be said to have "constructively received" the whole bonus; that is, if he had the right to take it all immediately. In that case it demands an immediate tax payment on the full amount of the bonus.

The constructive receipt problem is a ticklish one. To make sure that your deferred bonus does not fall under it, you should make a written agreement with the company specifying that the payment of bonuses as earned will be deferred. This agreement can state that your right to the bonus is a conditional one, i.e., contingent on your remaining with the company until the bonus is paid out.

Restricted Bonuses

Some companies prefer to create bonus arrangements that have various restrictions on when they can be activated. These generally take the form of such things as stock options (both nonqualified and qualified), warrants, restricted sale stock plans and phantom stock. All these are discussed below, explaining how they effect the executive and how they effect the company that offers them.

STOCK OPTIONS

One of the most prevalent and popular fringe benefits, the stock option, can be of great value to the executive. It is another way of giving him a personal stake in the corporation, geared to the market value of its securities. It allows him to make investments using a minimum amount of capital, or in some cases none at all, and to take advantage of rising markets with small risk to himself. However, it should be said that after what we all experienced in the spring 2000 stock market downturn, an executive would do well to temper his expectations about how much his stock options will contribute to his retirement nest egg and overall estate building.

A stock option is a right, in this case the right to buy corporate stock within a certain period of time. The option entitles you to purchase the stock at a fixed price—regardless of what the market price may be at the time you exercise the option. A few companies offer these options to all employees, or to all employees above a certain level, but generally speaking they are offered to key personnel only, or else as an inducement to lure key people away from one corporation to another.

Options usually aren't granted outright but on the installment plan. If the executive leaves before his option period has expired, he forfeits his right to the unexpired part of the option. In addition, companies usually add other restrictions. In some plans the executive must agree to hold his stock for investment only; he is prevented from selling in the open market. Sometimes the company requires that if the executive dies, the stock be sold back to the corporation (this, incidentally, can be a valuable right to an executive if the stock has no ready market and would thus be a nonproductive asset in his estate).

Executives like Mr. Key who are negotiating stock option agreements should look at these company restrictions carefully; they can result in a limitation, or conversely, an increase in their future profits.

What happens when the market price falls below the option price? If the executive has already exercised his option rights, he is now the owner of the stock and he loses just as any other investor does. If he hasn't bought the stock yet, he is under no obligation to do so and thus incurs no loss. In other words, the value of stock options is tied to the value of the corporate stock. They do not represent guaranteed benefits the way pension plans and some other items in the compensation package do.

A few companies, however, try to make up for this by setting up a variable option price within a certain range. Other ways to assure the benefits of stock options are to make provisions for reducing the option price under specified conditions, or to issue new options at a lower price when the market drops.

Stock options fall into two classes for tax purposes: incentive stock options and nonqualified stock options.

The Incentive Stock Option

The tax advantage of an incentive stock option (ISO) is that there is no federal tax at the time the option is either granted or exercised (tax treatment at the state and local level may differ); however, the spread between the option price and market value at the time of exercise is a tax preference item and is added back for purposes of calculating the alternate minimum tax (AMT). If this is not a problem, then profits may be eligible for the more favorable capital gains treatment.

To qualify as an ISO, there must be a shareholder-approved plan that requires the following restrictions:

- The stock granted cannot be sold within one year of exercising the option, nor within two years of the option being granted. (Otherwise it may result in taxable compensation to the holder of the option.)
- Options must be granted within ten years and an option must be exercised within ten years of grant.
- The option price must equal the fair market value of the stock on the date it is granted.
- Options to purchase no more than $100,000 worth of stock may be granted to an employee in any calendar year.
- ISOs are not transferable during the employee's lifetime. Only the employee can exercise the option. They are, however, transferable at death.
- If the employee terminated employment, the options must be exercised within ninety days of the date of termination.
- A disabled employee or the estate of a deceased employee, however, may, within twelve months of termination of employment, exercise an option.

Let's say that Mr. Key had been offered ISOs. In order to take best advantage of this program, he should meet with his tax planner. If they determine that he is *not* otherwise subject to the AMT, then he should plan to exercise his options over the life of the option (generally the ten years mentioned above). The advantages? He will be able to minimize the impact of the AMT, *and* he will be able to start the clock on one-year holding periods so that future sales of stock will receive the favorable rates for capital gains.

He should take further care not to incur ordinary income tax on the sale of stock from an incentive stock option exercise by assuring that he sells it *after* one year from the date of his exercise, or *two years* from the grant date, whichever is later. This way, he will be able to receive the more favorable 15 percent capital gains treatment.

Nonqualified Stock Options

In this type, the option price can be set at any amount and the option can be exercised at any time, limited only by what the stockholders of the company will approve. In a rising market, an executive can make a substantial profit.

It is true, of course, that the executive must pay ordinary income tax on the difference between the option price and the stock's fair market value at the time the option is granted. If the option is subject to a condition that affects its value, there's no taxation until the condition is met or removed.

Again, let's look at some actual figures. Suppose Corporation Americana agrees to give Mr. Key an option to buy 1,000 shares of Americana stock at $50 per share. The agreement states that Key can exercise the option in four installments of two hundred fifty shares per year, starting one year from the date of the agreement. There is a further condition that Mr. Key must still be employed by Americana at the time he exercises each of the installments.

At the time Key is given the option the market value of the stock is $75 per share. At the end of the first year, it goes up to $100 and Mr. Key exercises the first installment, paying the company $12,500 for 250 shares. On paper, he now has a profit of $12,500. This is the value of the first installment of the option, and therefore he must pay ordinary income tax on this sum. Mr. Key will also be subject to federal income tax withholding, social security, Medicare, state and local taxes at the time of exercise. (Some employers have written in provisions to allow the use of shares to cover withholding costs.) If Mr. Kay exercises his stock option, then sells the stock soon thereafter, his cash proceeds can be used to pay the withholding costs. If his profits from the exercise are substantial, some preplanning should be done to consider where he will get the funds to pay additional taxes when he files his tax returns.

If he sells the stock sometime in the future for $100 per share, he owes no taxes. However, if he thinks that the value of Americana stock is likely to rise due to its current success and future plans, he may want to exercise his options sooner rather than later. Why? Because though he'll pay ordinary income tax and withholding costs on any positive difference between his exercise price and the stock's fair market value at the time, any future increase in the value of the stock can be taxed at the more favorable capital gains rate. If he can afford to tie down his money while he waits for this increase, has the money to pay the income tax and withholding costs on his exercise, and considers it a priority investment, this could be a good strategy for him.

As if this were not enough for Mr. Key to think about, he should also evaluate how much of his own net worth is tied up in Americana's stock. The issue of diversification and how much he wants to depend on the future growth and stability of Corporation Americana should be considered. If his stock exercise is dependent upon his working at Americana at the time of exercise, he may want to evaluate his own prospects for staying on board at Americana.

To the corporation, the taxation aspects of unrestricted options are more advantageous. It gets a tax deduction for the value of what it gives the executive: the difference between the option price and the market price at the time the option becomes taxable to the employee.

Financing Stock Options

An executive is often faced with the problem of finding the money to exercise his stock options. There are a number of alternatives available to him.

1. He can arrange for a loan from the company or from existing pension or profit-sharing funds.
2. He can take a bank loan. In most cases collateral will be required, however. He will have to put up other securities in addition to the optioned stock. This is because the loan is made to buy stock and the usual margin requirements for this type of transaction must be met. Once again, the interest expense will not be deductible unless the loan is secured by a residence.
3. If the option is exercisable over an extended period of time, he can exercise part of the option and then use this stock to pay for the new stock as each installment is exercised, without gain on the stock used in payment.

Regardless of how he arranges his loan, of course, he will have to pay the money back. If he's bought in a rising market, however, that can be fairly painless. He can sell some of the stock, repay the loan, and still have his profit.

Stock Options and Estate Taxes

If an executive dies before he's exercised his stock options, what happens then?

Sometimes the options are not exercisable and therefore lapse. Or the estate may be allowed to exercise them. If so, they are considered part of his *taxable* estate. His estate will have to pay an estate tax on the value of the options, i.e., on the difference between the option price and the market price at the time of his death.

This estate tax liability, incidentally, occurs whether or not the estate actually exercises the option. Thus an estate tax can be assessed even though the estate doesn't receive any profit. This usually means that the estate will want to exercise the remaining options. But the cash to do this may be hard to get because of the margin limitations on stock-purchase borrowing. Key executives therefore would be well advised to provide for sufficient life insurance proceeds to make ready cash available for this purpose, especially if their stock options are substantial.

OTHER STOCK PLANS

Stock options are not the only way in which an executive can tie his fortunes to those of the corporate stock. Many other arrangements are possible, some well known, others not.

Stock Warrants

The stock warrant resembles a stock option. The difference is that the warrant is negotiable. It is a right to purchase a specified number of shares of a corporation's stock at a fixed price, usually within a stated period. There is no capital gain or loss when the warrant is exercised and the stock is purchased. A *subsequent sale* of the stock may incur a gain or loss, depending upon its value at sale. The tax basis of the warrant is added back to the sale price to make this determination.

The warrant itself is immediately salable at its market value. This is a way to make a quick profit in a rising market without paying out any money at all except in taxes. If the warrant was distributed as a nontaxable stock dividend, the owner's tax basis will be the difference between the proceeds from his sale and the fair market value of the warrant when he received it. If he received it as a taxable dividend, or it was purchased, a gift or an inheritance, he would realize a capital gain or loss based on the difference between his cost basis and the proceeds of the sale. Either way, careful tax planning is needed, and it is wise to consult a tax advisor prior to selling the warrant itself.

Letting the warrant lapse without exercising it is considered to have been a sale on the actual lapse date. If this results in a loss, the owner can only realize the loss for tax purposes if the warrant was acquired by a taxable dividend, or by purchase, gift or inheritance. If the warrant was received through a nontaxable stock dividend, the cost basis is zero for purposes of a lapse.

Stock warrants are often used as an inducement to obtain the services of an outside person, or as a bonus to a present key person. The value of the warrant (the difference between the market price of the stock and the warrant exercise price at the time the warrant is issued) is subject to income tax. Any profit above the market price at the time the warrant is issued is also subject to tax.

Restricted Sale Stock Plans

Restricted sale stock plans provide that the executive may purchase limited amounts of company stock at a discount from fair market value with after-tax dollars. In some cases the purchase is financed on an installment basis out of his dividend proceeds. If Mr. Key participated in such a plan, he might want to consider whether or not to include the value of the restricted stock in his income as he receives it. If it is included, subsequent dividends he is paid will receive the favorable 15 percent dividend tax rates. If he elects not to include the restricted stock in his income, he will pay ordinary income tax on them.

When he leaves the company, Mr. Key must sell the stock back to the company. The price he gets depends on the particular plan in force in his corporation. It may be based on the book value at the time of the resale or on a valuation based on earnings. Or there may be a set figure which is agreed to in advance, but adjusted periodically. If the stock is held for a sufficient period of time, he may receive capital gains treatment on profits at sale.

Restricted stock plans are particularly useful to small corporations. They give an executive all of the benefits of stock ownership except the right to sell on the open market. They keep the control of the stock within the company. They are frequently used in industries where turnover of top personnel is high.

Phantom Stock

Not too many executives in Mr. Key's position know about this unusual fringe benefit. It offers a unique way of participating in the increase in value of corporate stocks without investing any capital.

Shadow stock is a bookkeeping device. The executive doesn't actually receive stock at all, but he participates in stock appreciation and dividends just as if he did.

Here's how it works. A key executive is credited on the company books with a certain number of units equivalent to stock, but no stock is actually issued. Any dividends declared on the stock are credited to his account, paid out to him, or retained, depending on the provisions of the plan. He is also credited with any increase in the value of his mythical shares, and he gets the benefit of stock dividends and splits. When he leaves, reaches the end of an agreed-upon period of time, or retires, he receives an amount of money equal to the increase in value of his shares, plus whatever retained dividends have been credited to his account.

When he takes out his profits, the executive pays ordinary income tax on the gain. No capital gains treatment is possible. The tax impact can also be spread out if he takes his payments in installments. The corporation gets similar tax treatment. No deduction is allowed until the time of payout.

Phantom stock is often used by family-owned businesses and other closely held companies who want to provide incentives to key people without sharing the ownership or voting control in the company. Unlike stock options, the employee has no cash outlay (except taxes) upon receipt of the benefits. However, the company faces a potentially substantial cash drain when the benefit is paid. This benefit tends to be underused, due to the accounting requirements to make adjustments on the company books each year for the changes in the underlying value of the stock and dividends credited to employees.

DEFERRED COMPENSATION

The trouble with success is that its rewards are reaped during high-earning years and often don't carry over into later, less productive years. This is a key problem for all of today's key executives. They get their major salary increases at the time when they have to pay the largest taxes on them. How much more advantageous it would be if the increases could be paid out in retirement years, when the tax burden is lower. Or if the executive died, how much more secure his family would be if they could have the benefit of that salary increase then.

Actually, both these alternatives are available to the present-day executive, through corporate deferred compensation plans. These are payment devices which, in effect, level out the executive's earnings curve and spread out his compensation during his entire life instead of concentrating it during his working years. The resultant tax savings increase the amount of spendable cash available to him during his life. If he dies, his family gets the benefit of both the earnings spread and the tax savings.

Many items in the compensation packages, such as pension and profit-sharing funds, are really forms of deferred compensation. But because they are qualified, and hence nondiscriminatory (i.e., paid out according to a standard formula to *all* employees in the group), they are of limited value to the key executive. *The kind of deferred compensation we are discussing now is discriminatory and limited to selected personnel.* It is the result of an individual contract between the corporation and the executive, tailored to the needs of that particular executive.

Suppose our friend Mr. Key received an offer of a big salary increase from his company, Corporation Americana. Assume he decided that he wanted this increase deferred. What precisely does he ask for?

The Deferment Contract

Deferred compensation agreements generally provide that a salary increase—let us say $10,000—is not to be paid out at the present time but postponed until retirement or termination of employment, when the accumulated sum is paid in installments to the executive, either for the rest of his life or for a certain number of years. If the executive dies, his family gets the payments he would have received. Such agreements can be *pure* deferred compensation, where the employee agrees to defer a portion of his current compensation; or they can be *salary continuation plans* where the employer provides a cash benefit in addition to the employee's regular compensation.

Often these contracts also provide for the post-retirement consulting services of the executive. This assures the company that it will continue to have his valuable services, and that he will not go over to a competitor.

This part of the contract should be carefully worked out, however, in order to ensure that the executive will not lose the capital gains treatment, if any, of his package compensation deals (pension, profit sharing, etc.) because his employment hasn't "terminated." The dangers of his being taxed for constructive receipt must also be guarded against.

In actual monies received, how does the executive benefit? If Mr. Key takes a $10,000 increase immediately he will have only $6,700 left from it after his 33 percent tax. Under the deferment contract, he may have as much as $7,200 per year left after taxes, if he receives it during the lower-income-tax-bracket years of retirement.

There is a possible thorn in this rosebush called deferred compensation, which a key executive should keep in mind. Compensation can only be considered "deferred" if it is subject to substantial forfeiture, such as being subject to his loss if the employee leaves prior to a specified age. During this period of time when the employee has no vesting, the deferred compensation is a general liability of the corporation. The fund cannot be set up as a trust or set aside for the employee in any way which would remove it from the reach of the corporation's creditors. In the event of a bankruptcy, even the deferred compensation funds would be available to meet creditors' claims. This means there is always a possibility that a corporation may not be able to meet the obligations of the deferred compensation contract when the payout is due. If the company is relatively new, and not proven over time, this may not be a desirable arrangement for Mr. Key. With established companies the risk may be small, but it is still there.

The Use of Deferred Compensation Funds

During the years when part of Mr. Key's salary is being deferred, the corporation has use of these funds. By all rights they should be used by it for the benefit of Mr. Key and not the corporation. After all, if he hadn't chosen to have it deferred, the money would have been paid out and therefore wouldn't be available to the corporation. A common method of using these funds for the employee is to use the funds to buy insurance on the executive's life.

Key Person Insurance. When a company takes out insurance on a key person, it is, in effect, indemnifying itself in the event he dies and his services are lost. When key person insurance is used in conjunction with a deferred compensation agreement, however, it is also a way for the company to finance the deferred compensation. Should Mr. Key die, the proceeds from the insurance policy can be used by the company to meet the obligations of his family. If he retires, the cash surrender value can be used to meet its responsibility to him.

This insurance will often completely finance the company's obligation to Mr. Key and his family at no, or little, cost to the company. This is so because: (*a*) the premiums are paid for out of the after-tax amount that the salary increase would have cost the company; (*b*) the insurance proceeds are received tax-free; and (*c*) the benefits paid to Mr. Key or family are tax-deductible.

Thus the cost to Corporation Americana of, say, a $13,000 raise to Mr. Key would have been $8,710 after taxes. This amount more than pays the annual premium on a $200,000 paid-up-at-65 policy on him. If Mr. Key should die before retirement, let us say, at age 60, the company would get $241,400 (including dividend additions) of tax-free proceeds, or $157,920 more than it paid in premiums.

On that basis it would be possible for the corporation to pay out as much as $300,000 to Mr. Key's family over an extended period without dipping into any reserves. The $300,000 that is paid out is tax-deductible at a 34 percent rate, so the actual cost to the corporation is only $198,000—just $43,400 less than the company got in insurance proceeds.

On the other hand, if Mr. Key does not die but retires at age 65, the cash surrender value of the policy, including the dividend additions, is about $182,000. This is enough for the company to fund a deferred payout of $20,000 a year for fifteen years after its tax deductions, at a cost of $16,000 more than it received when it cashed in the policy. Thus Mr. Key has guaranteed a total of $300,000 to himself or his family whether he lives to retirement or dies anytime prior to it.

These are figures that Mr. Key should certainly have well in mind when he sits down at the bargaining table.

Split Dollar Life Insurance. For over forty years, split dollar life insurance plans have been a commonly used executive benefit. Put simply, they are an arrangement wherein the employer and the employee split the cost of paying premiums, and split cash or death proceeds. Literally speaking, *if the employee is the owner of the policy,* the employer "loans" the bulk of the premium cost to the employee. In the past, this operated like an interest-free loan, and no interest was deemed to be paid by the employee. A collateral assignment creates an obligation that the policy cash values or death benefit be used to reimburse the employer for any premiums it has paid. *If the employer is the owner of the policy,* the employer endorses a portion of the death benefit to the employee for his control. With deferred compensation plans, these arrangements have been used to help fill in any gaps in the plan. They have also been used in Supplemental Executive Retirement Programs (SERPs) to provide supplemental retirement income.

There has been a sea change in the use of this technique for providing selective benefits for key employees and owners of businesses. For plans entered into after September 17, 2003, there are new regulations governing split dollar plans. For those established prior to September 18, 2003, material modifications of the plan will trigger the application of portions of the new rules. These are very complex rules, but we will try to offer an overview of their effect.

The changes in the tax treatment of split dollar plans focus on the issue of policy ownership. *If the employee owns the policy* (collateral assignment arrangement), then any premium payment by the employer is considered a loan. The employee will owe interest payments to the employer at the Applicable Federal Rate (AFR). The loan payments can be structured as either a term loan (higher interest rates initially, but providing a cap—advantageous in a low-interest-rate environment), or as a demand loan (allowing a lower initial rate, but adjusted every month—or once a year if a blended rate is used). The employer will have to pay tax on the interest payments. The employee cannot personally deduct the interest paid.

If our Mr. Key already has such an arrangement, he would be wise to request a review of its status relative to the new rules, and have his or the corporation's tax advisor explain how he will be affected. This is especially true if his was a *collateral assignment arrangement* where Americana paid the majority of the premium, with Mr. Key being deemed to have received a benefit (or bonus) equal only to the pure term cost portion of his cash value life insurance.

If Mr. Key has an *endorsement plan*, the new rules will not apply unless he, as nonowner of the policy, is given access to some portion of the policy's cash value. If this occurs, he will be taxed on that amount.

If he negotiates for a newly established plan, he should discuss carefully with his tax advisor what the plan is meant to accomplish to be sure the plan will serve the right purpose.

The Sarbanes-Oxley Act of 2002. With the uncovering of corporate scandals and accounting irregularities, Congress passed the Sarbanes-

Oxley Act in 2002 to impose greater oversight and accountability on corporate accounting practices. As a result, it is unclear whether publicly traded companies can legally make what appear to be tax-free loans to pay for life insurance premiums on cash value policies. The act specifically prohibits corporate loans to the top five executives. In the past, split dollar funding of life insurance was a popular way of providing a key employee of a publicly traded company with an advance of premiums; in effect, a tax-free loan to pay for life insurance premiums on cash value policies. As a result of the new law, many companies are simply paying taxable bonuses to employees with existing split dollar arrangements, and letting the employees make the premium payments themselves.

To summarize, after September 18, 2003, new rules apply to split dollar arrangements. Collateral assignment plans will be treated as loans from an employer to an employee. Endorsement arrangements will continue to receive favored treatment to the extent that they do not make portions of the policy's cash value accessible to the employee.

Arrangements made prior to September 18, 2003, that are not materially modified thereafter should not be affected by the new rules. However, these new rules have many twists and turns. Key employees and their employers with existing plans should seek professional tax advice on how best to continue their arrangements.

Tax Implications of Deferred Compensation and Split Dollar Insurance in the Estate

Deferred compensation is subject to the estate tax in an executive's estate. It is also taxable to the beneficiary as income, although the estate tax paid can be a deduction from the income received. Even so, the income tax impact can be serious. When deferred compensation is paid to a widow, in addition to other income she may be receiving, her income tax bracket goes up, sometimes so much that the benefits from the deferred payments can be reduced. This heavy tax erosion of the deferred payments can be lessened by dividing up the payments among a number of beneficiaries, or making them payable to a trust which is taxed as a separate entity.

Split dollar insurance proceeds are also usually taxable in the estate. One possible way to avoid this is to transfer ownership of both the policy and the split dollar agreement over to the beneficiary, and thus take them out of the executive's taxable estate.

162 EXECUTIVE BONUS PLANS

Another way in which Americana can reward and retain Mr. Key is to provide a special bonus that is paid directly to fund a cash value life insurance policy on his life. The only cost of the premium for Mr. Key is the income tax paid on this bonus. Corporation Americana can even "gross up" the bonus to cover the tax incurred. As long as the amount of this bonused premium falls within a "reasonable" amount of compensation, it is deductible to Americana under Section 162 of the Internal Revenue Code. The corporation can pick and choose which valued people will be rewarded in this fashion.

Mr. Key owns the life insurance contract, can select the type of policy, can name the beneficiary and will have access to the policy's cash value. He now has an extra layer of financial security for his family should he die prematurely, and the prospect of accumulating a substantial tax-deferred cash value available upon retirement. This "frosting on the cake" has come very inexpensively for Mr. Key, and may have cost him nothing at all if he received a gross bonus that netted his entire life insurance premium.

Executive bonuses can also be given in the form of cash benefits.

RESTRICTED ENDORSEMENT BENEFIT ARRANGEMENTS

What if Mr. Key's employer wants to provide him with a "golden handcuff" that will give the company an immediate tax deduction, rather than deferring it to some future time, yet create a restriction on Mr. Key's access to it that keeps him on board? This can be accomplished using a restrictive bonus plan. On a selective basis, the company can provide cash value life insurance to just the key people it wants to reward and retain. It is a very easy benefit to install, and is paid simply as additional compensation by the employer.

How does it work? A written agreement provides that the employee will be the purchaser of a life insurance policy on his own life. He will be the owner, and will name the beneficiary of the policy. A restrictive endorsement is added to the policy that states that the employer's consent is required for the employee to do the following:

- Surrender the policy.
- Assign or pledge the policy to obtain a loan.

- Make a change in the ownership of the policy.
- Borrow from the policy's cash value.

The agreement will state conditions under which these restrictions will expire. Typical conditions include:

- The employee retires.
- The employee reaches a stated age.
- A stated number of years have passed.
- The employer decides to release the restrictions.
- The company is dissolved or becomes bankrupt.

A second written agreement provides for the bonus that pays for this benefit. Under this document, the employer agrees to provide a bonus to the employee in the form of premiums paid directly to the insurance company. The premiums are considered taxable income to the employee in the year the premiums are paid. For this reason, some employers provide a "double bonus" that covers the employee's tax on the bonus.

Often employees will add after-tax dollars of their own to these policies. Combined with their employer's premium contributions, the tax-deferred buildup of the cash value can provide a source for additional funds available at retirement. The money will grow tax-deferred, and can be withdrawn from the policy at retirement without tax up to the dollars paid into the policy. Additional funds can be withdrawn as tax-free loans (if the policy has not been overfunded in its early years and hasn't become a modified endowment contract.) This can be very attractive to a key person who is already contributing up to allowable limits into qualified retirement plans, and is looking for other tax-advantaged ways to save for retirement.

LONG-TERM CARE INSURANCE AS AN EXECUTIVE BENEFIT

Mr. Key's mother-in-law just passed away at the age of 86 after ten years of illness and years of expensive care. He never wants to worry about exhausting his own retirement funds, nor interrupt his children's lives due to his or his wife's future needs for costly long-term care. He requested and received long-term care policies for himself and his wife, paid for by the corporation. They agreed to buy him and his wife policies that are fully paid by his age 65. Corporation Americana will fully deduct the premiums as an ordinary and necessary business expense. Mr. Key will owe no tax on this benefit, and his eventual use of the policy daily benefits will be tax-free. This is, indeed, a valuable benefit that puts a meaningful safety net under the funds he is accumulating for a secure retirement. It could be worth hundreds of thousands of dollars to him and Mrs. Key.

THE ESTATE BUILT FROM BARGAINING

Can it be done? That is to say, could a key executive build an estate out of no more and no less than the best compensation agreements he can make with his employer?

The answer is yes.

Here is one estate we know of personally. It is composed of the following items: $325,000 in the pension plan; $65,000 from the profit sharing fund; $150,000 of group life insurance; $110,000 in stock purchased by the use of stock options; $150,000 in split dollar life insurance. It will amount to $675,000 if he dies before retirement, or provide him with $50,000 per year on his retirement.

Or, in other words, a good bargain, even though he is not a top executive in the organization.

Executives in an organization would do well to leverage their value in the company to negotiate a package of benefits that will make them want to stay with the organization, build its value, focus on their responsibilities and contributions to the progress of the company, and have peace of mind knowing that they and their family will have a secure future.

CHAPTER 6

Your Occupation and Its Opportunities: Self-help for the Self-employed

So much for Mr. Key Executive and his forerunner, Mr. Young Executive. As employees of Corporation Americana, their occupations offer them a unique and negotiable source of estate building. Yet not everyone climbs a corporate ladder, nor has the opportunity or inclination to do so.

For those reasons we want to introduce another character into the drama, a professional woman who is nobody's employee. Her name is Ms. Doctor, the young physician who nets $80,000 a year from her new practice. She has no compensation package and no negotiated benefits, no company to give her any of these niceties. Where are the estate-building opportunities in *her* occupation? Who is going to help her?

This, in a nutshell, is the situation of some ten million citizens of this country—all the doctors, lawyers, dentists, accountants, architects, engineers, writers, artists, and actors, other independent professionals, and along with them the independent businesspersons: the sole owners or partners of businesses, large or small, the entrepreneurs. These are the self-employed. They range from the actress who commands $100,000 for a single performance and the individual business owner who grosses a million per year, to the corner grocery store operator who nets only $35,000, or the writer who makes $60,000 in a good year, half of that in a bad one, and the Web page designer who has seen his business boom in the last few years, and expects it to keep on growing.

There are no *ready-made* pension plans, deferred compensation arrangements, or profit-sharing funds for them. They can put up to $3,000 a year into an IRA or $6,000 where there's a nonworking spouse and they file a joint return. (If neither of them participates in a qualified retirement plan they may make deductible IRA contributions. However, if they are active participants in a retirement plan, the $3,000 IRA deduction limit per person is phased out for single taxpayers with income over $45,000 in 2004; $50,000 in 2005 and thereafter. The phase-out income threshold for married taxpayers is $65,000 in 2004; $70,000 in 2005; $75,000 in 2006; $80,000 in 2007 and thereafter.) Unlike the rest of their fellow citizens, their occupations do not automatically provide them with substantial built-in tax shelters. They are compensated as well as or sometimes better than the corporate employee. But since all of this compensation is in the form of income, it is subject to tax.

The heart of their dilemma is in the very word that describes their economic situation: *self-employed.* Our tax laws were set up originally to benefit the employee, the person who works for someone else. Large though their numbers are, the self-employed used to be an economic anachronism in our economy.

Today there are a variety of opportunities for the self-employed to establish tax-favored savings plans for retirement. The fence that once separated the tax-sheltered employee from the nonsheltered self-employed person is no longer an issue. Over the years it has been opened more and more, until the Tax Equity and Fiscal Responsibility Act of 1982 gave the self-employed the opportunity to provide themselves with most of the same employee benefits that their corporate counterparts enjoy. Since then many changes in the tax law and many more retirement planning opportunities have been added.

"Self-help" is still the concept, however. More than large corporation employees, the self-employed have to take the initiative and put together their own compensation packages, and have to know about and utilize the various opportunities available to them for building funds for retirement and for building an estate.

THE PROFESSIONAL:
THEIR AVENUES TO SECURITY

First, just who is the professional? A person with advanced technical training—a lawyer, accountant, doctor, dentist, optometrist, engineer, architect and others—who performs a *personal service*.

"Personal" is the key word here. The very meaning of the corporate identity is impersonal. In law, if not in fact, it cancels the personal nature of the professional's relationship to his client or patient. Thus, until recently, society had been reluctant to grant most professionals the right to incorporate. At the same time, professionals had not been allowed to build up any tax-protected pension or retirement funds for themselves. These the government had reserved for employees.

This is no longer true. Today, there are many avenues open to professionals that will allow them to accumulate tax-sheltered capital, and thereby help them find economic security for themselves and their families.

Some of these avenues involve some form of corporate tax treatment for the professional. Some are concerned with compensation devices that afford advantageous tax treatment for professional income. Others allow professionals to build their own tax-sheltered retirement funds. Together, they make up a package of advantageous professional compensation ideas.

The Unincorporated Association: Avenue Number One

The first blow in the battle for fringe benefits for the professional was struck in 1948, in Missoula, Montana.

A partnership of eight doctors decided to form an unincorporated association. As members of the association, they set up a group pension plan for themselves. The U.S. Treasury demanded payment of ordinary income taxes on the amount in the pension reserve fund which had been allocated to Dr. Arthur R. Kintner.

Dr. Kintner became the man who carried the ball for his association, and as it turned out, for professionals all over the country. He paid the tax, but sued for a refund in U.S. District Court. His contention: His association, although unincorporated, was enough like a corporation to warrant the tax treatment of a corporation.

In 1952, the courts sustained Dr. Kintner, and after he won on appeal, the Treasury acquiesced. Now members of unincorporated associations which meet certain qualifications can take advantage of various corporate plans and benefits and receive either C corporation or S corporation tax treatment. The qualifications are:

1. *Continuity.* The association will not end if one of the members dies, retires, goes bankrupt, or becomes insane.
2. *Limited Liability.* No member can be personally liable for any of the debts of the association.
3. *Centralized Management.* A committee or a group must be given exclusive management of the business.
4. *Transferability of Interest.* Any member can transfer his interest to a nonmember without the approval of the other members, although he may be required to offer it first to them.

The Professional Corporation: Avenue Number Two

Wouldn't it be better to avoid the ambiguities of the unincorporated association and form a professional corporation instead?

By all means, and fortunately, that is now possible. The success of Dr. Kintner and others who followed in his footsteps led to the enactment of state laws giving professionals the right to incorporate. The majority of states grant the privilege to all professions. The others limit it to specified ones such as medicine, dentistry, and law. Needless to say, the professional who forms a corporation or association has really found the way out of the self-employed wilderness. Now he can avail himself of the fringe benefits that corporate employees enjoy: qualified defined benefit pension plans and profit-sharing plans; group life insurance, group disability insurance, group medical, accident, and health insurance; and deferred compensation arrangements.

The Limited Liability Company or Limited Liability Partnership: Avenue Number Three

Some states allow professionals to form limited liability companies (LLCs) or limited liability partnerships (LLPs). LLPs are business entities available to public accountants, law practices and architects. LLCs do not have these professional restrictions. While limiting liability, these business forms also provide for the establishment of a fringe benefit program. Professionals can thereby establish qualified benefit pension plans, defined contribution plans, group life insurance, group disability insurance, group medical, accident and health insurance.

Self-employed Retirement Plan—The Keogh Plan: Avenue Number Four

For the professional and the independent businessperson who cannot have or doesn't want either the unincorporated association or the corporation, an LLC or an LLP, there is another avenue open. It provides retirement benefits that are now similar to corporate plans.

This avenue was created by Congress in 1962, in the form of the Self-employed Individuals Tax Retirement Act, popularly known as the Keogh Act (also known as HR-10 Plans). This plan allows self-employed people of all types to set up retirement funds for themselves. Here's how it works.

Dr. Jones is a successful surgeon in the 33 percent income tax bracket. He has an earned income of over $225,000 per year. He can set up a retirement fund for himself under the provisions of the Keogh Act/HR-10 Plan in the form of a defined benefit plan or defined contribution plan. If he chooses a *defined benefit plan*, he can decide how much retirement income he wants, up to a maximum of $165,000 a year, adjusted for inflation. His annual contributions into the plan, actuarially determined, will be the amount needed to accumulate a fund sufficient to provide the fixed benefit he wants to receive after retirement. However, he will be required to make contributions each year based on the calculations of an actuarial service to build toward the provision of a defined future benefit. With a *defined contribution plan*, it is the amount of contribution that is fixed. In addition, his contributions are discretionary, so if he has an unprofitable year, he can lower or skip contributions to his plan. The legal maximum is 25 percent of earned income or $41,000, whichever is less. (It should be noted that a self-employed individual's *earned income* is determined by deducting from gross income all business expenses *and* contributions to his retirement plan. Thus, Dr. Jones must have *net earned income* of at least $205,000—$164,000 + $41,000—to make the maximum contribution.)

Dr. Jones's fund accumulates both income and gain, tax-free, just as it does in a qualified corporate fund. In effect, his $41,000 contribution can earn approximately one-third more income for him as it would if the income were subject to his 33 percent tax bracket.

Jones can take out his money anytime after he reaches 59½ years old, or he can take it out at any age, if he is disabled. He must begin making withdrawals, however, no later than April 1 of the year following the later of 1) the calendar year he reaches age 70½ or 2) the calendar year he actually retires. If withdrawals are made before age 59½, except because of death or disability, a 10 percent tax penalty must be paid. An exception to this would be to take substantially equal payments at least annually over his life expectancy, or the joint life expectancy of him and his spouse, or him and his designated beneficiary's *after* ceasing his self-employment

Suppose that Jones has employees—a secretary, an assistant, or a technician. Then his plan must also cover them. If it is a "top-heavy" plan—that is, the key employees' accrued benefits or account balances are more than 60 percent of those of all participants in the plan—there are special rules for nonkey employees. Dr. Jones's will be a "top-heavy" plan, so he'll have to make an annual minimum contribution of not less than 3 percent of each participant's compensation. Moreover, the employee must have a nonforfeitable right to 100 percent of the benefit either after three years of service or after six years with 20 percent becoming nonforfeitable after two years and increasing 20 percent each year thereafter.

For some professionals, particularly when office staff may change every five to ten years, this nonforfeitability provision can be irksome. On the other hand, it works out quite nicely for those who have valued employees they wish to retain and reward, or who have relatives as employees.

· Case in point: Jane Jones works for her husband, Dr. Jones, as a receptionist and bookkeeper, at a salary of $30,000 per year. He sets up an owner-employee plan and contributes $6,000 per year for her. Since this is tax deductible, this contribution costs him only $4,020. It is not reportable on their joint return as income to Jane.

Thus, Dr. Jones will be able to build a tax-sheltered retirement fund for himself and his wife totaling $47,000 a year. He gets a tax deduction on all of this.

All other things being equal, will Dr. Jones be better off with a Keogh plan or a corporate one?

Though the amount of the retirement fund he can build would be the same under each, a corporate plan still has certain advantages over a self-employed one. The self-employed can't deduct the portion of his Keogh contribution that goes to purchase life, health, or accident insurance, while premium costs are deductible for a corporate plan. Nor can he borrow from a Keogh plan, while he could, subject to certain limitations, from a corporate plan.

Moreover, the professional corporate employee can have wider benefits made available to him on a tax-free basis. The corporation can provide him with group term insurance. The premium cost on the first $50,000 of coverage will be tax-free to him. The cost of coverage over

$50,000 paid by the corporation will be taxable income, but usually he will be paying much less than if he were to purchase this added coverage with before-tax dollars.

Building a Retirement Fund Through Tax-exempt Institutions: Avenue Number Five

Ms. Successful Commercial Artist, like many independent professionals, is a woman of varied interests and varied activities. Partly because she likes it and partly because it adds to her prestige, she has for many years been teaching courses at an art school. Her salary for this work—$7,000 per year—adds little to her spendable income since it merely piles additional taxable income on top of her yearly income of $90,000.

Someone tells her that she should use part of that salary to build a retirement fund for herself, and so she investigates the possibilities. She learns about the tax-sheltered annuities available to her under a 403(b) Plan offered to employees of certain tax-exempt institutions. Seeing this as an opportunity to accelerate her retirement savings, she asks the school to take all $7,000 of her salary, and instead of paying it out to her, to use it to pay a premium on a variable annuity for her. Now she is getting no taxable income in salary from the school. There is no taxation on the $7,000 which is invested in the annuity contract. (As of 2004 the allowable deferral to 403(b) Plans was $13,000. Her employer does not match her contributions, but could for total contributions up to the lesser of $41,000 or 100 percent of includable compensation.) The variable annuity contract in which she is investing will be paid out in installments at age 65. She then will have to pay income tax on the annuity payments as she receives them.

If she dies before she retires, the variable annuity's value is paid out to her beneficiary. The beneficiary has to pay income taxes on it.

Can every professional who has a part-time job with a tax-exempt organization avail himself of this kind of arrangement?

Unfortunately not, since not all tax-exempt institutions can offer this tax advantage to their employees. However, the class that can is very broad and generally embraces charitable and educational organizations. These include public schools, colleges or universities, churches and charitable entities that are 501(c)(3) organizations.

There is another way, however, of providing retirement benefits through tax-exempt institutions. Any organization may set up a nonqualified retirement plan. Most corporations don't avail themselves of this opportunity because the contributions to such nonqualified plans are not tax-deductible when made. But this aspect is obviously not important to the tax-exempt organization. It can create a retirement fund for an employee in the following way. Instead of paying out a salary to the employee, on which she must pay income taxes, it makes the payments into a separate account to be paid to her when she retires.

Let's look at the case of Ms. Accountant, age 55. She agrees to handle the finances for her college alumnae organization on a part-time salary basis. Ordinarily the salary would be $6,000 per year. Because of her high tax bracket, however, she decides to ask instead that $3,000 of the money be put into a trust for her, to be paid out in installments when she reaches certain ages or on her death. Her right to the fund, however, is conditioned on her continued service—until the payout. Because it is a forfeitable right, this money isn't taxed to her at the present time. The income earned by the trust is taxable to the trust (as a separate taxpayer) at its tax bracket. When the installments are paid out to her as she reaches the specified ages, she pays income tax on them. Assuming that she is in a lower tax bracket then, she will have more spendable cash available to her.

Since January 1997, some tax-exempt organizations can adopt 401(k) qualified retirement plans, so their employees can now choose to defer up to $14,000 ($15,000 in 2006) of their earnings into such a plan.

Taking a Piece of the Deal: Avenue Number Six

This is the final—and sometimes the most lucrative—way in which a professional can accumulate capital as a result of his occupation. It is a method, incidentally, that is not available to the corporate executive.

We once knew an architect who built an entire estate in this way. He started his unique estate plan unintentionally back in 1970. In that year he agreed to design a commercial building for a fee of $35,000. When the time came for payment, his clients were unable to pay any part of it. They had become insolvent. They offered him instead a 25 percent interest in the property.

The architect had a choice between becoming one of their creditors or taking a share of what appeared to be worthless realty. He took the latter and mentally wrote off his fee as a bad debt. But the property interest somehow survived the financial difficulties without being foreclosed, and by 1982 it had become a profit-making investment. In 1988 the property was sold. His share of the proceeds: $260,000.

That experience encouraged him to take shares in other property. During the years from 1988 to 1998 he had frequently taken part and sometimes all of his fees for services in income-producing real estate. He ended up with an estate of $1,550,000—although his net income rarely exceeded $80,000 in any one year, and he was by no means a great or popular architect.

This is what we mean by "taking a piece of the deal." It is a method that many other professionals besides architects could well utilize. Often they are in an excellent position to judge the potential success of an enterprise with which they are associated.

Take the case of the attorney who accepts stock in a new company in lieu of a $20,000 fee. Assuming she is in a 28 percent tax bracket, she pays a tax of $5,600 on this stock. Three years later, she sells the stock for $35,000. She pays a long-term capital gains tax of $2,250 on her $15,000 profit. Her net gain on the whole deal was then $27,150 versus the $14,400 she would have netted from her $20,000 fee, after taxes.

Of course, every deal doesn't work out this well. Like most investments, the professional "deal" involves a risk. Bird-in-hand professionals will want to use more orthodox methods of estate building. The investment-minded lawyer, accountant, architect, and engineer, however, should examine the opportunities available here for a unique means of capital growth.

THE INDEPENDENT BUSINESSPERSON

Until recently the independent entrepreneur, the owner or partner of a business, was in an ironic position, compared to his executive counterpart, the manager-employee of a corporation. On the one hand, the independent's situation had greater growth potentialities. If the business went well and the times were propitious, it was possible for him to accumulate a fortune. The corporate executive's occupation generally affords him no such possibility.

On the other hand, the independent businessperson could not have the built-in tax shelters which were available to the corporate executive. His income might be greater but a large part of it was taxed away.

Over the years developments have given the independent many tax-advantaged opportunities. In fact, there is no reason why the independent now cannot avail himself of the same type of favored tax treatment as larger, more established companies. He is in business. Nearly every business can incorporate or adopt some form of business entity that comes under the sheltering spread of the tax-favored umbrella in some way that fits its particular needs.

Depending upon the number of owners, profitability, liability exposure and tax advantages desired, independent businesses can operate as C Corporations, subchapter S Corporations, Partnerships, Limited Liability Companies (LLCs) or Sole Proprietors. It is worthwhile looking at the opportunities for retirement savings and estate building afforded by each of these forms of business.

Some independents shy away from the idea of incorporation because of that famous bogey, double taxation. However, there are ways to enjoy the advantages of incorporation and overcome this problem.

But first, what is it?

THE MEANING OF DOUBLE TAXATION

Corporations are taxed on their profits. The first $50,000 of profits are taxed at 15 percent; the next $25,000 at 25 percent. Profits from $75,000 up to $100,000 are taxed at 34 percent. An additional 5 percent tax up to a maximum of $22,250 is imposed on income over $100,000 up to $335,000. Corporations with income of $335,000 up to $10 million will pay 34 percent. Between $10 million and $15 million the rate is 35 percent. Up to $18,333,333 it rises to 38 percent, and goes back down to 35 percent thereafter. Double taxation occurs when the profits are paid out as dividends to the stockholder. They are first taxed to the corporation at its brackets. They are again subject to income tax to the stockholder at special dividend rates. Under the 2003 Tax Act dividends are now taxed at a 15 percent rate for people in marginal brackets of 25 percent and greater. For taxpayers in the 15 percent bracket dividends are taxed at 5 percent when received. Thus, if the corporate net profit is $50,000 to begin with, the corporation pays an income tax of $7,500. Then, when the remaining $42,500 is paid as dividends to the stockholder, the tax is $6,375. A total of $13,875 in taxes is paid, leaving only $36,125 available for use by the stockholder out of the $50,000 original profit.

Naturally, no one likes the idea of paying taxes twice on the same income even though the tax on dividends has been greatly reduced. To see how it can be overcome, let's take the case of Mr. White, Ms. Brown, Mr. Green and Ms. Black. Each of them is independent; each of them incorporates his business but overcomes the double-taxation factors in a different way. In all cases, the money is put to personal or corporate uses that leave the business owners and/or their businesses with a better financial outcome.

Mr. White Draws Out the Entire Corporate Net Income in Salary

He is the owner of a small manufacturing firm. He wants to establish an employee benefit package in which he can participate fully, but wants to receive the company's profitability as income and pay tax only once. The company's net earnings are $60,000. White incorporates the business, but since its income is small, he can reasonably withdraw it all as salary. Now there is only a single tax on the income, the tax on his personal salary. His corporation gets a full tax deduction on the payments to him. The situation is essentially the same as before except that White is also now free to set up a program of corporate benefits for himself.

Ms. Brown Splits the Income Between Herself and the Corporation

Ms. Brown is the sole proprietor of a textile distribution business which has net earnings of $80,000. All this is taxable as ordinary income to her, and with a tax bracket of 28 percent, she pays a heavy tax bill—about $22,400. This leaves her with $57,600 per year of after-tax income.

Brown thinks she can get along on less than that. She incorporates her business as a C corporation and pays herself a salary of $60,000. Her income tax on that is 25 percent, or $15,000. The balance of the profits—$20,000—is left in the corporation. It is taxed now at only 15 percent, or $3,000. The total tax bill of Brown Inc. *and* Ms. Brown is $18,000, as compared with Brown's former tax bill of $22,400. She has reduced the total tax paid by $4,400.

Now, too, Brown can avail herself of all those corporate fringe benefits, using the income she leaves in the corporation which, if used to fund a retirement plan and group insurance program for Brown, would reduce the corporate tax still further.

Not everyone will want to follow in Brown's path, of course. Splitting income will depend upon the relative tax brackets of the corporation and the owner. There is also a limit on the amount which the corporation can reasonably accumulate without incurring certain tax penalties. In such cases, why not emulate Mr. Green?

Mr. Green Elects to Have His Company Taxed as a Subchapter S Corporation

Subchapter S refers to a section of the Internal Revenue Code which came into being in 1958 and was substantially revised by the Subchapter S Revision Act of 1982 and again by the Small Business Job Protection Act of 1996. Under it, stockholders of a corporation may elect to have their corporation considered as a partnership for tax purposes. The income, credits, deductions and losses are passed through pro rata to the shareholders. For all other purposes, the S corporation has the attributes and advantages of a corporation, including protection from personal liability for lawsuits brought against the company.

Mr. Green, the president of Close Corporation, Inc., Mr. Gray, the vice president, and Mr. Outsider, an investor, own the corporation equally. Green gets a salary of $60,000. Gray gets $40,000. The corporation has profits of $100,000. All three owners wish to lay claim to these profits for themselves equally, with the most favorable tax treatment.

Gray, Green, and Outsider decide to file an election under Subchapter S. Their goal is to have Close Corporation's income taxed to them as stockholders once, rather than first to a C corporation, then to them as dividends. Green and Gray are taxed on their $60,000 and $40,000 salaries. In addition, the three stockholders are taxed personally on their shares of the $100,000 profit, even though the profit is retained in the corporation. If the corporation later distributes that $100,000, it is not taxed again to the stockholders, and if retained, becomes part of the stockholders' basis in the value of stock in the company, should it be sold at a later date. These characteristics of S corporations fit the initial desires of all three owners to have the taxation of the company's income flow through to the stockholders subject to individual tax rates, rather than being first subjected to the possible double taxation of C corporation dividends.

The S corporation status of their company will offer other advantages as well.

1. Their company will not be subject to the Alternative Minimum Tax.
2. If they have a year when the business generates passive income, it can be used to offset passive activity losses from tax shelters they may have.

Green (and Gray) are able to enjoy the liability protection and tax-favored employee benefits of the corporate setup with one exception: an employee owning more than 2 percent of the stock of a Subchapter S corporation is not eligible for certain fringe benefits such as a tax-free accident and health plan and $50,000 of group term insurance.

For those who are interested in Subchapter S treatment, here are the qualifications, updated to 2004, which a company must meet to elect taxation under its provisions:

1. There must be no more than seventy-five stockholders, none of whom are nonresident aliens or a corporation or partnership.
2. The corporation must be created under the laws of the United States, or one of the fifty states, or one of the territories.
3. There must be no more than one class of stock outstanding, but there may be different voting rights among the shares.
4. All stockholders must consent to adopting S corporation status.
5. Prior to December 31, 1996, an S corporation could not own 80 percent or more of another corporation. For tax years after 1996, the Small Business Job Protection Act allows S corporations to own a "qualified Subchapter S subsidiary" (QSSS). To qualify, the subsidiary must be 100 percent owned by the parent S corporation, and the parent must elect treatment of the sub as a qualified Subchapter S subsidiary. Its income, deductions, credits, losses, etc., are treated as if directly owned by the parent S corporation.

If the corporation receives more than 25 percent of its gross receipts from rents, royalties, interest, dividends, annuities, and gain from the sale or exchange of securities, and also has accumulated earnings and profits, it will be taxed on that passive income. After three consecutive years of such income it will lose its Subchapter S status.

Many closely held corporations have elected S corporation status to take advantage of lower individual tax rates. As of 2004 income of up to $319,100 is taxed more favorably at individual rates than at corporate rates. You should review the desirability of S status in light of your own individual tax bracket, including state and local taxes.

Ms. Black Uses the Excess Earnings of the Corporation to Expand Her Business

Ms. Black is one of three siblings who own a small New England manufacturing corporation. Recently, the profits of the firm increased considerably. Black and her brothers took stock of their situation. What should they do with their profits?

Their salaries were already high, so much so that they couldn't raise them substantially. They didn't want to pay out dividends and be subject to double taxation, even though taxation of dividend income has been substantially reduced. Besides, their personal tax brackets were already high. They couldn't accumulate any more earnings in the corporation without being subject to the imposition of the 15 percent accumulated earnings tax (an additional tax imposed on accumulated earnings in excess of $250,000—$150,000 for personal service corporations—not justified by the reasonable needs of the business).

Their decision: to plough the profits back into the business, using them for an extensive advertising campaign. The result: because of the advertising campaign, sales tripled, the business is growing . . . and growing . . . and growing . . . until it has now become a national distributor, its chief product a household word. In effect, the pressure of high taxation forced Black and her brothers into a highly successful expansion they might otherwise never have undertaken.

RETIREMENT BENEFITS FOR THE INDEPENDENT BUSINESSPERSON

With no one to set up a retirement plan for them, the independent businessperson has the opportunity and the responsibility to learn about and select a type of retirement plan that fits their business. The consistency and amount of profitability, the need to attract and keep key people, the desire of employees to make contributions from their salaries and the amount of time until the owner's desired retirement age are some of the issues that need to be considered.

The Keogh Plan (HR-10 Plans)—Flexible or Mandatory Contributions

Keogh plans were designed to serve the needs of the self-employed person or partnerships. There is no need to have employees to establish these plans, though if employees are hired, they must be allowed to participate. One type of plan is a *defined contribution* design. There are set-up fees and annual administrative and filing costs, but it allows the businessperson to determine the amount they will contribute in any given year within certain limits. In 2004 the maximum for a sole proprietor or partnerships is the lesser of 25 percent of *net business income* or $41,000. For this purpose, *net business income* is calculated by deducting contributions made to the plan on his own behalf. Effectively, he would need *net earnings* of $205,000 ($164,000 plus $41,000) to make the maximum contribution. Within that limit contributions can vary from year to year, or even skip a year when profits are scarce. Moreover, the business needn't be conducted on a full-time basis to establish such a retirement plan.

Take the case of Mr. Wood. He makes artful turned bowls as a hobby after his "day job." He is so talented that his bowls fetch a handsome price in a local store featuring fine handmade items. In his "moonlighting" hat he is an independent businessperson, a sole proprietor, but not an actual *employee*. He hopes to retire early from his day job, and pursue his more enjoyable and lucrative hobby more fully. His accountant advised him to establish a Keogh (HR-10) plan to accelerate retirement savings using the income generated by the growing popularity of his craft. Since it is not a predictable flow, Mr. Wood decides on a profit-sharing Keogh plan so that his contributions to it can vary from year to year up to the allowable amount. This special qualified plan lends employee status to the self-employed for the purpose of letting them participate in the tax advantages a retirement plan can offer. He sets it up prior to the end of his fiscal year, and will have until he files his taxes (plus extensions) to put funds into the plan each year.

The other type of Keogh plan allows the businessperson to define the retirement *benefit* goal (income payout) they want to achieve; again, within certain prescribed limits. This is the *defined benefit* design. In 2004 the maximum is 100 percent of the participant's average compensation for the three highest consecutive calendar years during which they were active under the plan, or $165,000. This is a more costly plan administratively, since the services of an actuary are required to keep the plan on track.

Let's look at two partners who neglected retirement savings earlier in their careers and need to catch up. Dr. Rock and Dr. Stone have a very successful partnership as psychologists. Their income has a very predictable base, with even greater income in some years. Dr. Rock wishes to retire in about eight years, but has not yet put aside much for her goal. Dr. Stone is in a similar situation with slightly more savings, but a seven-year goal. Their financial advisor suggested they accelerate their savings and tax advantages by establishing a Keogh with a defined benefit (pension) design. Once the plan is set up, they will make mandatory contributions calculated by an actuary service that will determine how much they need to contribute year by year. The amount will be based on how well that year's investment performance kept them on track for reaching their respective goals, but in any case will allow them to put aside much more pretax income toward retirement than any of the other qualified plans available to them. Their contributions will be kept on target to build sufficient capital to produce the payout benefit they design into the plan. Unlike Mr. Wood, who can choose whether and how much he wants to contribute in any given year, the good doctors will be required to contribute each year to keep their plan on course. Their steady base of income makes this a sustainable solution for them.

Simplified Employee Pension (SEP)

What if the owner of a small business (could be sole proprietor, C corporation, S corporation, partnership, limited liability company, etc.) wants a very simple, low-cost plan, but wants a way to establish a retirement benefit to reward himself and employees from the profits of the business.

Take the case of Ms. Wright, who owns a Web page design business and has two employees. She values her fellow designers and wants to keep them on board by offering a retirement plan. If her goal is to give them pure incentive to make the business prosper, she may want a simplified profit sharing plan, and so could select a Simplified Employee Pension Plan referred to as a SEP. The costs to her for such a plan are low: almost no set-up fee or annual administrative fee beyond about $10 per person. She will be able to make annual contributions of up to 25 percent of their income (essentially 20 percent if unincorporated) to a maximum dollar amount of $41,000 (profits allowing). She'll be able to contribute what in effect will be 20 percent of her own earnings net of self-employment tax. She'll have very little paperwork or cost, but will be required to contribute for all employees if she contributes for herself. However, as with profit sharing plans, she is not required to make contributions, and in any given year she will have the discretion to determine whether and how much her profits will allow her to make contributions. All the contributions she does make to the plan will be 100 percent vested to her employees immediately.

SIMPLE IRA Plan

If Ms. Wright's employees want to set aside some pretax dollars from their own salaries *and* benefit from profit sharing, there's good news. Starting in January 1997, businesses with 100 or fewer employees and no other employer-sponsored retirement plan can offer a Savings Incentive Match Plan for Employees, referred to in acronym form as the SIMPLE IRA Plan. Ms. Wright and her two designers can defer up to $9,000 per year from their salaries into the plan in 2004. This will go to $10,000 in 2005 and then be indexed for inflation thereafter (but not more than 100 percent of compensation). Ms. Wright will have to match their contributions dollar-for-dollar up to 3 percent of her employees' salaries, or use a nonelective formula and make contributions that represent 2 percent of their salaries whether or not they defer a portion of their own salaries. If she uses the matching formula of 3 percent, she does have some relief in unprofitable years. In no more than two out of every five years she could drop her contribution for them to not less than one percent. Their money will grow tax-deferred until retirement. If they withdraw funds before age 59½, they will pay both income tax and a 10 percent penalty that rises to 25 percent on contributions less than two years old. Such a plan can serve both Ms. Wright and her employees well by providing tax-deferred savings and an incentive to help the business prosper, while keeping administrative costs at a minimum.

Selecting a Retirement Plan

The self-employed needn't wade through a confusion of possible retirement plans on their own. Making constructive use of financial advisors such as accountants, business and tax attorneys, and financial planners can help sort through the technicalities. Advisors can help the businessperson match the nature of their business, its profitability and prospects, and their own need for retirement savings with the possible plan designs to find the right solutions through many stages in the development of their businesses.

THE PAYOFF

When all is said and done, what is the payoff? Are the independents—businesspeople and professionals alike—as well off as their corporate brethren so far as their tax-sheltered estate building opportunities are concerned?

Though there are still some restrictions for the self-employed and Subchapter S stockholders, the independent has the opportunity to create his own tax-sheltered package almost equal to that available to the executive of Corporation Americana. The independent doesn't have the security of a large corporation and is dependent on his own ingenuity and success—meaning his business or professional fortunes—for his estate plan.

Yet he has a great advantage. He can, if he is successful, accumulate a real fortune from his business or profession, an estate which is truly worthy of the name. In the long run, this may be an occupational opportunity that cannot be equaled.

For this reason, adding an exit strategy for how to sell the business, take it public, or pass it on to the next generation without devastation from capital gains or estate taxes could be one of the very critical parts of his overall business and estate plan. (See Chapters 17 and 18.)

CHAPTER 7

INVESTMENTS: MAKING YOUR

CAPITAL WORK FOR YOU

Today nearly everyone is an investor in one way or another. The idea of accumulating money and putting it to work in the hope that it will produce income and perhaps appreciate in value appeals to all classes and all ages, though finding your way through today's volatile markets presents more of a challenge and has heightened the need for thoughtful planning. The investment programs of individuals, of course, differ widely, and should—based on your age, experience, timeline, available capital and tolerance for risk. Thus, a fourth-grader may put one-half of his allowance in a savings bank each week with his grandest goal a strictly limited one: the purchase of a new skateboard.

His father, on the other hand, buys stocks when and if he has the money to invest, and his eyes are fixed on broader, if somewhat vaguer horizons—who knows what the future in the securities market may bring?

Looking at the two investment programs from a strictly technical point of view, we'd say the boy has a definite edge on his father. His program meets the classical requirements for a sound investment philosophy. He has a fixed objective and a systematic savings and investment plan. What's more, the amount of his investment is realistic in relation to his resources, and its form, the savings account, is well suited both to his circumstances and to the attainment of his fixed objective.

But what about the father? In fact, his objectives are undefined. He vaguely knows he wants to ensure his family's security, or perhaps he hopes for riches. But his savings program is not systematic at all. Haphazard is the word for it. He buys stocks without any particular plan or sense of diversification. As a result, he never accumulates enough capital to really initiate and carry through a sound investment program. He lacks the two basic ingredients which form the basis of any estate planning investment program—objectives and resources.

It is not the purpose of this chapter to discuss how to make millions (and certainly not how to lose them). It is, rather, to set forth the essentials of an investment program and discuss the nature and meaning of investments from the estate planning point of view.

This point of view is long-range. It is not concerned with haphazard buying of securities, when and if funds are available, and then selling when cash is needed. An estate planner's program must be predetermined and conscientiously carried out over the period of his investing life, which may be forty to forty-five years or more. It is part of a larger plan, and its goals are the same as that larger plan: to provide funds for retirement, disability, and family security, both before and after the planner's death.

SURPLUS CAPITAL: THE BASIS OF INVESTMENTS

To invest you must have surplus capital, funds that are not needed for current family requirements nor for other aspects of estate building, such as insurance or the emergency savings account.

Thus, the estate planner–investor must, at some point in life (and that point is far better reached earlier than later), examine his resources, assess his needs, and put into motion a systematic savings plan. The funds devoted to it are for investment; not for a vacation, not for holiday gifts, not even for that second automobile or home.

There are all kinds of methods open to a person today to help him set up such a savings system: payroll deductions, corporate savings plans, banking programs, and mutual funds with automatic investment plans, to name only a few. And, of course, the time-honored method of budgeting family expenses to leave some surplus out of earnings, although painful, is always possible. Just about anything will do so long as there is regular saving.

The story of the eccentric who puts his money in a mattress is an old one, but we sometimes wonder if those who scoff at it aren't really missing its message. The fact is that he has succeeded in saving surplus capital. What's more, if this "savings program" of his is regular, i.e., if he takes a part of his weekly salary and stows it away over a period of years, he will end up with more money at retirement age than the great majority of his more sophisticated fellow citizens.

The real mistake of our hoarding friend is not *using* his excess capital; that is, in failing to put it to work so that it produces income or provides principal growth, or both. This is what we mean by investment and these are its prime attributes: income production and capital appreciation.

ESTATE PLANNING PRINCIPLES OF INVESTMENT

For the estate planner, investment acumen lies not so much in the ability to select a certain "right" security as it does in the ability to create a long-term, well-balanced investment program that will produce the capital needed to carry out estate planning objectives.

How you as an investor-planner accomplish this and how well you accomplish it is a highly individual matter. There are your aims and objectives; the amount of capital you have available; your age (how much time you have to carry out your program); your other resources; your experience and competence; the tax bracket you are in; the amount of risk you are willing to take or can afford to take; even your personality and temperament. All these factors enter into the success or failure of your investment program.

There is a wide, and often confusing, variety of investment opportunities available. When you come to the problem of selecting investments, each one should be assessed from different points of view. Most investment advisors, brokerages, mutual fund companies and variable annuity providers offer questionnaires that help you develop a good sense of your personal profile as an investor. In general they are best used in conjunction with the kind of dialogue you can have with a skilled investment advisor; someone who can help you review your portfolio, your own changing needs, and shifts in market conditions over time; someone who can keep you from over- or underreacting to change and keep you on track toward meeting your goals. To determine your own profile as an investor, the questionnaire and dialogue should consider at least the following:

1. *Diversification.* Does your portfolio show variety? You must seek to achieve diversification, not only in the relation of each investment to the others, but also in the relation to the rest of your assets and your sources of income. Does your portfolio include differing styles for buying/holding/selling; does it include different industries, companies of different sizes and potential; a balance between growth and income securities, domestic and international, suitable for your timeline?

2. *Safety.* How safe will the principal be? The amount of risk varies with each type of investment. Here the planner must balance the classic contradictions. On the one hand, since you are looking for safety, you should seek investments which carry a minimum of risk. On the other hand, low-risk investments usually offer low returns and little appreciation. How well can you tolerate swings in the value of your portfolio over short and long periods of time? How much loss can you tolerate in a downturn before an investment should be sold? When will you take profits and redistribute them to regain the portfolio balance you specified? There's also the issue of not abandoning common sense and certain fundamentals for the investment with enticingly wild claims. If it sounds too good to be true, it may be worth careful scrutiny.

3. *Timeline.* How long do you intend to invest toward a particular goal? The 35-year-old may have a portfolio that emphasizes growth and assumes more risk. She has twenty-five or thirty years to allow for swings in the value of her investments in her anticipation of long-term growth. The 68-year-old who has recently retired, and has all the capital he expects to put aside, may prefer a portfolio that protects his principal and provides him with income.

4. *Inflation Hedge.* How well will this particular investment preserve your capital against inflation? It is just as important to protect the purchasing power of your capital as it is to protect yourself against the possible loss of capital. In any inflationary period, it won't do to just maintain the number of your dollars. If that is all you do, you will still suffer an economic loss. Here again, the whole question of diversification enters the picture. A portfolio that is invested entirely in a savings account, returning 1 or 2 per-

cent, is often no protection against inflation. Only a portfolio based on a variety of investments—some with fixed returns and some with potential for capital appreciation—will do that.

5.   *Growth.* What is the growth potential? Here we are speaking of the inherent ability of the investment, not just to protect against inflation but, in addition, to appreciate the capital beyond a normal inflationary increase. Generally speaking, these investments are found in the industries which have great growth potential. In the early part of the century, it was the railroads and the steel industry. In recent years it has been first automobiles and chemicals, then electronics and biotechnology, then telecommunications and burgeoning global markets. Growth sectors change and shift, rise and fall, making diversification an essential factor. There's also the *style* with which you buy. Do you buy a good, quality stock when it is underpriced, then hold it for growth, or do you buy it when it's "catching fire" and already accelerating in value?

6.   *Income.* What is its expected income return? Here we refer to expected *future* income production as well as to current. Is the income guaranteed? Will the income return be available in the bad times as well as in good times? Is it fixed? Will the rate of return move up and down with general money rates so as to reflect the state of the economy and the probable changing costs of living?

7.   *Marketability.* What is its marketability? Is this a security that you can readily sell? Or will buyers perhaps be hard to find? There are many securities that are not readily marketable, but still make worthwhile investments. Obviously, however, your investment portfolio should not be weighted with these. Liquidity is extremely important to many aspects of estate planning.

8.   *Taxation.* How will taxation affect your program? As in many features of estate planning, taxation plays a fundamental role in the investment program. At this point it may be worthwhile to deal with some basic tax concepts which will be involved in our later investment discussion.

INVESTMENTS AND TAXATION

Your build-up of capital will be much greater if you utilize available tax shelters and thereby reduce the amount of taxation. This applies to the two aspects of income taxation—the taxation on income received from dividends, interest, rent, etc., and the taxation on profits that may occur from a sale of property or stocks.

In the former case (except for "qualified dividend income") the regular federal income tax rates of 10, 15, 25, 28, 33, and 35 percent will apply. The income you receive from your investments is taxed at a maximum rate of 35 percent to the individual. There are a few exceptions and exclusions. Interest is generally taxable; there is one major exception—interest on bonds that are issued by a state or one of its subdivisions. Net income from real estate is taxable also, but the deduction for depreciation can greatly reduce the tax burden. The same applies to the deductions and depletion allowances for investments in natural resources and cattle. Capital gain or loss tax treatment occurs when a capital asset is sold. Many investments you will make outside your business will come within the capital asset category, and so will qualify for such treatment. The types of properties which do not qualify are: copyrights and other artistic properties; assets held for sale to customers in the ordinary course of business; notes and accounts receivable acquired in the course of doing business; certain government obligations issued at discount.

The Basis of Capital Gains Taxation

When you sell a capital asset, the tax you pay is imposed on the difference between the sale price and what is called the "adjusted basis" of the asset. If the sale price is less than the adjusted basis, you have a tax loss; if it is more, you have a gain.

Generally, the "adjusted basis" is the price you originally paid for the asset, plus any additional capital expenditures you may have made on it. Thus, if you paid $20,000 for property and put capital improvements of $5,000 into it over the years, your adjusted basis would be $25,000. However, basis can be determined by more than just a purchase price. It could be based on its fair market value on a specific date, such as the date of death of a decedent when inherited, or a substituted basis.

However, the adjusted basis may be less than cost. The adjusted basis of a piece of real estate, for instance, is the purchase price (or its fair market value on a specific date, such as date of death of a decedent when inherited, or a substituted basis) plus added capital costs minus the depreciation allowance. (Gain attributable to accelerated depreciation may be subject to ordinary income tax.)

Other special rules apply. For gifts made before 1977, there are two rules for determining the basis, one for gain and one for loss. For gain, the basis is the same as the donor's basis plus the gift tax. For loss, however, the basis can be either the donor's basis or the fair market value of the property at the time of the gift (plus the gift tax), whichever is lower. If the asset is a gift received after 1976, the same two rules apply for determining basis, one for gain and one for loss. However, only that portion of the gift tax attributed to the appreciation over the donor's cost can be added to basis.

Sometimes these two rules make a tax no-man's-land out of the sale of gift property. Here's a father who gives some securities to his son. The father paid $10,000 for them, but at the time he gives them away, their market price is only $6,000. Sometime later the son sells the securities for $9,000. Has he incurred a gain or loss?

Under the rule for determining gain, he takes his father's cost of $10,000 as his basis. Since his sale price was only $9,000, he has no gain. Using the rule for determining loss, he takes as his basis the lower value, the fair market value of the securities at the time his father gave them to him—only $6,000. Again, since he sold the asset for $9,000, there is no loss. For tax purposes, he realized neither a gain nor a loss.

For inherited property, the estate tax valuation establishes its basis. The general rule is that property in a decedent's estate is valued at its fair market value on the date of death. The property gets a new basis that may be more or less than the decedent's. If less, the decedent's paper loss is never realized. If the fair market value of the property is greater than the decedent's basis, the step-up in basis means that the unrealized appreciation escapes the tax on capital gains. Suppose a woman invested in a new enterprise in the 1950s when its stock was selling at $100 a share. When she dies, it's being traded at $200 a share. Her daughter, who inherits her estate, gets a new basis of $200. If she sells it for $210, she has a taxable gain of only $10.

An exception to the rule that the basis of inherited property is its fair market value on the date of death is a special provision that permits real property used in family farming or by a closed corporation to be valued at its "actual use" value rather than its "best use" value. For example, a piece of property used as a farm might be worth $100,000, but as part of a shopping center, its best use, it would have a value of $300,000. If certain conditions are met, the estate can elect the actual use value for estate tax purposes.

There is another exception to the rule that property inherited from a decedent takes as its basis the estate tax valuation. To prevent an heir from giving appreciated property to a person on his deathbed in order to get a step-up in basis to market value at the time of death, there is no stepped-up basis for any property the decedent received as a gift within a year of his or her death if that property is left to the original donor or donor's spouse. Note: If the property passes to another person the step-up basis rule does apply.

The tax law permits the executor to value the estate's assets at their date-of-death value or the value six months later or, if sold or distributed within six months, at the value of the property when transferred. If the total value of the assets in the estate declines, the executor will usually elect the alternate value to save estate taxes. For estates of decedents dying after July 18, 1984, however, the alternative valuation date can only be elected if both the value of the gross estate and the estate tax are reduced as the result of the election. The alternative value can no longer be used solely to increase the basis of the assets in the estate.

Current Taxes on Investment Sales—and Qualified Dividend Income

The Jobs and Growth Tax Relief Reconciliation Act of 2003 (JGTRRA 2003) added provisions for more favorable tax treatment of *capital gains*. These provisions create opportunities for harvesting capital gains with lower tax consequences, at least until December 31, 2008, when the law will "sunset" and revert to pre-2003 rates. For now, a person in the 25 percent marginal tax bracket and above pays only a 15 percent capital gains tax on a capital asset held for at least twelve months, then sold. The rate drops to only 5 percent for 10 and 15 percent brackets.

Also under JGTRRA 2003, the same tax treatment applies to *qualified dividend income*, which used to be taxed as ordinary income. Qualified dividend income refers to dividends paid on domestic common and preferred stock and certain qualified foreign stock held for specific periods. A detailed explanation is beyond the scope of this book, but in general the more favorable treatment is designed to favor the holding of stocks for at least four months for common stock, six months for preferred stock.

There are exceptions to this favorable tax treatment on capital gains. For instance, the rate on long-term gains from selling depreciated real estate is 25 percent. Long-term gains from the sale of such items as art and antiques (collectibles) are taxed at 28 percent. So are half the long-term gains from the sale of qualified small business stock.

For your investment portfolio where the 15 percent or 5 percent rates apply, you may want to take advantage of these changes on long-term gains by reducing any large concentrations of highly appreciated securities, then reinvesting to give your portfolio greater diversification. Reevaluate tax-deferred investments you are contemplating, such as variable annuities, to see whether your after-tax withdrawals will exceed after-tax capital gains potential outside such vehicles. For instance, the choice of dividend-paying stock mutual funds and bond mutual funds within a variable annuity will benefit from the *deferral* of taxes, but when withdrawn the gains will be taxed as ordinary income; while quality growth stock investments might fare better being taxed at capital gains rates when all is said and done.

A further strategy might be to use an income-splitting technique to take advantage of the lowest 5 percent rates. Let's say you have highly appreciated stock and want to free up cash to fund college tuition. If you transfer the stock ownership to your children, or grandchildren, and have them sell the stock, their low tax bracket (if they earned up to $29,050 in 2004) will lower the capital gains tax on the sale to 5 percent. Of course, this only works if they are over the age of 14, otherwise the "kiddie tax" rules apply and *your* tax bracket is used, bringing the *10 percent* long-term capital gains tax to bear.

The distinction between capital gains and losses and other types of income, however, does still have significance. Capital losses are first deductible in full against capital gains. Thereafter, any additional capital losses may offset other income only up to $3,000 on a dollar-for-dollar basis in any taxable year. (This carryover amount may increase in the future . . . stay tuned.) Losses in excess of the $3,000 limitation may be carried forward to the following tax years. Under the Revenue Reconciliation Act of 1993, certain anti-conversion provisions keep taxpayers from converting higher-taxed ordinary income into lower-taxed capital gains. These include straddles, futures contracts and market discount bonds.

In certain instances, the law will not permit tax losses. Loss deductions, for example, are not allowed on "wash sales" (i.e., a sale of securities at a loss, made thirty days before or after the purchase of substantially identical securities by the same person). Nor are they allowed for losses that result from sales between closely related people, such as husband and wife.

Tax law changes in 1997 created another area for caution. Previously, transactions designed to lock in gain on appreciated securities without paying capital gains tax could be achieved by using the so-called "short against the box" transaction. An investor could make a short sale of securities identical to those that had appreciated in his portfolio, lock in his gain and not realize any taxable gain. The 1997 law treats such transactions as "constructive sales" as of the day they were opened. A gain equal to the difference between the proceeds of the short sale and the tax cost of the underlying stock is recognized. This change is effective for short sales opened after June 8, 1997. If you hold such a position that was opened on or prior to June 8, 1997, consider closing your position to avoid expensive income tax results, and the loss of a step-up in cost basis at death on the shorted stock.

TYPES OF INVESTMENTS

With these tax principles firmly in mind, the potential estate planner–investor is ready to look at the considerable variety of investments from which he can pick and choose.

Savings Accounts

These are the most common and some of the most conservative types of investments. They have their drawbacks—the principal is static so there is no opportunity for appreciation of capital, and no protection against inflation. But there is a guaranteed return. Rates, though usually regulated by the supervising governmental authority, tend to rise and fall with inflation and recession. Recently, passbook savings and savings and loan accounts have been returning extremely low rates, as have money market accounts and certificates of deposit, but they have been a kind of "safe harbor" from volatile markets for some.

Short-term savings accounts also offer liquidity. Ordinarily, when you deposit money in a savings account, you can take it out anytime you choose. Some institutions retain the right, however, in fine print, to condition withdrawals on sixty- or ninety-day notice. With certificates of deposit, interest penalties are imposed for early withdrawals.

Most savings accounts are insured, either by the Federal Deposit Insurance Corporation or the Federal Savings and Loan Insurance Corporation. Except for federal savings and loan associations, however, which are required to carry FSLIC insurance, the insurance need not be that of a federal agency. It can also be private. Depositors should always check on this. Generally up to $100,000 is insured per institution.

1. *Mutual Savings Banks.* These are state-chartered institutions that exist in approximately one-third of our states, chiefly in the East. They follow a conservative investment policy, since state laws limit their investments to prescribed securities. Currently, about 65 percent of their assets are invested in mortgages, the rest in government securities, gilt-edged corporate bonds, and a few common stocks.

2. *Savings and Loan Associations.* The return paid on this type of savings may be higher than that paid by other major savings institutions because savings and loan associations specialize in home financing. Therefore they can have large earnings to distribute because home mortgages will usually earn a greater return than government securities.

3. *Commercial Banks.* Many offer savings accounts, but the interest rates are usually lower than either the mutual savings banks or the savings and loan institutions because the Federal Reserve Bank limits maximum interest rates they may pay with respect to certain time deposits. The difference is generally about one-quarter of 1 percent.

4. *Credit Unions.* A credit union is an association formed by any group of people who have a common interest—employees of a particular company, professionals, church members, etc. The group pools its savings and makes them available for loans to members. They are federally or state-chartered. Credit unions are tax-exempt institutions and their administrative costs are low. This makes it possible for them to pay higher interest rates than most other savings institutions. Credit unions, however, do not have the professional management that most banks and savings and loan institutions do; therefore, some of them do not have the same degree of safety, although many of them do have federally backed insurance against depositor loss similar to banks.

Payroll Savings Plans

If you have made the decision to save regularly, but don't want to bother with the mechanics of deposits and purchases, or if you want to supplement your savings program, many employers offer savings plans in which deposits can be automatically deducted from your paycheck before you receive it. In some cases employers will contribute a percentage of your savings to your account.

Many companies offer *401(k) programs* that provide options for saving as well as investing. It is important to remember, however, that since 401(k) programs are actually retirement-type or tax-deferred funds, they are not really liquid. They come under the umbrella of a program that carries delays and penalties for withdrawal before retirement age. Among the options typically available in 401(k) programs are investments in money market funds and a selection of mutual funds consisting of a variety of asset classes from conservative to aggressive.

U.S. Saving Bond plans provide for regular deductions from wages to purchase bonds for you.

Government obligations are debts that the government owes. They are two types: marketable and nonmarketable securities.

Most people are personally familiar with the nonmarketable type, namely, U.S. Savings Bonds. They may not be sold or used as collateral, but their redemption by the government upon demand is guaranteed.

Series E and EE bonds offer a special tax advantage. The owner may report the income on his tax return as it accrues or in a lump sum when the bonds are redeemed. If they are redeemed for qualified higher education expenses (tuition and fees) for the investor, spouse, or dependents, there is no tax if redemption occurs in the year the expense is incurred. This tax feature is also of value in a retirement plan, since, having a number of years within which to redeem his bonds, he can wait until the lower income tax years of retirement to report this income. Holders of E bonds should make certain as to their maturities, even though they may be extended, because when the maturities are reached they may stop accruing interest.

Series H and HH bonds have no special tax advantage. They are sold at par (face value). The interest is paid semiannually and must be reported each year. They mature ten years after issue. They can be redeemed any time after six months from the date of issue.

Since 1998, *Series I bonds* have been available. They are sold at par and pay a fixed taxable interest rate for thirty years, plus a semiannually adjusted inflation rate that is tied to the consumer price index. When I bond rates are quoted, they are actually a combination of the two rates. The interest payments are added to the overall value of the particular bonds you hold and are not taxed until you redeem the bond, when they are subject to federal tax. Series I bonds issued after February 1, 2003, may be redeemed any time after twelve months. As with Series EE bonds, proceeds are tax-free if used for qualified higher education expenses such as tuition and fees.

Series Es, Hs and Is all have the advantage of *safety*; the credit of the United States government stands behind them. But since their return is fixed, and there is no potential appreciation in market value, they offer no protection against inflation, other than the potential rise in interest rates on Series I bonds.

Treasury bonds, on the other hand, are marketable securities that can be sold in secondary markets and are issued in the forms of bills, notes, certificates, and bonds. Unless the Treasury calls them in sooner, they are not redeemable until their maturity date. They are traded like corporate securities, and so their value is subject to the changes of the marketplace. At times their interest rates have been lower than many other fixed return investments.

But from the estate planning point of view, these lower interest rates (which causes them to sell at a discount) can make some of them attractive estate investments. On the owner's death, certain issues of U.S. Treasury bonds can be redeemed to pay estate taxes at their par values. The person who purchases these Treasury issues, which have been selling as low as $80, for example, can add to his estate an asset that will be valued at $100 at his death.

Municipal Bonds

The investment importance of municipal bonds is that their interest is tax-free both federally and in the state where they are issued.

Municipal bonds are issued by a state or its subdivisions (towns, cities, counties, and the like) or its agencies (highway, bridge, or other authorities). They are of three kinds: *general obligations,* which are backed by the credit and taxing power of the government entity; *revenue bonds,* issued for a specific purpose (such as financing a bridge or sewage system), the income and principal of which are payable out of the special project or enterprise; and *moral obligation* or *agency bonds* issued for purposes of financing state housing, hospital, and university construction. Although the latter type are basically revenue-type bonds, the state legislature is supposed to have a moral obligation to vote for allocating funds toward payment of interest and principal if the underlying projects do not generate sufficient income to do so. The general obligation issues are safer investments, but, being less risky, they usually yield a lower return.

Being tax-free, municipals are offered at a lower rate of interest than most corporate bonds. If you buy municipals and save taxes, will you end up with more spendable income than if you had invested in higher yielding corporate bonds?

For the person in a high tax bracket, the answer would definitely be yes. Take a taxpayer in the 35 percent bracket. A tax-free bond yielding 4.5 percent gives him a return equivalent to a taxable interest of 6.9 percent.

But there are disadvantages to investing in some municipals that should be weighed against their tax advantages. Many of them are not as readily marketable as United States government or corporate bonds. If the owner is forced to liquidate them in a hurry, he may have to sell them in a narrow market and below their face value. The estate planner who invests in them should consider them as long-term investments, not as a source of ready cash.

Furthermore the safety of municipals depends on the credit of the local government or the municipal project—often a difficult matter to determine. Recently, even some of the largest municipalities have had difficulty in redeeming bonds issued by them. Also, how dependable, for example, is the issue of a small town's sewage disposal bonds? This is obviously a question that can only be answered by experts. Anyone contemplating such investments should consult investment advisors who are specialists in the field.

All this means that the return from municipals should be substantially greater than the after-tax income received on other types of investments. Otherwise, the return doesn't compensate for their less desirable features.

Suppose an issue of municipals pays 5.5 percent. A taxpayer whose top bracket is 35 percent buys them and gets a return equal to 8.5 percent in taxable interest. A taxpayer with a 15 percent top bracket, however, would get a return equal to only 6.5 percent taxable interest.

I'd call this a worthwhile investment for the 35 percent person; he would likely receive a lesser yield from other investments. But the 15 per-center is getting little more than the return he would receive from a safe, liquid investment such as a U.S. government bond.

U.S. Government Securities (Treasury Bills, Notes, and Bonds)

U.S. government securities can be used to provide interest income, greater marketability than municipal bonds, and staggered maturities. Their interest income is free of state and local taxes. If held to maturity, you do receive your principal and promised interest payments. Do be aware, though, that rising interest rates can cause the selling price of your government securities to drop. If you are forced to sell before maturity to handle an emergency, you could lose money on your original investment.

For this reason, purchasing Treasury securities of various maturities may be a wise plan, say, two-, five-, ten- and thirty-year securities for greater availability of funds and opportunities to repurchase at possibly higher interest rates.

Corporate Bonds

When you purchase a bond of Company X, you are lending money to it, and it guarantees to pay a certain rate of interest, and to repay your loan in full by a specified date. Your bond may be *secured*, that is to say, it is backed, by a lien or pledge on all the company's property or on specific assets to ensure repayment. Or it may be unsecured, a *debenture* bond. The former is a safer investment. In either case, however, your claim takes precedence over stockholders'.

What are the investment features of a corporate bond? First of all it is marketable; second, it yields more than government obligations; third, it provides the security of a fixed rate of interest; fourth, it guarantees repayment of the face amount if you hold it to maturity; and fifth, it usually has an active market to ensure liquidity.

The chief disadvantage of the bond, however, is that since its interest is fixed, its market value will decline in a time of rising interest rates. One way to offset this effect is to buy convertible bonds. This type gives the bondholder the right to convert the bond into a certain number of shares of the common stock of the company.

Suppose you buy a convertible bond. Sometime later the stock of the corporation has a substantial market rise. You can either convert the bond to the stock, or sell it in the open market at a gain that will reflect the increased value of the stock to which it can be converted. Thus, a convertible bond offers the security of a fixed return investment as well as the growth opportunities of an equity investment. It is a hedge against both deflation and inflation, and therefore represents a most useful type of investment in an estate planner's long-term portfolio.

Taxation of Bonds

Bond interest, except for municipals, is taxable income. If interest is in default at the time you buy the bond or if you buy "income bonds" (i.e., bonds where the interest is contingent on earnings) on which back interest is due, when and if you eventually get the back interest, it is not considered taxable income but a return of capital. This reduces your basis.

When the bond is sold or redeemed, your taxable income is increased by this amount of paid back interest. Therefore, this is merely a deferral of income.

Similarly, if you buy a bond at a discount and then you sell it at a profit or it is retired, the amount of the discount (other than an original issue discount) is taxable income. Suppose you buy a bond, for example, at discount, purchasing it at eighty-five when it had been issued at one hundred. When the bond matures, the company retires it, and you have a taxable income of fifteen.

A final word on bonds: except for convertibles, they have growth potential only if general interest rates decline. Their safety is dependent on the soundness of the company that issues them and its continuing ability to pay interest and repay principal.

Stocks

Until now we have been concerned with fixed return investments. They are usually safe, they are conservative, and they should be included in a sound investment portfolio. But in most cases they must be balanced by investments with growth potential. The need for growth investments is twofold. They tie your capital to the prevailing economy. Thus, in an inflationary period they may protect your capital from a loss of buying power. Also, growth investments provide opportunity for capital appreciation apart from an inflationary rise.

Investments in corporate stocks serve this function. The holder of such an investment is not a creditor of the company like the bondholder; he is an owner. As such, he shares in both profits and losses. The expectation of increased profits provides the growth potential, but it should not be forgotten that loss potential is there also. That is why stocks are more of a risk; they traditionally offer higher yields than bonds of the same company.

Preferred Stock. This stands midway between a bond and a stock. There is a fixed return, but there is no specified maturity date. Usually preferred stock may be called, but the callability is an option that the corporation need not exercise. A preferred stockholder's claim is subordinate to those of the holders of bonds and other corporate indebtedness, but prior to those of common stockholders. In addition, his right to dividends is usually cumulative: that is, if dividends are in arrears, they must all be paid before any dividends are paid on the common.

Preferred, then, is like a bond in that its market value increases and decreases with prevailing interest rates. It is like a stock in that the payment of dividends is dependent on earnings. The preferred stockholder, however, is entitled only to the fixed dividend; everything over that belongs to the common stockholders. On the other hand, if the corporation cannot pay dividends, the preferred shareholder, in effect, participates in its losses.

There are two special types of preferred, however, which offer greater potential for appreciation by giving the preferred the opportunity to share in the company's growth.

Convertible Preferred: Gives the shareholder the right, after or during a certain period, to convert his stock into a fixed number of shares of common. Thus, if the market price of the common rises, he can sell his preferred (which will have increased in value), or he can convert to common at no additional cost.

Participating Preferred: Gives the shareholder the usual fixed dividend, but includes the right to share excess dividends with the common stock.

Convertible preferred is offered by many companies; participating preferred is rarely offered by public corporations.

Common Stock. The common stock of a company is junior to bonds and other indebtedness and preferred stock. A company may have only common stock outstanding, or more than one class of stock. When a company has more than one class, as a general rule it will have one class of common and one or more classes of preferred. However, it may have more than one class of common. Although common stock is the junior security, it usually has the voting power. Occasionally preferred stock has voting rights, but generally it is the common stockholders who control the corporation.

The common stock bears the greatest amount of risk along with the greatest potential for growth. In the average portfolio, common stocks are necessary because of their capital appreciation potential. The proportion of investment which should be made in common stocks will vary with each individual's particular circumstances.

For example, the stockholder of a closely held corporation will not have a great need for investing in common stock because part of his assets is already in a growth investment, his business. A corporate executive or professional person with a steadily rising income may not need as large a percentage of investment in common stock as perhaps a person with a fixed salary or retirement income requires. His increasing earning power and his increasing ability to put money aside are a hedge against inflation and an estate-builder.

Stocks vary greatly in quality from the "blue chips" to the "cats and dogs." The choice depends on how much risk one is willing to take. For a person who depends solely on investments for income, the amount and regularity of dividends are important. Dividends fluctuate, and there is no guarantee that dividends will be paid out at all. However, an investor can look to a corporation's past dividend record and its current earnings as a guide to its future dividend paying policy. In addition, the current more favorable tax treatment of cash dividends under JGTRRA 2003 lowers their taxation to 15 percent for taxpayers in the 25 percent bracket and higher, and to 5 percent for those in the 10 or 15 percent brackets. Until this law sunsets after December 31, 2008, dividend income plays an even more meaningful role in a portfolio than before.

Since the investment program of an estate plan is a long-range program, upwards of forty years, the element of long-term growth is an important factor. But how do you determine where to find it?

Potential for growth is not limited to new enterprises. Older companies may offer great possibilities of growth, as for example, public utilities located in areas of the country with expanding populations.

However, the greatest potential or opportunity for growth often lies in the common stocks of the riskier new enterprises. The estate planner with substantially all of his reserves invested in fixed-return or "blue-chip" securities can validly commit a small part to venture enterprises. He may risk the loss of a small part of his capital but might garner a windfall in the long run. Our products and services are constantly changing. A new product or invention may create a multimillion-dollar corporation or an entire industry in years to come.

Unfortunately, there is no scientific way of selecting the right industry or corporation. Not only determining what to buy, but when to buy, is difficult. Whether investing on your own, using an asset manager, or investing in mutual funds, diversifying across industries, or based on size and maturity of companies, helps to smooth out the variations in the value of your portfolio over time. This may include buying stocks in companies of proven strength, and taking a chance on the growth potential of newer companies; buying only U.S companies; or including global investing. The watchword is diversification. But diversify how? Knowing yourself as an investor is critical. How much time do you have to invest? How averse to changes in the values of your investments are you? Most mutual fund companies and asset managers have investor profile questionnaires that you can use to determine the type of investment mix that matches your personal risk tolerance and timeline and will help you put together a mixture of investments that can help you stay on course in good times and bad.

Special Investments for High Tax Brackets

The person in the high tax bracket looks for investments which provide large tax deductions and allowances for depreciation and depletion. The actual cost of these investments is often reduced by the amount of income tax savings. Such a person should investigate a number of special types of investments that we will merely indicate here. In the proper case they offer opportunities which should not be overlooked. There are specialists and brokers who handle only these types of "deals." Often they are individuals working on their own, or even "wildcatters." We would strongly suggest you carefully look into the background and experience of anyone you deal with. Your local bank or stockbroker can get you the names of the more reliable organizations that operate in these fields.

Oil and Gas Wells. There is a deduction for drilling expenses as well as depreciation on physical equipment purchases. However, the Tax Reform Act of 1976 provides for recapture (ordinary tax treatment) of past intangible drilling cost deductions when such interests are disposed of by the investor. If the well is successful, there is a deduction for depletion of 15 percent on income received for most investors (investors with an economic interest by way of a capital investment). When the investor's cost is recouped by depletion allowances, future allowances become tax preference items.

Cattle. There are substantial tax benefits. Expenses of care and feeding are deductible from ordinary income. The cost of purchase of the cattle can be depreciated over the scheduled lives of the animals, subject to taxation on the depreciation as ordinary income when sold. Breeding, dairy, or draft cattle get special treatment on sale, if they have been held for two years or more. If there is a loss, it is considered an ordinary loss, deductible against ordinary income if the taxpayer participates in the management or operations of the activity. If the taxpayer does not participate in the activity such losses can only be used to offset gains from similar investments. And as the herd increases in number and weight, there is a capital appreciation.

Timber. If you own an interest in timber, you will get a cost depletion allowance. This applies whether you own standing timber, have a right to cut the timber, or merely hold timber royalties.

Unit Investment Trusts, Mutual Funds, and Commercial Annuities

Investing on one's own is a difficult task. It calls for skill, experience, and above all, time. A person with large resources can afford to pay for individual professional assistance, but the small investor is usually dependent upon whatever information he can gather from disparate sources in the limited time he can devote to this effort.

Few so-called small investors attain success in the investment field. The lists to choose from are so long and the comparative values among stock issues are so difficult to assess. The amateur or part-time investor may be wise to turn his selection of investments over to a professional group. Here he gains not only experienced management, but also wider investment diversification than he would otherwise be able to afford.

Mutual Funds and Unit Investment Trusts. When you buy shares in one of these investment companies, you are investing in a company whose sole business is the investment of its capital in securities. Its capital is the pooled money of many investors, which it uses to purchase stocks, bonds or other types of securities. What type of securities, what areas of the economy it invests in, whether it is aggressive or conservative in its investment style, depends on the type of fund. Many investment companies have a wide variety of fund investment styles from which to choose, allowing investors to select one, a few, or many funds within one "family of funds" to create a portfolio suitably diversified for their purposes.

There are two types of investment companies: *closed end* and *open end*.

The *closed end* or *unit investment trust* operates like the ordinary corporation. It sells a *fixed* number of shares that are regularly traded on the market to investors. The company uses its funds for investments and pays the profits from dividends, interest, and capital gains to its stockholders.

The shares of these companies are subject to market fluctuations, just as are any other corporate shares. The price usually reflects the value of their underlying net assets, i.e., the securities held by the company. But they may sell above or below this value depending upon their success and market conditions.

The *open end* company, popularly known as the *mutual fund*, has no specific limit on the number of shares it can issue. With few exceptions, the more money it receives for investment, the more shares it will issue.

When you buy a share in the mutual fund the price you pay is based on the net value of the fund plus a loading or sales charge. Most mutual fund companies now offer what are generally referred to as A, B or C shares. A shares are charged a sales load every time you invest *new* money into the fund. Their advantage is that if you intend to invest $25,000 or more, you will typically incur a lower charge. Generally, as you reach invested amounts of $50,000, $75,000, $100,000, $250,000, and $500,000 you pay lower and lower charges on new money invested. These increments of lower charges are referred to as *breakpoints*. In general, at $1 million and above, no sales load is charged. Make sure that you find out what proportion of the price is accounted for by this loading charge; sometimes it can go as high as 6 or 7 percent on amounts below the first breakpoint. More typical is 5.75 percent. Check the prospectus of each fund to see what their breakpoints are, and how much the charges decline at each step. B shares have what is called a *contingent deferred sales* charge. They allow any new money to be invested with no initial sales charge, but do impose a sales charge that declines year by year for withdrawals that occur prior to (typically) five or six years. During this time, even if you stay invested, these shares have higher internal charges that do not disappear until, typically, the sixth year. At the end of this time, B shares become A shares. B shares offer *no* breakpoints, but may be useful for the small investor who intends to withdraw money within, say, five years. C shares have no up-front sales charge, and either no contingent sales charge period, or a short period and lower charges for early withdrawals. A few funds have no loading charges, but may have higher internal costs. Over long holding periods they may be more costly. It is critical to read prospectuses for mutual funds to determine the best purchase strategy to suit your needs.

Shares of mutual funds are not traded on the market. They are purchased and redeemed either directly by the company or through a broker. The redemption price is determined by the net asset value of the fund at the time of redemption plus (occasionally) a redemption fee.

Since the market value of the securities held by the fund fluctuates, the value of the fund's shares fluctuates as well. Thus, the price at which you buy or have your shares redeemed is determined by the market value of the underlying securities at the time of the transaction.

Many people establish a systematic investment program to put money aside on a regular basis, perhaps with automatic contributions directly from their checking account. To assure that you reach your accumulation goal you could accompany it with term life insurance and a disability insurance plan, so the investment plan can be completed even in the event of your death or disability.

Both closed and open end companies offer different types of investment portfolios. Some are balanced funds, investing in preferred and common stocks and bonds. Some are limited to a particular type of security, offering only common stocks or only bonds. Others limit their holdings to particular industries, such as chemicals or electronics and are referred to as sector funds.

In any case, these companies offer the investor a wide diversification of securities or diversification within a particular industry—much more than he could develop on his own. His costs will be the loading charge (unless it is a no-load fund), a possible redemption fee, and the investment fee charged by managers.

Commercial Annuity Contracts. Over the years we have heard more confusion about the nature of commercial annuities than any other type of investment. To clarify things some distinctions should be made. Annuities are investment contracts made between the investor and an insurance company. They can be purchased as a regular individual investment and are then referred to as *nonqualified annuities*. They can be purchased as part of a qualified retirement plan, including IRAs, and are then referred to as *qualified annuities*. The same contracts and investment choices can be offered for either purpose. It is generally a matter of indicating which it will be on your application.

When annuities are purchased for the purpose of accumulating funds over a period of time, they are in what is called an *accumulation phase* and allow for the deferral of taxation on investment growth and earnings until distributed. If funds are withdrawn prior to age 59½ these are taxed as ordinary income, and a 10 percent penalty is applied. Annuity contracts for this purpose can be *deferred fixed annuities*, in which case they will offer a fixed rate of return for a fixed period of time, then adjust to a different rate for the next specified period.

Generally these contracts include a type of "back-end" sales charge, referred to as a *surrender charge*. They are on a sliding scale that might start from, say, 5, 7 or 9 percent and decline year by year until the end of the five, seven or nine years. Periods and percentages vary. The important thing to realize is that withdrawals you make prior to the end of the surrender period can result in your literally "surrendering" a portion of your investment's value. For this reason, annuities should be used for long-term goals.

The deferred variable annuity is a newer development in the attempt to combine the security of the fixed dollar investment and the growth opportunity of the equity investment. It offers the deferral of taxation on the growth of your investments until withdrawn, but along with the tax deferral comes unfavorable tax treatment on gains of ordinary income tax and a 10 percent penalty if withdrawals are made prior to age 59½. Depending on the specific contract, some part of the funds you pay to the company for your annuity may be invested in fixed dollar investments. Thus, there is a guarantee that a certain amount will be available when the annuity is due for payout. Some variable annuities also offer riders that guarantee your principal if held for specified periods of time, despite declines in the underlying investments you have selected.

Another portion is invested in equity securities, typically in the form of mutual funds, sometimes from multiple investment companies and with multiple investment styles from which to choose. This, hopefully, ensures that if inflation continues, and the buying power of the fixed return portion is thereby reduced, there will nevertheless be an increase in value in the equity portion. Theoretically, the increase will roughly equal the increase in the cost of living, *but remember to evaluate these deferred gains against the now-more-favorable capital gains rates outside of annuities.*

A variation of this plan is based on the investment of a portion of the annuity payment in cash value insurance and a portion in equity stocks. Thus, if you die, your family gets a substantial death benefit. If you retire, the company terminates the policy and invests the cash value together with the equity value to produce the annuity return. There is no guarantee of what the return will be. If inflation causes the cost of living to rise, then the annuity payments should rise accordingly, but if it goes down, so too should the annuity. You should judge whether the taxation of deferred gains on variable annuities payout proceeds as ordinary income will offset the possible treatment of other long-term investments that may receive more favorable capital gains tax treatment.

The holder of the variable annuity, however, is placing his investments in professional hands. As with mutual funds, he is getting the advantage of experienced investment management.

At retirement, annuities can switch from *accumulation phase* to *annuitization phase*, or payout phase. At this point, you could begin taking regular fixed payments or variable payments out of the annuity as needed. For guaranteed income, you could place a sum of money either from an existing annuity or from other sources in a *Single Premium Immediate Annuity* to provide a guaranteed income for your life, or combined lifetimes with a spouse, or over a fixed period of time (say, ten years), or paid out over one or joint lives with monies left at death within a certain period of time (say, ten years) left to a beneficiary, such as a child.

A word of caution: Once funds are committed to an immediate annuity, there is no access to the principal. You trade the guarantee of a specific income for a specified period of time (or lifetime) for the flexibility of being able to cash out some or all of your funds for an emergency or an opportunity. Thus, it would not be wise to put all your capital into such a contract.

SELECTING A MUTUAL FUND

It is good to know that mutual funds are valuable investment media. But how do you, as a small investor, in the limited time you can devote to the investment of your resources, make an informed judgment of which funds best fit your individual investment objectives? You should try to choose a fund that meets your standard of safety, diversity, and return. Each mutual fund or group of funds has its own philosophy and approach to managing its investments. These are set forth in the company's prospectus, which can be a basic tool to help you assess whether you will achieve safety, diversity, and return. What you will need to know, then, is the performance of the fund over time and the types of investments that make up the fund. To obtain information on the funds that are available, simply look for their ads in major newspapers—usually in the business section. They will contain information about their performance and investment focus and give you an 800 phone number to call for a prospectus. You should send for prospectuses from several companies to make comparisons. Once you receive a prospectus there are several factors to look for which will help you make comparisons among funds, and to decide which one is right for you.

1. One criteria for making a selection amongst fund companies is past earnings. Look at their earnings/performance over many years. Look at their long-term growth, how they performed in good and bad markets during those years. This information is partially available in the prospectus. It can also be found with comparable data on other funds in *Investor's Business Daily* under the section labeled "Mutual Funds," with percentages of performance in the year to date as well as for preceding years. Yields

will always fluctuate with the market (unlike, say, a CD). Major newspapers provide information on the current prices of each of the mutual funds in their business sections on a daily basis.

As a starter, it is probably best to consider the established mutual funds with conservative, diversified stock or bond portfolios. As you become more experienced, more used to the fluctuations of the fund price in the market, and perhaps have more discretionary income, you might consider funds with portfolios that are less diversified, more invested in speculative businesses with potential for substantial growth, and thus involve greater risk.

2. Each fund details the assumptions upon which its projected growth is based, along with its philosophy of investing. This is subjective information, but will give you an idea of how it plans and makes investment decisions, and how aggressive or conservative it may be.

3. Most funds offer several types of portfolios with varying investment objectives and types of investments. Types of investments that make up each portfolio are given in listings. You can select a mixture of funds that suit your risk profile and timeline.

4. These days, many mutual funds have investor risk profile questionnaires to help you determine the mixture of investments that fits your risk tolerance and timeline. Many of these are available on their websites or through financial advisors. Also, most prospectuses will give you a guide for selecting amongst the various portfolios—investment objectives, types of investments emphasized in the portfolio, degrees of risk, and rates of expected return (i.e., low, medium, high) are provided. Some are balanced funds, investing in preferred and common stocks and bonds. Some are limited to a particular type of security, offering only common stocks or only bonds. Others limit their holdings to particular industries, such as chemicals or electronics. These are called sector funds. Many mutual fund companies will allow you to transfer your funds from one mutual fund to another within their assortment of funds as your investment goals change—at little or often no cost. This is important, because even if your goals remain the same, the proportion of money you initially allocate to various funds can get out of balance, as when one sector of the economy outperforms another. Take the late 1990s, when the technology sector skyrocketed in value. Investors who did

not sell amounts they accrued in that sector to reallocate according to their original plan of investment may have experienced much greater declines in their portfolio values than those who took profits regularly and redistributed them according to their original portfolio mix.

5. Making changes in your allocation of dollars to various funds can create additional costs, depending upon the type of shares you own in a mutual fund. As discussed above, the costs of getting into and out of the fund (load costs) depends upon whether you already paid a charge to buy the shares of the funds (A shares), purchased shares that incur a contingent deferred sales charge when withdrawn within an initial period of years (B shares), or have no charge to purchase or redeem, just higher internal fees on an ongoing basis.

6. If you are about to invest in a mutual fund, we suggest that you seek professional advice. It can help you pick the fund family and individual funds that are right for you.

QUALIFIED TUITION PROGRAMS: SECTION 529 PLANS

These are worth a special mention, because college costs keep rising, making it more of a challenge to put aside enough funds. There are a variety of tax-favored programs that offer various tax breaks for those earmarking savings for this purpose. The program with some of the more generous tax treatments are the *Section 529 plans*, also known as qualified tuition programs, that were first created by federal legislation in 1996. They have undergone a number of changes that have made them even more flexible, and have become very popular as a way of investing substantial sums of money to grow tax-deferred until withdrawn tax-free if used to pay for higher-education expenses. For the most part, these are primarily state-sponsored programs (though some are privately sponsored). All fifty states now offer some sort of Section 529 program, with most selecting mutual fund companies as the official investment managers of the invested funds.

Contributions are made with after-tax dollars in cash and are not deductible. Since these are treated as completed gifts, they are subject to the annual gift exclusion ($11,000 in 2004). It is possible to accelerate these gifts, making five years' worth in one year ($55,000 for an individual; $110,000 for a couple), but then not contributing more until the end of five years. The compounding effect of this can be valuable, since funds are growing tax-deferred. Anyone can contribute to an account for a beneficiary, such as parents, grandparents and friends. Overall contribution maximums vary from state to state, with some allowing as much as $250,000 to be contributed overall.

When you open a Section 529 account, you will be the "participant" and will have a custodial role, controlling the allocation of contributed funds across a variety of mutual funds selections, or so-called "age-based" portfolios that are adjusted for risk depending on the number of years until the beneficiary reaches college age. With most plans you may also name a successor participant in the event of your incapacity or death. The "beneficiary" of the plan is the person for whom higher-education funds are being contributed. Any person can be a beneficiary, including yourself. You may name one beneficiary only, but you can select a new one at any time. This would be important in the event of the death of a beneficiary, his or her change in plans, receiving a scholarship or simply falling out of your good graces. A rollover to the new designated beneficiary must occur within sixty days and can be to another "member of the family" (first cousins of the original beneficiary, your spouse, your child or his descendent, a stepchild, a sibling or stepsibling, nieces or nephews, aunts and uncles, in-laws, parents, stepparents, spouses of the above).

Withdrawals used for *qualified higher-education* expenses are tax-free. These expenses include such things as tuition, fees, room and board, supplies and equipment (e.g., a computer or lab equipment). Qualified expenses are reduced by the amount of any Hope Scholarship Credits or Lifetime Learning Credits (see below). At any point you could decide to terminate the plan, but withdrawals of funds not yet used for qualified expenses are subject to ordinary income tax on all gains plus a 10 percent penalty. In effect, you gave away the funds as a completed gift, but have the recourse of taking them back with a penalty. A most unusual feature.

When selecting a plan, you are not restricted to the one offered by your state of residence, though some states (not all) provide the added incentive of giving you a tax deduction for contributions. Be aware of the various fees charged on contributions (front-loaded, back-loaded), and the investment selections available to be sure the investment selections, program features and costs suit your needs.

As with other provisions of the Tax Relief Act, this program is due to "sunset" after December 31, 2010. Congress will have to decide on whether to extend it. If Section 529 qualified tuition programs are not extended, withdrawals will not be tax-free.

OTHER TAX-FAVORED WAYS TO PAY FOR COLLEGE

There are a variety of other tax-favored ways to provide funding for college costs, though not as generous as the Section 529 qualified tuition plans.

- *Coverdell Education Savings Accounts* (previously known as Education IRAs): In 2005 annual contributions of $2,000 can be made. Earnings accumulate tax-free. Account proceeds can be used tax-free for qualified education expenses for college and graduate programs, as well as elementary and secondary education. This K–12 provision "sunsets" December 31, 2010, unless extended by Congress.
- *Hope Scholarship Credit:* This provision allows you to take up to $1,500 of tax credits against $2,000 of qualifying expenses for each of the first two years of college for each student enrolled at least half-time. Tax credits are phased out for single taxpayers earning income between $42,000 and $52,000, and for married taxpayers earning income between $85,000 and $105,000.
- *Lifetime Learning Credits:* This is a very flexible provision that allows you a credit against income taxes on 20 percent of the first $10,000 of expenses associated with education. A maximum of $2,000 is available per year. The credit applies to any post-secondary education expenses. The studies can be for improving job skills, not necessarily for a degree, and students needn't be at least half-time. This credit cannot be used in the same year as a Hope Scholarship Credit. The use of these credits is phased out at the same income thresholds as for Hope Scholarship Credits.
- *Gifts:* Annual gift exclusions can be used to contribute to Uniform Transfer to Minors Accounts (see Chapter 13 for a full discussion) for a limited degree of tax-free growth, up to $1,600 per year in 2005. While the child is under age 14, earnings in excess of this amount are taxed at the parents' tax rates. After age 14, ex-

cess investment earnings are taxed at the child's tax rate. The accounts are controlled by a custodian (often a parent or grandparent) at least until the child reaches the age of majority, and can be used for the education, medical needs and support of the child as needed.

Special note: Grandparents can make payments for tuition directly to their grandchildren's schools, free of any gift or estate tax.

- *Series EE Bonds:* Interest on these bonds is tax-free if used for paying tuition and fees of one of your dependents. (In 2004 such treatment is phased out for single taxpayers with modified adjusted gross income between $59,850 and $74,850; for married taxpayers between $89,750 and $119,750.)
- *Financial Aid:* The federal government provides a formula to colleges and universities for determining who is eligible for financial aid. Factors include subtracting the expected contribution the family will make, its assets and income, and the assets and income of the child. If a child in your life is likely to seek financial aid, it would be better not to make a large gift directly to him or her.
- *Life Insurance and Annuities:* Suppose you have a need for life insurance, and want it to provide some living benefits. Suppose you will be at least 59½ years old when your child attends college. Consider the use of cash value life insurance and/or an annuity for tax-deferred buildup of funds for college. The funds accrued will not be included in the formula for calculating eligibility for financial aid. The life insurance can provide tax-free loans and, in the event of your death, immediate tax-free death benefit to cover college costs.

INVESTMENT ADVICE AND ASSISTANCE

If you feel that an investment company such as a mutual fund does not render the tailor-made service that fits your individual investment needs and believe you could put together a better package on your own, you will need advice and assistance from professionally qualified sources. Fortunately, there are a great variety of individuals and organizations that offer investment, informational and counseling services to the serious-minded investor.

Market Letters and Security Reports

Today there is a huge quantity of published material available to the prospective investor, especially now that these are offered over the World Wide Web, via fax or in print. It varies from the dope sheet put out by an individual operating from a hole in the wall to the comprehensive statistical reports issued by firms like Moody's or Standard & Poor's.

What do these services offer or purport to offer? Their information is theoretically based on independent investigations of the investment value of major corporations. To do a good job of this investigation, the service has to have competent research people who interview the heads of companies, study the records of the firms, and analyze the industries they represent. On the basis of this information, they make independent judgments as to the companys' financial condition and their prospects for success. Moreover, they put all this information and analysis into a readable and understandable form. All of this is something that the individual can't possibly do for himself; it is a full-time job and requires a large organization. Hence the great attraction of these services for the individual investor.

But you must realize that the information presented is general and does not necessarily reflect *your* individual needs. You must still make your own critical evaluations as to what such information means in terms of your own investment program.

Brokerage Houses

These offer advisory and investment services, and many are also equipped to take over the complete management of a portfolio. They are subject to the rules and regulations of the stock exchanges in which they operate and hence must measure up to standards of reliability.

When you deal with a firm that is a member of the New York Stock Exchange, the person who acts as its representative must have passed an examination given by that exchange. He will be registered with it, with the National Association of Securities Dealers, and, usually, with the state in which he functions.

Does all this automatically guarantee that you will get good service from any representative? Not necessarily, for the job he performs is a highly individualized one. He uses the research provided by his company and then adapts this research to your own individual needs. This takes acumen, judgment, and interest, things that can never be guaranteed by formal registrations or even examinations. Remember, too, the representative is paid to buy or sell. This gives him a personal stake in his dealings with you that could impair his objectivity.

The Individual Broker

Many investments cannot be traded without a broker. In an arena with so many possibilities and variables it is important to have a specialist whose focus and expertise can guide you through the investment maze. Service, proficiency, and general approach of these individuals will vary. You may need to interview a few to find one you feel comfortable with. The effort can be worthwhile, since individual brokers are of varying experience, competency, and conscientiousness. Their training and experience should enable them to succinctly explain how particular investment opportunities may meet your specific goals. Many brokers are trade-oriented. Although they offer advice on estate-oriented investments, their main emphasis is on day-to-day trading. Because of this you need to keep in mind that their earnings are based on fees charged to you for trading into or out of investments. Thus, you should carefully make your own decision based on information and your own judgment as to if and when to make such moves. Before placing any investment orders it is a good idea to meet your broker in person for a strategy session. In this way you can discuss and clarify your objectives, based upon the advice of a knowledgeable specialist with whom you have established a relationship of trust and confidence.

Online Trading

With the advent of investment brokerage trading systems via the World Wide Web, individual investors can now establish brokerage accounts and buy and sell securities for themselves online. During the late 1990s such activity gained tremendous popularity as stock prices rose to all-time highs day after day. Individual investors were rapidly buying and selling on a daily basis, many on margin (borrowing from the brokerage house to purchase more shares in targeted stocks). Many did so with no plan other than to cash in on easy profits, and lost tremendous amounts of money when the market fell rapidly.

Such activity has declined in volume since, but it remains clear that this medium of investing is best suited for those with sufficient knowledge of what they are buying and how they are planning to purchase, hold and sell their selections. For most people, it is still a good idea to work with a professional to determine a portfolio model and appropriate investment vehicles to suit their specific needs.

The Investment Counselor, Asset Management Programs

The advantage of this type of counseling lies in the fact that you will get individualized attention. Moreover, you can be sure that attention will be objective. The counselor has nothing to sell but his services, represents no other interests, either directly or indirectly, except those of the client, and earns only his fee that is based on the value of your portfolio. If you succeed, he succeeds.

If you select competent and experienced investment counsel you will get both the information and the professional advice you need to do a good investment job. Investment counselors don't guarantee success, of course, but your chances of winning it are much higher than if you tried to do it yourself. Some counselors offer asset management programs that put together portfolios of individual securities (mixtures of stocks and bonds using various investment styles) based on your specific needs. Others may also or exclusively use selected mutual funds to offer sufficient diversification to smaller parts of your portfolio.

One of the drawbacks is that most firms in this business cannot afford to take small accounts. You will need to have at least $100,000 as a minimum with some, $1 million with others, to invest before you can utilize such a firm. On this, you usually pay a fee representing a percentage of the managed amount.

Ordinarily this percentage gradually declines with the increase in the size of the account. Also, there is frequently special consideration made for government bonds and municipal bonds that are in the account and require little professional supervision.

A significant advantage to this type of management is continuity for a family. All too often there is one spouse who takes the role of money manager. If that spouse is the first to die, the surviving spouse may not have the skill to continue the management of their portfolio. Having an ongoing investment counselor can provide a means to continue or adjust the investment plan for the family without the survivor having to become an instant expert at a difficult time.

Your Local Bank and Trust Company

All the major banks, as well as many local banks, maintain trust departments. As a matter of fact, this tendency to create trust and custodial departments in the banking fraternity has increased substantially in recent years.

Essentially, these trust departments have as their objective the preservation of an estate, whether that estate comes as a result of an inheritance or is still in the hands of the estate creator.

In actuality, however, many of these trust departments do manage estates that have a growth objective. You should not therefore be deterred from inquiring at your bank as to the suitability of their trust department in taking over the management of your estate building plan.

Make certain that the bank you have chosen is set up for the aggressive, moderate or conservative type of investment action you may require.

There is also a question as to the minimum size of the account that can be accepted. In many of the larger banks and trust companies, the minimum account is $1 million, but there are many, especially in regional centers, that will take them from $100,000 or less. This, of course, precludes the use of this investment aid for the majority of the people who are starting to build an estate, and limits it to those who already have a substantial portfolio.

Fees tend to run along roughly the same lines as the fees outlined above for investment counselors. There again, there is a variation. One bank rarely has exactly the same fee structure as another.

To sum up, the selection of investments for the estate planner follows no magical formula. Your own portfolio's composition will depend upon your financial status, the state of the economy, your needs and taste for risk versus rewards, and most important, your objectives. Estate planning objectives are not meant to be tied to sudden success but to the accumulation of a sufficient capital base to supply income for major expenses such as college education for your children, and for disability, retirement, and death.

With all this as basic information you can now take a look at the resources provided in the Appendix on pages 399–424, which are designed to help you construct your portfolio and have an overview of the types of investments available.

CHAPTER 8

INVESTMENTS: PUTTING YOUR
CAPITAL IN REAL ESTATE

Of all investment opportunities, real estate may offer the big chance. Here is one area where property value is inherent in the property itself. Indeed, now, as in the past, the demands of a growing population tend to increase land value. As even such an early economic thinker as Henry George pointed out, land represents a basic need of society; as this need grows, so also does the value of real estate. Population pressures, in terms of both higher standards of living and a rising birth rate, create new and larger demands for both land and buildings. Land for development becomes scarcer and more valuable.

The past two decades dramatically illustrate this essential character of real estate. Its values—both rental and property—have risen sharply. Given a continuing increase in the population, a well-situated piece of real estate is almost automatically sure to rise, subject to the ups and downs of normal real estate cycles. At the same time, its income yield is unusually high. A 10 to 15 percent return is not uncommon. In addition, real estate has other advantages. It has special tax-sheltered opportunities. It protects its owner against the erosion of inflation; rentals and values move with the economy.

Why, then, do we so often hear that real estate should represent the later, not the first use of investment money for the part-time investor? If we can predict with more certainty that a piece of land will increase in value than a share of stock, why buy stock before buying real estate?

For two reasons. First, there is the problem of liquidity. Despite its great potentiality as an estate builder, real estate lacks ready liquidity. It is subject to cycles within the long-term growth pattern, and it is greatly affected by real estate market swings—local, temporary, and specific though they may be—which occur even when the overall trend is inflationary. The person who is forced to sell real estate to get liquidity during one of these cyclical periods runs the risk of incurring losses because he cannot find a ready buyer. Perhaps the area where his property is located is in decline, while areas nearby are undergoing renewal and renovation.

Second, there is the question of knowledge and experience. Real estate investment in improved property is really a matter for professionals or those who have available time and are willing to devote it to their investment program. It involves the management and, often, the improvement of property. Expert help is not easily obtained, and even if it is, it still must be paid for—sometimes to the extent of leaving small profits to the owner.

Thus, the place of real estate in the estate creation structure for the part-time investor is as one element in an overall program. It is an opportunity which may bring long-term capital returns. But it is also an asset that must be supported by more liquid properties such as insurance or securities and, if it is improved property, managed by someone with skill and experience.

The First Real Estate Investment: The Home

A person's first venture into real estate, however, contradicts what we have just said. Since he must live somewhere, no matter what his stage in life is, he is going to be concerned very early in the game with at least a peripheral aspect of real estate investment—the purchase or the rental of a residence. Thus, at the beginning of the estate planner's program, when the "five firsts" are being established—your occupation, savings, life insurance, disability insurance and residence—real estate investment questions enter into the picture.

Most people don't look at it this way. They place personal considerations above investment ones when they look for a place to live. We do not quarrel with this. Obviously, the personal factor is, and should be, paramount. But since buying a house usually represents one of the largest single purchases an individual makes during his life, he must also consider the investment aspects of the purchase. In fact, before buying a home he should, as an estate planner, weigh the advantages of ownership versus rental. Whichever road he chooses can have a long-term effect on his estate planning future.

To Rent or Buy?

Personal consideration aside, the question comes down to one of relative costs. Real estate agents will tell you that the person who pays monthly carrying charges of $1,500 for his home is better off than the one who pays the same $1,500 in rent because the home owner gets a tax deduction for the part that is taxes and interest, while the renter can't. Also, some part of that $1,500 is an amortization of the mortgage principal.

All well and good—if the $1,500 really represents the home owner's full cost. Too frequently, however, these blithe estimates overlook certain costs of home owning. There is commuting, the need to buy one or more automobiles, the purchase of larger amounts of furniture, and even with a new house, at least a certain amount of repairs, decoration, and land development. These are all real costs of home owning. And finally there is another hidden cost: the net income which the home owner could otherwise realize on the amount of capital invested in his home.

Or, in other words, the person who cannot decide which path to take—to rent or own—should calculate the true, not the supposed costs of his ownership. To do this he takes first his estimated annual home owning expenses; second, his capital investment in the house itself and its remodeling and improvements, prorated over a number of years, and the net income he loses by not investing this capital. He adds these together and then subtracts from this total sum the income tax savings from allowable deductions for taxes and interest. The figure he arrives at is his actual cost for home ownership.

Is it less than the rent he would have to pay for a comparable apartment? Then home ownership is cheaper for him. If it is higher, then renting may represent a better choice. Of course there are such things as possible appreciation in the value of a home that is owned over time, and the enjoyment and pride a family can derive from ownership.

HOME OWNERSHIP: INDIVIDUAL

If your decision is to buy, then you are making an investment. What should you look for from the investment point of view? What are the disadvantages and advantages of such ownership?

The limitations are clearly demarked. A house is not a liquid asset. Depending on market considerations it may take a short or long period to find a buyer for a house. Generally speaking, it is not a short-term investment either. The costs of buying and selling, and the capital expenditures involved, need to be amortized over a long period of time before the investment becomes a worthwhile one. Look at your house as a good short-term investment only if you are able to buy it below the market value. If you buy at the market, then your costs of buying and selling will almost always end in a loss on the deal.

On the plus side, count in your mortgage as a definite advantage. It represents a systematic savings plan. The amortization is a repayment of a loan, but at the same time it is a method of capital accumulation. Part of each monthly payment to the mortgage holder increases the home owner's net worth. In addition, the interest paid on the mortgage is tax deductible, if the mortgage is on your principal residence or on one second residence and does not exceed the original cost of each of these residences plus the improvements on them.

The potential for increase in market value is another advantage. Depreciation notwithstanding, homes have in the recent past sold for more than the amount at which they were purchased. The key factors in growth potential are location and timing. Is the prospective house in an area that is growing—not static or on the decline? Is it situated near public transportation, schools, playgrounds, shopping areas? Is it in an area in which the houses are well built and of comparable or greater value? Are the streets and public services well maintained? Is it close to major industrial or commercial centers of the area? Did you make your purchase at the top of a housing sale cycle, or near the bottom? All these factors influence the growth potential of your home purchase.

If there is a gain when you sell your principal residence, you will be entitled to a tax exclusion on this gain up to $500,000 for those married, filing jointly, and a $250,000 exclusion for single taxpayers. Furthermore, you can repeat this same exclusion of gain if you have treated a property as your personal residence for at least two of the last five years. This change is especially advantageous when you are ready to retire and move to a smaller, less expensive residence, become divorced, or are widowed. The bad news is that you can no longer "roll over" and defer gain that exceeds $500,000.

HOME OWNERSHIP:
THE COOPERATIVE APARTMENT

Individual home ownership is not the only possibility. Cooperative ownership has become increasingly popular in some parts of the country. The lure of the cooperative apartment is that it seems to offer all the advantages of home owning, with none of the burdens. Is this really true? Let's take a look at the way a cooperative works.

In the cooperative arrangement a corporation builds or buys a building, then sells its shares together with a proprietary lease to each tenant. The tenant does not actually own his apartment. He is instead a shareholder and lessee. As such, he pays a share of the costs of operation, maintenance, repairs, taxes, mortgage, insurance, and other expenses for the whole building, and in addition decorates and maintains his own apartment. The tenants, as stockholders, elect the board of directors of the cooperative.

While annual costs vary widely from one cooperative to another, a cooperative apartment will usually cost less than a comparable rented apartment. Since the cooperative is a nonprofit organization, there is no landlord's profit to be added to the rent. In addition, the cooperative owner gets the same tax deduction as the owner of a private home. The carrying charges paid by the tenant are applied partly to the amortization of the mortgage on the building and partly to his share of the mortgage interest and real estate taxes. Payments toward the amortization represent an increase in his equity interest. The mortgage interest and tax portion, which can run as high as 40 or 50 percent, allows him considerable tax savings since they are deductible from federal and, in some cases, state income taxes. However, mortgage interest is deductible only to the extent it is attributable to loans not exceeding the cost of the residence plus improvements.

Here, for instance, is a man in the 28 percent tax bracket paying $14,400 in rent annually. He has $20,000 to invest in a residence. If he puts it into securities and earns 8 percent, he will net, after taxes, about $1,248 annually. Suppose, instead, that he buys an interest in a cooperative or a condominium with the $20,000. Let us say he pays $14,400 annual carrying charges on this. Often, $7,200 of this amount will be deductible for his share of interest and taxes. This would mean a savings for him of $2,016 annually, or $768 more than he would realize renting and investing his $20,000.

Then, too, there is the fact that the cooperative owner has no maintenance and repair responsibility (these are taken over by a manager or management firm) and also that he is usually not personally liable on the bond and mortgage.

The picture is not entirely rosy, however. If real estate values decline, so will the value of the cooperative. Carrying charges are not fixed. They can rise as well as decrease. Moreover, if the tenant cannot meet the carrying charges, he may have to sell or sublease. If he is unable to find a buyer or lessee, then he must vacate the apartment and surrender his stock. This places a greater burden on the other tenants, since assessments will have to be increased to pick up the tab for the defaulting tenant.

Other disadvantages? The cooperative owner does not have the freedom of the sole owner. On the one hand he is not responsible for his own maintenance, but he usually then cannot make alterations without the approval of the board of directors of the cooperative. His interest is also less marketable than a home because he can't sell or assign his apartment without the board's approval. And usually he cannot assign his stock as security for a loan. Thus, he cannot use this asset as a collateral security.

HOME OWNERSHIP: THE CONDOMINIUM

This is a popular type of ownership that is also cooperative but has certain advantages over the original type. The condominium owner actually owns his own apartment; he is taxed on it as a separate entity, and he can mortgage it. He also owns the common parts of the building (halls, land, stairways) jointly with the other owners, and pays a proportionate carrying charge for these facilities.

Unlike the cooperative owner, the condominium owner usually has the right to sell the apartment, although here, too, he may need consent or may have to offer it first to the other owners. He is responsible for the taxes and mortgage on his own apartment, and if he defaults in the payment of these, his interest may be foreclosed. The other owners' apartments are not substantially affected, however. There is also more mortgage money available to the condominium since each apartment is considered a separate private home. Mortgages on homes are available up to 90 percent of their value, while those on cooperative buildings usually do not exceed 75 percent, if any, since some lenders will not offer loans on a property not directly owned.

True Real Estate Investment

Home ownership is only a peripheral form of real estate investment, of course. True real estate investment implies investment for investment's sake. It can take many forms. Let's take a brief look at the two major areas of opportunity: unimproved and improved real estate.

UNIMPROVED REAL ESTATE

As an investor in unimproved real estate, i.e., in vacant land, you are not buying the property for the purpose of improving it but for its own sake. You get no income from it, and except for the deduction for mortgage interest and taxes, realize no tax savings (since land is not a depreciable asset). You are conducting a holding operation, betting on the possibility that the land will increase in value over a short or long period of time. This is risk investment and usually it is long-term investment. It is a commodity bought for the purpose of resale.

Whether it is to be famine or fortune depends again on that hallmark of real estate investment: location and the movement of the real estate market. With hindsight we can see what Mr. Astor saw in Manhattan. With foresight, today's investor can select locations that offer if not the same prospects, quite favorable ones.

The wise investor of today looks to the patterns of living and the movements of people to find the favorable locations. Our population is moving to the West and the Southwest. With the growth of industrial areas in these states, real estate continues to increase in value there. But there is still potentially valuable vacant land in the highly populated areas of the Northeast, and other built-up areas, as the boundaries of suburbia widen and what was once open country becomes a part of the metropolitan center.

When there is a growth in leisure time, the need for recreation and vacation areas steadily increases. Vacant land at the beaches, lakes, or in winter sports areas becomes valuable as people go farther and farther from the cities to find space. The rise in popularity of a single sport, such as skiing, can make land acquisition in hitherto desolate areas a valuable property, and a valuable addition to a real estate portfolio. Property in sparsely populated resort areas has an additional advantage. Taxes are low since the community does not have to provide schools, fire protection, roads and public buildings. For the investor who can afford to wait, such land may be worth buying and holding, if it appears to have resort potential.

IMPROVED REAL ESTATE

Investment in improved real estate—whether it is a parking lot or a large office building—involves two major considerations: how to finance its purchase and how to manage the property. Later on, we will be going into the management problem in connection with various types of real estate ownership. At this juncture, let's examine only the financing situation.

The usual method is through mortgages; they play an important role in making these investments attractive. First of all, the investor does not have to put up the full purchase price. Second, if the value of the property increases, the entire increase belongs to him. Here's Ms. Investor. She buys a small apartment house for $400,000. She puts up $100,000 in cash, takes a mortgage for the rest. Later she sells the property for $550,000. That increase of $150,000 belongs to her. In other words, she realizes a gain of over 100 percent on her original $100,000 investment, a gain made possible by the $300,000 mortgage.

Mortgage financing can also mean tax savings. If Ms. Investor is a real estate professional for at least half her working activity and for more than 750 hours a year, she will be able to deduct her mortgage interest against her net income from the property, thus reducing the cost of borrowing through tax savings.

Further, the depreciation allowance on the property means additional tax savings. This is an important tax shelter. The depreciation is on the entire value, not just your equity. The tax-sophisticated investor looks for mortgage financing that provides a depreciation allowance in excess of his payments for amortization of the principal. Accelerated depreciation is a tax preference item and may be subject to the 26 percent or 28 percent alternative minimum tax for property that was in use before 1987. Except for this, he is using tax-free income to pay off his mortgage. In effect, he increases his equity in the property with untaxed income from the property but will be taxed on his gain upon selling. If the rental property owned was placed in service after 1986, and straight-line depreciation was used, then upon sale the owner will not be subject to recapture if he has held the property for at least one year.

Ownership: Sole or Participating?

For the investor who has the time, the experience, the money, and the necessary skill, sole ownership of a real estate investment can be a worthwhile venture. But few part-time investors possess these attributes. For them the answer lies in some kind of participating interest. A number of opportunities are open.

Partnerships

Here is a typical investment situation. A person with a small amount of capital to invest wants to buy a small apartment building. He has sufficient capital to make the purchase. His problem, however, is management. Even a three-story apartment building requires continuing professional administration if he is to realize a good income from it. His solution is probably to join hands with a partner—someone he knows and trusts, and who has some capital and real estate experience. If they pool their capital and experience, the investment has a greater chance for success.

This is especially true where a fairly substantial investment is to be made. Here, a group of people with limited capital (including one experienced manager) can join forces. With their combined capital and available outside mortgage financing, profitable and productive opportunities can be developed. If you are interested in local real estate investment this method is highly effective. It has proved to be one of the more successful ways of entering the real estate investing field. It makes possible the establishment of a substantial fund for the investment; mortgage financing is usually available because of personal relationships between the participants and lending agencies; management is supplied by experienced personnel within the group itself on a low-cost owner-interested basis.

The Syndicate

The syndicate is the real estate market's equivalent of mutual funds. In essence, it is a partnership in which a large number of investors pool their funds for large-scale investment, a further development of the small partnership group. The investments can be limited to special types of real estate or to certain geographical areas. The syndicate might, for example, be set up specifically to seek high income or capital gain. On the other hand, syndicates can be widely diversified in type of operation or investment.

The investor in a syndicate owns a fractional share of the total syndicate investment. Usually he is a limited partner, not personally liable beyond his own interest for the debts and liabilities of the partnership.

Most syndicates are concerned only with single properties. Some, however, are more broadly based: these give the investor an opportunity to spread out his investments with a limited outlay.

There are other advantages too: high income return and income tax deductions for depreciation, mortgage interest, and real estate taxes are chief among them. As with individual real estate investments, if tax deductions exceed income, investors are allowed to deduct their proportionate share of any excess against their other income. However, the deduction for investment interest is limited to the amount of net investment income. Tax deductions are usually greater in the early years of the life of the syndicate, thereby increasing the actual yield. But even though they go down later, the gross income may increase as the mortgages are amortized.

Drawbacks? The same as for most real estate investments, that is to say, the problem of liquidity. When the syndicate is doing well, the investor usually has no difficulty in finding a buyer for his interest. In bad times, however, he may run into a good deal of trouble if he wants to liquidate.

Syndicate management offers some problems, too. The success of the enterprise depends on the managers. They are given a percentage of the profit as an incentive. But while this helps to ensure professional management, it can also take off a lot of cream at the top.

Very careful consideration should be given to the reputation and competence of the syndicators. Conflicts of interest between syndicators and the unit investors can occur. In some cases marginal properties have been syndicated at inflated values.

THE REAL ESTATE CORPORATION

The real estate corporation is similar in form to any other corporation. Its major business is the buying, selling, and ownership of real estate. Being a corporation, its income is subject to double taxation. The corporation is taxed first on its profit, and then the distributed dividend is taxed again in the hands of the stockholders.

This treatment tends to eat away much of the profit. Ordinarily this is a great drawback to the corporate form of organization. The rule doesn't always apply to the real estate corporation, however. Since its assets are in real estate, it has large deductions for depreciation which, together with real estate taxes, interest, and operating expenses, can reduce the tax bite. Its taxable income is lessened or offset by these deductions so that it may end up with no taxable earnings or profits, or even have a loss for tax purposes. Since distributions to stockholders are taxable dividends only if the corporation has earnings and profits, if there are none, payments to stockholders are not considered dividends, but a return of capital. This reduces the basis of their stock; on later sale of the stock these distributions are, in effect, taxable income.

It sounds strange to say that investing in a corporation with tax losses can be profitable unless you realize that tax losses are a form of tax shelter. A corporation is allowed to carry its excess losses forward (and back), and thus reduce present and future earning for tax purposes.

Added point: the real estate corporation is one of the few types of real estate investment that offsets to some extent the problem of lack of liquidity. Like other corporations, its stock is traded on exchanges and over the counter, and can readily be sold at the prevailing quoted prices.

At times real estate corporation stocks might sell below their asset values, especially when their returns have been comparatively low, but one advantage they do have is that their values and returns will move with the general stock market trends, and thus act as an inflationary hedge. Remember, too, that with public issues in real estate corporations, the investor is often not so much concerned with the income return as he is with the potentiality they represent for capital appreciation.

REAL ESTATE INVESTMENT TRUSTS (REITs)

A Real Estate Investment Trust (REIT) is a taxable corporation, trust, or association investing primarily in real estate and/or mortgages. It has the corporate features of limited liability, centralized management, continuity, and transferability of interests, meaning that you can sell your shares in a REIT in much the same way you would sell a stock. It is managed by one or more directors or trustees for the benefit of the investors who are shareholders or beneficiaries.

REITs were first introduced through an act of Congress in 1960.

They are structured similarly to mutual funds in that they allow investors to pool their resources and invest indirectly in income-producing real estate of various kinds.

For the estate builder who has neither the capital nor the expertise to own real estate as an investment, a REIT offers the opportunity to include real estate in his portfolio without having to buy actual properties. Some REITs purchase properties and invest in the equity. These are called *equity REITs*. Some invest only in mortgages for the purchase of commercial properties and are referred to as *mortgage REITs*. Others are hybrids and purchase both.

The entity must distribute at least 90 percent of its taxable income to shareholders every year. The income of the REIT that is distributed is only taxed once. It passes directly to the shareholders, where it is taxed, as opposed to corporate income, which is taxed first to the corporation and then to the stockholders. Shares in a REIT can be sold in much the same manner as you would sell a stock or shares in a mutual fund, and so offer a level of liquidity not found with personal ownership of real estate.

This is all good, but not quite as good as the tax treatment given to the syndicate. The partners of the syndicate can use excess tax losses against their other income but the REIT's excess losses are not available to the beneficiaries or shareholders.

In selecting a REIT for an investment portfolio, there are several factors to consider. Be aware of the *types of investments* held by the REIT. They can invest in such things as hotels, resorts, apartment buildings; retail properties such as shopping malls; office buildings; health care facilities; and other types of real estate. As always, location of real estate is critical, so be aware of the *geographical location* of the holdings. Look for the degree of *diversification* within an individual REIT or what you can achieve with several REITs. The *dividend yield* and potential for *growth in earnings* are factors that can help you decide if a specific REIT will help you do better than owning stock. Lastly, and very importantly, review information on who is providing the *management* of the REIT. Look for extensive real estate experience and whether there has been continuity of leadership. Constant changes in managers may not be a good sign. A good website run by the National Association of Real Estate Investment Trusts (NAREIT) is www.nareit.com. This is another area where the services of an investment advisor with experience in dealing with REITs can be very strategic.

MASTER LIMITED PARTNERSHIPS

Master limited partnerships are hybrids that have characteristics of stocks, bonds, and traditional real estate investments. They are traded like a stock, have partial tax-exempt yields like those on municipal bonds, and are subject to depreciation benefits and appreciation of property values as with any other real estate deal.

The master limited partnership is a group ownership of specific collections of properties, such as a shopping center, an office building, a mobile home park, senior citizen residential complexes, etc. Once the package is put together, you can buy shares of the partnership and later sell them like stock. The yields in the form of dividends are generally quite reasonable, and are generally 50-60 percent tax exempt. There are also depreciation benefits.

This investment also has sell-out capabilities to offer you liquidity in what is traditionally a nonliquid investment. The danger in this, however, is that because real estate values can fluctuate, you may be tempted by a slow market to sell out and cut what appear to be losses before the property has a chance to reach or even exceed its project values. If you decide to hold onto the investment, you are in until the properties are sold—hopefully at appreciated values.

MORTGAGE-BACKED SECURITIES

Most people know these investments by their trading names: Ginny Maes, Fannie Maes, and Freddie Macs. What they represent are home mortgages that are purchased from various banks and then pooled. These are then resold in the form of shares in the pool to investors. The mortgages are guaranteed by agencies of the federal government, meaning that if a home owner defaults on his home loan, the federal agency guarantees continuing payment on the loan, and forecloses on the owner.

Earnings come from the interest rates charged on the mortgages, minus a management fee. For instance, if the interest rate on a mortgage was $5\frac{3}{4}$ percent, the investor may be getting $5\frac{1}{2}$ percent with the $\frac{1}{4}$ percent going to manage the pool.

A Special Consideration:
Where to Get Advice

The prospective real estate investor has some special problems. Expert advice and help are not freely available to him as they are in the securities market. There are no market letters; reliable and independent analysts are usually not available. Where does he go for help in selecting a property investment?

If he is to go it alone, his solution must be the real estate broker. He is undoubtedly the most informed person he can find. But when he goes to him for advice, he should remember that, like the stockbroker, this broker is not a disinterested party; his object is, after all, to sell real estate. The best course is to seek out a well-established broker, one who enjoys a good reputation, get submissions on property within a selected type and financial range, and then ask your lawyer or accountant to review them.

If the investor is to participate in syndicates or trusts, REITs or limited partnerships, then the information has to come from prospectuses and offering bulletins. Unless you have an expert ability to assess this type of literature, we would recommend you have an experienced real estate broker, investment advisor with experience in this area of investing, or perhaps your banker or attorney review it for you.

Looking Ahead

The last few years have seen incredible booms in real estate values, and historically low interest rates; investors saw their properties soar in value. Historically, as with any investment cycle, the contraction of the overall economy during a recession has seen real estate values drop and create losses for some, buying opportunities for others. The recent accelerated purchases of real estate during this time of low rates may also have precluded some from making further purchases for the next several years. This, too, could mean a period of low demand and declining prices in the near future.

The estate planner's role is to make *long-term* judgments and assessments that evaluate the broader, ongoing character of various types of investments, not just their cyclical fluctuations. Viewed in this manner, real estate well selected and managed will continue to be a form of investment that can yield high income and capital returns for long-term investing and has its place in the estate builder's overall investment portfolio.

♲

THE DAY THE WORK STOPS:

DISABILITY AND RETIREMENT

If you are 35 now, you have just about a three-to-one chance that you will live to 65. If you reach that age, you can add almost seventeen more years to your life expectancy—seventeen years, probably, of retirement from your active earning career.

But if you are 35 now, there is also a one-to-three chance that you will at some time in your life become disabled for a period of three months or more. Moreover, the chance that you will have a long-term disability before 65 is greater than the likelihood that you will die before that age. If total disability does strike, and you are the major family income earner, this can be more of a financial disaster than death. You become one more mouth to feed, and medical expenses can become a lingering burden.

Does your estate plan take any of these events, fortunate or unfortunate, into account?

DISABILITY

A young executive whom we know is an indefatigable do-it-yourselfer around the house. Independent, strong, and somewhat self-willed, he has a tendency to take on jobs that are too much for him. One time, he decided to install a 300-pound staircase to an upper terrace. He hoisted the staircase onto a 2 by 4, and then onto his shoulders. In the process the staircase tipped and fell, missing his back by a fraction of an inch.

This near disaster had a sobering effect on him. He stopped his work and went inside and had a beer. His hands were trembling so that he could hardly open the beer can. What unnerved him so, he said later, was the thought, not that he might have been killed, but that he might very easily have been disabled for life.

As he sipped his beer and gazed out the window, contemplating the fallen staircase, he realized that he didn't even have the faintest idea what kind of income, if any, he could expect if he ever became permanently disabled. Did his life insurance cover disability? Were there any company benefits—after all, he'd been working on his own time, not the boss's. Would the government give him anything? If he got anything out of these sources, would it be for life or just for a short period of time? What on earth, he wondered, happened to people who had accidents of this sort?

Mr. Do-It-Yourself was not alone in his quandary. Most people today have no more than a vague notion of what kind of protection is available to them if they become disabled either through sickness or an accident. They don't know that there are different meanings of disability as the law or various agreements define it. They are at a loss as to what kind and what amount of protection to buy—that is, if they think about buying any at all.

All of this represents a serious default in estate planning. Disability, while not inevitable, is certainly a possibility.

Mr. Do-It-Yourself had an unusual experience that dramatically illustrated this, but the fact is that the possibility of disability looms in the foreground for everyone. What's more, as life expectancy increases, so do the chances of contracting debilitating diseases that maim but do not kill.

Planning for support to cover disability, then, is just as much a necessity as planning for support to protect one's family at death, or for a retirement income.

The Disability Picture: What Is It? Who Gets Protection?

The Estate Planning Worksheets in the back of the book will help you analyze the income you can expect if you become disabled. It is probable that the disability income column will be the one that shows the greatest gap between what will be available as against what you will need. You will undoubtedly find that you are covered by some type of government or employment disability program. But will this be enough? Will it, together with unearned income from all other sources, be sufficient to support your family for an extended period of disability?

The answer will depend on the type and amount of coverage you have. What will be the amount of the payments? Are they taxable income? After what length of disability do they begin? How long do they last? What type of disability is covered? If you make bonus income or commissions beyond a salary, are the additional earnings covered? (Usually not.)

Only when these questions are answered is the true disability-income picture revealed, and the directions of its improvement indicated.

If you think of disability as an inability to work caused by an accident or sickness, that's simple enough. But the plans or laws providing coverage include a number of variations within that meaning. Some define disability as an inability to do any kind of work at all. Some broaden it to cover an inability to work at your regular occupation. Some cover you for partial disability, such as when an illness or injury keeps you from working at full capacity and reduces your predisability income. Some limit the definition to an impairment that is "reasonably certain" to last for life; others to one that is merely "expected to continue indefinitely." Some will give you coverage for a limited period of time, others permanently.

The point is to know what you can expect and from what sources.

Source Number One: Federal and State Governments. There are five prime sources of government protection against disability—state workers' compensation, state sickness disability, social security, veterans' benefits, and government insurance policies for people in the armed forces or veterans.

Most of these will not provide anyone with more than a subsistence level of support, and some of them are limited to those with low incomes. Nevertheless, it's as well to know just what you can expect from them— for you must take them into account in your disability estate planning.

Workers' Compensation—State: This is limited to accidents or diseases that occur as a result of your job. The disability income replacement portion of these benefits is generally designed to replace two-thirds of lost wages, but with a very low maximum. For instance, in 2004 the cap on payments in California is $728 per week. The compensation is awarded by a board or hearing officer and is based on the extent of the disability, its estimated duration, and incurred medical expenses.

Sickness Disability—State: A few states also have compulsory coverage for disabilities that occur as a result of nonoccupational injuries and sicknesses. There are only five states in the country that participate in these programs: California, Hawaii, New Jersey, New York, Rhode Island and the Commonwealth of Puerto Rico. Under the California State disability law, for example, a worker is entitled to a weekly allowance (paid biweekly) if he is unable to perform the regular duties of his employment. Currently, in 2004, he receives an amount equal to 55 percent of his average weekly wage, up to a maximum of $728 per week, for a maximum period of fifty-two weeks. This is really coverage for a short-term disability, and although $728 per week isn't enough for support, it is of some help to the person who has a savings account reserved for just such an emergency.

Social Security Disability Benefits—Federal: You can get a monthly allowance for a long-term disability under liberalized provisions of the Social Security Law. Previously, there was a minimum age limitation, which has now been completely removed. To be eligible, you must have been covered by social security for varying periods, depending on your age, before you become disabled. Lesser periods of coverage are required if you are blind.

There is a five-month waiting period before benefits are available, but they continue as long as the disability does. The monthly allowance is based on average monthly earnings, and is the same as the amount which you would receive as old age benefits at age 65 though a different formula is applied. There is a dependency allowance for unmarried children under 19 who are attending school full-time, and totally disabled children over 18 who become disabled before that age. There is also one for a spouse of any age if she has children in her care who are eligible for dependents' benefits, as well as for a spouse 62 years old or older.

The protection is designed for long-term disabilities. The law defines disability here as an illness or injury so severe that it is expected to result in death, or to make the applicant unable "to engage in any substantially gainful" occupation for at least twelve months.

Veterans' Benefits—Federal: These are important, because so many people may qualify for them.

If your disability is service-connected, you are entitled to compensation either from the Veterans Administration or from your branch of the service. You can get this no matter what your income is. Amounts for a disability, whether wartime or peacetime, vary from a low to a high range of monthly benefit, depending on the degree of disability, with specific rates in severe cases. If the disability is rated 30 percent or more, there is an additional allowance for dependents.

If your disability is not service-connected, you can get a pension, provided your income is not above a specific threshold for a single person with no dependents, or higher for a married person with dependents.

If you already get social security disability benefits, you still qualify for the service-connected compensation, but if it is non-service-connected, your social security above what you paid in will be counted as part of your income, and therefore may affect your eligibility.

G.I. Insurance—Federal: There are two types, United States Government Life Insurance policies for those who served before World War II and National Service Life Insurance for those who served during and after World War II.

If you carry USGLI, you can get payment for a total and permanent disability that keeps you from working in "any substantially gainful" occupation and that seems "reasonably certain" to continue for life. The proceeds will be paid out in monthly installments of $5.754 per $1,000 of coverage for a total and permanent disability. If you die before 240 installments have been paid out, the balance is paid out as death proceeds.

Does your policy have a Total Disability Income Provision? If it does and you incur a total (but not necessarily a permanent) disability before you are 65, you will get $10 per month for each $1,000 of insurance in force. These payments do not reduce the amount of the insurance.

If you carry National Service Life Insurance, your benefits are somewhat different. These policies provide for a waiver of premiums if you become totally disabled for six months or longer before the age of 65. This doesn't give you any income, of course, but it does remove the burden of keeping up the life insurance premium payments.

NSLI also has an extra premium provision that gives you disability income payments. It's for total disability prior to age 65 (defined here as the inability to follow "any substantially gainful" occupation without injuring your health). It provides $10 a month for every $1,000 of insurance in force up to $100 a month for as long as the disability lasts. Payments do not reduce the amount of your insurance.

You can see what this melange of government benefits add up to. They provide only a minimum income, unquestionably, not sufficient to meet the support needs of your family. For that, we must turn to other sources of disability income.

Source Number Two: Your Occupation. For the corporate executive, his job may offer other opportunities for disability protection, most of them available in the corporate compensation package.

Voluntary Employer Aid: Generally, employers will continue an employee's salary for a period of time during disability. Others will supplement existing disability payments which are paid by state or federal governments. But since such employer aid is not required by law or an employment contract, it is apt to be short-lived. Most such benefits are limited to a short-term salary continuation, usually for a few months or, at most, a year. It should be added that some employers cover this risk with group short-term disability insurance, rather than bearing the full cost of self insuring.

Group Health Insurance: Depending on the type of program your company offers, you are likely to find that your group health plan covers all or part of your hospital expenses, and your medical and surgical care, plus a certain amount of physical rehabilitation, subject to your deductibles and co-payments.

Group Long-Term Disability Plans: It is becoming increasingly common for employers of medium and large-sized companies to provide group insurance for disabilities lasting more than six months or a year. For example, a policy might pay monthly benefits of 75 percent of salary for the first year of disability, 50 percent for the next two years, and 25 percent from then on. Another type of policy pays a straight 60 percent of salary for twenty years or until age 65. Often there is a cap on monthly benefits that the plan will pay, such as $5,000, or even $10,000 for those with higher salaries.

What about taxes on these disability benefits? Often it may be possible to avoid any income taxation at all. Thus:

1. If the employee pays the premiums, there are no taxes on the benefits.

2. If the employer pays the premiums, the premiums aren't taxable to the employee, but the benefits are. However, the exceptions are very broad. Thus, there is no income tax to be paid on benefits that reimburse an employee's actual medical expenses, or on payments based on certain types of illnesses or injuries such as the loss of a limb.

A very important note: If you receive commissions or bonuses beyond your salary, these earnings are generally not covered—often only your base salary is covered. Read your group benefit description carefully. If you routinely receive this type of additional income and it is not covered by your group policy, you should obtain a personally owned disability income policy to replace this part of your compensation during a prolonged disability.

Profit-sharing Plans: Disability income provisions are often included in these qualified plans, and are one of the exceptions to being charged a 10 percent penalty for withdrawals prior to age 59½. They may take the form of a payout in weekly installments of taxable income. They can, however, provide for a lump sum distribution of the vested account.

Pension Plans: Some pension plans pay out retirement funds if the disability is "permanent and total." Payout plans vary. They are usually connected in some way to the vested pension rights that have accrued before the disability. Some of them reduce payments if you are getting social security or state disability benefits. Other plans, however, separate disability benefits from retirement funds, and the amounts bear no relation to each other. This can be advantageous, for in some of these plans both retirement and disability benefits are paid. The same tax treatment applies as in the profit-sharing payouts.

Self-employment Retirement Plans: Under the retirement act for the self-employed, funds can be withdrawn upon disability. The withdrawals will be taxed in the same way as retirement distributions.

Draining retirement funds during a disability should be a last resort. Better to assure that your sources of income during a disability come from other sources.

Source Number Three: Your Own Plan. After you determine what you will receive from all sources for disability, as well as all sources of other unearned income, you may find that additional income will be needed. Except in rare cases, some form of additional disability insurance protection is required—particularly in younger years when the estate has yet to be created.

Disability insurance policies vary widely. You should know precisely what you are getting, and be aware of the many nuances, exceptions, and definitions contained within these policies. Your support will be affected by such details if you ever become disabled.

Individual Disability Insurance: These policies vary greatly from company to company; you should be sure to compare the following key points:

1. What type of disability is covered: total, or partial, or both?
2. How does the policy define disability? Some policies consider it to be an inability to perform the duties of your regular occupation; some say it's inability to work at any occupation; some define it as the inability to work in any gainful occupation for which you might be considered "reasonably fitted" by education, training, or experience; some define it as a loss of income due to disability. Still others combine one or more aspects of these various definitions.
3. What is the "elimination period?" Will you start getting benefits immediately from day one of your disability, or is there a period of waiting before payment begins?
4. What is the duration? Will you get benefits for one year, two years, five years, or until you reach 65? (These days few policies pay out for life.)
5. Is there a cancellation clause? Can the insurance company cancel at will? If there is such a clause, the company can terminate your policy, or refuse to renew it, or increase the premium rate.
6. Is there a waiver of premiums during the period the monthly indemnity is being paid?
7. Can the company increase or reduce the monthly indemnity payments during the "guaranteed renewable" period?
8. Is there aviation coverage?
9. Must you be confined to your house in order to qualify for disability payments?
10. Is there a liberal "recurrent disability" clause?
11. Is partial disability covered?

12. Is a return-to-work bonus provided?
13. Can it be tailored to "wrap around" the group coverage you have at work?
14. Is there a rider to replace contributions you would have been making to your retirement plan?

Group Disability Income Insurance: We are not referring to corporate group insurance but to insurance offered by many associations to their members. This type is common, for example, among county or state medical and bar associations as well as other professional groups. The premiums are lower than individual coverage, and it continues so long as you remain a member of the group and meet the age requirements. *Don't substitute it for individual insurance, however. The insurance company, as well as the group, can terminate the policy at any time.*

Disability Overhead Expenses Policy: Are you a self-employed professional, an independent proprietor, the owner of a small business? Then you might consider this kind of insurance. It covers your overhead expenses while you are disabled, paying up to a stated amount a month for validated expenses (including people needed to replace your efforts until you recover). It generally provides benefits for periods of one or two years.

Waiver of Premium on Life Insurance: During a period of disability, all fixed obligations should be reduced to a minimum. You should therefore consider having waiver of premium riders added to your life insurance policies. It is precisely during the period of illness (when the need for the life insurance protection may be greatest) that the funds for continuing the policies may not be available. We have always felt that the small extra premium to buy this rider represents a worthwhile investment. Some insurance companies not only pay your life insurance premium for you while disabled, but allow you to convert term coverage you may have with them to cash value insurance. They pay the new, higher premium and the cash value builds up in *your* policy. If you expect to be permanently disabled, this can be significant. If you expect to return to work, be sure you will be able to resume paying your own—now higher—premium.

The Final Analysis on Disability: It is extremely important from an estate planning point of view to run the numbers and determine the amount of *after-tax* income you would receive from all sources during a disability. If you have a substantial shortfall from your customary income, you could face the prospect of draining savings, investments and retirement plans to meet ongoing expenses. If that is the case, obtaining personally owned disability insurance buys you an invaluable financial safety net. It can bring your coverage up to the maximum possible and cover income shortfalls you would otherwise suffer. If you subsequently recover from your disability and return to work, you are then in a position to resume the building of your estate.

RETIREMENT

Disability is a misfortune. It has to be planned for, but one hopes that it will never come about. Retirement is different. By all rights it should be viewed as the goal toward which one works, the fulfillment of an active life, a time when serenity replaces struggle, and aspirations give way to contemplation, to new adventure and the time and freedom to explore oneself and the people and world around one.

The concept of retirement has changed for many. People are living longer, healthier lives. Preventive health habits have made their way into the awareness of the general public to a greater degree. Retirement has frequently become a time to pursue interests, spend time with family and friends, travel, become involved in the community, pursue an avocation, or even start a new business. Many retirees become even more active than they were while working, with more time for keeping fit—pursuing a fitness program or sport that keeps them vigorous to older ages.

When age and health problems do impose restrictions, there are more medical options for treatment, and modes and venues for care that help to maximize one's quality of life (see Chapter 10 on long-term care).

All this means that you may possibly be living in retirement for as many years as you worked for a living. With this in mind, it is more crucial than ever to take stewardship over your own financial needs—for the future you—and apply real focus to preparing for a secure and enjoyable retirement.

Personal Planning

The plan should be both personal and financial. By personal, we mean deliberately preparing yourself for what you want to do with your retirement years. This can mean all sorts of things—preparations for continued work of some sort, either as a part-time worker in your field, or perhaps in a "second business" that you have built up during your active working years; decisions on where and how to live; most important, the building up of a backlog of interests, hobbies, and lifetime purposes, perhaps volunteerism that can enrich your mind, enrich the world around you and occupy you fruitfully in your later years.

This is where most people fall down, incidentally. A default of personal planning, which is to have no idea of what to do with your newfound time, can be just as serious as the financial default we have been stressing so much. The high rate of heart attacks and disease among the retired is no accident, according to American Medical Association studies; it is a direct result of an inability to readjust to life in retirement, a psychological blow which takes its physical toll.

Financial Planning

Let's return for a moment to the Worksheets in the Appendix. There are three income columns that need to be filled in, if you remember: your family's income after your death; your own and your family's needs in the event you are disabled; and when you retire.

We are concerned now with the column dealing with your retirement financial needs. How can this be calculated? It takes a bit of figuring and planning. Assuming you are 65 at retirement and that your children are grown-up, married, and on their own, presumably your income can be smaller.

But how much smaller? There is the standard of living to be considered. People who have been accustomed to a comfortable mode of life for many years find it especially hard to adjust. It may be more difficult for them to lower their standard of living than it is for the young and adventurous person. Then there are the physical problems. Comfort isn't just a psychological matter; it's also physical. Substandard or cramped housing, rigorous weather, lack of domestic help—all of this takes a physical toll on the elderly person. You may have additional problems as well—needy grandchildren, indigent relatives, a retarded or handicapped adult child of your own who will need your support for the rest of his life.

What does it all add up to? Only you can know that. Suffice it to say that you should make sure you do know as early as possible in your working life. The sooner you begin to plan for retirement, the better.

Sources of Retirement Income

There are four main ones—social security, corporate employment plans, commercial plans, and your personal capital.

Social Security. National elections were fought on this issue in 1934 and will be again in the years to come, especially with the "baby boomer" generation" approaching retirement and fewer younger workers to support their expected benefits. Today social security remains one of our country's most famous social welfare laws. Here are some of the main things you, as an estate planner, should know about it.

Who Is Covered by Social Security? Almost all employed and self-employed persons are covered for old age benefits. A federal retirement system covers federal employees.

What Does Social Security Provide For? Currently, it provides the greatest monthly retirement income for a person over 65 (the "Full Retirement Age") who has received social security credit for forty quarters (about ten years); or a permanently reduced amount if benefits are started from age 62. A dependent spouse is also entitled to benefits, even though he has never worked, if he is 62 or older; or at any age, if he is caring for a child eligible for dependents' benefits. A widow or widower age 60 or over is also entitled to benefits. There are also additional allowances for unmarried children under 18, up to 19 if in high school, or to any age if disabled prior to age 22, or surviving dependent parents at 62.

For those of us born after 1937, the age when we can start collecting full social security benefits is being moved forward. If born in 1938, you'll have to wait to age 65 and two months; if in 1939, you'll have full benefits at 65 and four months, and on it progresses. Finally, anyone born after 1959 will only get full social security benefits if they start collecting them at age 67. If you can afford to, or wish to wait until age 70 to collect social security benefits, your monthly payout amount will be even greater than what your full payout at 65 (or 67) would have been. Age 62 will still mark the earliest age for collecting monthly retirement payouts.

How Are the Amounts Determined? Retirees get a fixed amount, depending on their average yearly earnings before retirement. A spouse gets one-half the worker's benefits. There are cost-of-living increases in benefits, determined each December for the following year. If you're looking up your benefit on social security tables, the dollar amount of your benefit is referred to as the "Primary Insurance Amount" (PIA). The PIA is based on "Average Indexed Monthly Earning" (AIME) and the year you were born.

Should a Wife Wait Until She Is 65 to Claim Benefits? This question usually arises when wives are a few years younger than their husbands. Which is better? Claim her benefits at 62, or wait three years to get the higher rate?

It may be good to consider the first, because of the mathematics of the situation. A wife entitled to the maximum wife's benefit at 62 will get $91 less per month than if she waits until she is 65. But during the three years between 62 and 65, she will accumulate a total of $14,724. In order to equal or exceed that amount of income at the higher rate, she will have to live nearly 13½ years after 65.

Can I Still Earn Money and Get Social Security? Yes, you can, as follows:

1. *After* the "Normal Retirement Age" (NRA—gradually increasing from age 65 to 67) you can earn any amount and your social security benefits will not be taxed.
2. If you are *under* NRA for the entire calendar year, receiving benefits and earning an income, you can earn up to $11,640 in 2004 and not be taxed on your social security benefits.
3. If you reach NRA during a calendar year, but do not exceed $31,080 (in 2004), your benefits will not be taxed.

The amount of your benefits to be subject to tax depends upon the amount of your income plus 50 percent of your social security benefits. This combined total is referred to as your *base amount*. Depending upon your tax filing status the amount of income in excess of your *base amount*, can cause portions of your social security benefits to be included in taxable income as follows:

Base Amount Limitations	Percentage of Social Security Benefits Includable in Gross Income
Single Taxpayers	
$0–$25,000	0%
$25,000–$34,000	Up to 50%
$34,000 and above	Up to 85%

Base Amount Limitations	Percentage of Social Security Benefits Includable in Gross Income
Married Filing Jointly	
$0–$32,000	0%
$32,000–$44,000	Up to 50%
Over $44,000	Up to 85%
Married Filing Separately	
Over $0	Up to 85%

However, during your first calendar year of drawing Social Security, you still qualify for full benefits in months when you don't receive earned income over the amount of your monthly benefit.

A word of advice: In order to get full benefits, it is necessary that your social security records be complete and correct. It is therefore important that you check your account to make certain all contributions on your behalf have been fully credited to you and that your qualifying periods have been correctly adjusted. You can get a record of your account and have any questions on social security answered by obtaining a Request for Social Security Statement (Form SSA-7004-SM) from your local social security office, or call and request one through their toll-free number, 1-800-772-1213.

Corporate Employment Plans. A lot has already been said in this book about the retirement aspects of these plans. Let us only add that such things as deferred compensation agreements and qualified retirement plans should provide the *bulk* of retirement funds for the corporate executive. The person who bargains well and wisely for these should have no difficulty with retirement income, provided he maintains his employment through retirement.

You can depend upon your payments from a pension plan because the amount is actuarially determined. The payout on a deferred compensation agreement is normally a set amount and, depending upon the solvency of the corporation, can also be relied upon.

But profit-sharing plans and stock benefits, while important and usually reliable, cannot be counted upon to provide a fixed income. You can only estimate how much these will eventually bring in. Time and the economic cycle have a way of altering your estimate radically. There may be no profit for the corporation to contribute into the plan. The plan's investments, as well as the stock of a corporation, may also decline in value and in their ability to produce income, possibly delaying your retirement.

The method of payout, however, is in any case an important factor in retirement planning. The plans usually offer a lump sum or a variety of installment payments. The means you select will depend on your own retirement picture. For example, how many and what dependents you will have to support; and, importantly, how to receive the income so as to minimize erosion from income as well as estate taxes. The proceeds, for instance, may be rolled over in an IRA to defer taxation until later withdrawal; or you may want to arrange for equal payments over your lifetime. It's best to make these decisions before you retire by doing some projections and laying out a financial plan. If you leave it to the last minute, you may find there are limitations on your choice, or you may hurriedly make decisions you later regret.

Self-employed Retirement Plans. In Chapter 6 we dealt with the tax shelter and retirement opportunities of these plans. Here, however, we want to emphasize that the withdrawal of the retirement fund should be made in the years of your lowest income. This is so because the taxable portion of this payout will be subject to income taxes at your bracket. For those who turned 50 prior to January 1, 1986 (born prior to 1936), this is especially so if they make a lump sum withdrawal of the entire fund. They may elect ten-year averaging of the tax on the ordinary income portion of their distributions. They may also make an election for capital gain treatment on the portion of their distribution that can be allocated to their participation in the retirement plan prior to 1974.

Commercial Sources of Retirement Income

1. *Immediate annuities as retirement income insurance* can offer a guaranteed annual income from the time you retire to the day you die. This income represents both interest and a return of principal; its unique aspect is that you can elect a payout option where the income never ceases while you live, but continues as long as you live.

    Thus immediate annuities function chiefly as an alternate or substitute for personal investment, which frequently cannot offer the same security. Suppose, for example, that after age 65 you find that your income from investment and/or other resources isn't enough to support you. You begin to use up your principal. But how can you be sure that this principal will last all your life? You may live past your life expectancy and outlive your capital. The risk as to how long you will live is something you cannot afford to take. If you buy an immediate annuity policy, the insurance company takes that risk for you.

Actually, you can buy one of several types of immediate annuities. If you want to guarantee security for your spouse as well as yourself, you might consider the *joint and survivor* annuity payout option. This pays income to you during your life, and when you die, the income is continued for your spouse for the rest of his or her life.

Or there is a *period certain annuity* payout option. This pays income for your lifetime but also guarantees payments for a minimum period of time, usually ten or twenty years. Thus, if you die before the period is up, your beneficiary gets the fixed income payments for the balance of the period. Your return is a little less, but you are not running the risk that your early death will cause a complete loss of the annuity fund.

Even if you have sufficient retirement income from investment sources, you may want to consider putting some of your assets in annuities. The security they offer is psychological as well as economic. You are relieved of the strain and effort that an investment program involves. Beyond this, a program that balances annuities with growth stocks operates as a hedge against unpredictable changes in the economy. The stocks are there to meet an inflationary trend; the annuities, a possible deflationary situation. What we do not recommend is the sole use of immediate annuities. Once you start the payout, you have no access to the principal to handle emergencies or opportunities beyond the scheduled payments. Part of your retirement capital should be available to provide flexible access to funds.

2. *Whole life insurance* can be used for retirement purposes. Let's assume that, at retirement age, you find you don't need all the insurance coverage you had previously carried. The cash value that has been accumulating tax-deferred within the policy offers you some options for retirement income. You could withdraw an amount equal to your premiums paid, then borrow out a portion of the balance, all tax-free. Another option is to do a tax-free exchange of the policy and its cash value for an immediate annuity.

You can then select from among the same annuity payout options described above.

3. *Endowment insurance* is a classic example of life insurance that can be used for retirement purposes. If you die before the time of endowment, the face amount of the policy will be paid out as a death benefit. If you survive to the time of endowment, say, 65, the amount is paid to you in a lump sum, or it can be paid out as a retirement fund.

   You can select various endowment times such as ten years, twenty years, or age 65, as an example. Cash is building up tax-deferred for you and can either be annuitized or drawn out in a tax-free income stream of cash surrenders up to the amount of premiums paid, then as loans should you wish to maintain a death benefit.

Personal Investments

If, over a term of years, you have followed a systematic program of personal investments, by the time you retire you should theoretically have accumulated a substantial amount of capital—enough to produce income for you during your retirement. That is the significance of investment income. It takes over for you when you are no longer an active earner.

When you reach retirement, however, you should take a fresh look at your investment pattern. You may find that the time has come to alter it. If, for example, you have used your investments for capital growth, you may want now to switch to safe, fixed-income investments. On the other hand, if you own annuity accumulation policies or other fixed-return investments, then perhaps you will want to put a part of your assets in growth stocks. Or perhaps you were heavy in tax-free bonds during your high-earning, high-tax years. Now that you are in a lower income bracket, you may want to choose higher income producing securities. In any event, this is the time to get together with your financial advisor for a complete reappraisal of your financial portfolio.

A LAST WORD ON RETIREMENT: DECIDING WHERE TO LIVE

Change of residence is common among retired people. Sometimes it is due to the desire to live near family members. Many of them move to the warmer retirement states of California, Arizona and Florida. Before you join the trek, however, you should check on the various estate and income tax situations in each of these states. If your estate is sizable, the tax situation can make quite a difference.

Arizona: The income tax goes up to 5.04 percent on net income in excess of $150,000. The estate tax is equal to the maximum credit for state death taxes under federal estate tax law, as discussed below.

California: The income tax goes as high as 9.30 percent on net income above $38,291. The estate tax is equal to the maximum credit for state death taxes under federal estate tax law, as discussed below.

Florida: There is no income tax and no estate tax. The federal estate tax allows a credit for death taxes paid or to be paid to a state, according to a schedule. Florida will receive the amount of this credit as the death tax due to it. There is, however, an annual tax on intangible property (stocks and bonds, money market funds, mutual funds, loans, notes, a portion of accounts receivable and limited partnership interests, including qualified IRAs, employee retirement plans and deferred compensation plans). In 2004 the first $250,000 as assets are exempt; $500,000 per couple.

It is also important to be aware of the level of property and sales taxes in states you are considering for residence, since this will impact your ongoing cash flow directly.

CHAPTER 10

LONG-TERM CARE: THE
RETIREMENT BUDGET BUSTER

What if, after all your careful planning, saving and investing, your expenses after retirement suddenly jumped an additional $5,000 per month, or more—without warning? That is what many retired Americans experience every year when they or a spouse require extended care at home, in an assisted living facility or perhaps in a nursing facility.

Take Jake and Susan as an example. Jake suffered a stroke, spent some days in acute care in the hospital, ten days in the skilled nursing wing, then moved on to the first stages of rehabilitation in a nursing home. Eventually Jake came home, but needed help in accomplishing everyday activities. The moment Jake's care changed from skilled care to custodial care (needing help with activities of daily living such as bathing, continence, dressing, eating, toileting and transferring—such as moving from a bed to a chair), he and Susan had to pay for his caregivers. For Jake, this began while he was still in the nursing home, and the bills piled up fast.

Then there's Daniel and Nora. For some time Nora had been showing signs of forgetfulness. Having been athletic all her life, she was physically very fit, but her mental faculties were fading at an alarming rate. When she was diagnosed with Alzheimer's disease, she and Daniel were devastated. They knew her condition would only worsen. Within a year and a half Nora needed someone to be with her at all times. She had become dangerously confused by every new moment. Daniel was alarmed to find that Medicare and their Medicare Supplemental policy did not cover the new expense. When Nora eventually had to be confined to a nursing home, Daniel found himself spending far more of their retirement nest egg on her care than either of them had planned.

THE NEED FOR LONG-TERM CARE

No one plans to become disabled as they grow older, but the truth is that about 48.6% of people in the U.S. age 65 or older may spend time in a nursing home.[1] About 71.8% of the same group receive custodial care in their own homes.[2]

As of 2003, the *average* annual cost for long-term care in a nursing home generally ranges from $57,000 to $65,000. We know of cases where it has been a great deal more. Taking this out of a retirement nest egg can devastate the best-laid plans for a long, comfortable life. The specter of running out of money then robs the retired of their peace of mind. It may put their adult children in the role of providing care for their parents in the form of personal caregiving, or adding the expense of hiring caregivers to their own family budgets.

Americans are living longer. The portion of the population age 80 and older is expected to increase by more than 200% by the year 2050 as projected by the U.S. Census Bureau's report entitled "Population Projections of the United States: 1995–2050." The longer we live, the more likely we are to experience disabling illnesses at some point.

This reality makes it imperative to include planning for long-term care needs as part of our retirement and estate planning strategies. There are a variety of ways in which these costs can be covered, depending on your financial resources and how insurable you are based on the state of your health.

---

[1] "LTC Choice: A Simple, Cost-Free Solution to the LTC Financing Puzzle," Center for Long Term Care Financing, September 1999.
[2] Long-Term Care: "Knowing the Risk, Paying the Price," Health Insurance Association of America, 1997.

How Do You Cover the Costs of Long-Term Care Out of Pocket?

For most people it is hard enough to save for retirement just assuming a healthy, long life. People do not, as a rule, attempt to create an extra fund to cover the possibility of paying for long-term care for themselves, or for a spouse if they are married. So how do people handle paying for care once the need arises? Let's take a look at some of the ways this can be done.

- *The Wealthy:* If you have enough wealth, you may be able to cover the cost of care out of your own cash flow, by liquidating or repositioning assets, putting them to use in new ways. If you are wealthy enough, this may not put you in financial jeopardy. Even so, self-insuring may not be the most *cost-effective* way to handle the expense. Many wealthy families purchase long-term care insurance, knowing that the premiums are far less than the cost of paying for care themselves. Still others obtain it to avoid hesitation on anyone's part to "spend the inheritance."

- *Those with No Choice; Exhausting Income and Savings:* What if your financial resources are not substantial? What if you have to self-insure long-term care costs? You may have to exhaust your income sources, such as pension income and Social Security, and then begin invading your principal (individual investments, IRA Rollovers, etc.).

  Having to sell and spend assets not only diminishes your retirement savings, but may have adverse tax consequences and create market losses. You may also impoverish a spouse and exhaust the legacy you had hoped to leave to your heirs.

- *Using the Equity in Your Home—The Reverse Mortgage:* Suppose most of your net worth is tied up in the value of your home and you need that money to pay for long-term care? Should you sell your home and move to a more modest one? Should you borrow from the equity and incur monthly loan payments?

  What if you could get money from your home and not have to move or make loan payments? A reverse mortgage would let you do that. It is a loan against your home that requires no payments as long as you continue to live there. You can receive money monthly, all at once, or take money as you need it. The amount of the loan grows as you take out funds. The money is paid back in full (including interest and fees) when you die, sell your home or move out for good.

The amount you or your heirs receive when the home is finally sold depends on the amount of debt that has to be repaid first, but you never owe more than the value of your home when it is sold.

If you own your own home, condominium or townhouse and have built up a substantial amount of equity, and if you are over the age of 62 and all owners agree, a reverse mortgage may provide enough supplemental income to help you afford the cost of long-term care. If you plan ahead while you're still healthy, you could use the income to purchase long-term care insurance and pay the premiums.

- *Using Life Insurance Policies:* Depending upon your age and how an illness or disability has affected your life expectancy, you may be able to receive some cash benefits from your life insurance policies during your life. *A caution:* Be sure the beneficiary of the policy can manage without the death benefit or its reduction.
- *Cash Value:* If you have permanent life insurance and have built up sufficient cash value, you may be able to take out some of the cash to help pay for care either by taking out a lump sum or amounts as needed. Generally, you can take out amounts tax-free up to the premiums you have paid, then borrow the rest that is available.
- *Accelerated Benefits Rider:* This provision, depending on the policy, allows some percentage of the death benefit (generally less than 50%) to be given as a living benefit to cover long-term care costs, or costs of a terminal illness.
- *Life Settlements:* A life insurance policy can be sold to a third party in exchange for a cash settlement in excess of the policy's cash surrender value, but less than the death benefit. Generally, the amount is 50%–85% of the death benefit, depending upon your life expectancy. The older you are, the more ill you are, the larger the settlement you receive.
- *Viatical Settlements:* In some states these are deemed to be the same as life settlements, but when used as a separate term, it refers to the sale of a life insurance policy on an insured who is terminally or chronically ill for a cash settlement that is also greater than the cash value of the policy, but less than the death benefit.

With either of the above transactions, you no longer own the policy and no longer pay premiums. The new owner will name a beneficiary of the policy who will receive the death benefit proceeds.

- *Using Annuities:* Purchasing an immediate annuity with a lump sum of money can be done to provide a predictable monthly income that cannot be outlived. In exchange for this guaranteed lifelong income, you give up any further access to the principal during your lifetime. Couples trying to help an ill spouse qualify for Medicaid coverage of long-term care costs may transfer their asset spend-down amount to the well spouse, who uses the money to buy an immediate annuity. This may help the well spouse while they remain healthy, but may cause problems later if they also need to qualify for Medicaid.

A few companies offer immediate annuities that combine regular monthly payout amounts that increase if long-term care needs arise and are certified.

HOW DO HEALTH INSURANCE, MEDICARE, AND MEDICARE SUPPLEMENTAL INSURANCE COVER LONG-TERM CARE?

Mistakenly, many people think these health insurance plans will pay for long-term care. The truth, as we saw in the example of Jake and Nora at the beginning of the chapter, is that they have severe limitations. Medicare covers only skilled care for twenty days, and only if it is a follow-up to a hospital stay. It pays a portion of the next eighty days, then nothing further, and only in Medicare-approved facilities. A Medicare Supplemental policy (Medi-gap) pays for the portion not paid by Medicare during the eighty days, then nothing further. If the need for care changes to custodial care during these first hundred days, no benefits are generally provided at all—whether in a nursing home or in your own home.

As to health insurance prior to being on Medicare, read the "limitations of coverage" section in your policy. Most will not cover custodial care in any setting, though they may provide for limited skilled care.

What Does Medicaid Cover, and How Do You Qualify for Coverage?

Medicaid pays health care costs for people whose income and assets are very limited. It is operated jointly by federal and state governments. It provides only limited coverage for long-term care. For instance, it is designed to cover costs only for skilled care and only in Medicaid-approved facilities (or, under some very strict limits, skilled care at home). It does not pay for the kind of long-term care most of us hope for, such as custodial care at home, or care in an assisted living facility. Its real intent is to be the payer of last resort.

To qualify, you must have spent down most of your assets and must use most of any income you receive to pay for your care first. Well spouses are allowed to keep limited income and assets for their own needs. To guard against people simply giving away assets to heirs to qualify for Medicaid, there is a look-back period of three or five years before you would then qualify for benefits. Doing such planning is very complicated with many pitfalls, and should be pursued with the help of an attorney who specializes in Medicaid planning.

HOW DOES LONG-TERM CARE INSURANCE COVER THE COSTS OF CARE?

First, let's not underestimate the monetary value of being insurable. Planning for long-term care while you are healthy gives you choices—a lot of them. If you choose to and can afford to purchase long-term care insurance, you are likely to pay for any care you ultimately need at pennies on the dollar.

As of 2003 more than four million Americans had a long-term care policy in force. We are becoming educated about the need to protect retirement savings. The peace of mind this coverage provides can touch people in several ways. For people approaching or in retirement, it means a safeguard from spending down their retirement nest egg on this type of extended care.

For adult children of aging parents long-term care insurance means the peace of mind of knowing that their parents will get the care they need. This is especially important for several reasons. For the most part, gone are the days of the extended family living close at hand. Members of families are often scattered across the country—sometimes as far as other countries—and are not geographically available to provide personal care. Insurance coverage allows the adult children to attend to the needs of their own immediate families and the demands of their careers. It keeps the aging parents from feeling they have to "tough it out" silently at home, not wanting to be a financial or physical burden to their children.

Take the case of Nate, age 86. A widower for four years, he began to experience pain from his arthritis that really slowed him down. Not wanting to interrupt the life of his daughter and her family, not wanting to incur the cost of a caregiver, he kept quiet about his diminished abilities to care for himself. He shopped for food less often, didn't feel like cooking much and often ate very little. He became malnourished, weakened, and took a nasty fall while trying to tidy up his house. Now, with a broken hip, surgery was needed. He suffered a stroke while in rehabilitation, and died a few months later. Had he felt the ease of knowing a long-term care policy would cover the costs, he could have hired a caregiver, had a better quality of life, with the dignity and comfort of staying in his own home, and would likely have had many more years to enjoy his family. Instead of managing a crisis, his family could have overseen the management of his quality of life.

For this reason, when parents cannot afford long-term care insurance for themselves, their children sometimes join forces to share in the payment of premiums for policies on Mom and Dad as part of an overall family financial plan.

Employers have seen the importance of their employees having this coverage for themselves and their parents. Many now either sponsor or pay for employees to obtain long-term care policies and to purchase coverage for spouses and parents at a discount. They know the wisdom of assuring that valued employees won't lose time or concentration at work due to the need to care for a spouse or a parent.

An example of this problem is the case of Janet, age 55, a vice president of a community bank and a key person in its operations. Her mother, age 80, suffered a stroke that left her only partly functional. Janet was quite close to her mother, and could not bear the thought of her being in a nursing home. Instead, Janet took early retirement, moved her mother to her home, and provided the care herself. It was a major loss for the bank, which had relied heavily on her leadership.

A popular executive benefit is a long-term care policy for key employees paid for by the employer, where premiums are paid up by retirement. The employer can deduct the premiums as a business expense. If the company is a C corporation, the owners can purchase coverage for themselves and deduct those premiums as well.

Even *people with substantial financial resources* prefer the cost effectiveness of purchasing long-term care insurance to the more costly prospect of paying for extended care out-of-pocket. In some cases the cost of premiums paid for ten years can be recouped within one year of receiving care paid by a long-term care policy.

Take, for example, Mr. Rich, a man of considerable means. He is just turning 65, selling his valuable business and thinking about ways to enjoy retirement. A factor in his planning is his experience with his mother, who was extremely ill for the last ten years of her life, requiring costly care. Being a good businessman, he compares self-insuring for his own possible long-term care needs (which he can easily afford) with purchasing a long-term care policy. Here is what he assumed and what he found:

- For a $200 per day benefit; thirty-day elimination period; 5% compound inflation rider; ten years of benefits, his premium would be $6,936 a year. (It would be less if his wife applied as well.)
- Based on family health history he assumes he might need long-term care in about ten years. The costs of $200 per day ($72,000 per year) would inflate by at least a compounded 5% per year ($117,280 in ten years).
- If beginning at age 75 he had, say, a seven-year illness, his after-tax costs would be $954,898. Assuming a combined federal and state tax bracket of 40% his money would have to gross a total of $1,336,857 in investment earnings to net the needed amount.
- In just the first year, the costs for care would be at least $117,280. If these were covered by his long-term care policy, his tax-free policy benefits would more than return, *in under a year,* the $69,360 he paid in premiums over the ten years.

His conclusion? To his mind, the more cost-effective way to cover possible costs is to insure them. If he never needs the coverage, it's the mistake he'd rather make.

A FREQUENT FINANCIAL PLANNING TOOL

The endorsement for including long-term care insurance in a financial plan is coming from many sectors. Attorneys, CPAs, financial planners, employers, and federal and state governments all endorse the necessity of this type of planning.

Baby boomers who have had the experience of caring for someone in their family are including long-term care insurance in their plans for their own retirement. About a third of those who purchase individual policies are under the age of 65.

Even families with strong cultural histories of caring for relatives within their own families are purchasing long-term care insurance. They may still open their own homes to the elder family member, but can use the insurance coverage to hire appropriate caregivers, and not have to take time from careers or family routines to provide the care themselves.

The federal government and the states know that Medicaid programs cannot continue to bear what will be an increasing need for long-term care—especially as the first of the baby boomer population approaches retirement age. Nearly half the states now offer long-term care coverage to their employees. The federal government has a plan available to federal workers and has seen the need to offer tax incentives for the purchase of individually owned long-term care coverage.

FUTURE NEEDS FOR LONG-TERM CARE: IS LONG-TERM CARE COVERAGE HERE TO STAY? YES, AND CONGRESS THINKS SO, TOO.

When long-term care insurance first appeared, it was primarily designed to cover the cost of nursing home stays and had many limitations. Over the past nearly two decades, policy benefits have evolved to include care at home, assisted living, respite care and hospice.

Though some hybrid products exist that link long-term care coverage with life insurance, disability insurance or annuities, most coverage is specifically devoted to providing just long-term care.

As more and more people have purchased coverage and gone on claim, they have experienced for themselves how much it contributes to their quality of life and a sense of aging with dignity. Family and friends noted these differences, and the word has spread. As a result there has been an increase in the kinds of benefits, services and facilities that are available to provide the proper care. This constructive evolution will likely continue. The U.S. population of people age 65 and older is expected to double over the next thirty years and comprise 20 percent of the population. This will clearly increase the demand for long-term care services.

In recognition of this rising demand, Congress passed the Health Insurance Portability and Accountability Act (HIPAA) in 1996. In so doing it recognized the need to provide tax incentives for Americans to purchase long-term care insurance for themselves.

Congress specified certain standardized benefit provisions that would allow policies to qualify for these tax advantages. Such policies are referred to as *Tax-Qualified Long-Term Care Insurance Policies*. The premiums now qualify for federal tax deductions in the category of health expenses. Close to half the states (twenty-one) endorse the importance of having this coverage by offering either tax deductions or credits for the premiums.

If you apply for coverage you will have the choice of a Non-Tax-Qualified Policy or a Tax-Qualified Policy. What is the difference?

Tax-Qualified Policies	Non-Tax-Qualified Policies
Premiums are deductible, up to a maximum limit (taxpayer must itemize deductions and have medical costs in excess of 7.5% of adjusted gross income).	Premiums are not deductible.
Benefits you may receive from your policy are not counted as "income" for tax purposes as long as they do not exceed a per diem amount ($230 in 2004).	Benefits received from your policy may or *may not* count as "income." As of this publication, the U.S. Department of the Treasury has not issued a final ruling on this matter.
Benefit triggers are two out of six activities of daily living. You must be unable to perform these activities without substantial assistance.	Benefit triggers are not restricted to two out of six activities of daily living.
Disability must be expected to last for at least ninety days.	Disabilities needn't be required to last for ninety days.
A "medical necessity" cannot trigger benefits.	A "medical necessity" or other criteria for disability can be used to trigger benefits.
Cognitive impairments must require "substantial supervision" to trigger benefits.	"Substantial supervision" need not be required to trigger benefits for cognitive impairments.

How Are Qualified Long-Term Care Policy Premiums Deducted?

If you have a "tax-qualified" policy and itemize your deductions, you may be able to deduct some or all of your premiums. To determine this, you add your annual premiums to your other deductible medical expenses. If the total exceeds 7.5% of your adjusted gross income you may be able to deduct some or all of your premiums on your federal tax return.

The amount of the deduction depends on your age, and should be reviewed with your tax advisor. The table below shows the limits on deductions as of the year 2004:

Age	Limit on Deduction
40 or less	$260
41–50	$490
51–60	$980
61–70	$2,600
71 and over	$3,250

WHAT IS A LONG-TERM CARE NEED? WHAT SORT OF CARE DOES IT INVOLVE?

Physical illnesses, disabilities or cognitive impairments such as dementia or Alzheimer's disease can create chronic conditions that result in mild to severe limitations. Long-term care is designed to overcome the limitations as much as possible. The services may include such things as help performing activities of daily living for people with physical illnesses or disabilities. Supervision, verbal cues and protection can be provided for those with cognitive impairments. Depending upon the condition, benefits are available for home health care, adult day care, respite care, or care in a nursing home, an assisted living facility or one's own home.

Skilled care is whatever must be provided by registered nurses or professional therapists. To be covered it must be ordered by a doctor and be needed on a twenty-four-hour basis. Most often the setting is a nursing home, but nurses and therapists might also come to your home.

At a less skilled level is *custodial care*, where one is helped with the activities of daily living mentioned above. These include bathing, eating, dressing, toileting, continence and transferring (as from a bed to a chair). Non-tax-qualified policies generally also include ambulation as a trigger. This care is provided in a wider variety of settings such as one's own home, an assisted living facility, adult day care and nursing homes.

Care coordinators provided by the insurance companies help families and their doctors establish a plan of care that suits specific needs and adjusts services and settings for care as needs change over time. At its best, good care management can even help the insured recover and return to an independent life.

WHERE CAN YOU GET LONG-TERM CARE INSURANCE?

There are several types of policies available for this coverage. Typically they fall into the following categories:

Individual Policies: These are sold through agents, or directly through the mail. There are many companies and combinations of benefits from which to choose, so this requires careful shopping and comparison.

Partnership Programs: These policies are available in only four states: California, Connecticut, New York and Indiana. To those who purchase them, these policies allow policyholders to qualify for Medicaid, yet protect some or all of their assets (but not income) from paying back Medicaid benefits. The amount of asset protection varies, depending upon the state's program. If you live in one of the four states, check for the specific manner in which its policies will protect your assets from having to be used for Medicaid benefits.

Partnership policies must meet certain strict criteria. They must have inflation protection (not as an option), include a benefit for care management, or have a plan of care that is designed by "access agencies" at the time of claim. These special policies are offered only through certain approved companies, and must be sold only by agents who have been certified to sell partnership policies. This certification is meant to assure that those applying will be able to make an informed purchase.

Since the federal government does not want to encourage Medicaid enrollment, it is doubtful that there will be any additional state programs.

Employer Group Plans: Depending on the number of employees in a company, coverage may be available to you with little or no medical screening, and at a possible discount. The employer may or may not cover your premium. Often, relatives are able to acquire the coverage, but have to qualify medically. Be sure to ask if you can keep the coverage after you retire, whether it must be converted to individual coverage, and whether benefits and costs then change.

WHAT LONG-TERM CARE INSURANCE BENEFITS ARE AVAILABLE? WHAT SHOULD YOU LOOK FOR IN A POLICY?

When you shop for this coverage, ask a lot of questions, and look through various companies' "Outline of Coverage" to see what benefits are described, how they are triggered, how they work, and how they pay.

Typical Policy Benefits

Settings Where Care Is Provided: When shopping for a policy, be sure to look for the services it covers and the settings in which you can receive care. All policies are not alike. There may be specifications regarding required licensing for facilities. Specific facilities may not be covered at all, such as personal care homes, homes for the aged and rest homes. The following may be available:

- Nursing home care
- Home health care
- Personal care in your home
- Services in an assisted living facility
- Services in an adult day care facility
- Services in other community-based facilities

A few companies offer benefits for care provided outside the United States. Some have a restricted set of countries where they will cover you. If you plan to live abroad part of the time during your life, this may be a benefit you want included in your coverage.

Home Health Care Provisions: These days most people are looking for policies that will let them receive care in their own home as the need for long-term care arises. As a result, home care benefits are in high demand. Not all policies are equal in how home care benefits are defined, so it is important to look for the types of care and care providers the policy will pay for.

- Is care in your own home paid for only if you use care providers from licensed home health care agencies?
- Or . . . will the policy also cover licensed health care providers who are not from a licensed agency?

Both of the above can include licensed practical nurses, occupational, speech or physical therapists, or licensed home health care aides.

Some policies will cover home health care aides who are neither licensed, nor from a licensed agency. Home health care aides can help with your personal care.

- Some rare policies will cover homemaker or chore worker services. This type of policy would cover someone who comes to your home to do chores, to cook for you, or to run errands.
- In general, adding home care to your policy will increase the premium, but will give you more flexibility for your care.
- Some insurance companies offer riders to pay benefits for family members who provide you with care in the home. This is a costly feature, and the physical, emotional and time burden for family members may not be a sustainable demand, regardless of the monetary compensation.

HOW DO YOU SELECT BENEFITS TO INCLUDE IN A POLICY?

The amount of coverage is determined using several variables. Determining how you select these is highly individual, depending on your circumstances. As you read through the information on any given policy, be aware of what is an option or a rider, and what is included in the policy benefits.

- *The Daily or Monthly Benefit Amount:* Currently, the amounts available range from $50–$300 per day, or $1,500–$9,000 per month. This is for care in a nursing home. A few companies offer even higher daily benefits. (Remember that daily indemnity benefits exceeding $230 per day in 2004 may not be considered tax-free.)

    How much do you need? It is important to know current costs in the setting where you expect to receive care—your community, the community where your children live, or in the area in which you plan to retire.

Some people plan to pay for a portion of their care out of pocket. They purchase a long-term care policy to pay for the amount they could not afford, or are not willing to pay out of their own pocket. Others want the policy to cover the costs as completely as possible.

- *Home Care Benefits:* Home care benefits are sold as a percentage of the daily benefit. So, as an example, if you want the same dollar amount for home care as for a nursing home, you need to specify that home care benefits are 100% of nursing home daily benefits.
- *The Elimination Period:* This is the period of time during which you would pay for your own care out of pocket before your policy benefits begin. Generally, the periods available are 0, 30, 60, 90, 180, and 365 days, depending upon the insurer.

    Consider your own financial resources including direct income (such as from a pension, an annuity and/or social security) and your liquid assets. Ask yourself how long you could afford to pay for your own care before you would be uncomfortable or would start to jeopardize your savings. The shorter the elimination period you select, the higher your premium will be.
- *The Benefit Period:* This benefit choice requires a bit of art, a bit of science. After all, you are asking yourself to predict how long you will require care once you qualify for benefits. Generally, people think back to the period of time they have seen elder family members being impaired and needing care. It is also good to assess your personal sense of physical and mental well-being. Typical benefit duration choices are two, three, five, six, ten years and lifetime.

    Lifetime or unlimited benefits are becoming more difficult to qualify for as insurers are seeing the amount of time policyholders are staying on claim. Some companies are now issuing such policies only to people rated as "preferred" risks.

    Since lifetime benefits are the most expensive, the earlier such policies are purchased, the better. Many people purchase this benefit if they have seen family members suffer very long impairments from dementia, Alzheimer's disease, stroke or arthritis. Others purchase it for the peace of mind in knowing they would never run out of benefits, no matter how long the illness or disability.

    Since some amount of coverage is far better than none, purchasing a benefit duration you *can* afford (even if it is not "unlimited") is a sound move if you are concerned about preserving your retirement assets.

- *Inflation Protection:* No one knows how many years it will be until they need long-term care, if they ever do. A person purchasing a policy at the age of 55 might not need care for twenty or thirty years or more. To keep their daily or monthly benefit meaningful so far in the future, it is critical to purchase a rider for inflation protection. For example, a $150 per day benefit in 2004 would have the buying power of $57 in twenty years if average inflation for long-term care rises at 5% (which it typically does—and more). To look at it another way, with a 5% compound inflation rider our same $150 per day benefit would rise to $398 per day in twenty years. Typically, this option is offered at 5% compounded increases, or 5% simple increases. The younger you are at the time of purchase, the more a compounding increase will matter. Some policies limit the amount the benefit can be raised, such as two times the original daily benefit at time of purchase.

- *Waiver of Premium:* This benefit allows you to cease paying premiums once you either receive care for a number of specified days, enter a nursing home or receive care for your policy's elimination period. It is important to know what a policy offers in this regard, since eliminating the premium bill during a disability can make a big difference to your cash flow when expenses can be high.

  Some policies offer the provision of adding the waiver of premium for home health care as well, but charge extra premium for this benefit. Others build it into the policy.

- *Notice to a Third Party:* Suppose as you age that a failing memory causes you to forget to pay your long-term care insurance premium and your policy lapses—just as you are starting to need it. To avoid this, most insurance companies have a section right on the application that allows you to name someone the insurance company can contact if your coverage is about to expire due to nonpayment—someone who would be in a position to see to it that the premium gets paid. In most cases, the insurance company will send you a form each year to change the contact person, in case the previous one is no longer available or appropriate.

  The person you name can be a friend, relative, bookkeeper, or advisor (such as an attorney or accountant). Generally, this benefit comes without an extra cost. Some states require that it be part of the policy.

A good way to help avoid this problem is to have the premium taken out of your checking account automatically. The issue then, of course, is to take measures to assure that your bill-paying account maintains a sufficient balance.

- *Restoration of Benefits:* If you purchase a benefit duration of less than "lifetime" or "unlimited," you could possibly run out of benefits at some time because of a prolonged illness or disability.

  Say you have a long-term care policy with benefits payable for three years at $200 per day. Since most policies have a "pool of benefits" design, this comes to $200 per day × 365 × 3. This is a pool of dollars equaling $219,000. If you suffer an illness that causes you to go on claim and require care for six months of daily custodial care costing $200 per day, you would have used $36,000 of benefits. If, after your recovery, you use no further benefits for a specified period of time (often six months, but check the policy), the $36,000 would be restored to your pool of benefits. This can be comforting later on when, during your last years of life, prolonged custodial care is needed.

  This benefit may or may not be included in any given policy. Again, it is important to read the policy's "Outline of Coverage" to see whether this is included, or is available as a rider.

- *Nonforfeiture Benefits:* Suppose after twenty years of paying premiums on your long-term care policy, you discontinue your coverage. If you have a nonforfeiture benefit in your policy you may be able either to receive back a portion of the money you have paid in premiums, or to receive a "reduced paid-up policy" with the daily benefit you bought, but for fewer years of coverage. Either way this is a costly benefit that can add between 10% and 100% to the cost of premiums.

  We do know of an exception to this. There is a version of this benefit that will return to your named beneficiary, or your estate, all the premiums you paid into the policy, regardless of how long and how much you received in benefits. Although this is an expensive rider, it does allow families that do not want to pay for long-term care expenses out of regular cash flow or the liquidation of other assets, to have insurance cover their costs of care. Upon their death, the full cost of every premium they paid, including the cost of the rider, is returned to their estate. The family is not disinherited for the cost of purchasing the insurance.

- *Premium Refund at Death:* Long-term care policies can not only protect against spending down retirement savings to cover the cost of sustained, lengthy care; they can be structured to return premium dollars that may have diminished an estate.

    Riders that provide refunds at death pay your estate the total dollars you paid in premiums, minus the dollars the insurance company paid out in long-term care benefit costs.

    Although this adds to the overall cost of premiums, this benefit appeals to families who want to "hedge their bets." Even though they want the protection of a long-term care policy just in case they need prolonged care, they are betting they'll never need it, or not for long, and want their premium dollars returned to their heirs.

HOW DO YOU QUALIFY TO RECEIVE BENEFITS ONCE YOU ARE COVERED?

In a policy's Outline of Coverage, there is a section usually called "Eligibility for Benefits." It will describe such things as:

- The type of assistance you need with at least two of six or seven activities of daily living. These are generally listed as bathing, dressing, continence, eating, toileting, and transferring. Non-tax-qualified policies may also specify "ambulating."
- Doctors' certification that you are expected to be disabled for longer than ninety days (with tax-qualified policies). Non-tax-qualified policies may pay benefits if your doctor documents that medical care is necessary. (Not available in tax-qualified policies.)
- Cognitive impairment triggers. It is possible to be able to do all the activities of daily living, but suffer mental incapacity. Most policies provide for tests of mental abilities as a trigger for benefits.
  - Some states have certain required factors to trigger your receiving benefits.
  - You may also find that companies differ in their criteria for triggering nursing home benefits versus home care benefits.

Remember, too, that the waiting period you select will determine how long you must pay for your own care before the policy pays your daily benefit.

How Are Policy Benefits Paid Once You Go on Claim?

Insurance companies specify one of two ways they will pay benefits for your care:

1. *The Reimbursement Method (the Expense-Incurred Method)*: If the insurance company agrees that you are eligible for benefits, they pay them to you or to your care provider only when actual care is provided. You are reimbursed, or the care provider (such as a nursing home) is paid directly for actual costs incurred, up to the maximum daily benefit of your policy.

   Let's look at the case of Anna, age 82, who is receiving care at home while she copes with the aftereffects of a stroke that has left her speech impaired and physically weak on one side. Her recovery has been slow, but she is expected to regain most of her previous functions with time and therapy. Her husband, Jon, is well, but unable to lift her and assist with her personal care.

   On some days, only an aide comes to their home to help her bathe and dress. The aide charges $50 a visit. So for those days, Anna is reimbursed $50. On other days, she receives physical therapy at a cost of $90 per visit, and speech therapy at $75 a visit. When these visits overlap in a day, her overall costs for the day come to $215. Her daily benefit is $150, leaving her and Jon with costs of $65 to cover out of their own pockets.

   Check the Outline of Coverage for such policies. Some allow for costs to be pooled over a maximum weekly budget (seven times the daily benefit). In such a case, a total of $1,050 in actually incurred costs could be reimbursed.

2. *The Indemnity Method (Per Diem Benefits)*: Under this payment method, once the insurance company agrees that you are eligible for benefits, you will receive your entire daily benefit on any day you receive care that is part of your personal plan of care, regardless of the costs you incur.

   So in Anna's case above, she would receive $150 for any day she receives care and would be able to literally "bank" dollars not needed on one day for costs incurred on another. Some companies have even more generous indemnity benefits that pay your daily benefit to you regardless of services or days provided. These are generally referred to as "Cash Benefits."

WHEN SHOULD YOU PURCHASE LONG-TERM CARE INSURANCE?

While there is no one magical age at which one should purchase this coverage, there are two critical issues to be considered.

1. The older you are when you purchase coverage, the more expensive the premiums will be.
2. If you wait too long, a change in health could make you difficult or impossible to insure.

    If you have a preexisting condition it is important to reveal it at the time of your application. Not revealing it may cause the insurance company to refuse to pay benefits for that condition later on, or even to cancel your policy. Revealing it and having it underwritten and approved means you will receive benefits when you eventually need care, even if the need is caused by that same preexisting condition.

    It is a good idea to ask how particular companies will evaluate a preexisting condition you may have. If it is severe, you may not qualify at all. If it is minor, or under successful treatment, you may be accepted for coverage, but at a higher premium rate. Being aware of the higher cost ahead of time can help you prioritize essential benefits you want to buy, and others that simply add too much cost to your coverage. If you work with an agent, they should be able to check with underwriters at various companies to give you an idea of how your condition would be evaluated and what rates you would be charged.

MAKING IT PERSONAL; GETTING INSURANCE QUOTES

If you have learned the costs of care in your area, or the area in which you expect to receive care, it is time to get some quotes. Whether you use an agent or shop on your own, get quotes from several companies and read their Outlines of Coverage.

Most companies will give you one main quote for a specific set of benefits, then back it with additional pages that show those benefits with various waiting periods, inflation provisions and all the possible benefit duration periods they offer.

Below are checklists of information to assemble and request when getting quotes:

Information on Yourself: Insurance companies will need certain information about you to give you a quote. Be able to give them the following data:

- Your name
- Date of birth
- State in which you live
- Whether you plan to cover only yourself or also want coverage for a spouse, or someone with whom you have an extended live-in relationship
- Information about preexisting conditions such as:
  - Name of the condition and its date of onset
  - Medications you take and their dosages
  - Your height and weight (if you feel you are overweight)

Information About the Coverage You Want Quoted:

- The amount of daily benefit you want (some companies use monthly benefit amounts, so $150 per day would be $4,500 in monthly benefits, for example).
- The length of the waiting period (during which you could afford to pay for your own care).
- The duration of benefits you want (typically two years, three years, five years, six years, ten years, or lifetime depending on the insurance company).
- Whether you want an inflation rider; if so, do you want simple 5% inflation, or compound 5% inflation of your benefit?
- Whether you want Home Health Care to be covered; and whether you want benefits to be paid even if a family member provides the care.
- Look at the brochures from each company you contact to see what optional benefits are available. For example, some companies include Restoration of Benefits provisions in their policies; others offer it as a rider.

- If you are in your peak earning years and want the option of paying premiums only for the next ten years, or to age 65, ask for quotes showing the (higher) annual cost of shorter payment periods. You may want the option of not paying premiums at some point in time, say at or after retirement.
- Don't be shy about asking for quotes with more than one combination of benefits. Find out for yourself if optional benefits you like are affordable.

HOW DO YOU MAKE A FINAL DECISION WHEN PURCHASING A POLICY?

Once you know the benefits you want and have found the insurance companies that offer them, you can begin to narrow your choices. One caution: Do not just price shop at this point. The soundness of the insurance company you select can be critical, especially if decades pass before you need long-term care benefits.

For one thing, ask if they have ever raised premiums on existing policyholders. Companies reserve the right to do so, though many states have now made this a difficult procedure for companies to carry out.

The soundness of a company can affect things like possible increases in premium costs over time, readiness to pay claims and services to insureds when on claim, to name a few factors. Insurance companies are analyzed and rated for their financial strength by several insurer rating services. Ask to see these ratings, or look them up for yourself.

Below are the rating services to consult and their websites.

A.M. Best Company: http://www.ambest.com

Standard & Poor's Insurance Rating Services: http://www.standardandpoors.com

Moody's Investor Service, Inc.: http://www.moodys.com

Fitch IBCA, Duff & Phelps, Inc.: http://www.bankwatch.com

Weiss Research, Inc.: http://www.weissinc.com

For further consumer guidance consult *A Shopper's Guide to Long-Term Care Insurance* published by the National Association of Insurance Commissioners.

The bottom line? Planning for retirement includes protecting your financial resources from the potentially devastating costs of needing care for an extended period. Having a plan in place before you need that care can mean a longer life with quality and dignity. It can prolong your independence, your ability to feel in control of your everyday life, and your enjoyment of family and friends.

Part Two

CONSERVING AND TRANSFERRING YOUR ESTATE

ESTATE TRANSFERENCE:

THE PROBLEM AND THE GOALS

Suppose you had a parent or grandparent like this: In 1962, Robert S. Kerr, United States senator and former governor of the state of Oklahoma, died. The senator was not only a zealous and determined public official; he was, while alive, a zealous and determined estate builder. During his lifetime he put together an estate that has been estimated at somewhere between $35 and $50 million.

At the time of his death, Senator Kerr had been discussing the making of a new will with his attorneys. One had even been drawn for him but was not executed. The old one, made in 1939, was obviously outdated. It failed to take advantage of the important tax savings offered by a law passed in 1948—the estate tax marital deduction. As a result, the taxes on his estate could be $25 million if his estate proved to be $35 million— almost $37 million if it turned out to be $50 million.

Because the senator, like many other successful and hardworking people, pressed from every side by demands on his time, never did get around to revising his will, it stood as his instrument of transfer.

With a will using the marital deduction, estate taxes of from $13 million to $19 million could have been saved. In fact, the utilization of a variety of techniques—lifetime gifts combined with charitable bequests and the full use of the marital deduction—could have resulted in even greater tax savings and possibly an estate transfer without any taxation at all.

This story is a dramatic illustration of the need to keep a will up-to-date. Tax laws change, and can create new opportunities and pitfalls. But it is more than that; it illustrates one of the basic laws of estate planning. When you have created an estate, you have completed only half of the job. Unless the creation is accompanied by a well-designed plan of transfer, much of what you have so painstakingly built up runs the danger of being dissipated, and with it the goals and objectives you have sought to achieve.

ESTATE CONSERVATION

A person plants a stand of trees. His idea is to eventually build for himself a nursery that will be a going business. The trees are his resources, which supply the business with its product. When they reach maturity the nursery is completed, but his work is not. Now he must preserve and maintain those trees, and allow for their future growth as well. It is the job of a lifetime, of several lifetimes if the nursery is to continue. This is what we mean by conservation.

Conservation—the preservation of what you have—is an indispensable element of estate transfer, indeed almost a synonym for it. Substitute the capital that makes up your estate for the trees that make up the nursery and you see its relation to the transfer program. If you want to conserve your family resources for the future use and benefit of your beneficiaries, then you must find ways to prevent erosion of these resources, just as you would have to find methods of halting soil erosion in your forest.

THE PROBLEM OF EROSION

Halting erosion is indeed an important problem, which faces the estate planner in this second phase of his program. Its threat is omnipresent throughout the estate building process, but is most likely to happen at the time of transfer of resources, when the estate owner passes all or some of his property on to his beneficiaries, usually his spouse, children, grandchildren, or parents.

The agents of erosion are several. There are the costs of transfer and administration; the liquidation losses which occur when assets have to be sold to meet the need for cash to pay estate costs. Then there is poor management, a personal factor which can dissipate capital just as surely as taxes and estate costs can. And finally there is taxation—usually the most powerful and vigorous erosive force. In property transfer it is estate taxation primarily, but gift and income taxation play their parts as well.

Tax erosion is not inevitable. It can be enormous, sizable, minimal, even nonexistent, depending entirely on the methods you use to transfer your property and the modes of ownership you set up for it. There is a great variety of these methods available to you, so many in fact that the choices presented sometimes seem to resemble a labyrinth. The job of finding your own right path through the labyrinth is tedious and challenging but the stakes are large; the outcome is of great personal and financial importance to every estate planner.

In the course of the second half of this book, we will discuss the ways of reducing erosion and of achieving estate objectives. We will explore the concept of lifetime giving, examine the living trust, see how to minimize taxes, set forth the principles of charitable giving, point up the need for a will, and explain how to assess your estate in order to make that will. Finally, we will look at the question of estate management: how to choose the people for this job and how to find the experts who will help you plan your transfer.

We will also discuss the current and changing impact of the Economic Growth and Tax Relief Reconciliation Act of 2001, with its expected expiration on December 31, 2010, when estate taxes are due to revert to pre-2001 rates.

ANALYZING YOUR OBJECTIVES

Do you remember the definition of estate planning set forth in the beginning of this book?

"The creation, conservation, and utilization of family resources to obtain the maximum support and security for the family during the lifetime and after the death of the planner."

These goals—family support and security—are basic objectives of practically every estate plan. They operate just as strongly in the conservation and transfer phase of the planning as they do in the creation. In that earlier phase the struggle to achieve these objectives, while dynamic and challenging, was a comparatively short-term one. Now the character of the problem changes. It is long-term; its impact reaches out beyond the span of an individual life and covers future generations. Now you are planning for the happiness of your family, not only in the present but in the future.

PLANNING FOR YOUR BENEFICIARIES

When you begin to plot your transfer program you must think of the specific people who will receive your property. You will have to assess their needs, both future and present; determine whether this person or that one can handle property; predict as well as you can what problem may crop up in their lives that you would want to prepare them for or help them cope with. How else can you make a fair distribution or decide who gets what, and how?

Your children, for example: The needs of an adult child are different from those of a younger one. So are those of a handicapped child versus an able one. One child has different abilities and capabilities than another; one has different needs and desires. All this will have to be taken into account when your distribution pattern is charted.

When you come to your spouse—the person who you probably think of as the focal point of concern in your transfer plan—you must think in terms of the meaning of widowhood, of the problems and situations your spouse will encounter. Does a man subject his wife to the bewildering details that administration of property often involves if she has had no experience with them? Does a wife cast her husband into a position where he will be in conflict with his own children over the distribution of that property? Or perhaps at odds with and defenseless against her former business associates? Does anyone want to involve a spouse in situations where relatives, his or her own, make continuous financial demands on them?

Your goal in this case is not only your spouse's financial security; it is also his or her peace of mind. This, too, you can help create for each other by proper methods of transfer.

Finally, there are your other dependents. Somehow you must fit them into this fabric that you are to weave into a harmonious pattern. These can include your own parents, relatives, even people outside your family. Sometimes these people are forgotten in a transfer plan with unforeseen consequences. We remember a situation where a man who had been the sole support of his own elderly parents left his entire estate to his wife. The wife remarried. The man's son, with an already inadequate income, took over the entire burden of their support. Certainly the father never intended this to happen. Like so many people, he simply never conceived of the possibility that he would die before his parents.

To all, or nearly all, of these beneficiaries, you have another responsibility, too: the responsibility to educate them to handle their property *during* your life *and* after your death. Family education is essential to the success of both property conservation and transfer. Property is inanimate; whether or not it grows, shrinks, is preserved, passed on, or is dissipated depends in large measure on the abilities of the people who administer and use it. When you are gone, this will be your family's task. It is up to you to see that they are prepared to assume it.

More than property values are at stake here. If human beings can affect the eventual fate of your property, remember that the opposite is also true. The money that you pass on can bring happiness to your family or it can bring disaster. It can build character and it can destroy it. If you transfer your assets in trust in such a way as to prevent your children from developing into responsible, stable adults, you may be setting the stage for unhappiness, helping to create dependent instead of self-sufficient people. On the other hand, if you transfer it so that your children are encouraged to take on responsibility and to use their money wisely, you are building the environment for their future well-being and maturity.

SECONDARY OBJECTIVES

Most people have other motives beyond the primary ones of security when they struggle for success, or work to accumulate capital. These may be called secondary objectives, motivations of the planner which are not family-oriented.

For some there is the hope of achieving personal immortality—the estate they leave behind them represents for them a concrete symbol of a lifetime of accomplishment. They may die, but their estate does not die with them. For others the building of the estate is motivated by an all-too-human ambition, the desire to attain power through the accumulation of capital.

What else? Family obligation and duty—the responsibility felt by many possessors of inherited wealth to pass on the estate intact to the next generation. Or business loyalty—the desire of a person to make sure that his business and those who helped build it will not suffer on his death. The wish to help a good cause or a charity is another important objective. In fact, there are probably as many individual goals as there are individual planners.

The point: motive—both family and personal—is at the core of conservation and transfer. Behind all the legalities and the technicalities, it operates as a driving force. Determining your overall purpose is the first step in planning your estate transfer—and one that only you can take. It will drive all that follows.

WHERE TO BEGIN

Like all elements of estate planning, conservation and transfer are continuous. They begin when your estate begins; end only when you die (and in a sense, not even then, for the conservation and transfer plan that you have structured will continue on after your death). But this point in your planning, the time when you assess what you have created and begin charting its future, is a particularly crucial one. As you marshal your assets and put them into place for orderly transfer, you are producing a master plan that (while it can be altered at many junctures and in many situations) will eventually control the financial lives of your family.

The Estate Planning Worksheets should be put to good use here. Working with them, the pattern of your estate and its transfer problems and potentialities become clear. Together with the general information contained in the following chapters, they should help you to set your house in order.

But where, specifically, to begin? With the first problem of estate conservation and transfer—understanding the unified system of taxing lifetime gifts and transfers at death.

CHAPTER 12

THE UNIFIED ESTATE AND
GIFT TAX AND HOW IT WORKS

QUESTIONS AND ANSWERS ON THE GIFT TAX

Here's a bit of shifting history: Prior to the Tax Reform Act of 1976, gifts made during one's lifetime were a way of transferring property to members of the family and saving substantial amounts in estate taxes. The gift tax law was very liberal. There was an annual exclusion of $3,000 per donee and we each had a lifetime exemption of $30,000 in addition to the annual exclusion, before any gift tax became payable. For every gift to a spouse, there was also a 50 percent marital deduction. The gift tax rates were only three-fourths of the estate tax rates and, moreover, the property was removed from the donor's top estate tax bracket and was taxed at the bottom rungs of the gift tax scale. With good planning, hundreds of thousands of dollars could be transferred with little or no tax.

When the donor died, except for gifts made within the last three years that were deemed to have been made in contemplation of death, the slate was wiped clean. The estate got a $60,000 exemption and a possible marital deduction of one-half the adjusted gross income. The estate tax was applied to the balance.

Lifetime giving became such a widespread way of avoiding estate taxes that Congress decided do something about it. As of January 1, 1977, it set up a unified structure for taxing lifetime gifts and transfers at death. The reasoning behind it was that a person should pay the same tax whether he transferred his estate at death or before.

Congress decided not to tax small gifts and kept the $3,000 annual exclusion. It replaced the former $30,000 gift tax and $60,000 estate tax exemptions with a unified credit, which was phased in from 1977 to 1981, when it reached $47,000 and was essentially equivalent to an exemption of $175,000.

Then came the "summer of '81." In the Economic Tax Recovery Act of 1981, Congress recognized the effects of inflation and tax bracket creep. It made sweeping changes in the estate and gift tax law but retained the unified structure for taxing them.

Let's look at the broad picture of the unified system of taxation of estates and gifts as it is evolving today before getting into specifics.

First, there is the "use it or lose it" annual gift exclusion. In 2002–4, the annual gift tax exclusion was increased to $11,000. This permits a person to give away as much as $11,000 a year (with no carryover if it is not used) to each of as many persons as he wishes without making a taxable gift ($22,000, if the spouse consents). This is adjusted for inflation using the Consumer Price Index and rounded to the lowest $1,000. Not great news in low inflationary times.

Then there is the separate ceiling on gifts beyond the annual exclusion that can be given anytime during life or after death that are exempt from gift or estate tax. The Economic Growth and Tax Relief Reconciliation Act of 2001 (EGTRRA) has begun to split out lifetime gifts from gifts after death. As of 2004, the lifetime gift exemption is $1,000,000 (a tax credit of $345,800). But EGTRRA established a scale for increasing the amounts exempt for estate transfers after death on a different scale. The two sets of exemptions and their corresponding tax credits are scheduled to increase until no transfer tax is imposed in 2010. However, in 2011 this law "sunsets" and tax rates return to pre-2000 rates unless Congress votes to retain them.

Here, then, is the still-shifting picture as projected through 2011:

GIFT TAX CREDITS / EXEMPTIONS

For Gifts Made in	The Unified Credit Amount Is	The Equivalent Exclusion Amount Is
2002–9	$345,800	$1,000,000
2010	$330,800	$1,000,000
2011	$345,800	$1,000,000

ESTATE TAX CREDITS / EXEMPTIONS

For Decedents Dying in	The Unified Credit Amount Is	The Equivalent Exclusion Amount Is
2004–5	$555,800	$1,500,000
2006–8	$780,800	$2,000,000
2009	$1,455,800	$3,500,000
2010	$0	$0
2011	$345,800	$1,000,000

EGTRRA is also reducing the top tax brackets for estates and gifts on amounts that exceed the Exclusion Amounts as follows:

2004	48%
2005	47%
2006	46%
2007–9	45%
2010	35% Gift Tax Only; 0% on Estates
2011	55%

No gift tax is payable until the credit is used up. The gift tax is cumulative. Prior gifts are added to current ones in figuring the credit used and tax payable. The tax rates for gifts and estates are the same except in 2010.

At death, all gifts made after December 31, 1976, except those coming within the $11,000 annual exclusions and those which qualify for the marital deduction, or made in 2010, are called "taxable gifts" and are added to the taxable estate. A tentative tax is figured to the total, and then the unified credit plus any gift taxes paid on lifetime gifts are subtracted. The credits exemption equivalent works like a charge account. Taxable gifts are charged against this balance until it is exhausted. The unused balance at death is then applied against estate taxes.

Here's how the unified system works: Ms. Donor, a widow, made taxable gifts to her children above the $11,000 annual exclusions, totaling $100,000. She paid no gift tax because she hadn't used up her credit. When she died in 2004, she left an estate of $1,900,000. In calculating the tax on her estate, the $100,000 of gifts must be added back and the tax figured on the total. The tentative tax on $2,000,000 is $780,800. Against this the credit of $555,800 allowed in the year 2004 is subtracted, leaving a tax due of $145,000.

All lifetime gifts and transfers at death from one spouse to the other that qualify for the marital deduction are tax-free. All outright transfers qualify as well as transfers in trust if they meet specific requirements (see page 280 for discussion of the types of trusts which will qualify for the marital deduction).

Let's turn now from the general picture and get down to some questions and answers on the implications involved in making gifts, for despite the changes brought about by EGTRRA 2001, the shifting picture of estate and gift taxes means planning ahead can make a difference.

SHOULD I MAKE GIFTS AND HOW MUCH SHOULD I GIVE?

Making gifts may be advisable from a tax point of view. But this does not mean that lifetime giving is always financially advantageous. There are other considerations besides taxes.

How much can you afford to give away? That is the heart of the matter. No one should ever give so much money away that he jeopardizes his own financial independence. A person transfers a large part of his estate to relatives and then comes up against a radically changed economic situation, a depression, or a recession. Or perhaps he suffers a reversal of personal fortune. What happens then? A true gift is irrevocable. That is something that all would-be givers should remember.

There is also the question of age. A person of 30 would obviously not want to give away as much as one of 70. It is not only that no one can predict the future; it is also that money given away is no longer available for investment and capital accumulation by the donor. However, properly used planned gifts can transfer future appreciation of value to a next generation and prevent such growth from increasing estate taxes in the donor's estate.

With these thoughts in mind, let's take a look at some of the workings of the gift tax.

WHAT DOES THE GIFT TAX TAX?

Generally speaking, the tax is imposed on the transfer of property by gift during a person's lifetime. The tax applies to all gifts except gifts between spouses and charitable donations. Also excepted are payments made on behalf of anyone for tuition or medical care directly to an educational institution or a provider of medical services. The donor pays the tax, not the donee. But if the donor defaults on the tax payment, the government has the right to collect it from the donee.

HOW IS THE VALUE OF A GIFT DETERMINED?

In the case of any kind of property other than cash, the value of a gift is considered to be its fair market value on the date the gift is made.

Thus, if the gift were securities, the value would be the current market price. The market value of real estate is usually arrived at by using expert appraisal, the assessed value, and the sale price of similar properties as guides. Business interests of closely held corporations represent a more complex problem. There are various methods and combinations of methods for arriving at the value of these: book value, capitalization of earnings, expert opinion, as well as many other criteria. The services of an accountant and attorney are required to make a proper valuation. You may also need the help of expert appraisers. (For a fuller explanation of the valuation of business interests, see Chapter 19.)

HOW DOES THE ANNUAL EXCLUSION WORK?

Any person may give away as much as $11,000 a year to each of as many people as he wishes without paying any tax at all. This exclusion is available to both a husband and a wife. They can therefore give away together as much as $22,000 per year to any person, even though it all comes from the property owned by the husband, for instance. In order to take advantage of this provision, called "gift splitting," a husband need only have his wife sign a consent to his gift on the gift tax return; it is not necessary for her actually to give any property of her own. The two exclusions then amount to $22,000. As noted previously the $11,000 annual gift exclusion will be indexed for inflation starting January 1, 1999, and lowered to the nearest $1,000 based on the Consumer Price Index. If the cost of living were to rise only 5 percent between 2004 and 2007, no adjustment would be made, since $500 would be less than $1,000.

The annual exclusion is applicable only where there is a gift of "a present interest," meaning that it can be claimed only when the recipient of the gift can immediately use, enjoy, or benefit from the gift. This has particular significance for gifts made in trust. When, for example, you make a gift in trust to a beneficiary who does not have the right to the income or principal of the property immediately, then you have made a gift of a future interest and it will not qualify for the annual exclusion.

Take the case of the person who makes a gift in trust to his daughter and grandchildren. The daughter gets the income during her lifetime and the principal is to go to her children at her death. The annual exclusion applies to *her* part of the gift (the right to the income) but not the grandchildren's part (the right to the principal). Since the right to the income during her life vests in her immediately, her interest is a present one. Since the grandchildren's right to the principal can be enjoyed only after their mother's death, their interest is considered a future one.

With minors, if your gift meets certain conditions, then the entire gifts in trust will qualify for the annual exclusion.

Suppose, for example, that you want to make a gift to your minor son, age 10. If you put it in trust and provide that the income and principal could be used for his benefit now with the remainder going to him at 21 (or, if he died, to his estate or according to his will), then the gift would qualify for the annual exclusion. This is so even though the age of majority has been reduced to 18 in your state. Exactly the same applies to gifts made under the Uniform Gifts to Minors Act, which also qualify for the annual exclusion.

Many donors do not want trusts for minors to end at 21, but still want the tax savings of the annual exclusion. They can have both if the income may be used for the minor and any accumulated income is payable to him when he reaches 21. The value of his right to the income qualifies for the annual exclusion (although the remainder does not). If the trust principal is large, this right to income may exceed the annual exclusion.

How Are Gifts Made Before 1977 Treated?

Generally the gifts you made before 1977 have no effect on your estate. You get a fresh start, but with exceptions. If you used part of your former $30,000 exemption between September 8, 1976, and the end of that year, your new tax credit is reduced by 20 percent of the exemption used. Also, in figuring the tax on post-1976 gifts, prior gifts are added back, the gift tax is then computed and the tax on those prior gifts under the new rates are subtracted. The result is that it is possible that the pre-1977 gifts may put your post-1976 gifts into a higher tax bracket.

When Must a Gift Tax Return Be Filed?

No gift tax return need be filed for gifts that come within the $11,000 annual exclusion. If a spouse consents to a gift, though it may be $22,000 or less for the year, a return must be filed. A return is not required for interspousal transfers that qualify for the marital deduction. Returns are due on the April 15 following the year in which the gift was made. However, if you have an extension for filing your income tax return, you get the same extension for filing the gift tax return.

What About Annual Gifts That May Increase in Value?

Since 1997 there has been a three-year statute of limitations on the IRS for challenging gift valuations after death. To lock this in and start the three-year clock, you need to file a gift tax return (even if no gift tax is being paid). Prior to the Taxpayer Relief Act of 1997, the statute ran only if you paid a tax. This is great news if you 1) owe no gift tax on a gift, 2) want to protect the value of an appreciating gift (such as stock or real estate) from challenges by the IRS, and 3) transfer future gains to your recipient.

WHAT ABOUT GIFTS MADE WITHIN THREE YEARS OF DEATH?

Before 1977, gifts made within three years of death were presumed to have been made in contemplation of death and taxed as part of the estate unless the executor could prove the gifts were made with lifetime motives. As of 1977 *all* gifts within three years of death were automatically included in the estate except for gifts that qualified for the annual exclusion.

Now only gifts of life insurance and certain other transfers where the decedent has retained or has been granted powers over the property are includable in the taxable estate. Other gifts made within three years of death that exceed the $10,000 annual exclusion, though not part of the taxable estate, are *added back* in calculating the estate tax and the unified credit. It is important to note that since the latter are not part of the taxable estate, they don't get a step-up in basis.

CAN HUSBAND-WIFE GIFT-SPLITTING BE USED FOR ALL GIFTS?

As described in connection with the annual exclusion, gifts can be made from the property of either spouse. If the other consents, the gift is taxed as though each made a gift of one half of the value of the property given. However you must be aware that the consenting spouse will be using up some of his or her unified credit if the gift is over $22,000.

ARE TRANSFERS BY SALE EVER TAXED AS GIFTS?

Yes, when the sale price of the property transferred is less than the fair market price. In this case, the amount of the difference is considered a gift. For example, if you sold your daughter a hundred shares of Blue Chip Corporation for $5,000 at a time when they were selling for $8,000, on the basis of a market price of eighty, you would be making a gift of $3,000.

ARE GIFTS IN TRUST SUBJECT TO THE GIFT TAX?

Yes, the gift tax applies to gifts in trust as well as outright transfers, when the gifts are complete. If the trust is irrevocable and you have retained no power of appointment, or right to alter or amend it, it is a completed gift and it is subject to the gift tax.

WHAT ABOUT JOINT OWNERSHIP OF PROPERTY?

What happens when you take property of your own or purchase property with your money and put the title into a form of joint ownership with another person? Is there a taxable gift? The answer is no, if he or she is your spouse; otherwise it depends on a number of things: the type of property involved and whether he contributed money or "consideration" toward the joint ownership; also whether or not the gift is considered to be a completed one—i.e., one in which the donor has given up any of his interests in the property. Thus:

Joint Savings Accounts. When you make a deposit of your own funds in a joint savings account with your son, for example, there is no gift until he makes a withdrawal. Then you have made a gift to him of the amount he withdraws, and that amount is subject to taxation.

Joint Ownership of U.S. Savings Bonds. Much the same principle applies. If you buy these bonds and list your son as co-owner, there is usually no gift until he cashes them in. At that point a taxable gift has been made.

Joint Ownership of Securities. Whenever you put stock, bonds, or mutual funds into joint names and your co-owner doesn't contribute one half of its value, you are making a gift. Joint brokerage accounts are an exception to the rule.

Joint Ownership of Real Estate. Purchase or transfer of real property into joint names is ordinarily a gift where one does not contribute consideration. Thus, if you bought a house and put the title in the names of both your daughter and yourself, you would have made a gift to her of more than one half of the value of the house, based upon your respective life expectancies.

What Are the Estate Tax Rules on Joint Property? The basic estate tax rule is that property in joint names is fully taxable in the estate of the first to die, except to the extent that the survivor can prove his own contribution. So it is possible to make a gift, such as by putting stock into joint names, and still have 100 percent of the property included in the donor's taxable estate.

However, there is a special rule for property held in the joint names of a husband and wife. Each spouse is treated as owning half. On the death of the first to die, only the value of half of the property will be included in the decedent's gross estate, regardless of which one paid for the property. There will be no tax on the property because of the unlimited marital deduction. However, only the half that is included in the gross estate gets a step-up in basis. This is especially wasteful in a community property state where holding title, say, to a home, as community property means the entire property receives a step-up in basis at the first death—a significant advantage for a surviving spouse who could want to sell the house he or she may now find too large or difficult to maintain.

WHAT ABOUT GIFTS MADE DURING LIFE BUT NOT PAYABLE UNTIL THE DEATH OF THE DONOR?

Again, there is a distinction made depending on whether you relinquish control and interest over the gift during your life. U.S. Savings Bonds, for example, registered in your name but payable on your death to your niece, are not gifts, since she has no right to the proceeds until you die. At that time, ownership of the bonds passes to her, but they are includable in your taxable estate.

Gifts of insurance depend on how the insurance policy is written. If you make your niece the beneficiary of an insurance policy, you have not made a gift if you continue to own the policy or retain the right to change the beneficiary. However, if you designate her as the beneficiary irrevocably or if you assign the policy over to her, then you have made a gift.

Are There Other Financial Advantages?

Making gifts not only saves on estate taxes, it also reduces the size of your estate and thus reduces the cost of the administration of your estate if you only have a will. These administrative costs can run as high as 5 to 10 percent of the total estate, so it pays to keep the estate as low as possible.

Savings can often be obtained when a gift is made because the future income from the property may be transferred to a member of the family with a lower income tax bracket than that of the donor, and the future appreciation in the value of the property is removed from the donor's estate with a consequent savings in estate taxes in his estate.

IS THERE A STATE GIFT TAX AS WELL AS A FEDERAL ONE?

The states of Louisiana, New York, North Carolina, Oregon, South Carolina, Tennessee, and Wisconsin, as well as Puerto Rico, have gift taxes. The rest do not. If you, as a resident of a non-gift-tax state, make a gift of real property that is located in a gift tax state, however, then you are subject to both the federal gift tax and that of the state in which the real property is located.

CHAPTER 13

GIVING DURING YOUR LIFETIME:

THE BENEFITS OF FAMILY

OWNERSHIP OF PROPERTY

To most people the phrase "estate transfer" means transfer after death. It summons up images of wills, bequests and legacies, funerals, lawyers, and family conferences.

But this is only one side of the coin. *Lifetime transfers,* that is, the making of gifts to your family while you are still alive, is just as important an aspect of estate planning as after-death giving. It has advantages to the whole family, both economic and personal.

THE PERSONAL SIDE

People who suddenly inherit large sums of money often do not understand the dynamics of money in our world. Because the amount is substantial, it seems to them as if it will last forever. After all, my grandparents, my parents, or my spouse had it and managed to hang on to it over a period of years; why shouldn't I be able to do the same? So the reasoning usually goes.

These innocents—and innocents they truly are—realize too late how ephemeral money really is, how rapidly it can disappear whether invested or merely spent. It takes experience to walk the tightrope of economic planning. Even the very most astute administrators are sometimes hard put to know how best to handle investments in a fluctuating market. How, then, is it that we expect inexperienced people to do it?

This is where lifetime transfer comes in. It prepares and educates the family—spouse and children both—about all the problems and skills needed in the management of property. It provides learning's most priceless asset, experience.

The Spouse

Let's use as an example a widow whose estate, inherited from her husband, included a block of stock worth $200,000 in a blue chip corporation. She knew little about the world of investment, but learned rapidly. Or so she thought.

Shortly after her husband died, the company announced a stock split. Seeing in the papers that the stock was now listed at a lower price, she got panicky, thought she was losing money, and sold off her stock, all $200,000 worth.

Next, she put the proceeds into a speculative stock (recommended by a friend she met at a cocktail party). Within two years, the value of the stock dropped from $200,000 to $50,000. Had she kept her investment in the original firm, it would have been worth $250,000.

It's easy enough to criticize or ridicule the unfortunate heroine of this little drama, but in doing so, we miss the point.

Was it her fault she acted so foolishly? After all, she never handled or owned any sizable amount of property in her life. Her husband had never "bothered her with money matters."

The World of Finance—Not for Men Only

In the past, many men (and their wives, too) considered the management of property and investments to be exclusively the prerogative of the male. According to this philosophy, women didn't understand the world of finance; they weren't interested in it; they weren't capable of grasping its finer and more subtle aspects.

But now women receive higher educations, vote, hold down jobs, play responsible roles in the community, become executives, politicians, scientists, engineers, doctors, and lawyers. So does it make sense to presume that they cannot tell the difference between a stock and a bond? In fact, we know of many couples where the wife handles the investments, and the husband has no interest.

What's more, acting on the presumption that a woman cannot understand finances is not only illogical but dangerous. We know from the actuarial tables that most wives outlive their husbands. Twenty percent of all married women become widows by the time they reach the age of 55; almost one-third by 65; and two-thirds by 75.

It's a fact that most women in the United States are going to be faced with the problems of administering property, sometimes large amounts of it. It is important that the world of finance be familiar to women.

The woman who has shared the ownership *and* management of property with her husband during their lives together is far luckier than the average widow. She can tell the difference between sound and poor investment advice. She isn't likely to fall prey to "hot tips" gleaned at the gym or proffered by well-meaning friends. If her husband dies, she will have to surmount the shock of his death, but it will not be heightened by fear and panic about money matters. Fortunately, it is ever more common that women take an interest in investing and family financial matters and attend, with their husbands, the meetings with account money managers. It is a healthy and needed trend that allows for continuity in how money is handled.

The Children

When it was suggested to a client that he start making gifts of property to his 21-year-old son, he looked skeptical. "Give him money? Why, he'll go right out and buy a sports car with it. He thinks money grows on trees."

Not knowing his son, we don't know whether he was right or wrong, but we do know that if the son is going to buy a sports car with the $20,000 his father gives him now, he may spend the one million he will inherit at his death just as unwisely.

But isn't it true that you can get around this problem by leaving all your property in trust for a child for the rest of his life? It is. Have you ever come across any of these trust-sheltered children?

We have, and the picture they present is not a pretty one.

One "trust fund baby" that comes to mind was 50 years old, married several times; at this juncture single once again. He didn't work. His life was made up of two important monthly dates. On the first of each month he received his stipend from the trust. By the fifteenth he had succeeded in drinking it up and began borrowing against the next payment.

The man who gives money to children during his life cannot guarantee that they will handle their inheritance wisely, but he has done far better than either the parent of the prospective sports car owner or the parent of the trust fund baby.

Through judicious giving, he has guided his children, helped them plan, taught them responsibility. When the time comes for them to take over, they may not be financial wizards, but they will certainly not be neophytes.

Let us make clear, however, that when we say "Give to your children and let them take responsibility for the gift," we're not speaking of young children. We are referring to young adults.

The pattern of lifetime transfer should be planned, and carried out in installments: so much at one age, another amount in five years, and so on. About 18 is a good age to begin with a small gift, say, a few thousand dollars. Once the gift is given, you should back it up with advice—but if the young person doesn't want to follow it, we recommend letting him have his way and making investments as he wants. He may lose—but win or lose, he will surely have gained in experience.

The Donor

It is not only spouses and children who learn from the experience of receiving gifts. Donors have a good deal to gain too. If they have the opportunity over a period of years to see what their children and spouses do with the property they have given them, they will be in a much better position to make the always difficult decisions on the distribution of their property after their death.

Will this child be able to handle their bequest? Or should the money be put in trust? Is this one capable of taking over the business? Would she be enthusiastic about it? Or do her interests lie elsewhere? Does the spouse take an intelligent interest in property? Or is the spouse genuinely and permanently not interested?

All these questions are much better answered in the framework of lifetime giving.

THE ECONOMIC SIDE

Lifetime giving opens up opportunities for saving, from which both the family and the individual estate planner can benefit. These opportunities are many and varied, but they can be summed up in a single phrase, tax savings.

Income Tax Savings

Spreading ownership of property among the family not only saves taxes, it increases the spendable income available to the family unit after taxes, in many cases by a substantial amount.

This is particularly true when unearned income is piled on top of earned income. At this point taxes become so heavy that the added income does not actually add very much cash to the family treasury.

But if the high-bracket individual who is receiving all this money divests himself of some of his income-producing property and gives it to a member of his family who is in a lower income bracket, or not previously a taxpayer at all, total taxes will be lowered and more after-tax money will be left. In short, it is axiomatic that one of the ways to save income taxes is to create new taxpayers or to level out income among the family members.

Thus, a person who is in the 25 percent tax bracket will ordinarily pay $250 in taxes on each added $1,000 of taxable income. But if he transfers property producing $1,000 of that income to his son, who is in the 15 percent tax bracket, the son will only pay $150 on the same income return. The donor has, in effect, added $100 to the family's spendable cash. These tax savings apply to any family gifts except to the spouse. Since most married couples file joint returns, there is no point in diverting income from husband to wife. For tax purposes, what's hers is his and vice versa.

The income tax savings factor has a number of other applications as well. Often it can help a family meet obligations that would otherwise pose heavy burdens. If you have a dependent parent, for example, why not make a lifetime gift to him? In this way he will be paying taxes on the income return in his low tax bracket. With income thus spread, the after-tax money available for the support of your parent will be increased.

Estate Tax Savings

This is important, in spite of the unified estate and gift tax, and in spite of currently diminishing estate taxes (but due to return in 2011).

The principle is simple: the more an estate is depleted by lifetime transfers, the smaller it becomes and the less taxes have to be paid on it. The results are often quite dramatic.

Take, for example, the mythical (but nonetheless typical) case of two women: Ms. A and Ms. B, who happen to have identical estates of $3,000,000. Both are widows and both plan to leave all their property to their children.

Ms. A keeps everything until her death in 2005. Her children pay an estate tax of about $705,000 plus administration expenses of $120,000, and end up by receiving $2,175,000 from their mother's estate.

Ms. B, on the other hand, makes tax-free gifts of $11,000 to each of her four children over a period of ten years, amounting to $440,000. When she dies, she leaves an estate of $2,560,000, subject to tax of $493,800 and with administration expenses of $102,400.

In all, Ms. B's children have received $2,843,800 from their mother, or $668,800 more than the children of Ms. A.

What to Give and How to Give It

The would-be donor of lifetime gifts has a wide choice as to the kind of gift he makes. It can be almost anything of value—cash, jewels, fine art, or stocks and bonds. But some gifts are better to give than others; tax savings can be greater depending on a number of factors. Gift giving, in fact, is a fine art. It takes a good deal of information and knowledge to make the proper choice in the proper circumstances.

Here are some general rules about what kinds of property to give.

Give Income-Producing Property

You save on *income taxes*; the *future profits* follow the gift, not the giver. But don't forget, your cost basis goes with the gift; you shift all capital gains to the recipient.

Give Appreciated Property

You can save on capital gains taxes if you give property that has increased in value. As a matter of fact, if you are in a tax bracket of 25 percent or higher, you may want to consider the possibility of *giving* appreciated property instead of selling it.

Take the case of the man in the 25 percent tax bracket who wants to take his profit on a stock which has risen in value from $4,000 to $10,000. If he sells the securities, he will have to pay a 15 percent capital gains tax on his $6,000 profit, or $900. But if he gives the stock to his daughter who is in a 15 percent bracket, she can sell it and pay a 5 percent capital gains tax of only $300.

This strategy becomes even more dramatic when capital gains are taxed at higher rates.

Give Property That Has a Potential to Increase in Value

If you expect that certain property will greatly appreciate in the future, a gift of this property will permit the donee to take advantage of the appreciation. This could be stock, real property, collectibles; things you may want to remove from your taxable estate before they increase further in value.

Insurance is ideal for giving. It is taxed only at its cash value at the time of the gift. The recipient gets the face value when the donor dies, but does not have to pay estate taxes on it. If the cash value of the policy when originally given is less than the $11,000 annual gift tax exclusion, and subsequent premium payments by the donor do not exceed the annual exclusions, nothing would be includable in the estate of the donor, unless he dies within three years of making the gift of the policy.

Gifts of insurance, however, have to be absolute (meaning that the ownership of the policy goes to the recipient, with no strings attached). If you retain any kind of control over the policy, the insurance will be considered part of your estate and therefore subject to estate taxes.

OTHER TYPES OF TRANSFERS:
SALES, SALES AND LEASEBACKS, ANNUITIES

Sometimes it is wiser to sell than to give. This is especially true since the amount of a gift over the $11,000 annual exclusion is included in figuring the taxable estate at death.

Gifts can cause family difficulties too. Often one member of the family will resent the fact that the gift goes to someone besides himself. Finally, you may not be able to afford to give property away.

The answer in all these cases is usually some form of sale. The sale, however, must be a true sale, for tax purposes; that is, it must be sold at its fair market price. If it isn't, you may have to pay gift taxes on the value of the property in excess of what is paid for it.

Installment Sales

When you substitute a sale for a gift, however, you may be bypassing the gift tax, only to run into capital gains tax. If your profit on the sale is substantial, then even with low capital gains tax treatment you may have to pay a fair amount in tax. If you receive only part of your profit in cash, and the balance in notes, you would have to pay the entire tax in the year the sale is made, perhaps paying in tax more than the cash you received from the sale. However, the installment sale provisions of the tax law allow you to spread the taxable income over the period the installments are to be paid, while transferring future appreciation of the asset to your family member.

Thus, on a sale of an asset which was originally bought for $120,000 and is now sold at a price of $200,000 there is taxable gain of $80,000. The tax on it would be a maximum of $12,000 at the highest current capital gains tax rate of 15 percent.

But if the sale were an installment sale, payable, say, over a ten-year period at $20,000 per year plus interest, payments would be divided into three parts. 1) In this case $12,000 of each payment would be a nontaxable *return of capital* (the price originally paid for the asset). 2) The other $8,000 of each payment is treated as *taxable gain.* 3) *Interest* included in each payment is taxed as *ordinary income.* With installment sales the child's obligation to his parent can be secured. Payments are due even after the parent (seller) dies and are payable to his estate.

It should be said that capital gains treatment has historically existed on shifting ground. When gains are taxed at higher percentages or as ordinary income, the spreading of the income over a period of years reduces the total annual income more dramatically, and thus you avoid paying a large amount of tax at once on a lump sum. This may reduce the overall taxes you have to pay on the profit of the sale. Moreover, in times when capital gains tax rates are higher, or treated as ordinary income, your tax savings could be greater when the installment payments are received in low-bracket retirement years. Under JGTRRA 2003 the portion of payments on installment sales that represent gain will receive the 15 or 5 percent capital gains tax treatment until December 31, 2008, when that law "sunsets." After that the capital gains rates are *scheduled* to revert to pre-2001 rules that require a five-year holding period to receive 18 or 8 percent capital gains tax treatment.

Sale and Leaseback

This device is often used by business enterprises, but it is just as applicable to the family group. A father who owns business property, for example, can sell it to his son. The son then leases it back to his father. Both parties save on taxes in this kind of arrangement. The father can take a deduction for the rent or royalties he pays. The son also has deductions for depreciation and operating expenses.

The Private or Family Annuity

Although rarely used, it occasionally can be a useful form of lifetime transfer.

The private annuity is similar to a commercial annuity except that the transaction occurs among members of the family group—usually between a parent in a high income bracket and his children, or between the donor and a family-controlled trust.

The idea of the private annuity is that in exchange for an outright transfer of an income-producing business or property by the parent to the children, they agree to pay him a reasonable annuity for the rest of his life. When the parent dies, the payments stop and the children have no further obligation to his estate, unlike the installment sale. Thus a valuable estate is transferred to children but there are no estate taxes to be paid.

The private annuity also has a number of unique income tax advantages. Usually it reduces the parent's income taxes without reducing his income return. It can also allow the parent to transfer appreciated property in exchange for the annuity without paying an immediate income tax; the tax on the gain is deferred and spread over the parent's life. It gets special annuity tax treatment; most of each payment is considered a return of capital, and the remaining portion is taxable income.

The private annuity probably has as many disadvantages to a child as it has advantages to the parent. First of all, the child is taxed on the income from the property. He receives no deduction for the payments he has to make to his parent. Furthermore, the annuity payments may greatly exceed the income on most property so that the child has to use his own resources to pay income taxes, as well as make up the difference between the property's income and the annuity payments. If the child sells the property, he may be eventually liable for substantial taxes because his final cost basis amounts to only the annuity payments paid by him to his parent.

Lastly, the private annuity must be an unsecured transaction to qualify for the favorable tax treatment to the annuitant. Although a parent may trust his child, there's the risk of a child's untimely death. As a result, he may have to enforce the obligation on his child's estate. Life insurance on the child for the amount due can eliminate this risk.

The usefulness of the private annuity must be evaluated for each unique case.

GIFTS TO MINORS: A SPECIAL PROBLEM

There are many instances when it is advisable to make a gift to a minor child. If you want to do this, be sure that you make the transfer properly, or you may find yourself restricted in the use and transfer of your child's property at some future date. The minor's freedom to deal with his property is limited by law. In addition, the income tax consequences of transferring income-producing assets must be considered.

Cash gifts or U.S. Savings Bonds usually pose no problems. A minor can deposit and withdraw money from a bank or redeem savings bonds, if he has reached an age of sufficient maturity.

The trouble arises when the gift is one of securities or real estate. In both cases, a court-appointed guardian will be needed to deal with the property owned by the minor. This is burdensome and costly.

A friend of ours ran into this situation a few years ago. He had been a foresighted estate planner in that he had been transferring property to his son ever since he was born, anticipating the eventual high cost of a college education. But when the boy entered college and the father tried to sell some of the stock he had put in his son's name, he found it couldn't be done without going through all the red tape and expense of having a guardian appointed. The father ended up borrowing the money.

You can avoid this kind of transfer problem by setting up a trust for your minor instead of making an outright gift. Trustees (who should not be the donor) can be given broad powers to manage, to buy and to sell, without being tied down by judicial supervision. Trust income will be taxed at the trust's tax rates, which can be high, so low- or non-income-producing assets might be most suitable. On the other hand, income distributed for the minor's needs are taxed at the minor's tax rate.

If you plan to give securities or cash, a simpler solution is to utilize the Uniform Transfer to Minors Acts, which now exist in most states. This permits you to give securities and cash (and in some states, insurance and real property) to a minor by transferring them to a custodian. The custodian has broad powers similar to those of a trustee. He maintains control of the property until the minor reaches 18 or 21, depending upon your state's law, and can use the income and principal for the minor. When the child reaches 18 or 21 the property is turned over to him.

If income-producing assets, such as real estate or securities, are transferred to a child under the age of 14, unintended tax consequences may result. The Tax Reform Act of 1986 provides that for a child under 14 years of age, unearned income over $1,600 (in 2004) will be taxed at the rate of the parent (if higher). If the minor is over 14 years of age, the income can be taxed at the child's rate.

To avoid this problem, children under the age of 14 may be given non-income-producing assets, such as EE bonds, state and federal tax-free municipal bonds for your state of residence, or growth stocks, in order to defer the recognition of income until the child reaches 14. These gifts will still provide important transfer tax benefits by reducing the parent's taxable estate.

Of course for now there are also the Section 529 Qualified Tuition Plans discussed in Chapter 8 that allow accelerated annual gifts of up to five years ($55,000 per donor or $110,000 per couple in 2004) at a time, or a maximum gift of up to as much as $250,000 in some states, to be made as completed gifts. Growth and earnings of these accounts are tax-free and can be distributed tax-free when used for the qualified expenses of higher education.

FAMILY PLANNING

Earlier, we spoke of the estate planner and his obligation to provide for his family. But there is another parental responsibility that enters into the picture—that of his own parents, who may themselves possess a substantial estate.

If you have expectations of inheriting property from your parents, the planning of their estates is an integral part of your own estate plan. Whatever the size of their estates, the manner of disposition may have an effect on your plans for your family's security and on your tax picture. For this reason, we encourage intergenerational collaboration on the subject of estate planning.

If your parents are in the top income tax bracket and they make gifts of their income-producing property to you (assuming you are in a lower tax bracket), there will be, of course, an overall income tax savings. In addition, there will be an eventual estate tax savings when they die, since their estates will have been reduced to the extent of the subsequent income and appreciation thereon. Of course, they will be passing on their own cost basis in the property. If you later sell the property, this leaves you to pay capital gains tax on all the gain accrued since their original purchase.

If your income tax bracket is higher, or just as high, gifts to your children rather than to you would be more advantageous. If your children are minors, the gifts can be made in trust and the income accumulated until needed. The trust is a separate tax entity, so depending on the amount of income it is taxed to the trust or to your children at rates lower than yours or your parents' (in certain circumstances). Here is a means of creating a fund with a minimum cost in taxation which will be available for future use in educating your children. Not only has the property been removed from the erosion of estate taxes in your parents' estates, but by bypassing you, any estate tax that would have been imposed on the property in your estate is avoided.

If your tax bracket is low or you need additional income, it still may not be advisable for your parents to make outright gifts of property to you, but rather to make them in trust. The trust can specify that the income, and as much of the principal as the trustees consider necessary, be paid to you and that after your death (or at some specified time), the trust property be paid to your children. In this way you have use of the income, and as much of the principal as you need. Because of the generation-skipping provision, however, the value of the trust may be taxed as though it were a part of your estate at your death, subject, however, to a lifetime exemption of $1.5 million (see page 245 for generation-skipping transfers). If your parents' estate is substantial, this could serve to reduce your eventual estate once you receive your inheritance.

You should discuss with your parents the amount and type of inheritance you expect to receive from them. They might be conferring a burden instead of a benefit. Remember that any property you inherit becomes part of your estate, and the income earned on it will be taxable to you. Inheritances can be renounced. But the renunciation creates the possibility of gift taxes, problems in estate administration, and could disrupt your parents' estate plans. Further, if your own estate plan includes a program of annual gifts to your children, an unwanted inheritance can frustrate the accomplishment of that program.

When there is bad planning (or no planning), the sins of the parents can be visited on successive generations.

Here is a classic example of this maxim. A man had a substantial estate of his own. When his father died, he inherited $400,000 from his estate. He didn't want to give up the inheritance, but, on the other hand, he didn't want this additional property increasing his own taxable estate. Moreover, the income on the property meant little to him because of his high tax bracket.

Obviously, his father should never have left him that property. Better to have transferred it to his grandchildren. Better still, in trust for them. The bottom line here is that estate planning is best coordinated across generations.

FAMILY COMMUNICATION

Unfortunately, the case we have just cited is not unusual in the annals of estate planning. It is the exception rather than the rule that two generations enter wholeheartedly into a mutual plan that will benefit everybody all around.

Yet such plans are a necessity. And furthermore, the planning has to be on an individual family basis because the circumstances of each family are different. What to give and whom to give it to (children versus grandchildren, for instance) depends on the various estate and income tax positions of the two generations *and* the skill and personalities of individual heirs. All sorts of variables are possible.

Behind the failure of most families to do planning for lifetime transfer is the old problem of communication between generations. On the one hand, the children are reluctant to bring the matter up; it involves asking their parents to give them money; it sounds grasping, selfish, a bit morbid. On the other hand, the parents hesitate because—and this is a common failing—they still tend to look on their children, whatever their ages may be, as children. There is also an all-too-human tendency to hang on to what you have while you are still alive.

In actual fact, intergenerational planning presents a wonderful opportunity not only to employ more advantageous strategies for estate transfer, but also to mentor successor generations on the management of the assets to be inherited. It provides a chance to pass along family values and financial acumen that are as important a set of assets to transfer as anything else the family owns.

Somehow, perhaps through an impartial third person such as the family lawyer, perhaps by reading a book like this, perhaps through general discussions that lead to specific ones, the problem must be broached and the family communications barrier breached. For family planning is the essence of lifetime transfer and sound estate planning.

CHAPTER 14

USING TRUSTS TO TRANSFER

YOUR ESTATE

LIVING TRUSTS

Ms. Thrifty has heard that her estate will have to go through a costly and time-consuming probate proceeding after her death. She wonders whether she can pass a large part of her estate directly to her beneficiaries, in the shortest time and least expensive way, by avoiding a court proceeding.

Mr. Successful has a unique problem. At age 57 he controls a number of corporations and travels all over the United States and abroad handling their affairs. This leaves him little time to manage his own sizable portfolio of investments. He knows that he isn't giving them the attention he should, but what can he do?

Mr. Disappointed Father has four grown children. Three of them have turned out to be all that a parent could wish, but one, his middle son, is a true black sheep: a spendthrift and an ingrate. Mr. Disappointed would like to cut the Black Sheep off and leave the bulk of his estate to his other children. But he shrinks from the idea of all the publicity such a will would receive and the embarrassment it would cause his family. He is looking for some way to disinherit his son without having everyone know about it.

Ms. Cautious Parent would like to distribute some of her hard-earned and considerable wealth amongst the various members of her family while she is still alive. For one reason or another, she doesn't feel that any of them are capable, at this point, of assuming responsibility for large sums of money. What should she do?

Ms. Plan-Ahead's oldest child is now only seven years old. Nevertheless, Ms. Plan-Ahead is already thinking about his college education. She has started a savings fund for that purpose, but is having a difficult time increasing it. In her 35 percent bracket, a great deal of income is being drained away in taxes. Isn't there some way she can get the income of the fund out of her taxable income?

Mr. Worried is not sure that he has made the right plans for disposing of his estate after his death. Sometimes he wishes that he could repeat Tom Sawyer's famous adventure, get a chance to attend his own funeral, and see how his estate plan would work out. He supposes that is a silly idea, but is it really?

Ms. Real Estate Investor is concerned about a different aspect of after-death estate transfer. Her estate consists primarily of large real estate holdings scattered all over the country. When she dies there will have to be a proceeding in each state where the property is located. If only all these administration proceedings could be dispensed with!

All of these problems and many more—some of them commonplace, some of them unique—can be solved by a marvelously flexible device for lifetime transfer, the living trust.

If you transfer your property to a trust, you can avoid the problem of having your estate administered in the courts (Ms. Thrifty and Ms. Real Estate Investor); get professional management for it (Mr. Successful); keep the transfer private (Mr. Disappointed Father); protect your beneficiaries against their own inexperience (Ms. Cautious Parent); preview the management of your after-death estate (Mr. Worried); and realize greater after-tax income in order to achieve important objectives such as providing a fund for education (Ms. Plan-Ahead).

In short, of all the devices for lifetime giving, one of the most useful is the living trust. It can do almost anything that the grantor can do with his property—and yet still have additional advantages that are not open to him as an individual.

WHAT IS A TRUST?

The device dates back to feudal times, but the basic concept has remained the same over the centuries. When you give property in trust, you give it to another person (or group of persons or institution) to be used and administered for the benefit of a third person (or group of persons or institution) or yourself. In other words, you are trusting somebody else to handle your property for the benefit of your beneficiaries.

Trusts are two types, *testamentary* and *living* (the latter, in legal parlance, called "inter vivos"). Testamentary trusts are those you create by will, which become effective at your death. Living trusts are created during your lifetime by an agreement but may, and often do, continue on after your death. This chapter is focused on the uses of the revocable living trust and several other types of "inter vivos" trusts, but much of what we will discuss also applies to the testamentary trust. (For more on testamentary trusts, however, see Chapter 17.)

How It Works

Here's a simple example of how a trust works. Uncle and Aunt Bountiful give their best friend, Mr. Trustworthy, 1,000 shares of Top Grade, Inc. Trustworthy agrees to hold and invest the property for the benefit of the Bountifuls' nephew, Peter, and for Peter's children.

The trust agreement provides that Trustworthy will pay all the income of the trust to Peter so long as he lives. When Peter dies, the property will be turned over to his children.

The Bountifuls are the *settlors* of the trust, or they may be called the *grantors*, *trustors*, or *donors*. Trustworthy is *trustee* and he becomes the legal owner of the trust property. He is the Bountifuls' personal representative, empowered to carry out Uncle and Aunt B's objectives. The Bountifuls could have had more than one trustee, and they could also have designated substitute or successor trustees to take over in case Mr. T becomes disabled, resigns, dies, or cannot act for any reason.

Peter and his children are the *beneficiaries* of the trust. Peter is called the *life tenant*, because he has the right to the income of the trust for the duration of his life. His interest is called a *life estate*. Peter's children are called *remaindermen*, meaning that their interest is a remainder one—the right to the property when the life estate ends.

Unborn or unknown persons may be beneficiaries of trusts. If, under the Bountifuls' trust, the remaindermen were to be Peter's children, the beneficiaries might include children as yet not born. If instead the remainder were payable to Peter's wife (without naming her personally), the remainderman might be unknown or unascertained, since his wife will be the woman to whom he is married at the time of his death.

The stock which the Bountifuls gave to their trustee is called the *trust fund*, or *corpus*, or *principal*. In this case the fund was stock, but it might have been real estate, cash, insurance, or even a business. A trust fund may be composed of any kind of property that can be owned or assigned. It can also change as new investments are made.

Two factors dictate what the trust does and how it will operate: state laws and the terms of the trust agreement.

State Laws

The laws governing the operation of a trust vary from state to state. They are concerned with placing various limitations on the powers of the trustee and on the length of time the property can be held in trust. No state will allow a trust to operate indefinitely (except in the case of charitable or employee trusts). A trust can be created to last a long time—in most states for a period measured by the lives of a reasonable number of living people, plus twenty-one years.

In one famous case, for example, a trust was created in 1926 to continue until twenty-one years after the death of all the lineal descendants of Queen Victoria who were then living. There were 120 lineal descendants of the queen at the time.

When creating a living trust you usually have some choice as to which state you want your trust to be governed by. The only rule is that the trust have some material connection with the designated state. It could be the location of a piece of real estate, for example, or the residence of either the settlor or the trustee.

THE REVOCABLE LIVING TRUST AGREEMENT

Except for the limitations of state law, the settlors can make their own rules about how the trust is going to operate.

Thus, the settlors designate the purpose of the trust; they determine the amount and type of property it will contain; they set the length of time it will last; they pick the beneficiaries; they direct how much they get and when they will receive it. Further, they can set forth conditions that a beneficiary must meet in order to receive income or principal. (Uncle and Aunt Bountiful might have said, for example, that Peter's children weren't entitled to the principal until they had reached certain ages, or had earned a certain income themselves.) They can provide alternate dispositions in case their conditions aren't met or the circumstances change.

Moreover, they can set the rules that the trustee has to follow, and they can make these as broad or narrow as they want. Their trustee can become their alter ego, possessed of powers both of management and disposition, which will permit him to handle the property as changing circumstances require, and dispose of income and principal according to his own discretion.

The settlors' ability to set their own rules makes the living trust not only an important instrument of lifetime transfer, but also a means of estate creation and death transfer. The rules the settlors lay down will depend upon what the trust is to be used for. One trust may play many different roles in an estate plan. Though a trust may be principally created for one purpose, it can achieve other objectives at the same time.

Much, in fact all, of the ability of a trust to accomplish these aims, however, depends on the ability of the settlors together with their lawyer to devise the proper rules. For would-be trust creators, professional advice is a must. In addition, they should have a general understanding themselves of the many paths of trust creation that are open to them; equally, of the many opportunities for income and estate tax savings.

Providing for your incapacity: Even more important is the ability to provide for your own best interests should you become disabled and unable to manage your own financial affairs, or make your own health-care decisions. Accompanying your living trust (or will) should be a durable power of attorney for financial management and durable power of attorney for health care. Depending upon their abilities and your relationships, you may want to appoint the same or different people to take over for you in these capacities. Should you recover from your disability, all powers return to you.

Ease of estate transfer: Other great features of revocable living trusts are their ability to remove property from your ownership as an individual to your ownership as a trustee of one's own estate during life. This is significant because the assets you transfer will not be subject to the delays, expense and public exposure of the probate process. Instructions provided in your living trust become irrevocable upon your death and provide a set of instructions for distribution of your estate that bypass the need to be probated. Assets are literally reregistered in the name of your living trust while allowing you to retain all rights of ownership and control during your life. You and your spouse can be the settlors, the cotrustees and the beneficiaries during your lifetimes enjoying all the benefits of property ownership without incurring the burden of probate proceedings for your heirs.

Flexibility as times change: The revocability of living trusts means that your instructions for distribution of property can change. As tax laws, family needs, or your attitude toward specific family members or charitable organizations change, you can amend your instructions for how your estate will be distributed.

Preserving a spouse's unified credit: Between spouses a plan for dividing the estate into two parts at the first death can preserve each spouse's ability to apply some or all of their unified credit to the transfer of *both* halves of the estate. Take the case of Mr. and Mrs. Familiar. They currently have an estate worth $5 million. In 2004–5 the unified credit will allow *each of them* to transfer $1,500,000 to their two children without incurring estate tax. Let's say Mr. Familiar dies first. If his $1,500,000 goes directly to Mrs. F., then his $1,500,000 is now in her estate along with her $1,500,000 and the other $2 million of their estate. When Mrs. F. eventually dies, she will have only her own unified credit to apply. Mr. Familiar's $1,500,000 will be taxed at the applicable estate tax rates at the time of Mrs. F's death as part of her overall estate—a loss of a valuable tax advantage. Instead, the Familiars take the advice of their attorney and include a provision in their living trust to establish a *bypass trust* (also known as a credit shelter trust) at the first death. Thus, Mr. Familiar's $1,500,000 would be transferred to the bypass trust that would hold his $1,500,000 during Mrs. F's life. She will have access to income and principal should she need it. If the assets in the bypass trust appreciate in value during the remainder of her lifetime, the appreciation escapes estate taxation when transferred to their children.

Special caution: Between the writing of this edition and 2011, caution should be exercised in the wording of this provision. The unified credit equivalent is rising as high as $3.5 million in 2009. The estate tax will be repealed entirely in 2010, then reverts to $1 million in 2011. Married couples would do well to consider actual dollar amounts that should go to a bypass trust at least for the next few years. This can avoid the possibility of transferring all or some inappropriate proportion of the estate to the trust, leaving the surviving spouse with little or no money of their own.

The Revocable Trust as an Estate Management Tool: A trust is revocable if the trust agreement provides that the grantor can revoke, alter, or amend it at any time. This permits him to terminate the trust and take back the property if he wants to. Or it gives him the right to change the terms of the trust, including the names of the beneficiaries and the amounts, and the manner in which they are to get their shares.

Revocable trusts *by themselves* have no tax advantages. Whether or not the grantor receives income from it, he must pay income taxes on the trust income. The principal is taxable in his estate.

But there are many nontax reasons for creating a revocable trust. It can allow for professional management, guarantees privacy, saves administration expenses, gives a preview of the after-death estate, allows for change as needed—provides, in short, all the inherent nontax advantages of a trust.

Take the case of Mr. Successful; he wanted to be relieved of the burden of managing his property, if you remember. He places this property in a revocable trust, with himself as the beneficiary, and makes a person he has confidence in or a professional institution, such as a trust company, the trustee. The trustee will take over the property, manage it, invest it, and do all the day-to-day things necessary to conserve and increase its value. Mr. Successful will have all the advantages of his property without the headaches connected with management.

Revocable trusts of this type (where the donor is also the beneficiary) are often profitably used by independent entrepreneurs or owners of small businesses. Here the owner transfers his business to a living trust. While he is alive, he continues to receive income from it. After he dies, the trust remains in force with the family as beneficiaries. This ensures the continuance of professional, experienced management for the business without interruption when the owner dies or if he becomes incapacitated.

QUALIFIED TERMINABLE INTEREST PROPERTY TRUSTS (QTIPS)

In certain circumstances, spouses may want to maintain control over their half of the estate even after their death. Take Mr. Certain, who is in his second marriage. He had children from his first marriage and wants to be sure that they ultimately receive whatever is left of his half of the estate after his second wife dies. The combined families are on great terms, but Mr. C worries about what might happen if his second wife remarries after his death and/or if she and his children from his first marriage have a falling out.

Luckily for Mr. C there is a type of trust that will help him achieve his goal. Having done some basic estate planning, he already has a living trust and has provided for his estate tax exemption ($1,500,000 in 2004 and 2005; see Appendix, page 369) to be placed into a bypass trust upon his death. His children are the beneficiaries of that trust. But what of the rest of his estate that he has now merged with that of his second wife? He can now provide for his half of the remaining estate to be placed in a Qualified Terminable Interest Property Trust, or QTIP Trust, as it is more commonly known. His second wife will receive income from this trust during her remaining lifetime, but upon her death his children will be named irrevocable beneficiaries of any remaining assets in the QTIP Trust.

The assets in such a trust will qualify for the unlimited marital deduction, so no estate tax will be due at Mr. C's death—only after the death of his second wife. This tool is most valuable in such multimarriage situations, or whenever there is a desire to control the ultimate distribution of one's own half of an estate after death.

THE GENERATION-SKIPPING TRANSFER TAX

As demonstrated by the trust created to last until twenty-one years after the death of all the lineal descendants of Queen Victoria then living, it is possible to have a trust that can last a hundred years or more. Before the Tax Reform Act of 1976, this meant that property could be used by successive generations without it being subject to estate taxes as it passed in trust from one generation to the next.

The 1976 act gave birth to an entirely new transfer tax, separate and apart from estate and gift taxes. It is a tax on generation-skipping transfers and applies to trusts—living and testamentary—and to similar arrangements designed to last for more than one generation. This might apply as well to insurance proceeds paid under an installment option.

In its simplest terms, the tax was originally imposed on a trust having younger generation beneficiaries (that is, beneficiaries in generations below the testator's or grantor's) if they are in more than one generation. An example of such a trust is one for the life of the grantor's son, Able, that goes on his death to his child, Baker. Here there are two younger generations: Able is the first tier and Baker the second. On Able's death, there is a generation-skipping transfer to Baker.

The Tax Reform Act of 1986 expanded and imposed the generation-skipping transfer tax on "direct skips." A direct skip includes an outright transfer to a beneficiary at least two generations younger than the grantor. An example would be a transfer from grandparent to grandchild.

The tax is payable on Able's death and is computed as if the value of the trust property at that time were added to his estate. It is designed as a substitute for the estate tax Able's estate would have paid on that property if his father had given it to him outright. However, it's the trust that pays the tax.

Since 1990 each grantor has been allowed a lifetime exemption of $1 million for generation-skipping transfers of any type. So, in the case of married couples, husband and wife are each allowed $1 million exemptions. As of 1998, the generation-skipping exemption has been indexed for inflation for transfers made on or after January 1, 1999. The increases will be made in $10,000 increments rounded to the next lowest multiple of $10,000. In 2004 and 2005 the amount is $1,500,000, and rising identically with the estate unified credit until 2010, when the GST is repealed for that one year based on EGTRRA 2001. This law "sunsets" at the end of 2010, reverting to the 2003 indexed amount of $1,120,000.

Planning Note: There are opportunities between 2004 and 2009 to allocate increasing amounts to the generation-skipping exemption as follows:

2004–5	$1,500,000
2006–8	$2,000,000
2009	$3,500,000
2010	Not Applicable
2011	$1,120,000 and indexed for inflation

During 2010 estate transfer taxes are repealed, so no amounts should be allocated for the generation-skipping exemption, since no exemptions apply that year. In 2011, the exemption returns and is scheduled to be $1,120,000, and indexed for inflation thereafter as described above.

The test of whether a trust will be taxed is the number of tiers of younger generation beneficiaries. Many commonly used trusts won't be caught because they have only one such tier. Here are some examples of trusts not subject to the generation-skipping tax:

A Trust for a Wife and Children That Goes to the Children at the Widow's Death. There is only one tier of younger beneficiaries, the children. A grantor's spouse is always treated as being in the same generation as the grantor, regardless of age.

A Trust for a Child, Then to His Children, but if There Are None, to the Grantor's Other Children. If the grantor's child dies without offspring, the property goes to his sisters and brothers. Then all the beneficiaries will be in the same tier. (See also Chapter 18 under "Using a Charitable Trust" for a way to maximize a gift to a grandchild.)

THE IRREVOCABLE TRUST

An irrevocable trust is one that cannot be revoked or terminated. Why make a living trust irrevocable? For two reasons: the irrevocable trust—if properly set up—can result in both income and estate tax savings.

Income Tax

If you set up an irrevocable trust, you will not have to pay any income tax on the trust fund's income, provided that (1) you do not receive any of this income; (2) it is not used to support someone you are already legally obligated to support (e.g., your minor child); (3) it is not used to discharge your legal obligations; (4) it is not accumulated for you or your spouse; (5) the income is not used to pay premiums on an insurance policy on your life or your spouse's life; and finally (6) the assets of the trust will not revert to either you or your spouse.

Under such conditions the irrevocable trust can be a prime means for the high-income estate planner to shift high personal income taxes, while still keeping the property within the family. The trust operates here just as the lifetime gift does: taxes are diverted by creating new taxpayers.

Be aware, however, that trusts are now subject (since 1994) to higher taxes on income they receive. Any amount over $9,350 (in 2004) is taxed at the maximum rate for trusts of 35 percent.

Estate Tax

The unified estate and gift tax has discouraged many from making large taxable gifts, because the value of the gift when made is added back in figuring the estate tax on the donor's estate when he dies. However, donors desirous of eliminating future income and growth on estate assets are able to transfer large amounts of such assets before they have to pay a gift tax on them. Each donor or spouse who has not used any of his or her unified tax credit in prior giving can make gifts up to $1,500,000 (2004–5) without having to pay a federal gift tax. This large exemption comes about because it is the amount that is equivalent to the unified credit allowed.

This credit is $345,800 in 2004–5 and gradually increasing to $1,455,800 in 2009. For one year, in 2010, the estate tax is repealed by EGTRRA 2001, a law that "sunsets" December 31, 2010. After this the exemption amount returns to $1,000,000 with a unified credit of $345,800. Remember, this is the amount that can be given without paying gift tax. Thus, by making substantial gifts, larger amounts of income from and appreciation on such assets will be removed from the donor's subsequent estate. (See page 215 for a table of these increases.)

One can also protect such income and growth from the impact of estate taxes by transferring the underlying assets to an irrevocable trust. But in order to do so there must be no strings attached. The donor may not have any right to the income or retain any power to alter or amend the trust or control the enjoyment of the property. He can be a trustee, but his power as trustee must not go beyond the standard administration of the trust, as distinguished from any power which could alter or modify the beneficiaries' interests. Moreover, he cannot retain any voting rights in stock of a corporation he controls.

In setting up a trust designed to remove income and appreciation on assets from the settlor's taxable estate, the settlor is making a completed gift. He is not only giving up the ownership of his property, he is also losing its uncontrolled use and benefits. Therefore, before taking the step, he should carefully and thoroughly weigh the gift as he would any other type of irrevocable transfer of property.

Let's assume a grandfather set up a trust for his son and three grandchildren, which at creation in 2004 had a value of $1,500,000. This used up his unified credit equivalent that year, but he allocates all of it to the 2004 Generation-Skipping Tax (GST) exemption which is $1,500,000. Let's assume further that the trust appreciates to $1,750,000 when grandfather dies in 2011. What did he remove from his estate without the imposition of any tax? First, he removed all the income from the property, which continues to be paid by the trust to his son and grandchildren in their lower income tax brackets during the life of the son. Second, since only $1,500,000 was reported in his estate as a taxable transfer, then the $250,000 difference, representing the appreciation, escaped estate taxation. Third, he allocated the full amount to his generation-skipping exemption, so any growth in the trust's assets eventually goes to the grandchildren tax-free.

If grandfather had the means, he could have continued to contribute assets to the trust taking advantage of the increasing GST exemption

($2 million in 2006–8; $3,500,000 in 2009). In 2010 there will be no GST, therefore no GST exemption, so grandfather should not make any contributions that year, since they could not be allocated to the GST exemption. In 2011, the GST exemption reverts to just a little over $1 million, so grandfather would have exhausted his entire GST exemption at that point. Of course, all along the way, he could have also used the annual gift exclusion to further increase the value of the trust by making gifts of $11,000 to each of his three grandchildren.

Assuming, at the son's eventual death some years later, the trust property has appreciated to $2 million and is now distributed to the three grandchildren under the terms of the trust. This value would be exempt from tax on its growth, since, at the son's death, a generation-skipping transfer is deemed to have occurred. Because the trust has GST exempt status, the additional $500,000 in appreciation goes to the grandchildren tax-free.

Nontax Benefits

In addition to tax savings, grandfather has achieved another result. He has controlled the disposition of the property to be made at his son's death. If he had given the property to his son outright, it might have been dissipated, reached by his son's creditors, or given to the son's wife when he died, with the ever-present possibility of its reaching the hands of a second husband or children of another marriage.

Powers of Appointment

If grandfather is more concerned with giving maximum flexibility to the trust than with controlling its ultimate disposition, he can give someone, the son or grandchildren, for instance, power to change or direct the flow of distribution of property without adverse tax consequences.

He confers what is called a *power of appointment*. This allows the recipient of the power to select or change the beneficiaries or their interests. So long as the person who holds the power of appointment cannot exercise it for his or his estate's benefit, the trust property will not be taxable in his estate. Grandfather could have given his son a nontaxable power by providing that the son could appoint the trust property among his children.

Suppose then that ten years after the trust was created, the family situation was such that one child needed more than the others or that one was greatly more deserving than the others. At that point, the son could bequeath that particular grandchild all the trust property or a large share of it.

Such a power of appointment gives more than mere flexibility; it also has a psychological value. It is the prerogative of grandparents to spoil their grandchildren, but no grandparent wants to destroy parental authority. The grandchild who can count on a substantial inheritance from his grandfather's trust at his father's death may flout parental control, if he chooses. But with the use of a power of appointment, the father controls the disposition of the trust and maintains his authority as head of the family.

TRUSTS WITH GRANTOR RETAINED INTERESTS

One other category of irrevocable trusts deserves mention. If you have a substantial estate these can help lower estate taxes and work especially well with assets that are growing rapidly in value. What are they? They are called trusts with grantor retained interests. They allow you to transfer assets such as securities, investment real estate, a personal residence, or art, and retain the right to receive income from or have use of the asset for a specified period of years. Your use over the period of time chosen reduces the value of the asset at the time it passes to the beneficiary you have named. Most often this is a child or grandchild.

When you create this type of irrevocable trust, you are considered to have made a gift in the present of the value that remains in the future when your use has ended. If you have, say, rapidly appreciating stock, real estate, art, or a home, this could mean a substantial reduction in your taxable estate now and in the future.

People we know who have been attracted to this technique have been single, widowed, or divorced and in need of some substitute for the marital deduction, or married with a need to further reduce their taxable estate at the second death. They had substantially large estates and were looking for astute ways to ensure that a child, grandchild, niece, or nephew for example, would receive as much of their estate as possible.

There are three types of these special trusts that can be used. The examples below will give you an idea of how to select the appropriate one.

Grantor Retained Annuity Trusts (GRATs)

This type of trust allows you to specify a fixed percentage of the value of the trust's asset that you will receive at least annually. The payout is mandatory and is based on the value of the asset when it is placed in the trust. If you specified a ten-year payout, at the end of that time the asset would pass to your named beneficiary. You would have received a fixed income for the ten years, and the value of your gift would have been reduced by the value of your ten-year income. If this was rental real estate, for example, and the property had grown half again in value over the ten years, the increased value would pass to your beneficiary free of further gift, estate, or generation-skipping taxes.

Take, for example, Mr. Widower, who lives in Arizona. He has commercial real estate rented to a major bank on a busy street in Los Angeles. He wants to travel for the next eight years, with extra income to do so. His estate is substantial in size, and although he and his wife did careful estate planning, there will still be a big estate tax bite. He adores his only grandson and wants to pass on this valuable piece of real estate to him without paying generation-skipping tax. He also wants to avoid the complexity of estate administration in two states, since everything else he owns is now in Arizona. Mr. W places the bank building in a grantor retained annuity trust (GRAT) and receives a fixed amount of income for the next eight years. The building is now worth a little over $1 million. His eight-year income stream will reduce this value substantially and keep it well under his $1 million limit for skipping a generation. This reduced value will be the value of the gift being currently made to the trust. When his grandson receives the building in eight years, any appreciation in its value will not be considered a part of the gift.

There is a catch: If Mr. W should die before the end of the eight years, the building will be pulled back into his estate and the gift would not have been completed. To guard against this possibility, Mr. W has created an irrevocable trust to purchase a life insurance policy on his life for the estate taxes that would be due.

Planning Note: Mr. W could also make the life insurance trust the beneficiary of the GRAT, further protecting his grandson from problems of his own possible divorce, death or incompetency.

Grantor Retained Unitrusts (GRUTs)

This type of retained interest trust operates in a manner similar to the annuity trust, but has a payout that is based on a fixed percentage of the net asset value of the trust determined annually. This means that the grantor's income could be greater or less in any given year.

Ms. Astute Investor has such a need. As a very successful business owner and personal investor, she has built a sizable estate over the years. She has not had time to marry and raise a family, but is very fond of her sister's college-aged son, who has shown promise in financial skills. With no husband to reduce her taxable estate with an additional estate tax exemption ($1,500,000 in 2004–5), Ms. Investor is looking for a way to ensure that she can effectively transfer her estate to her family and give a special reward to her clever nephew.

Enter her attorney with the idea of placing a portion of her investment portfolio into a grantor retained unitrust. She expects to need additional income from her investment portfolio for the next twelve years while she finishes building the value of her company for eventual sale. After that sale, she could easily afford to release some of her investments to her nephew. During that time she expects to coach him in the art of managing an investment portfolio. She has chosen to take an annual payout from her unitrust of 7 percent of its fair-market value as determined each year. Given her track record, she expects the portfolio to double in value over the next twelve years. The additional growth in value will not be considered part of her gift to her nephew. Her taxable gift will be the current value of the investments placed in the trust, reduced by the value of her projected income over the next twelve years. The value is expected to be just over $1 million, helping her to make very good use of her estate tax exemption. As with Mr. W, she has created an irrevocable trust that purchased a life insurance policy to cover possible estate taxes, just in case she does not live to the end of the twelve years.

Qualified Personal Residence Trusts (QPRTs)

With this type of trust you can remove your residence or vacation home from your taxable estate, continue to live in your home or make use of your vacation home for a period of, say, ten years, and pass it on to your beneficiary at a much reduced value for gift purposes. Again, even if the value of the property increases a great deal, your gift is the current fair market price reduced by the value of your use over the period of years you select.

Take the case of Mrs. Dynasty, who loves the family home and knows her son and his wife would love to inherit it someday. Mrs. D is concerned about the size of her estate and the taxes that will be due upon her death. She is afraid that the home may have to be sold to raise cash for taxes and wants to both reduce her estate and ensure that the home stays in the family. She decides to place her lovely home in a qualified personal residence trust (QPRT) and specify that she will live in it for the next ten years. Given her health, this seems like a good possibility. At the end of the ten years, the home will belong to her son. Her $2,000,000 home is valued for gift purposes at $1,000,000. If it grows in value over the ten years, the increase will not be considered part of her gift. If she dies before the end of the ten years, the home will be considered part of her taxable estate. Her good health makes it possible for her to create an irrevocable trust that obtains life insurance to cover the estate taxes that would be due should this occur.

QPRTs can be complex in nature and must be carefully constructed to suit your specific needs. They are not for everyone, but can enhance the estate planner's ability to accomplish a variety of personal and family goals.

ACCUMULATION TRUSTS

This is a method of setting up a trust so that the income is not paid out to a beneficiary but allowed to accumulate within the trust. The purpose is to save or shift income taxes by taking advantage of the fact that the trust is a separate tax entity. However, trust income over $9,350 (in 2004) will be taxed at the maximum 35 percent rate (see Appendix, page 367, for income tax tables).

Income received by a beneficiary from a trust is taxed to the beneficiary at his bracket. If this income is not paid out but is instead allowed to accumulate in the trust, the income will generally be taxed to the trust. But when the accumulated ordinary income is finally paid to the beneficiary, he is taxed on it under a special method designed to tax the income as if it had been paid to him in the years it was earned. He receives a credit for the taxes paid by the trust up to his computed tax liability. This is known as the throwback rule. Even though the beneficiary ultimately pays, the growth of the fund, while accumulating income at the trust's brackets, under current tax bracketing may be the same or less than it would have been had the grantor tried to build a fund at his own bracket. Should tax brackets be changed such that trusts are taxed at a bracket lower than the highest brackets for individuals, this could provide a more favorable accumulation device.

However, there is a very important exception to the throwback rule. Income accumulated while the beneficiary was under 21 or before he was born is not subject to the throwback rule. It is only taxed to the trust.

For example, a parent wants to provide for her minor child's education. When the child is young, say 7 years old (as in the case of Ms. Plan-Ahead), she takes $30,000 of securities that produce an annual income of $2,400 and places them in a term trust to last for eleven years. The income may be accumulated or paid out and, when the trust ends, the accumulations and principal will be used by the child for his college education.

On the $2,400 of income, the trust will pay a tax of $840, leaving a net return of $1,560. In Ms. Plan-Ahead's 35 percent bracket, she would have netted the same on those investments. So for now, she might be better off using a Section 529 Qualified Tuition Program where the funds can grow tax-free and be distributed tax-free if used for qualified higher education expenses, which is her intent.

For purposes other than college education, accumulation trusts can still provide a control factor; a way to accumulate funds where it is desirable to pay out income to the beneficiary periodically, but restrict his access to the principal.

LIFE INSURANCE TRUSTS

When you set up a life insurance trust, the trustees will either own the policy or be its beneficiaries, or both.

Life insurance trusts (like all trusts) can be either irrevocable or revocable.

The Irrevocable Insurance Trust

Irrevocable life insurance trusts are generally created to provide estate and income tax-free funding for the payment of estate taxes at a discount. The trust avoids estate taxes because the death benefit is not included in the settlor's estate when he dies. The death benefit proceeds are paid out on an income tax-free basis to the trust. The policy proceeds are generally far greater than the premiums paid, so funds to pay estate taxes are created at a discount to the settlor.

If a preexisting life insurance policy is assigned to the trust, any cash value it has accumulated and any subsequent premiums paid are considered gifts. To the extent they do not qualify for annual exclusions of $11,000 (in 2004, plus increases for inflation), these gifts will be added to the settlor's estate in computing his estate tax.

Irrevocable insurance trusts can also help shift income taxes if they are funded, though with trusts currently having a maximum tax rate identical to the maximum rate for individuals, this advantage will not save tax, but merely shift it to a separate entity. A funded trust is one where the trust principal consists of property in addition to the insurance. Prior to 1994, trusts had lower income tax brackets than individuals and this principal could earn greater net income after tax. Now, however, any trust income over $9,350 (in 2004) is subject to the highest bracket of 35 percent, the same highest bracket as for individuals. Placing assets in an irrevocable trust can still be done. Up to $1,500,000 (in 2004, and increasing to $3.5 million by 2009, then returning to $1,000,000 in 2011 after estate taxes are repealed for one year in 2010) per individual settlor could be used and thus remove from the taxable estate the amount exempt from estate tax during life. Of course, funding with amounts over the estate tax exemption would incur gift taxes (except in 2010).

Can a settlor achieve this income tax shifting by funding a trust of insurance on his own life? No—generally the income will be taxed to him if it is used to pay premiums on insurance on his own life. However, if an "adverse party" such as a beneficiary (or the guardian of a minor beneficiary) must consent to or approve the use of trust income to pay the premiums, then this income will not be taxed to the settlor but to the trust.

The funded insurance trust may be used in a variety of situations. A parent could use it to create an education fund for his child by the purchase of endowment insurance. By beginning an insurance program for his child at an early age, he can take advantage of the low premium rates for children. One could use a trust to finance a retirement income policy on the life insurance of a dependent relative.

Funded insurance trusts are also a means of saving estate taxes in successive generations. Grandfather wants to pass on a substantial sum of money to his grandchildren free of estate taxes on his and his child's estate.

He also wants to protect his grandchildren in case their father dies prematurely. He transfers $100,000 of securities to an insurance trust for the purchase of insurance on the life of his 30-year-old son. The grandchildren are the beneficiaries of the trust. The net income after the trust's taxes of $2,450 would buy $724,000 of insurance coverage. At their father's death, the grandchildren will have the $724,000 of insurance, plus the $100,000 of securities, a total of $824,000, tax-free.

The $100,000 in securities represents a taxable transfer (gift) by grandfather and will be added in figuring grandfather's estate taxes. It will bypass his son's estate. However, upon the son's subsequent death the $724,000 in insurance will pass to the grandchildren completely free of taxation in grandfather's or his son's estate.

Irrevocable trusts can also be unfunded (that is, not originally contain an underlying investment asset) and achieve tax advantages. One of the ways of achieving this is to fund the trust with annual gift-exclusion dollars paid by the grantor. A $10,000 annual gift exclusion (plus increases for inflation) can be taken for each beneficiary, if the trust is properly worded and certain procedures are carefully followed, allowing large amounts of money to be transferred out of the taxable estate and into the trust, and with no gift taxes incurred. To achieve this, the annual transfer of funds must be subject to a brief window of time during which beneficiaries can take out their share of the gift and use it for some other purpose. If they do not, the trust then pays the premiums and instantly provides for a tax-free death benefit that is far greater than any investment the same gifted dollars could have yielded.

The Revocable Insurance Trust

This is a very practical form of life insurance trust. While the revocable trust does not have the income and estate tax-saving advantages of the irrevocable trust, it is a more flexible device. Being revocable, it can be changed by the grantor anytime he wishes or at any time his objectives should change.

At the same time, it is an excellent instrument for making sure that his objectives *will* be carried out when he dies and his life insurance proceeds are paid into the trust. Suppose, for example, that a husband feels his wife should be protected against the risk of her lack of experience in managing money after he dies. He assures this by putting the property in trust for her, as we have seen. But unless he also puts his life insurance proceeds, which may constitute a large part of his estate, in trust, he may end up by defeating his original purpose. Hence the importance of the life insurance trust.

But what if he had the insurance payable to his estate and then provided for trust distribution under his will? Wouldn't this method accomplish the same result?

Yes, but this method lacks certain other advantages of the living insurance trust.

For example:

1. Insurance proceeds paid to a living trust are generally not subject to the claims of creditors. This is not true when they are paid to the estate.
2. In many states insurance proceeds payable to a living trust are exempt in whole or part from state inheritance taxes. This may not apply to proceeds that go to the estate.
3. Insurance proceeds in a living trust are not part of the probate estate, hence not subject to administrative costs. Not so when the *estate* is the beneficiary.
4. The living insurance trust has the advantage of immediate liquidity. Insurance paid to an *estate* is subject to the delays and costs of probate. The trustee of a living trust presents his proofs of death to the insurance companies, collects the proceeds, and begins the administration of the trust.

In some states insurance paid to a testamentary trust will enjoy some of the advantages the living trust enjoys.

Insurance Owned by the Wife. The revocable insurance trust can take care of another common problem. What happens when a wife has been made the owner of insurance policies on her husband's life in order to prevent their proceeds from being included in the husband's estate? How can trust protection be gained for her then?

Enter the revocable living trust again. Here the wife and not the husband creates it, and all the same advantages pertain. Such trusts are made revocable only during the insured's life. Once he dies, the trust becomes irrevocable and the wife is thus protected for its duration.

A word of warning here, however. If the wife makes the policy on her husband's life payable to a person other than herself (the trustee is such a person), even if she is the income beneficiary of the trust, she makes a gift of a part of the proceeds of the policy when it is paid. This gift is subject to the gift tax. To avoid this, she should retain the right to the income of the trust and a power of appointment to provide for the distribution of the remainder of the trust when she dies. This prevents the gift from being completed, and hence avoids the payment of gift taxes. The trust principal remains subject to estate taxes in her estate, however.

Pouring Over. A final word on revocable insurance trusts. They *can* be used as the basic after-death transfer instrument, a depository for most of the estate assets. In most states an estate owner who wishes to do this can provide in his will that all his probate property on his death be "poured over" into the trust. The trust then carries out all his estate-transfer objectives. The will becomes merely a subsidiary vehicle for bringing all his property together in the living trust. It is possible to do this, of course, with any kind of living trust, but at times it is the life insurance trust that is used as the receptacle for the pour-over.

The Contingent Insurance Trust

A common problem in estate planning is what to do with insurance that a husband owns on his own life if his wife dies before him, or if they die in a common disaster. His wife is the beneficiary of the insurance and he wants her to receive it outright, if she survives. But what does he do about his minor children if she doesn't survive? Normally they are named as contingent beneficiaries. Lump sum payout to them is not advisable. There are settlement options available under his policies, but rarely can they approach the flexibility of a trust.

What he needs is a trust that will receive the insurance proceeds if his wife doesn't survive him. In other words, a contingent insurance trust to handle the proceeds on behalf of his children.

THE SMALL TRUST

Many people have the mistaken idea that trusts should be limited to use by large taxpayers and large estates. This isn't necessarily true. The advantages to be gained from a trust still exist for the smaller estate, although perhaps reduced proportionately. There will be initial costs in the creation of the trust and the transfer of securities or other property, yes. But if the long-range benefits are important enough, and cannot be attained in any other way, then the costs are worthwhile.

What about finding trustees? And the problem of commissions?

Often relatives or friends will serve without commission. And while corporate trustees generally will not take the administration of small trusts, they will undertake them when they can be combined into a common trust fund. Under a common trust fund, the bank administers a group of trusts as one fund. This keeps down the costs of administration and permits the bank to charge standard commissions.

PROTECTING YOUR BENEFICIARIES

Up to this point we have been talking about trusts as if they were primarily tax-saving devices. In the long run this aspect, important as it is, is only a subordinate one. The true importance, and the chief reason, for setting up trusts is to transfer property in such a way that it will be most useful for one's beneficiaries. The trust, both living and testamentary, often does this better than the outright gift or bequest for two reasons. First, it can be made as flexible or as rigid as the grantor wants to make it. A well-planned trust is able to take care of the needs of each beneficiary according to his station in life, his age, and his abilities.

Second, there is the unique function of the trustee: someone who, in effect, carries on for the estate planner, protecting his family and meeting their needs, acting as he would, in accordance with the changing conditions and situations that arise. This makes the trust a unique instrument of protection.

The Spouse

Many spouses feel insulted or hurt if their husbands or wives leave property in trust for them. The spouse may feel that it shows a lack of confidence or faith in them. If he has not had previous experience, however, he may not be prepared to handle large sums of money. If this is true, he himself would not want to be burdened with administration of the property. Or perhaps he may be capable but not interested. Perhaps he's too busy with his career to have time for financial matters. The ability is there but not the inclination. In this case, too, outright gifts could be a burden to him.

Beyond all this, a trust acts as a buffer against the demands and pressures that a widow or widower is frequently subjected to. When one comes into substantial property, it is difficult to resist requests for loans or gifts—especially when they come from relatives; more especially, from one's own children. We know of one widow who was left $300,000 outright. She lent $100,000 to one son, then felt guilty toward her other son. When he demanded a similar loan to buy a house, she lent him an equal amount. The sons realize their obligations; they both pay interest on their loans, but just the same she is left with only $100,000 of ready cash available. If she needed the money in an emergency, or if they stopped paying the interest, what could she do about it? She would have been happier if the money had been put in trust for her.

We're not saying that all bequests or gifts to spouses should be made in trust. In many couples both have the ability and the willingness to handle property and end up with the survivor doing a better job of it than their spouses did. Such a person has no need of a trust. We are saying, however, that a trust implies no lack of faith, or even a desire to restrict a person's freedom. Its purpose is protection.

The Children

Here is certainly an instance where the elasticity of the trust device comes into play. It can be used to cover all kinds of situations that require special handling. Obviously, minor or incompetent children need the protection of a trust. It obviates the necessity for a guardian of property (for the minor) or a conservator (for an incompetent), and at the same time it permits greater flexibility in the management of the beneficiaries' property.

As we have said, a trust can be used to protect irresponsible adult children against themselves. If you do have such a child—one who simply cannot handle money in any way except to spend it—you might consider setting up a "spendthrift trust." This prevents the beneficiary from assigning or selling his interest in the trust and places it beyond the reach of his creditors. The very existence of organizations that specialize in buying trust and estate interests for as little as 15 or 20 percent of their potential value testifies to the need for this kind of trust provision.

Trusts that have "spendthrift" provisions usually provide that the trustees, instead of giving the beneficiary large sums outright, are free to use the money in his behalf as they see best and exercise their own discretion. For example, a trustee could pay the person's rent and provide him with the necessities of life, but otherwise conserve his money for him.

On the other hand, your adult child (or other young beneficiary) may be unpredictable at this juncture. There is no way of knowing if he will eventually be able to handle his property wisely, but you don't want to restrict him forever with a rigid trust. The answer might be to set up an "incentive trust." For example, the amount of income payable to him could be gauged to his own earned income. Or payments of principal could be conditioned on a minimum amount of earned income over a specified period.

In many families the problem is not with the children, but with their spouses. A donor may be worried about the possible effect of a large gift of property on a child; they too may be subject to pressures from their spouses. He wants to protect his child against this, to make sure that the property his child receives from him will remain within the family, and not go ultimately to the child's spouse. The trust is again the solution. He can use it to assure final distribution to grandchildren or other members of the family or to carry out some other family purpose.

A Special Device: The Sprinkling Trust

But suppose you have no way of knowing precisely what your family's future needs may be. After all, no one is omniscient. Who can tell whether there might not come a time when one beneficiary will need an extra amount of money, another time when his share should be less? There may be special types of events you want to provide for, such as a wedding, a down payment on a first home, or funds for other milestones that can enhance the lives of your heirs without detracting from their own senses of purpose and achievement.

Enter the trustee. You can give him the power to use his discretion in such instances by setting up a trust which allows him to "sprinkle" or "spray" income among a group of beneficiaries. Not only does this give the trust flexibility, it can also aid in keeping family tax costs at a minimum.

Suppose, for example, that a grandmother creates a trust with the income payable to her children and grandchildren in such amounts as "the trustee may determine." Some years later, the settlor's oldest grandchild enters law school. It will take about $33,000 per year to pay for his higher education. If his father called on the trust for help, he would have to receive about $44,550 from the trust in order to pay the $33,000 fee, since he is in a 35 percent bracket. But because the trustee has sprinkling powers, he can pay the money to the grandchild instead. Then he need take only about $36,300 of the trust fund's "distributable net income" to produce the $33,000 at the grandchild's 10 percent bracket.

GUARANTEEING PRIVACY

All of the above applies to both living and testamentary trusts. But the living trust also provides another protection for the settlor and beneficiaries: it guarantees privacy. Mr. Disappointed Father, if you recall, wanted to cut one son out of his will but shrank from the idea because of the publicity the will would engender. Not everyone has such exotic problems, but no one likes to have his dirty linen washed in public. A living trust ensures this won't happen. It is a personal agreement between the settlor and his trustee. It is not a matter of public record as the will is, because it doesn't have to go through the courts.

Mr. Disappointed Father, for example, could set up a living trust that contains almost all his property. Three of his children would be the beneficiaries of the trust; the trust property would pass to them at his death. His will, however, could leave all his remaining property (of which there would be little left) to his four children equally. As far as the outside world would know, he had treated all four children equally.

PREVIEWING THE AFTER-DEATH ESTATE

The living trust has one final advantage. When it is created consciously as the after-death transfer plan, there is a unique opportunity to give the entire estate-transfer program a dress rehearsal. The planner can work with the trustees to acquaint them with the problems and duties he wants them to assume. He can familiarize his family with the trustee. He has ample opportunity to see how his plan will work while he is still alive. He may be able to correct weaknesses or oversights before it is too late. In his estate plan he gets what most people want but few ever get: a second chance.

CHAPTER 15

WHY EVERYONE NEEDS A WILL

Everyone?

With the popularity of revocable living trusts as a means for transferring an estate, there may be a tendency to think that having a will is no longer necessary. The truth is that even if you have such a trust, at least a "pour-over will" is needed to direct certain assets not reregistered in the name of the trust. These would be assets that you do not wish subjected to probate and want funneled into the trust upon death, in order that they are distributed according to the terms you have specified.

Let's examine for a moment a reason why an estate owner may want to use a will rather than a living trust as an estate transfer vehicle. There may be a need for creditor protection for the beneficiaries of your estate, such as for certain high-risk professions or businesses, since creditors are given notice and a finite opportunity to make their claims against your estate. Once the deadline for their claims has been exceeded, your beneficiaries can receive your assets free and clear.

But what about the young person whose estate consists primarily of a few stocks and bonds, a little insurance, and a house that isn't paid for? What good would a will do his family? Surely his spouse is bound to inherit everything, including the debts.

Or the husband and wife who own everything jointly? What's the point of a will in this case? The survivor gets everything, doesn't he?

And the wife who owns little or no property in her own name? Does she need a will if she has nothing to pass on?

The truth is, they all do. The wife of the young man with the "small estate" is not going to get it all; state laws provide that children or relatives are entitled to a portion. Death in a common disaster may upset the plans of the couple with joint property. The wife with "nothing" forgets that someday she may inherit property from her husband and that wills not only dispose of property, but also provide for the guardianship of children.

By means of a will, a person exercises his legal right to express his postmortem objectives: to provide for the welfare of his family, to distribute his assets as he thinks best, and to secure the efficient management of his property. Implicit in these rights also is an opportunity—the opportunity to save taxes by means of a well-drawn will that takes advantage of available tax shelters.

For the estate planner who does not make lifetime transfers, his will is his entire property transference program. It is the sole expression of his intentions and the only way he has of carrying out his ultimate objectives. Without a will these objectives will not be met. Without a properly designed will the desired results will not be achieved.

The underlying aspect of a will, then, is the maker's *intention*. Though the planner's attorney draws the will, it is the planner who must determine what he wants his will to do. He is, after all, the only one who knows his family needs and how he would like to see them met.

If the planner does not use his right to make a will, the law will step in and make one for him—but the results may be quite different from what he had envisioned.

THE STATE OF INTESTACY

If a person dies without leaving a will, we say he died *intestate*. The law takes over and directs how his property will be distributed; in effect, writing the will *he* failed to make. The law's writing is as fair and equitable as possible; the major trouble is that it is done blindly.

It is based on general principles regarding the disposition of property; general principles for the guardianship of children; general principles as to the rights of relatives; and general principles as to who shall manage the estate. It is therefore impersonal and by necessity rarely coincides with the particular interests and objectives of the individual who has died.

The law in question is the law of the state in which he had his domicile and the state where his real property was located. It varies from state to state but there are certain general patterns of distribution in all intestacy laws.

If you die without a will, what happens?

Your Spouse's Share of Your Estate May Be Smaller Than You Intended

Many people think that a husband or wife automatically inherits everything when the other spouse dies. This is not always so, though it may be in some community-property states. Depending on the state in which you live, your spouse will be entitled to from one-third to one-half of your estate. In some states, the widow's share is equal to a child's share. What she gets depends on the number of children. If there are five children, the widow only gets one-sixth. For example, the wife of a man with a net estate of $300,000 who had five children would get only $50,000. Is this what her husband would have wanted?

When the average married individual disposes of his or her property, their chief aim is usually to ensure the protection of their surviving spouse. But the laws of intestacy may run counter to that concept. When they prevail, say, as in the example above, a widow may not have enough to support herself; she may become dependent on her children. While the estate owner is alive his wife enjoys a standard of living that matches her husband's $300,000 estate. After his death she can't live on the income from her $50,000 capital. How long will the income and principal last when she has to dip into this fund year after year to meet her financial needs?

Moreover, she is restricted in her freedom to use her minor children's inheritance to provide and care for them as she thinks best. This means that the children can also suffer from their father's intestacy.

The hardship may be greater if the estate is a small one. The young father who doesn't make a will because he hasn't much to leave is a husband and parent who is not facing up to the problems his surviving family will have. His wife will need the entire estate to support herself and the children. If he were to leave an estate of $75,000, he would probably want her to have it all and not just one-third, for example. In the absence of a will, his widow, in some states, would get only $25,000.

The balance of $50,000 would go to his children, but his wife would not have free use of it.

But what if there are no children? Many childless couples assume that each will automatically inherit everything from the other in the absence of a will. They should be aware of the fact that under the intestate distribution laws of many states, the survivor shares the estate with the deceased spouse's parents or brothers and sisters, or even nieces and nephews. The results are sometimes appalling. The bottom line: know the intestacy laws of the state in which you live. Your attorney will be able to assist you with this.

Children Get Equal Treatment

Except for what goes to the surviving husband or wife, the children will be treated alike. If there is no surviving husband or wife, they share the entire estate to the exclusion of all other relatives. Children of a deceased child inherit the share their parent would have taken.

This equal treatment may be equitable when a fixed standard has to be set, but it cannot and does not take into consideration the needs and desires of the individual child. One child may be disabled and entirely dependent on his parents, but his share will be the same as his healthy brother's. One daughter may have cared for her parents through illness and old age, but she will receive no more than her sister who had deserted the family.

Inheritance by Minors Will Be Affected

If you do have children and they are minors you have even greater need for a will. Property that minors inherit belongs to them, but its use is restricted until they reach their majority. An outright inheritance by a minor, as occurs in an intestacy, results in the need for appointment of a guardian to deal with the minor's property. This involves the trouble and expense of a bond for the guardian, periodic accountings by him, and judicial proceedings for authorization to act or for approval of acts already performed. The mother who has been appointed guardian of her children by the court may be indignant to discover that in order to use their funds for tuition, she must bring a court proceeding for authorization. She may, as their mother, know best, but as their guardian she is subject to judicial supervision.

Sometimes a guardian of the person of the minor (as distinguished from the property of the minor) must also be appointed. A parent, as a child's natural guardian, has the primary right to both these appointments. However, if the surviving parent is unfit to be guardian or dies before the child reaches adulthood, someone else has to be selected.

In one celebrated family, a father of considerable wealth died. His estate passed one-half to his wife and one-half to their two-year-old child. A court proceeding was brought for her appointment as guardian of the person and property of her child. A few years later she died in an auto accident. Another proceeding was necessary in order to have her executor account to the court for her acts as guardian and to have a new guardian appointed. Each grandmother sought the appointment to the exclusion of the other, and a bitter fight ensued. The issue was finally resolved by their appointment as co-guardians, but the dissension remains to this day.

Expenses Will Be Greater

The cost of administering an estate may be greater when there is no will. The administrator of an intestate estate must furnish a bond in most states. The bond protects the beneficiaries and creditors of the estate, but the cost of the premiums must be paid either out of the estate or out of the administrator's fees.

The administrator is also limited in his actions by the laws of the jurisdiction in which he is appointed. In order for him to sell property, compromise claims, or distribute the estate, he may need judicial authorization. The cost of each proceeding for authorization or approval is paid out of the estate.

The Administrator Is Not a Free Agent

The limitations set upon the administrator are again for the purpose of protection—in this case, protection of the estate. But, in fact, they can be a hindrance to sound management. For example, administrators may be restricted to specified percentages and types of investments. The estate may consist solely of high-grade common stock, but if the law of the state does not permit full investment in common stock, the administrator must sell some of it or risk personal liability. If the asset that must be disposed of is a business, people other than the members of the family may also suffer.

An unfortunate case was brought to us by the surviving partner of a growing business. He and his late partner, whom we shall call Joe, started the business on a combined capital of $10,000 and had built it into a successful enterprise. When Joe died, he left a wife and three young children but no will. His wife inherited one-third and his children two-thirds. The attorney for the estate had informed the surviving partner that, by law, he had to liquidate the assets of the partnership and pay Joe's share to the estate. He didn't believe it. We could only confirm the fact that liquidation was required by existing partnership law.

Although provision could have been made for continuation of the business (such as having a buy-sell agreement funded with life insurance on each partner), this hadn't been done. Since Joe's children were minors, they could not agree to continuation. The liquidation meant an economic loss to all involved. As a going business it had provided each partner with a minimum income of $50,000 a year. The operating value, of course, would not be realized on liquidation.

The Law Picks Your Administrator

The law—and not you—selects the administrator of your estate if you die without a will. As a general rule this means that the surviving husband or wife has the first right to be appointed. But is this always desirable? How about the man whose wife gets one-third and whose children by an earlier marriage get two-thirds of the estate? Would the husband—even if he were to agree to this disposition—want the wife to administer it? It would hardly make for family harmony.

If the surviving spouse doesn't want to be the administrator or if there is no surviving spouse, what happens then?

The general rule is that the children have an equal right to be appointed. But would all parents of all children want this, supposing there was an irresponsible or spendthrift child?

Sometimes the court will appoint all of the children jointly. We know of one case in which this happened. The children (there were four of them) had never liked each other, never got along together. Now they carried their jealousies, their bitterness, and their petty quarreling over into the administration of their father's estate. Every step taken, large or small, meant a family quarrel resulting in the inefficient and costly administration of the estate.

There May Be Unnecessary Taxes

Intestacy is the opposite of planning. It means leaving things to chance—
the chance of what the law will be in the state in which you are living at
the time of your death; the chance as to who will survive you. It may cost
your estate unnecessary taxes because your spouse receives less than the
full amount she could have been given tax-free. If your spouse receives
more than the amount needed to eliminate tax on your estate, the excess
amount may be needlessly taxed in her estate.

If your parents turn out to be your heirs, they may not welcome an
addition to their own estate that causes an increase on their estate taxes.
The child with a substantial income of his own may realize only a small
net return on his inherited property after the bite of income taxes. Instead
of savings there is waste.

Tax savings is a prime ingredient of estate planning. As we will see in
the following chapters, the carefully planned estate can minimize losses
from unnecessary taxes, both income and estate, simply by taking advantage of existing laws. But little can usually be accomplished toward this
end without the aid of a will.

With a Will There's a Way

So much for intestacy. Let's look at the other side of the picture, and examine some of the advantages to be gained through a will.

A will is a plan or a design for the distribution of property. It is custom-
made, created by one individual for the benefit of his family. That is its
great advantage. With a will you can:

Choose Your Beneficiaries

Instead of letting the law select the people who will share your estate and
determine their respective shares, you can choose those upon whom you
wish to confer your bounty. Take the situation of the widow who received
only one-sixth of her husband's $300,000 estate—the income of which
was not enough to support her. By means of a will, her husband could
have left her a larger share of the estate and could have made provisions
for a trust for the rest. This would give her sufficient income for a continuing comfortable support.

Only by means of a will can a parent provide for the special financial security of a dependent, disabled child or compensate the worthy child in preference to the undeserving.

What's more, the person with a will can determine not only *who* his beneficiaries will be, but *how* and *when* they will receive this inheritance. If he wants, for example, to leave his spouse's share in trust, he can do this through his will. If he wants one person to have the use of the property for a certain period of time, and then to have another succeed him, this can best be done through his will.

Leave Property to Minors the Better Way

If minors are to receive property it should be set up so that it can be most efficiently and economically administered for them. The trouble with their inheriting property by intestacy is that they become outright owners. The fact that they are underage limits their ability to deal with their property and requires that it be handled by a guardian in their behalf.

A will can dispense with the need for a guardian of the minor's property, and the bond, accountings, and judicial supervision that accompany it. If a guardian of the minor's person is needed, he, too, can be designated in the will.

Take the case of the struggle between the two grandmothers we cited before. A will could have prevented family friction as well as needless expense. If the father had left the child's share in trust, the trustee could have managed the property for the minor without the need for a guardian of the property. The mother or any other person could have been designated as trustee and a successor named in the event of her death or resignation. Furthermore, to ensure continuous management, uninterrupted by possible death, a trust company could have been selected as trustee or cotrustee.

Save Administration Expenses

A person who makes a will can generally dispense with bonds for his executor and trustee. In an estate of some size, the savings may be thousands of dollars. In a small estate, even the few hundred dollars saved is meaningful. By giving your managers broad power to deal with the property, you may enable them to administer the estate without having to resort to court proceedings for authorization and approval. One sentence in a will, for example, giving the executor power to sell real estate can save the costs of a proceeding for judicial approval of such a sale.

Set Your Own Rules for Managing Your Estate

Again, with some limitation the person who makes a will can make his own rules. He can confer extensive powers on his executor or trustee in the administration of the estate or trusts. On the other hand, he may want them to have more restricted powers than the law would otherwise allow. In any event, the powers that he gives them should enable them to deal effectively with property he leaves. They should be flexible enough to permit changes as the needs of the surviving family and economic conditions change.

A partner in a business, such as Joe, should give his executor and trustee power to allow the business to continue and permit the estate to participate as a partner. The executor is in that way free to choose his course of action in the light of the best interests of Joe's family and the economic conditions then prevailing.

Choose Your Own Managers

The person you name in your will to administer the estate is your executor or executrix. The one designated to manage the trusts is your trustee. The court will accept the person (or persons) nominated by the testator unless he is a felon or lunatic. Some states have restrictions on the appointment of nonresidents.

One member of the family may be designated by the testator to the exclusion of all others. Coexecutors or cotrustees might be advisable for soundest management or family harmony. The person with an irresponsible beneficiary can prevent him from running the estate. The person with an irresponsible family can put the estate into the hands of competent, reliable outsiders.

WOMEN AND WILLS

The number of male intestacies may be great, but it is surpassed by the female intestacies. Unless they possess wealth of their own, many women just don't think about making a will, and often their husbands don't either.

A will can solve situations where the husband already has a large estate, which will be subject to high estate taxation at his death, and doesn't want to inherit additional property from his wife. Better for her to leave it directly to the children or grandchildren.

This problem crops up most frequently in families where the wife owns insurance policies on her husband's life. He has transferred them to her in order to keep the proceeds from being included in his taxable estate. But if she dies without a will, he could find himself the owner of the policies. This can be avoided by having her will transfer the policies to the next generation. When the husband dies, the proceeds go tax-free to the children (or to a trust for them).

As the possessor—potential or actual—of property, then, a woman, just as her husband, has the problem of disposing of this property in the most effective manner.

For women who are also mothers, the responsibility is especially strong. If there are minor children, the necessity for their property being left in trust and for making provisions for guardianship is doubly important. A husband's will may provide all this, it is true, but ordinarily his will would pass all or most of his estate to the wife if she survives him.

If she dies without a will, then the original plan for the distribution of the entire estate is defeated. The property that she has received from her husband will go outright to the children and not have the trust protection they require. In addition, her opportunity to nominate a guardian of her choice for them will be lost.

Can't she wait to do all this until she is a widow? This is playing with fire. There is no assurance that if she neglects it now, she won't neglect it then. Nor does she have any sure way of knowing that she might not become incompetent to make a will. Moreover, the threat of death by common disaster (husband and wife both dying in an accident, such as a plane or automobile crash) is always present, particularly in today's world. If it can be established that he died before her (even minutes or seconds before her), then she is the survivor—a survivor who may have died intestate, with all that that implies.

WILLS AND JOINT PROPERTY

What happens to joint property when both owners die simultaneously? Many people mistakenly think that if all their property is jointly owned with their spouse, there is no need for them to make a will; the survivor will take it all. This holds true, but not in a case of simultaneous death, as in a common disaster. If there are no wills, the joint property is divided in half and each half distributed according to the laws of intestacy. Is this what the husband and wife wanted? If not, a will could have provided for this situation and disposed of their property as they wished.

BEWARE OF JOINT AND MUTUAL WILLS

A joint will is *one* instrument executed by two people as their respective wills. Mutual wills are separate instruments executed by two people as their respective wills, but the wills are similar or reciprocal. Husbands and wives execute joint and mutual wills in the mistaken belief that it makes things simpler. Or they believe that they guarantee that the survivor ultimately has to dispose of the property as the first to die would have wished. They want to be sure where the property will go after the deaths of both of them.

A joint will—one document executed by both—doesn't simplify matters. It should be avoided if for no other reason than the fact that the probate on the death of the survivor is needlessly complicated—particularly if the survivor dies in a state other than the one in which the will was first probated. The simplest method is by separate wills.

Both joint and mutual wills are ambiguous things. Take the question of whether the survivor has the right to make a new will. Sometimes the courts have held that if there is no agreement not to revoke, the survivor is free to go ahead and dispose of the property as he or she chooses. On the other hand, sometimes the mere making of a joint or mutual will has been found to imply sufficient agreement not to revoke. Then the provisions are binding on the survivor whether or not they are intended to be.

Thus, if you do decide to make a joint or mutual will, you should be sure to spell out your agreement, whether it is to allow revocation or to prohibit it.

Moreover, you should not make agreements not to revoke without the fullest consideration of the pros and cons. The husband who is convinced that after his death his wife will give his property to a second husband, or the wife who fears the same thing in reverse, can both achieve their objective through other means—a trust, say, or an annuity. Moreover, even if the will is irrevocable, the survivor might be able to circumvent or violate the agreement by using up the property, wasting it, or giving it away.

If both have faith and confidence in each other, then tying the survivor's hands is certainly unwise. Circumstances may change radically after one of them dies, and call for a different disposition. The survivor, however, would be powerless to make it.

And finally, joint and mutual wills can be invitations to litigation. If the survivor rightfully or wrongfully makes a new will, the stage is set for a court battle between the beneficiaries of the old will and the beneficiaries of the new.

The bottom line: A living trust with husband and wife as settlors and cotrustees would likely handle the intentions that would be put forth in a joint or mutual will.

DON'T PROCRASTINATE

Intestacy seems to be a universal failing. The person who doesn't make a will is in illustrious company; Abraham Lincoln, to name one famous instance. No doubt the millions of people who followed in his footsteps and died without a will never meant this to happen. They were procrastinators. They meant to make one sometime soon, maybe not tomorrow, but soon.

But a will should not be put off like this. There may not be time to do the job later. Or conditions may change, and the prospective testator become incompetent to make a will. The will should be made now—as if death were imminent—to cover present needs and foreseeable future ones. It can always be changed. A will is ambulatory. It has no effect until death. When a situation alters, it can be altered. But if it is not made now, it may never be. That is the point.

CHAPTER 16

AN OUNCE OF PREVENTION:

MEETING THE PROBLEM OF

TAX EROSION

In the course of estate planning, it may sometimes seem to the planner that the primary beneficiary of his estate is the Internal Revenue Service. A feeling of frustration develops. One elderly lady, on being informed of the estimated amount of estate taxes her executors would have to pay, indignantly said, "If the taxes will be *that* much, I'd rather not go."

If death and taxes are inevitable, unnecessary tax erosion is not. Unnecessary tax erosion is the wasting of estate assets through the payment of taxes which, with proper planning, could have been avoided. The prevention of tax erosion, or, in other words, tax savings, is an essential element of estate transference.

At the risk of being repetitious, let us emphasize again that the purpose of estate planning, whether it be in the creation or the transference stage, is not tax savings. The purpose is security for the family. Planning that keeps taxes at a minimum, leaving as much as possible for the family, helps to achieve that goal. Tax savings, then, is not an end in itself but a means.

Even if a planner doesn't care about tax savings (although we have yet to meet one who didn't), he must know what the tax on his estate will be in order to determine how much he will actually be leaving to his beneficiaries. His gross estate and his estate after taxes may be two very different things. He must work with the net figure if he wants to have a true picture of what he is actually transferring.

Even with the current schedule of diminishing of estate taxes and their repeal in 2010, they are due to return in 2011. From a planning point of view, it makes sense to plan on their existence as an ongoing factor, since none of us is very good at predicting the time of our demise, nor the future of tax law changes.

WHAT ARE THE TAXES?

In tax planning, various taxes come into play. The major one is, of course, the federal estate tax. Other death taxes must not be overlooked, however. The state in which you live at the time of death will impose a tax, which may be called an "estate" or "inheritance" or "succession" tax. Real property located in another state may also be taxed by that state. Property in a foreign country, even stock of a foreign corporation, may be subjected to death duties of that country.

The variations among these state and foreign taxes are so great that it is not feasible to discuss them here. As a rule, state taxes are small in comparison with the federal estate tax, and they may be allowed in part or wholly as a credit against the federal tax. They should be considered, however, in any final calculations.

Proper planning also calls for consideration of income taxes, that is, the taxes the beneficiaries will have to pay on the income from the property they receive from your estate (when added to their other taxable income). Any nonspouse will also owe ordinary income tax on the entire value of any qualified retirement accounts you leave to them as beneficiaries. The ultimate figure that determines whether your sought-after objective, family security, has been achieved is, in the end, the net income your beneficiaries will have after the payment of all taxes.

WHAT THE ESTATE TAX TAXES

The federal estate tax is a tax on the transfer of property at death. The tax is imposed on the "taxable estate." Since the taxable estate is arrived at by calculating the gross estate and subtracting from it the allowable deductions and exemptions, your first step is to determine what will be included in your gross estate.

A person normally considers the property he owns, or the property that will pass under his will or living trust, as being the assets of his estate—the stocks, bonds, real estate, business interests, cash, and personal effects which he thinks of as his. However, his gross estate for tax purposes may include other property—property he owns together with someone else, property he once owned, and even property he never owned.

Here are some items that a planner may not know are includable in this gross estate for tax purposes, or items that can be easily overlooked.

1. *Gifts Made at Any Time Under Any of These Circumstances.*

    If you retain the right to the income or a power to designate who shall enjoy the income, or

    If possession or enjoyment of the property can only be obtained by the beneficiary if he survives the donor and there is a possibility that the property may return to the donor or his estate, or

    If you have retained a right to change the beneficial enjoyment of the property by a power to alter, amend or revoke that right.

2. *Transfers Made Within Three Years of Death.* Gifts of property made within three years of death are generally no longer includable in the gross estate, with the major exception of life insurance. In addition, if the decedent set up a trust or similar arrangement but retained a life estate or power to revoke or which didn't become effective until his death and he released his rights in the property within three years of his death, the property is taxable as part of his estate. The same rule applies if he released a general power of appointment (see page 297) within that time.

3. *Annuities.* The value of an annuity payable to a survivor is includable to the extent of the contributions made to it by you or your employer.

4. *Jointly Held Property.* Each spouse is treated as owning half of the property in their joint name, so only 50 percent of the value of the property will be included in the estate of the first spouse to die. The total value of property held jointly by you and another person or persons with right of survivorship will be included in the gross estate of whoever dies first. There are two

exceptions. If the survivor can prove he contributed to the purchase price, then the part represented by his contribution will be excluded. If the property was received from a third party by inheritance or by gift, then the survivor's percentage of interest in the property is not included.

5. *Insurance on Your Life.* Its death benefit will be includable in your gross estate if it is payable to your estate or if it is payable to other beneficiaries and you had any incidents of ownership in the policy. Incidents of ownership may be something less than what one commonly thinks of as ownership. They may be the right to change the beneficiary, to surrender or cancel the policy, to assign or pledge it, or to borrow against the cash surrender value.

6. *Insurance on Another's Life.* This is an asset like a stock or bond or any other piece of property, but it is frequently overlooked. It includes business owners who have a cross-purchase buy-sell agreement and own life insurance on each other. Generally speaking, the amount of the cash surrender value of the policy will be included in your gross estate.

7. *Income Payable After Death.* At the time of death there is generally some income that has been earned by the decedent and will be paid to his estate or beneficiaries. It may be salary, commissions, royalties, or a share of partnership income. While it is sometimes difficult to forecast what unpaid salary or uncollected fees will be due at the time of death, there are income items that can be estimated. These include renewal commissions, installment payments under a contract or other agreement, and employment benefits paid under a nonqualified plan.

8. *Power of Appointment.* Strange as it may seem, property that you never owned may be included in your gross estate. This will happen if you are given a general power over property—that is, a right to designate who the property will go to including yourself, your estate, your creditors, or the creditors of your estate. If the power was created after October 21, 1942, the property will be included in your gross estate whether or not you exercise the power. If it was created on or before that date, however, it will be included only if you exercise it.

9. *Distributions from Pension and Profit-Sharing Plans.* Such distributions are fully taxable for estate tax purposes.

While the following items are not truly part of your gross estate, they will enter into how the tax on your estate will be computed.

10. *Taxable Transfer Made After December 31, 1976.* Post-1976 gifts that exceeded the annual exclusions, other than gifts that qualified for the marital or charitable deductions, are taxable transfers and are added to your taxable estate. However, you may have a credit for gift taxes you paid (the unified credit).

11. *Generation-Skipping Trusts.* If someone a generation older than you established a trust for your benefit by will or trust agreement, and such trust eventually passes to beneficiaries a generation younger than yourself (i.e., children, nieces, or nephews), the trust might be taxed as though its assets were added to your taxable estate (see generation-skipping taxation on page 245).

12. *Half of Community Property Interests.* If you live in a community property state, your half of the assets are included in your taxable estate.

13. *Assets Transferred under the Uniform Gifts to Minors or Uniform Transfer to Minors Act.* If you die while still the custodian of assets you yourself transferred to a minor, those assets are deemed to be includable in your gross estate.

14. *Cumulative but Unpaid Distributions on Retained Interest in Corporations or Partnerships.*

15. *The Lapse of Certain Voting or Liquidation Rights in a Corporation or Partnership.*

DEDUCTIONS

Expenses and Debts

Once having arrived at the gross estate, the next step is to determine your deductions. The costs of your funeral and the expenses involved in the administration of your estate, such as executors' commissions and attorneys' fees, are deducted from the gross estate.

These generally average from 5 to 10 percent of the gross estate, depending on the size of the estate, the commissions allowed by the particular state to your fiduciaries, and the problems which may arise in connection with the probate or administration of your estate. A will contest or tax litigation can run up the cost considerably. To have a figure to work with, we recommend taking 7½ percent of your estate as your estimated administrative expenses.

In addition, your debts, whether it be the mortgage on your home, unpaid taxes, or an electric bill, should be deducted.

When expenses and debts have been subtracted from the gross estate, the figure arrived at is the adjusted gross estate. Next comes the most valuable deduction of all—the marital deduction.

The Marital Deduction

Under the unlimited marital deduction, any property left by a husband or wife to his or her spouse that qualifies for the marital deduction passes tax-free. Before 1982, the maximum marital deduction was limited to 50 percent of the adjusted gross estate or $250,000, whichever was greater. In the Economic Recovery Tax Act of 1981, Congress decided that a married couple should be treated as one economic unit and to permit them to postpone the taxation of their estates till the death of the survivor. By deferring any tax until the second death, the family has the use of the money that would otherwise have been paid out in taxes for producing additional income during the life of the survivor. That is why the marital deduction is easily the most valuable tool available for alleviating estate tax erosion.

How to Qualify Property for It. This deduction isn't an automatic one. It is allowed only for property that does actually pass to the surviving spouse under conditions that make it includable to her taxable estate when she dies, if she still has it. Knowing which kinds of property transfers qualify for marital deduction is critical, so as not to lose its great benefits.

Property that qualifies for the marital deduction includes property passing outside your will as well as under your will so long as it is includable in your gross estate. Insurance proceeds payable to your spouse that are part of your gross estate will qualify. So, too, does the half of the joint property that she takes by right of survivorship and that is includable in your gross estate. In community-property states she receives her husband's half of the community property. Both halves of the community property then have a new cost basis at current fair market value.

Property given to her in trust can also qualify, provided the trust provisions meet specific requirements set down by tax law. For a gift in trust to qualify, the principal of the trust must pass to her estate at her death (an estate trust) *or* she must receive all of the income of the trust (a quali-fied terminable interest trust).

The estate trust is useful for large estates or when the surviving spouse has large income from other sources. The estate trust, unlike the qualified terminable interest trust, does not require that all of the income be paid to the survivor. It can either be accumulated in the trust or paid to the survivor at the discretion of the trustees. As a result, the trust income is not piled on top of other taxable income and thereby taxed away. Income being retained in the trust is taxable to it. The only requirement is that to qualify the trust for a marital deduction, the principal and accu-mulated income must pass to the survivor's estate at his or her death and be subject to distribution as part of the estate.

With a qualified terminable interest property trust, popularly known as a "QTIP trust," not only must the surviving spouse be entitled to all the income, but no one can have a right to direct the use of income or principal for anyone other than the surviving spouse during his or her lifetime. A provision, for example, permitting the trustees to use the prin-cipal for the support of someone else would disqualify the trust for the marital deduction.

On the survivor's death the property can pass to the beneficiaries des-ignated in the will or trust agreement. Alternately, the surviving spouse can be given a power to appoint the trust principal, but the planner should provide for the disposition of the trust principal should the sur-vivor fail to exercise the power.

There are special estate and gift tax rules for property passing to a spouse who is not a citizen of the United States. To qualify for the estate tax marital deduction, a noncitizen spouse may become a U.S. citizen be-fore the estate tax return is filed so long as the spouse was a U.S. resident at the time of the decedent's death. In addition, all property passing to a noncitizen spouse qualifies for the marital deduction if the property is as-signed to a qualified domestic trust before the estate tax return is filed.

The Charitable Deduction

A deduction is allowed for property included in the gross estate that is given to charity. Unlike the income tax law, there is no percentage limita-tion (although the state of your domicile may limit the amount you can leave to charity). The gift need not be exclusively for charity. For exam-ple, you might have a trust with the income payable to your children, and the remainder to charity. The value of the remainder interest will qualify for the charitable deduction. (This important deduction has many ramifications. For a full examination of them, see Chapter 18.)

THE FEDERAL UNIFIED CREDIT

Because of the unified credit, which is equivalent to $1.5 million (rising to $3.5 million in 2009, with a repeal of estate tax in 2010 and the return to $1 million in 2011), an estate of that amount or less is no longer liable for any federal estate tax and no estate tax return need be filed. A married man or woman with an estate greater than that could leave his or her children, relatives, or friends an amount up to the exemption equivalent, or put that sum into a nonmarital trust and leave the balance to his or her spouse. No matter how large the estate, the combination of the unified credit and use of the unlimited marital deduction for the balance in excess of this exemption makes it nontaxable.

FIRST STEP IN TAX PLANNING:
THE DRY RUN

The first step in tax planning is to determine how much your estate taxes will be. This calls for a bit of pencil work. Your Estate Planning Worksheets have the necessary forms and instructions for you to estimate the amount of these taxes.

This estimate, of course, includes only federal estate taxes, not state inheritance taxes. There may also be credits for state and foreign taxes, which your attorney can calculate for you, and certain credits that can't be determined beforehand. But the figure you arrive at in the Worksheets is your starting point for any estate planning you will want to do.

SECOND STEP IN TAX PLANNING:
REDUCING TAXES

If the figure is higher than you would like it to be, the next step is to see what can be done to bring it down without sacrificing your basic objectives. Estate planning being an individual matter, what can and should be done depends upon your particular circumstances.

Here are some suggestions for ways and means of bringing down the tax bill.

Reduce Your Gross Estate

The major way to reduce your gross estate is by making lifetime gifts. However, as indicated in Chapter 12, taxable lifetime gifts and estate assets are taxable under one unified tax system. Nonetheless, by making maximum use of annual exclusions and available deductions, some portions of gifts otherwise taxed can be eliminated from all taxation. In addition, large taxable gifts, if timely made, can exclude a good amount of subsequent capital growth and income from taxation even though the value of the gift itself is taxable. If you have already made gifts where you have retained some right or power over the property, such as a right to revoke a trust, you might release the right or power. This should only be done after careful consideration, however. Giving up a right or power can mean a taxable gift.

If you have a general power of appointment under a trust that was created on or before October 21, 1942, in order to keep the value of the trust out of your gross estate you must be careful not to exercise it or else take steps to release it.

Make Use of the Marital Deduction

Unless there are strong nontax reasons against it, it is wise to take full advantage of the marital deduction when your combined estates—both husband's and wife's—will be less than the amount of the estate exemption. That is obvious. But what about the case where both husband and wife have approximately equal and sizable estates?

One theory has it that the marital deduction should not be fully used. This logic says that while the use of the deduction reduces taxes on the husband's estate, for instance, it ends up piling his property on top of his wife's (i.e., adding the property which qualified for the marital deduction to the wife's estate). When she dies, her estate will be in higher estate tax brackets and her estate taxes greatly increased. The combined taxes on the estates of husband and wife may be larger than if the husband did not fully use the marital deduction.

One cannot quarrel with the logic of this reasoning. But it can result in a situation where taxes are not postponed, but instead are paid out immediately. On the whole, we think this is inadvisable. Here is a case where taxes should be postponed, for two reasons.

First, when taxes are postponed, additional money is available for investment. This can produce income for a widow and/or family over the period of the wife's lifetime. If the wife is 50 years old when the husband dies, this could mean twenty-five years or more of capital appreciation and income production on money that otherwise would have been paid out in taxes.

Second, why assume that the wife's property is going to be conserved intact until she dies? It may well be that she will give some of it away, or be forced to spend a large part of it on living expenses. Also, no one can foresee what the course of the economy will be over such a relatively long period of time. A severe recession or negative stock market could shrink values to the point where the property left at her death would be subject to less estate taxation than can now be anticipated.

But not *all* of one's property *has* to go to a surviving spouse in order to provide for their needs. If the estate is large enough, why disregard the ability to shelter one's unified credit equivalent (currently $1,500,000)?

Get Maximum Mileage from the Unified Credit

It is still important to get maximum mileage from the unified credit in the estate of the first spouse to die, because the estate of the second will be subject to tax on everything above the exemption. An amount equal to the exemption can be "sheltered" by using a nonmarital trust, so as to give the survivor the full benefit of the estate without all of it being taxed in his or her estate.

Take a couple with assets of $3,000,000—$2,000,000 in his name and $1,000,000 in hers. The husband could leave all $2,000,000 to his wife and there would be no tax on his estate because of the marital deduction. But then, let's look at hers. She has a potential $3,000,000 estate. She would only be able to apply her unified credit of $1,500,000. The other half of the estate would be subject to estate tax.

If instead of an "everything to my wife" will, this husband shelters the $1,500,000 exemption equivalent in a nonmarital trust and leaves the balance of his estate ($500,000) to his wife, there will be no tax at his death. However, now his wife's estate will be only $1,500,000—her original $1,000,000 worth of assets plus the $500,000 she inherited from her husband. Thereby there will be no tax on either estate. He could give his wife access to all the income from his nonmarital trust during her lifetime, and the right to demand annually either $5,000 or 5 percent of the trust's value, whichever is greater. If he did this, the extent of her demand rights would be taxable in her estate.

Make Full Use of the Annual Gift Exclusion

A very effective and underused estate planning tool is the ability of anyone to make annual gifts of $11,000 (indexed for inflation in the future) in cash or other assets to as many beneficiaries as they wish. In a large estate these relatively small-sounding amounts can be very effective in reducing the current and future size of a taxable estate. Remember that for married couples the limit rises to $22,000 by opting for "gift splitting." No gift tax return need be filed (unless you want to start the three-year statute of limitations running on the IRS's ability to challenge the value of an appreciating gift upon your death, or unless you live in a non-community property state). Furthermore, the annual gift exclusion does not reduce your estate tax exemption (currently $1,500,000), and equally importantly, does not fall under the timeline of so-called deathbed gifts (a provision whereby gifts made within three years of death are pulled back into your estate as if they had never been made).

Here are some opportunities to make use of annual gifts:

1. When you establish a durable power of attorney, be sure it includes the power to make gifts on your behalf. This could allow for deathbed gifts of $11,000 to a number of beneficiaries, even hours before your death and even if you have become incompetent or physically unable to issue checks. *Be sure such gifts are issued as certified checks in case you should die before the checks are cashed.*

   If you have an estate too small to incur estate taxes, but have only a will and no living trust, such last-minute gifts could reduce the probate fees that are directly related to the size of your gross estate.

2. Use your annual gift exclusions as gifts to an irrevocable trust that holds life insurance on your life. This will vastly expand the dollar amount of the gift your beneficiaries receive.

3. Consider making annual tax-free gifts of minority interests in a business or other assets to a family limited partnership. (See page 342 for a description of the family limited partnership.) The size of your gift for estate valuation purposes will receive a

substantial discount by being a minority interest and having restricted marketability.

4. Checks could be issued, even just prior to death, to make tax-free gifts of tuition or payment of medical expenses for your family or a friend. The amounts can be entirely free of gift or estate tax if issued directly to the school for tuition costs or directly to the medical provider. We know of one such deathbed gift in which the last two years of tuition at M.I.T. were paid for a grandson and did not count against the annual gift exclusion or as part of his generation-skipping allowance.

Here are some rules to follow to be sure your annual gift exclusion gifts of $11,000 to each recipient are allowed.

- Be sure the gift is completed. It must actually be received by the recipient.
- Attach no strings to the gift. You must not restrict how or when the gift can be used by the recipient.
- If you give annual gifts to a trust, be sure there is an opportunity for the beneficiaries to withdraw the gift amount for some specified period of time. The mere availability of the gift for this period will qualify it as a "present interest," i.e., capable of being received in the year given. This is crucial to it being allowed for the annual gift exclusion.

Other Last-Minute Deathbed Planning Strategies

1. If you live in a non-community-property state, consider the strategy of giving some assets to the sickly spouse to better equalize the estates and allow for use of the estate tax exemption ($1,500,000 in 2004). The ill spouse would need to live a year and a day after the transfer, but there is no penalty attached to it, so why not give it a try?

2. Consider transferring appreciated assets to the ill spouse's estate so they receive a step-up in cost basis at his or her death. There are certain types of trusts that will avoid the need for a spouse to survive a year and a day, so if substantial amounts are tied up in appreciated assets, you should consult an attorney.

3. If there are securities in an ill person's estate that are trading at a loss, these should be sold prior to their death. The losses will go

on their final income tax return for the year of death. If not sold, any unrealized capital losses would expire at death.

4. If you are a family member and executor who wishes not to accept an executor's fee so as not to reduce the estate that passes to the family, consider taking the fee, reducing the size of a probatable estate and then writing checks within the $11,000 annual gift exclusion to family members to distribute it after all.

Save Taxes Through "Wasting"

You can realize even greater tax savings, both estate and income, and assure adequate support for your spouse with a "wasting" marital deduction trust. This is done by creating two trusts, one of which qualifies for the marital deduction. Support for your spouse is provided by using both the income and principal of the marital deduction trust for her benefit. The income of the other trust is accumulated and this second trust is not used until the marital deduction trust is exhausted.

Case history of a wasting trust arrangement: Mr. Green will have a net estate of $2,000,000. His main objective is to make sure that his wife will receive $100,000 a year in addition to the income from her own substantial assets.

Under his will, he creates two trusts. The first, a marital deduction trust, will have a principal of about $500,000 and the second, the non-marital deduction trust, the balance of $1,500,000. The marital deduction trust pays her $100,000 a year: first all of the income, then principal as needed to make up the balance. She will pay tax on the income. The amount she receives from principal is not taxed. Over the years, as the principal of the trust is used up, the portion of the $100,000 annual payments that comes out of the principal will increase while the income portion of it will decrease. This means that her income taxes will continually decrease.

Meanwhile, the income of the second trust is accumulated, and income taxes are paid on it, by the trust as a separate tax entity. If and when the marital deduction trust is exhausted, the income and principal of this second trust are used to make the $100,000 annual payments.

When any accumulated income is paid to Mrs. Green from the second trust, it will be treated roughly as though distributed to her in the year it was accumulated. This is done through a shortcut averaging method. She will be liable for any increase in tax that would have resulted had that income been distributed to her in those prior years, but with a credit for the tax that the trust paid on it. Therefore, because her taxable income will be continuously decreasing while the marital deduction trust is being exhausted, use of the averaging method could result in a situation in which she will have to pay little or no additional tax on the distribution, after using the credit for taxes paid by the trust. Moreover, in spite of the additional tax that may be due, the family benefits from having the use of the deferred tax monies until the tax actually becomes payable.

At widow Green's death, whatever remains of the second trust passes to the beneficiaries under her husband's will without being taxed in her estate.

What has Mr. Green accomplished? First of all, he has provided the support that he wants for his wife. Second, there is no estate tax at his death. Third, his wife's support is backed by the property of his entire estate. Fourth, there can be an overall savings in income taxes. Fifth, this plan will help reduce the estate tax on his wife's potential estate by using up the property of the marital deduction trust (which would be taxable in her estate) and preserving the property of the second trust (which is not taxed in either estate).

Provide for a Marital Deduction in Case of Common Disaster

To get the marital deduction there must be a surviving spouse. What happens when the couple dies in an accident or disaster so that the order of deaths cannot be established?

As we know, generally the laws provide that each is presumed to survive the other. Therefore, neither will inherit from the other, and so no marital deduction.

It is possible, however, to change this presumption. The change should be made if the two estates are disproportionate in size. By a simple provision in the will, trust, or insurance contract, the beneficiary can be presumed to have survived and the property will pass to him. When one spouse has little or no property and the other has a substantial amount, such a provision in the latter's will can mean considerable tax savings in their combined estates.

Take the case of Mr. and Mrs. Brown. He has an estate of $2 million, but she has no property of her own. His will "shelters" an amount equal to the exemption and leaves the rest outright to Mrs. Brown. If they were to die simultaneously in a common disaster, under the law of their domicile, Mr. Brown would be presumed to have survived his wife and she would inherit none of his estate. Without a marital deduction, the federal taxes on his estate would be $780,800 if they died in 2004. If he were to insert a provision in his will that, if they were to die in a common disaster, she is presumed to have survived, then $500,000 of his estate would pass to his wife tax-free under the marital deduction. There would then be a $1,000,000 and a $500,000 estate—both of them exempt from federal tax. Tax savings: $780,800.

Save Income Taxes by Spreading

Some items may be taxed on your beneficiaries as well as being subject to estate taxes. Pensions, annuities, renewal commissions, fees, royalties, and salary continuation payments all fall into this category. There is, however, an income tax deduction allowed for estate taxes paid on any income items. By dividing these benefits and other forms of income among a number of beneficiaries, and other forms of income among a number of beneficiaries or trusts, income taxes can be saved. In addition, even greater savings can be realized by giving them to low tax bracket beneficiaries. Give other assets to those in high brackets.

Save Income Taxes by Sprinkling

If you have a number of beneficiaries, it may be advantageous to have the trustees or some other person determine how much income is to be paid to each. Ms. White has, let us say, three daughters, each of whom has children. She creates three separate trusts, one for each family group, and provides that the income of each trust shall be paid out among the members of the particular family in such amounts as the trustee shall see fit. The trustee can then "sprinkle" income within each group according to individual needs and tax brackets.

THE NEED FOR TAX PLANNING

Many people do their tax planning in a hit-or-miss fashion. That is not the approach to this chapter, as you can see. It calls for a conscious and continuing effort. It's worth it, however, for the most elementary of reasons. The stakes are high, the possible savings to be realized—for large estates—in the millions. For small ones it is perhaps not as dramatic. But to the family of the person with a modest estate, each dollar saved can be of greater importance than to his wealthier counterpart. This is the point to remember: tax savings are always important; tax planning is for everyone. It is important to talk through the objectives you have for various members of your family with your estate planning attorney. Doing so means that the proper available tax-saving strategies can be applied to an estate plan designed to carry out the wishes you have for yourself, your spouse and your heirs.

CHAPTER 17

ASSESSING YOUR ESTATE: WHAT TO LEAVE AND HOW TO LEAVE IT

One way to look at estate planning is to view it as a jigsaw puzzle. Here is one piece called "taxes," another known as "lifetime transfers," others labeled "investments," "charitable giving," "corporate benefits," and so on. As a planner you yourself have dealt with these pieces and so created your estate and prepared it for transfer.

Almost, but not quite. The pieces of the jigsaw puzzle are still separated from each other, and until you fit them together, you will not have a coherent picture of your estate or its transfer plan—no real way of knowing what's going to happen to it after your death.

A preview or dress rehearsal of the estate transfer is basic to all estate planning. It is as if you were to give a piece of machinery a trial run. You note its defects and its strong points. You prepare it in the best of all possible ways for its eventual use: by testing it.

The test is often focused on a key element in the estate transfer plan: your will, or your living trust. We'll deal first with the will. The will is the fundamental instrument in many plans of after-death estate transfer. The success of your particular plan will depend on how well you make your preparations for it.

Previously we have talked about the need for making a will or a living trust. Now we want to discuss, first, *how* to make a will.

Contrary to the usual procedure, the making of a will should not be simply a matter of consulting your attorney, listening to his advice, and then signing a document. A lawyer's function in estate planning is not to tell a client what he should do with his property. It is to advise him on what can be done and to create the means for carrying out the wishes and objectives the client wants to achieve. The initial preparation for a will must be undertaken by the client himself. This is best done before his first conference with his attorney.

THE "DISTRIBUTABLE" ESTATE

You should begin by examining exactly what you will have to distribute. Before you can decide on what property or how much property you want to give to any particular member of your family or to your family group, you must first find out what your *distributable* estate will amount to.

Distributable estate means the property that will be left after taxes, funeral and administration expenses, debts, and any losses or costs incurred in the liquidation of assets to meet these cash requirements. Most people do not realize that, both in volume and content, the distributable estate is not the same as that which a person may have enjoyed during his life. The only way to know what it really will be is to subject your estate to a hypothetical administration: a trial run.

This is also the time for you to crystallize your objectives; to determine what they are generally and specifically; to decide which are primary and which are secondary. Unless your estate is large, you will not be able to accomplish everything you might wish to. As in other phases of life, the more important things must take precedence over the less important, and compromise may have to be made. This aspect of preparation necessarily involves analyzing your beneficiaries and weighing their needs against what you are able to provide for them.

Only when you know what you have to work with and what you want to accomplish can you begin to chart the "distribution flow" of your estate—what property is to be distributed to whom, and how.

Outside Taxation but Inside the Estate

If you have done your homework and filled out the Estate Planning Worksheets, you already have a list of the assets that are includable in your gross taxable estate.

To find out what your distributable estate is, however, you must now do some additional calculating. The distributable estate includes anything which will pass to your beneficiaries at your death, *whether or not it is then subject to taxation.* If your plan has focused on steps to reduce tax erosion, you may find that this nontaxable but distributable property is quite substantial. Property in your distributable estate but not in your taxable estate could include:

- A living trust that has been designed to remove some of the property from estate taxation.
- Your spouse's half of your jointly held property.
- Insurance on your life that you do not own and over which you have no incidents of ownership.
- Property over which you have a limited, not a general, power of appointment.

In order to formulate a plan of distribution you must include all such items. You may not have the power to direct the disposition of some of these, it is true, but they do affect your overall plan and your beneficiaries, and must be incorporated within it.

Inside Your Estate but Outside Your Will

The inventory for your trial run is different in another respect. Property that passes under your will constitutes your *probate estate* and is controlled by the directions in your will. But as we have seen, the will is not the only means by which property passes at death. Property can also pass outside of the will by living trust, by right of survivorship, by beneficiary designation, or by contract. Your will does not control the disposition of these assets, unless, as we shall shortly see, they become payable to your probate estate.

In almost every estate there will be some property that will not pass under the will. In fact, often the value of the nonprobate assets exceeds that of the probate estate.

Your inventory, therefore, must separate the property passing *outside* of the will from the property passing *under it*, for two reasons.

First of all, you must know what and how much property is controlled by your will. Otherwise some of its provisions may fail.

For instance, a widow plans to have her estate go to her children, but she wants her sister to have payments under a deferred compensation agreement. She makes her will accordingly, bequeathing the deferred compensation to her sister and the rest of the estate to her children. She knows that the value of her deferred compensation contract will be in her taxable estate and so mistakenly believes it will pass through the probate estate.

Ms. Widow has forgotten that the terms of the contract provide for payment to her children. At her death, what happens to the bequest to her sister? It has no effect. The terms of the contract, not her will, determine the disposition of its proceeds.

In an extreme case the will may turn out to be nothing more than an empty shell, because nothing passes under it. If this is what the planner intended, fine. The estate plan may have been designed to have everything pass outside the will. In that case the will is made to take care of certain events that may occur such as the premature death of a beneficiary. It is also drawn to take care of nominal or miscellaneous property that has not been otherwise provided for.

But if the will was designed to transfer substantial properties and it turns out to be such an empty shell, then the estate plan will necessarily fail.

The second reason for separating property into "outside" and "inside" the will is the need for an integrated master plan. Where it is possible to do so the disposition of nonprobate assets can be altered to fit into the plan. For instance, the beneficiary of an insurance policy can be changed. But this is not always possible, and so the will must be drawn so as to compensate for, or coordinate this factor into the plan.

Take the case of Mr. Equalizer. He had set up trusts for his two older children but never created one for his youngest child. His financial affairs are such at present that he is unable to create a trust for the youngest. He believes in equal treatment but the living trusts can't be altered or amended. He must compensate for this imbalance by means of his will so that the total property received by his children, both the living trust and his probate estate, will be equally divided among them.

Therefore, it is important to know how each item of your property will pass. Let's look at some of the assets that commonly pass outside the will.

Jointly Owned Property. Property in the names of two or more persons, where there is a right of survivorship, passes by operation of law. This means that on the death of one owner it automatically goes to the survivor or survivors, and is unaffected by the decedent's will.

Take a certificate of stock that is jointly held. The registration will read something like "John Shareholder and Jean Shareholder, as joint tenants with right of survivorship, and not as tenants in common." The one who outlives the other takes all. Note, however, that if you have a stock certificate or deed or other certificate of ownership that reads "as tenants in common," there is no right of survivorship. Each owner controls the disposition of his share of the property and it passes under his will.

Most people put the family home in the joint names of the husband and wife. This form of ownership is known as a "tenancy by the entirety" but it is simply a joint tenancy with right of survivorship between husband and wife. The principle is the same. The survivor takes all. *Note:* In community property states, you may want to own a home as community property since the entire value of the home will be "stepped up" in its cost basis, meaning the surviving spouse who may later sell the home will have any gains calculated from the entire fair market value of the house when the first spouse died, *not* half the original purchase price; a possibility for enormous tax savings.

People often rent safe deposit boxes in joint names. This does not generally affect the ownership of the property in the box. In a few states, however, the property in the box may pass by right of survivorship.

One other type of property commonly held in joint names is U.S. Savings Bonds. If a bond is registered "Peter Patriot or Polly Patriot," the survivor automatically becomes the sole owner.

Savings bonds can also be registered in the name of "Peter Patriot P.O.D. Polly Patriot." The initials P.O.D. stand for "payable on death." This isn't a joint ownership. Peter is the sole owner while he lives. But if Polly survives, the net result is the same. She becomes the owner of the bond.

Living Trusts. The trust instrument, not the settlor's will, controls the disposition of the trust. But if the settlor reserves a power of appointment over the trust property exercisable by his will, or if the trust by its terms specifies that the property returns to him, then the will takes over and determines the disposition of the property.

Insurance. Your life insurance is an asset of major importance that passes outside your will or living trust (unless you have made your estate or the living trust the beneficiary). This applies to annuities as well. The terms of the contract determine not only to whom it is payable, but also how it is to be paid—in a lump sum or under options.

Employee Benefits. Although they may be payable to your estate, specified beneficiaries are usually named to receive profit-sharing, deferred compensation, pension, or other benefits.

Business Agreements. Contracts for the purchase or sale of a business interest at the death of a partner or stockholder frequently provide for payments to be made, not to the deceased's estate, but to specified people, such as the spouse or children.

Under the Will: The Forgotten Property

If it is important to know exactly what property passes outside your will, it is equally important to know exactly what is passing under it.

Too often certain items are overlooked. What will happen to the jointly owned property, or the P.O.D. bonds if your co-owner doesn't survive you? What happens if the beneficiaries of your insurance or employee's benefits die before you, and you haven't designated secondary beneficiaries? In all these cases the property passes under your will. Obviously, you can't predict who's going to survive. If your estate plan does not call for alternative dispositions in case a beneficiary dies before you do, then you must be sure to include this property in your calculations.

Suppose you have a distributable estate of $400,000, and $300,000 of this is jointly held with your husband. You figure that only $100,000 will pass under your will. But if he dies before you do, then the figure jumps to $400,000. In planning your will or living trust you must take care of this contingency.

Remember that you need not specifically devise or bequeath property in your will in order to have the property pass under it. Your will includes a residuary clause that reads something to the effect: "All the rest, residue and remainder of my property, both real and personal, of which I may die seized or possessed or to which I may be entitled, I hereby give, devise and bequeath to . . ." Whatever you haven't disposed of before in your will passes under this clause.

In addition to property that falls into your probate estate because a co-owner or beneficiary doesn't survive you, there are certain items that are commonly overlooked, or that the planner doesn't realize he is bequeathing by his will.

Insurance on Someone Else's Life. A policy owned by you on someone else's life is your property just like any of your other assets, and therefore is transferred by your will or living trust. The fact that a third person is a primary or contingent beneficiary has no effect on the ownership of the policy. Let's assume you own a $50,000 policy on your wife's life. Your children are the beneficiaries. Under your will, your wife receives your residuary estate. The insurance policy on her life will go to your wife at your death, not to your children.

Living Trusts. As we know, the property will pass under your will in certain instances: if you specifically provide in the trust agreement for this or if the trust property is to be returned to you when the trust ends.

Employee Benefits. There is one type of employee benefit that is always controlled by your will: the restricted stock option. One of the restrictions is that it cannot be transferred except by will (*or by the laws of intestacy*).

Inheritances. Why is it people tend to think property isn't theirs until it is actually in their hands? Suggest to someone who has been left an inheritance that he revise his will to provide for his changed circumstances, and his answer is frequently, "Why should I hurry? I can wait until it's paid to me." In truth he should not wait. Whether or not he has actually taken possession of the inherited property, it is his by law and it passes at his death just like any other property he may own.

Powers of Appointment. So far we have been mainly concerned with powers of appointment from a tax point of view. Let's look at them now as they affect estate transference.

You give yourself a power of appointment when you create a living trust and reserve the right to change the disposition of the trust property. Usually, however, the power of appointment is given to you by someone else, either in his will or in a living trust.

Powers are of two types: general and special (or limited). Under a general power of appointment, you have the right to appoint the property to anyone you choose, including yourself, your estate, or your creditors. Under a special power you can appoint it to any individual or group, but not to yourself, your estate, or your creditors or those of your estate.

If you have a power of appointment, you can control the disposition of the property and so you must include it in your planning. You must decide whether or not to exercise it from the point of view of your overall estate plan of distribution and its tax consequences.

There is a major drawback in having power of appointment. You can have a power without knowing about it and exercise it without intending to. This can throw an estate plan completely out of kilter.

Listen to the sad tale of a New York lady who evidently didn't know she had a power of appointment. She was a widow with a son and a grandchild, and lived on the income from an $800,000 trust created for her by her husband. She thought the principal of the trust would pass to her son at her death.

She often visited her son and grandchild at their home in Texas. One day while there, she decided to make a will. She told the Texas attorney whom she consulted that, since the principal of the trust would go to her son, she wanted to leave her own small amount of property to her infant grandson. The will was duly drawn and executed.

It was only after her death that it was discovered that she had a power of appointment over the $800,000 trust. Her will left everything to her grandson. Did this include the trust property?

The courts of New York, whose law governed the exercise of the power, said it did. In New York, then, as in many states, a residuary clause in a will automatically exercised a power of appointment unless the will specifically stated that it should not. Even though the evidence showed that she had believed her son would receive the trust property at her death and that she wanted him to, her will gave it to her grandson. Without knowing it, she had disinherited her only child.

Figuring Your Distributable Estate

If you have inventoried all your assets and arrived at a grand total, you are now ready for the second step. This one involves not addition, but subtraction. Refer to the "Estate Cash Requirements Schedule" in the Worksheets and get the total of your debts, expenses, and estate taxes. These are subtracted from your grand total. You now have an estimate of your distributable estate, assuming, of course, that there will be no further losses caused by liquidation of assets in order to pay estate taxes and costs.

ESTABLISHING LIQUIDITY

At this point you know *how much* is available for distribution but not *what* is available. One task remains to be done on your inventory: establishing liquidity to pay the taxes, debts, and expenses. One or more of your assets must be used for this purpose. It may be that your inventory indicates that your estate will have enough cash to pay these items. If so, you have no problem. Make the appropriate entries in the column headed "Property to Be Liquidated" and you are ready to go on to the next step.

But if there will not be enough ready cash, you must select assets that will have a ready market, such as savings bonds or actively traded securities.

In Chapter 7, we pointed out that if your security portfolio contains U.S. Treasury Bonds, then your estate may be able to use them to pay the taxes and realize a profit on the transaction. This is because certain Treasuries (the Federal Reserve publishes a list of them) owned by a decedent may be redeemed at par to pay estate taxes. If an estate contains these, they should be used for this purpose.

In addition, a planner (especially an older person who is about to make new investments and may have insufficient life insurance) should consider the advantage of investing in such Treasuries in an amount up to his estimated federal estate taxes. Because their interest rate is below the going rate, they are currently selling below par. The planner can buy an issue at the market price and, when he dies, the estate can redeem them at 100 percent by having the proceeds applied to the payment of the taxes. Though the estate realizes a profit—the difference between the purchase price and par—the profit will not be subject to capital gains tax. Since they can be redeemed at par to pay taxes, the estate's basis will be par.

It is important, in determining if there will be sufficient available cash or liquidable assets, to remember that the property listed on your inventory as passing outside your will does not go to your executor and so may not provide the needed liquidity. Suppose, for example, a woman has a $100,000 certificate of deposit that she figures will cover her estate expenses and taxes. However, the certificate is in her name and her son's as joint owners. On the death of the mother, the CD automatically goes to the son, who doesn't have to turn it over to the estate. The most the son could be required to contribute would be his share of the estate taxes on that $100,000. Establishing liquidity may call for changing ownerships of assets so that they pass to your estate instead of outside the will. Many estate planners use the leverage of life insurance owned by an irrevocable trust (not personally owned) to provide for all the liquidity needs, leaving all other assets untouched.

It may be, however, that your trial run shows that there will not be sufficient cash or readily marketable assets available to pay taxes and the other costs. A valuable property may have to be sacrificed to meet these obligations. This indicates a serious defect in your estate picture.

Now—while you have the opportunity—is the time to alter or reorganize your assets, to buy additional life insurance, or to take steps to reduce taxes. Otherwise, your estate plan may run into difficulties.

REVIEWING YOUR BENEFICIARIES

Now that you know what you have to distribute, you are ready for the next phase in your analysis: a review of your beneficiaries and your responsibilities to them. This is the time to set forth your objectives as clearly and completely as you can.

If you have had an opportunity to judge your beneficiaries as to their ability and responsibility in handling property, either through lifetime giving or through other means, you have a guide to base your judgments on. If not, you must still decide on some pattern of distribution because you need a will now. You can't wait until you are sure. You devise the best plan for the present and change it, if necessary, when you have more knowledge.

Unless yours is a very large estate indeed, you will have to establish preferences among the various claimants to your largesse. You must choose your primary and secondary beneficiaries. The selection should be based primarily on two major factors: the needs of each and the resources of each.

Is the support of your spouse your primary objective? Or does the fact that she has an estate of her own put her in the secondary beneficiary category? Is her estate so substantial that your wisest course would be to omit her entirely?

Should your children be treated equally, or is there a disabled or incompetent child whose welfare must be given special attention? Have you considered your grandchildren—present and future ones? Have you thought of the often neglected daughter-in-law who might need financial assistance on the death of your son?

Do you have dependent parents? Perhaps they don't need financial assistance now, but might they in the future? Are there other relatives who might be in need of support such as a widowed sister or invalid brother?

Your plan of distribution must be based first on the needs of these people who look to you for support and care. Don't forget bequests to friends and relatives, however. These tokens of affection and respect, albeit a financially insignificant part of your transfer plan, should also be taken care of.

At this juncture, gifts to charity also enter into the deliberations. You don't need to make large charitable gifts like those envisioned in Chapter 18. Even though your means are limited, you may still have charitable objectives.

When mulling over your list of beneficiaries, don't be so coolly rational that you neglect an important human element in estate planning: the preservation of family harmony. You may give more to one child than to another for reasons that are quite proper. But are you sure that the "neglected" child isn't going to resent it? These resentments can be amazingly strong. The hostility and passions they generate can last for years, even pass from generation to generation. You may find it wiser, in the long run, to treat all your children equally even though their needs and resources are far from equal. Of course, your decision will be influenced by the *degree* of differences in need.

If the possibility exists of creating resentment or disharmony over unequal treatment (or possibly equal treatment), it may be wise to scrap a sound plan of distribution in favor of one designed to promote harmony. Remember, it takes only one person in a family to create disharmony.

FREEDOM OF DISPOSITION

You may think that you can dispose of your estate pretty much as you please. While this is generally so, there are certain legal restrictions on what you can do.

Freedom within Reason. A few years ago, a man died in New York, leaving a will he had drawn up himself with a number of unique provisions. Among them were directions for a fund to be set up to pay the salary of a uniformed guard to watch over his grave. The court refused to allow this provision to be carried out, failing to see the need for guarding the dead.

Your disposition must be reasonable or it will not be given effect. You might want your executor to dump your securities in the ocean, but the courts won't permit such waste. Nor would they permit a provision to be carried out directing that all your personal property be used for your funeral pyre.

Freedom Consistent with Public Policy. The law will not allow you to dispose of your estate in a way that offends the public policy or law of the state. Your estate can't be used to promote illegal or immoral acts such as illegal gambling or insurrection or prostitution. A condition attached to a legacy that induces conduct contrary to public policy will not be upheld. If you make a bequest to a daughter on the condition that she doesn't marry or she divorce her husband, it won't hold. Restraints on marriage and promotion of divorce are generally deemed to be against public policy and so the testator's condition will be disregarded.

Freedom to Choose Your Beneficiaries: The Special Status of the Surviving Spouse. The major restriction on your choice of beneficiaries is your spouse's right in your estate.

In medieval days, when land was wealth, a widow automatically received a life estate (the right during her lifetime to the income from and the use of property) in one-third of all the land her husband had owned during their marriage. This is known as *dower.*

A husband, on his wife's death, received a life estate in all of the lands she had owned, not just one-third. The husband's right is known as *curtesy.* For the husband to be entitled to curtesy, however, there had to be a child born of the marriage and heard to cry "within the four walls." As a result, when the lady of the manor was about to be delivered of her firstborn, the lord gathered his men to act as attesting witnesses to the birth. They listened outside the lady's bedchamber for the wail that would give their lord his curtesy. The child only had to be born alive. Legally it made no difference whether he survived. The sound of the baby's cry signaled the start of the feasting and revelry in celebration of the lord's good fortune.

In some states, these feudal laws, though not the rituals, are still retained in modified forms. But in today's nonagrarian society, where wealth is usually made up of personal property, dower and curtesy are of little protection to a surviving spouse. For instance, a millionaire in New Jersey who owned no real estate could cut his wife off completely until as late as 1981.

Other states that have retained dower and curtesy give the surviving spouse a right to part of the decedent's personal property as well, or permit the spouse to relinquish dower or curtesy for a share of the entire estate.

In many states dower and curtesy have been completely abolished. The widow or widower is given instead an absolute right to a fractional share of the estate that is known as a "statutory share." If the decedent's will doesn't give the survivor a minimum amount set down by law, he or she may claim the statutory share.

In community property states the survivor automatically gets one-half of all the community property.

Although these rights are conferred by law, a spouse can relinquish or alter them by an antenuptial or postnuptial agreement. In addition, these rights of one spouse in the estate of the other are lost on divorce, abandonment and, sometimes, separation of the parties.

Freedom to Disinherit. With the exception of your surviving spouse, you can generally disinherit anyone else, including your children. There is one exception—the state of Louisiana. There the children automatically get a portion of the estate, their share depending on the number of children.

In order to exclude your children, however, you may have to spell out your wishes in specific terms. If a child is born after the execution of the will, he may be entitled to his intestate share (what he would have received if you had died without a will) unless it appears that after-born children were intentionally excluded. In some states this applies to living children who were not mentioned in the will. This doesn't mean that you can't exclude your children. It means that if you don't make your intentions clear, the law may assume that it was an inadvertent omission, and so remedy it. Note that spelling out your intentions doesn't mean the necessity of spelling out your *reasons*. Leave the vitriol out of your will.

Freedom to Be Charitable. Odd as it may seem in a charity-oriented society, there may be limitations on your right to give to charity at your death. In some states, bequests and devises to charity are invalid unless the will was executed a specified time before death. This was to prevent a dying person from trying to buy his way into heaven at the last, desperate moment. Other states limit the portion or percentage of the estate that can be left to charity if you leave certain descendants or heirs.

These are vestiges of English feudal law, when church and crown were vying for power and the crown was trying to combat the church's increasing wealth. Nowadays, however, the motive is different. Protection of the family is the reason for these laws.

PREVIEWING YOUR TRANSFERS

Once you have determined who your beneficiaries will be and apportioned your estate among them, what kinds of testamentary transfers can you, and should you, make?

As with lifetime transfers, your after-death gifts may be outright or in trust. They may be:

1. *Bequests.* A bequest is a gift of personal property by will. It may be a sum of money—"$1,000 to Aunt Jennifer"—or a specific piece of property—"my automobile to my wife." It can be a share of the estate, such as "one-third of my net estate to my sister, Matilda." Or a bequest might be in the form of a direction to the executor to sell certain property and pay the proceeds to a beneficiary.
2. *Devises.* When the property given is real estate, as, for example, when you leave your home to your spouse, it is called a devise. The devise might be made entirely to one person or it might be a gift to one person for use during his life, or for a period of years, with the property then going to someone else.
3. *Residue.* As we have already seen, the residue is the balance of your estate after all other bequests and devises. Every will needs a residuary clause. Although it is possible to dispose of everything through the prior bequests and devises, and have no residuary estate, there will almost always be some property that hasn't been taken care of. In addition, if any bequests or devises should fail because a beneficiary died before the testator, or for any other reason, the property falls into the residue. Without a residuary clause there would be a partial intestacy.

A typical will includes gifts to relatives and friends, the secondary beneficiaries. Caution must be exercised because the residue is only the amount left over after payment of the prior legacies. If your property should decrease between the time of the making of the will and the time of your death, your primary beneficiaries could be left with little or nothing.

Here's a case history in point: a man with a half million dollars made a will leaving a bequest of $5,000 to each of his nieces and nephews, and the residue to his children. When he died eight years later, his estate was worth only $135,000. Each niece and nephew got $5,000. There were nineteen of them in all. Thus his children were left with less than $40,000, while their cousins inherited a total of $95,000.

This planner should, of course, have reviewed his estate plan during those eight years and made the necessary revisions. Even failing this, he could have protected himself against such a fiasco by including a simple provision in his will that limited the $5,000 legacies to a fixed proportion of his ultimate estate. Thus, his primary beneficiaries would have been assured of receiving the bulk of his estate.

The Testamentary Trust. After-death gifts by your will, including the residuary estate, need not be outright. They can be in trust.

Although the form of a testamentary trust, as well as the motives for creating it, may be different, it is similar in most respects to the living trust.

There is the same flexibility and variety of arrangements possible with both types. Income can be paid to one or more beneficiaries, be accumulated, be paid out in the discretion of the trustee or a third person, or be sprinkled or sprayed among a group of beneficiaries. There can be an arrangement to have the trust pay the beneficiary an annuity, guaranteeing that he will receive a stated sum or minimum amount, regardless of the income earned by the trust.

As to the principal, it can be paid in specified sums, at specific times or ages, on the happening of certain events, at the discretion of the trustee or a third person, or at the demand of the beneficiary. Making the decision as to when and if principal payments should be made to beneficiaries can be a difficult one. When, for example, should you let a child receive principal? When he is 21? Not until he reaches 50 or 60? For use upon specific occasions such as a down payment on a first home, a child's wedding, a sabbatical from work after at least ten years of work? Perhaps never?

None of these choices is necessarily a perfect solution. A 21-year-old is still usually immature; he could squander away the property within a few years. A person who has to wait until late middle age to receive principal may be too old to use and enjoy it to its fullest extent. The business he wanted to start, the home he wanted to buy, or the education he wanted to give his children—the opportunities to achieve any of these things may have gone by.

Or the person who never receives any of the principal may at some time find himself in serious need. How much security and protection has the trust, created for his benefit, given him if he suffers a prolonged or serious illness or finds himself in unexpected financial difficulties, with the assets of the trust beyond his reach?

One practical solution to the problem is to have the principal paid out in installments; fixed amounts or portions at certain ages or times. For example, your will might provide for payment of one-fourth of the principal to your beneficiary at ages 25, 30, 35, and 40. If he dissipates the first quarter, he may still handle the second or third more wisely.

Another solution is to leave it to the trustee or a member of the family to decide at what time or times, or for what reasons, payments of principal should be made. They could also be given the power to terminate the trust and distribute the remainder to the beneficiary if they consider it to be in his best interest.

Another possible way of handling the problem is to specify the purposes for which principal may be used: for education, buying a home, establishing a business, etc. With an extremely irresponsible beneficiary, your list might be more limited. It could be restricted to serious emergencies or special needs, such as medical care. We remember one trust for such a young man where one of the purposes for which principal could be used was the payment of his medical expenses. He persisted in forwarding his liquor bills (which were substantial ones) to the trustee for payment, on the grounds that the liquor was for medicinal purposes.

Fortunately, many trust beneficiaries are mature, responsible people. Trusts are often created for them for tax or management reasons, sometimes only for convenience. A planner might well give such a beneficiary the right to demand principal—either an unlimited or restricted right.

However, if tax savings is one of its purposes, the beneficiary's right to demand principal should be limited to $5,000 a year, or 5 percent of the value of the trust principal. Otherwise, he may find all the trust property taxable in his estate when he dies. If he wants or needs it, then he can take up to the specified amount in any year. If he doesn't, the principal is left undisturbed or subject to be paid out at the trustee's discretion. Don't assume that a beneficiary will invade principal just because the trust says that he may. Many people are so conditioned as to the sacredness of principal that they are by nature reluctant to use it, even when necessity demands it.

This reminds us of the turn-of-the-century story of the reunion of a group of graduates of a very fashionable finishing school. The well-groomed, well-dressed ladies were shocked to discover that one of their classmates was obviously a prostitute. Her former friends took her aside to find out why this had happened to her. She explained that she simply needed the money. "But what happened to the trust left you by your father?" they asked. "Oh," she said, "the trust is still there, but the income has dropped considerably and I know Daddy wouldn't like me to dip into principal."

In creating a trust, give some thought to using a power of appointment. The trust, remember, creates future interests. No one can predict the future with any degree of certainty. No matter how carefully an estate plan may be worked out today, it may not adequately meet the situation existing twenty or thirty years hence. You can provide the necessary flexibility to handle unforeseen situations and changes in circumstances through powers of appointment.

With such a power you give someone else the opportunity to reassess the family needs at a later date and make any necessary or desirable changes in your plan. He could have the power to do this during his own lifetime or at his death by his will, or both.

You must also decide whether this power is to be a general one so that he may appoint the property to anyone, including himself or his estate, or a special or limited power. A general power naturally gives greater flexibility, but as you recall, it results in tax erosion. The property of the trust is includable in the gross taxable estate of the holder if it is a general power, but not if it is only a special power. If the income beneficiary of a trust has a power which can be exercised during his life, whether general or special, and he exercises it, he makes a taxable gift.

We have seen that a power can be inadvertently exercised and the havoc that can thus be wrought. To avoid such accidents, your will can and should require that, in order to exercise the power, the donee must specifically refer to the power you have given him. Furthermore, there should always be a disposition provided for the trust property in case the power isn't exercised. If the disposition is satisfactory, the donee need not exercise the power. If it isn't, he can change it.

Pouring Over into the Living Trust. Have you already set up a living trust or are you planning to do so as part of your program of lifetime transfers? If so, as you recall, it can be the after-death, as well as the lifetime, transfer vehicle. Probate property can be added to it, or in legal parlance, "poured over" into it when you die, by having your will provide for this.

Outright or in Trust. How does one choose between making an outright testamentary gift or leaving it in trust? If it is outright, it is the beneficiary's to use and dispose of freely. A trust limits the beneficiary's rights in the property, but should the dead hand of the testator control the living?

It should be in trust:

- If your beneficiaries are minors—at least until adulthood.
- If your beneficiaries are incompetent, irresponsible, or simply imprudent.

- If you want to save estate taxes on the estates of future generations.
- If you want to keep a particular asset, such as a family business, within the family and out of the hands of outsiders.
- If you want to assure professional management of the property.

The planner who has confidence in his beneficiaries should consider consulting them on the form in which they want their inheritance. You might feel that a mature person should receive the property outright, but he might prefer tax savings to freedom of use.

In the long run it is up to you as the estate planner to make your decisions, weigh the problems—psychological, economic, and personal—and arrive at the best possible solution for your family.

THE FINAL PICTURE

If you have followed the steps suggested for the trial run, you have a picture of what your distributable estate will look like and how it will be distributed.

Now you can figure out, on the Estimated Income Schedule in the Worksheets, the *estimated available income* for your family after your death. This will show whether your family will have the support you want for them from your estate.

Study the picture carefully. If there are flaws or gaps, you have the opportunity to change it, to correct errors and touch up weak spots. Now is the time to seek professional help—to work with your attorney to make the necessary changes and revisions to guarantee that your after-death objectives will be achieved.

☽

IT PAYS TO BE CHARITABLE

In 2003, $240 billion was donated to charity in the United States. Seventy-five percent of this was from individual contributions.

Bill Gates, the founder of Microsoft, and his wife, Melinda, have endowed the Bill and Melinda Gates Foundation with approximately $24 billion from their personal fortune to focus on global health, education libraries and Pacific Northwest giving. It is Mr. Gates's expressed desire to give away the bulk of his fortune during his lifetime. A host of other such megaphilanthropists have dedicated enormous sums of money to a wide variety of charitable causes. When disasters strike, the response in donations from the general public for both domestic and worldwide needs is immediate and generous. Where else is the impulse to give so strong and motivation for giving so varied?

Every year billions of dollars are given away to charity by Americans, both individually and collectively. The donors range from rich to poor, from corporations to private foundations to individuals; and the recipients from great institutions such as large public charities to the local library, school, or church. Solicitations are made by mass mail or advertising campaigns, door to door, by nationwide television marathons, and by individuals, both great and small; from the famous movie star to the boy down the street.

People respond to the onslaught of appeals for an amalgam of reasons. For some the motive is a noble one, a desire to help those in need. For others it is a matter of personal satisfaction or the need to repay one's debt to society, or a way of advancing medical research for a disease that has touched their family, or to support certain principles and beliefs. For others the charitable impulse is stirred more by ambition than by altruism. Philanthropy is a means of attaining status. A person's worth in a community is often measured by the amount he gives away; the larger it is, the larger you believe his fortune must be. What better way of assuring immortality than by giving funds for a wing of a hospital, an endowment to a university, a collection to a museum, or helping to cure Alzheimer's, cancer, malaria or AIDS, to name a few?

Adding to all these personal motives—and promoting them as well—is the admixture of tax savings. Our tax laws encourage charitable giving. When you give to charity you pay no gift tax; you receive an income or state tax deduction; in some cases you may even reap a profit from your gift.

The tax aspects of charitable giving make it a significant element in estate planning. Although your philanthropic motives may be of primary importance, it behooves you to plan your program of giving in a way designed to give you maximum tax savings. If philanthropy can pay extra dividends, why not plan them? A sound program of charitable gifts can mean giving more than you might otherwise be able to afford. It can even provide greater security for your family and/or yourself. It can help preserve a family business. It can be a means of carrying out your family values and objectives. It may also appeal to a desire to leave the world better than you found it. The tax code with respect to charitable gifts allows you to self-direct what might otherwise have gone solely to the federal budget as estate taxes. Through well-thought-out charitable gift planning, you may be able to direct portions of your hard-earned estate to causes and organizations whose work improves the world in ways dear to your heart. Either way it is "social capital." Charitable gift planning places the focus on your social and fiscal priorities rather than those of the federal budget. It can be a very gratifying part of your estate planning.

What Is Charity?

Not every gift you make with a philanthropic purpose in mind qualifies for tax deduction under the federal law.

Your gift will qualify for a deduction under these conditions—if it is made to the United States or one of its states for public purposes; or if it is made to religious, charitable, scientific, literary, or educational organizations, provided their income doesn't inure to the benefit of any individual and provided no substantial part of their activity consists of carrying on propaganda or attempting to influence legislation. It is also important to note that whatever the gift, the charity must receive some benefit from it.

If you make a gift of $250 or more, you will need to keep your cancelled check (if you made a cash donation), and obtain a receipt from the charity with the amount and date of the gift, and stating the item given if not cash. The charity will also have to note the value of any services or goods you received in return (a dinner, a seat at a ball game, etc.).

If your gift exceeds $5,000 you will need to obtain a qualified appraisal of its value and associated information about your contribution to the particular charity.

Although the definition covers a multitude of circumstances and organizations, note that it does not include every nonprofit organization. A donor can sometimes run into trouble in claiming a tax deduction for a "charitable" contribution. A case in point involved the estate of William Nelson Cromwell. The donor, a prominent Wall Street lawyer, left part of his residuary estate to three bar associations. The government denied the estate a charitable deduction for these bequests. The executors, one of whom was John Foster Dulles, sued for a tax refund of over $2 million on the grounds that these associations qualified under the tax laws. The lower court denied the deduction. The organizations, it stated, existed primarily for the benefit of the members of the profession; in addition, they engaged in activities to influence legislation. On appeal, however, the higher court found that the organizations were conducted in the interest of the public and granted the charitable deduction.

This story had a happy tax ending, but nevertheless, the moral is clear. Before making a gift, look into the organization you are planning to benefit and find out if it qualifies. Just because it is a nonprofit organization doesn't mean that your donation to it will be tax-deductible.

THE TIMING OF YOUR GIFT

When should you make a charitable donation: while you are alive or at your death? Putting aside personal considerations and viewing it solely from a tax point of view, your decision should be made on the basis of whether you want to save *income* taxes or *estate* taxes. If you give during your lifetime, you will save on the first. If you give at your death, you will save on the second. But sometimes it is possible to arrange matters so that you get both income and estate tax deductions for the same gift.

Generally speaking, lifetime charitable giving is not of as much significance to the person in the lower income tax brackets. He saves little and so may be better off with a plan that gives him an estate tax deduction. The high-bracket planner, on the other hand, may wish to reap income tax benefits during his lifetime to increase his spendable income, and so, too, his ultimate estate to heirs.

LIFETIME GIVING: THE INCOME TAX APPROACH

All of us make lifetime gifts to charity in some form or other. We make a donation, take our deduction on April 15, and let it go at that. Perhaps we are being careless and are paying out unnecessary tax dollars. A bit of foresight and planning can reduce the actual cost of charitable giving or increase the amount of the gift.

How the Income Tax Deduction Works

Unlike the estate and gift tax laws, which carry no restriction on the amount deductible for charitable contributions, the income tax deduction is a limited one. Here's how it works for taxpayers who itemize deductions:

Fifty Percent Deduction Limits: You are allowed a deduction up to 50 percent of your adjusted gross income, if your gift is a contribution to a publicly or governmentally supported organization, or if it is to certain types of private operating foundations or conduit foundations that will be described later. Thus, a taxpayer whose adjusted gross income is $80,000 may deduct all of a $40,000 gift to these types of organizations.

Thirty Percent Deduction Limits: However, if your gift to these same organizations is one of long-term capital gain property, or *for the use of* these same organizations, or given to most private foundations, you may only have a deduction up to a maximum of 30 percent of your adjusted gross income. Certain exceptions are made to this 30 percent rule. You may have up to a 50 percent deduction if the gift is made to (1) a private nonoperating foundation (usually a family foundation) and if the foundation distributes the contribution to a 50 percent charity within 2½ months of its reporting year, or (2) to a private operating foundation, or (3) to a community foundation that pools the contributions it receives from many people and administers these contributions as a common fund (large cities and many small ones have them). An interesting point about the community foundation is that the gift to the common fund is kept in a separate account in the name of the donor and he may designate the charities that are to receive the benefits of his contribution.

Twenty Percent Deduction Limits: In the case of long-term capital gain property given to most private foundations, the limit will be the *lesser* of 20 percent of your adjustable gross income, or 30 percent of your adjusted gross income *minus* allowable contributions you made to 30 percent types of charities.

Charitable organizations are referred to as 50 percent or 30 percent charities depending upon the maximum deductions allowed for gifts made to either type.

If your gift to a 50 percent charity exceeds 50 percent of your adjusted gross income, you may carry over the excess for the next five years. There is also a five-year carryover permitted on gifts to 30 percent charities. Thus, if you have given amounts exceeding 30 percent of your adjusted gross income to your family foundation, you can deduct the excess in the current year or in future years.

For corporations, the charitable deduction is different. A corporation gets a deduction of up to only 10 percent of its taxable income.

In addition to determining how much to give, the planner should consider the kind and form of gift. One type of gift may give better tax results than another.

Gifts in Kind

Suppose you want to make a gift of property—whether it be securities, real estate, or insurance. You will get an income tax deduction equal to the fair market value of the property at the time the contribution was made. The fair market value is the price at which the property would have changed hands between a willing buyer and a willing seller. Gifts in kind are particularly valuable when they consist of appreciated property. They will cost the donor less than an equivalent gift of cash and, in some cases, they may even result in a profit to the giver.

Your college asks you, for example, to pledge $5,000 to the college's building program. If you pay the pledge in cash, you receive a deduction for the $5,000. If you are in the 28 percent bracket, then the amount of your deduction is $1,400. If you choose instead to satisfy your pledge with securities worth $5,000, which originally cost you $1,500, the cost of your contribution would be less and the tax savings greater, because had you sold rather than donated, you would have paid capital gains tax of 15 percent on the $3,500 of gain. By donating the stock you have an income tax savings of $1,400 and a capital gains tax savings of $525. Total tax savings: $1,925 by giving appreciated stock, versus $1,400 for donating cash.

There are limitations on appreciated property of which you should be aware.

1. You are only allowed a deduction up to 30 percent of your adjusted gross income if your gift to a 50 percent charity consists of appreciated property.
2. Generally speaking, if the gift of appreciated property is given to a 30 percent charity, the deduction is limited to 20 percent of your adjusted gross income.
3. If the gift consists of property that, if sold, would give rise to ordinary income, the deduction is based on your cost. This is also so for property, such as works of art, books, and letters, created or prepared by the donor.
4. If the gift is of tangible personal property such as a stamp or coin collection, gems, or art, and it would be subject to long-term capital gains tax if sold, your deduction for the gift may or may not be as favorable as you would like. If the gift is related to the charitable purpose of the organization (such as a painting to a museum), then your deduction will be for its current fair market value up to 30 percent of your adjusted gross income. If the property given is unrelated to the charity's purpose, your deduction will be based on your original purchase price, plus the cost of any improvements you may have paid for (i.e., your adjusted cost basis).

Depreciated Property

Don't make a gift to charity of property that has depreciated in value. You are better off selling the property and donating the proceeds. The charity doesn't suffer because it will receive cash equal to the value of the property it would have otherwise gotten, and you will have a loss deduction in addition to the charitable deduction.

Present Gifts of Future Interests

In order to get a charitable deduction, your gift need not be one that the charity receives immediately. You can make a gift of a remainder interest under any one of three prescribed conditions and still get an immediate deduction for the present value of that interest.

These are the conditions under which a charitable remainder gift will qualify for a deduction:

1. A gift in trust under the terms of which the donor or other beneficiary is to receive a specified annuity (at least 5 percent of the value of gift) during the term of the trust and the charity receives the remainder upon the expiration of the trust.
2. A gift in trust with the donor or other beneficiary entitled to receive annually a fixed percentage (at least 5 percent of the value of the trust property) as determined each year during the existence of the trust, and with the remainder going to a charity at its expiration. In both of these situations the trust must end at the death of the donor or beneficiary or within twenty years of the creation of the trust.

    Examples of 1 and 2: In both, a donor creates a trust and funds it with $100,000. In situation 1, she is to receive an annuity of $6,000 during her lifetime, and upon her death the remainder goes to a charity. In situation 2, the donor is to receive annually 6 percent of the value of the principal of the trust *as determined each year* during her lifetime, and upon her death the remainder goes to a charity. Note: Effective July of 1997, trusts under 1 and 2 above that pay income to the donor or other beneficiary are required to have a remainder interest for the charity whose present value is worth *at least* 10 percent of the initial fair market value of the trust. (See further information ahead in this chapter under "The Charitable Remainder Trust.")

3. A gift of a residence or farm to a charity, with the right retained by the donor and his spouse to use it during his or her lifetime or for a specific period of years.

    Example: Mr. Country Squire, a 71-year-old property holder, owns a large country estate worth $450,000. He wants to enjoy it during his life, but he plans to leave it at his death to a nearby college. At the same time he'd like to make some lifetime charitable gifts. The tax savings would also mean a lot to him.

    His solution is to donate to the college an interest in the property worth approximately $30,000 each year, but retain the right to live on it during his lifetime. The gift to the college is a gift of a remainder interest—the right to the donated property at Mr. Squire's death.

    He gets a tax deduction of approximately $12,500, which is the remainder value of property worth $30,000 at the end of the life expectancy of a man aged 71 (see the Treasury table in the Appendix). In his 35 percent bracket, this deduction means an annual tax savings of $4,375.

    As Country Squire grows older, he can donate interests worth less than $30,000 each year, since, as his life expectancy decreases, the proportionate value of the remainder interest given to the college increases. As long as the value of the remainder interest he gives away each year is worth $12,500, he will find himself with $4,375 more of spendable income.

    Addendum: he might, if he wishes, arrange the gifts so that he retains the right to live on the estate for a certain number of years instead of for his life. Or he might wish to have his wife enjoy it after his death. In this case the college will not get possession of the estate until after his wife dies. Then the remainder interests (the value of the gifts to charity) will be reduced by the joint life expectancies of Mr. Squire and his wife, meaning a lower deduction for him each year.

Charitable giving can be used to provide secure retirement income for the giver. You arrange to give your favorite charity a sum of money or property. In return for this gift, the charity agrees to pay you or your spouse an annual income for the lifetime of either or both of you for any stated period. These are the ways it may be done:

The Charitable Annuity Trust. Under this arrangement a trust specifies an annual amount to be paid to you. This guarantees that you will receive a specific amount that you can depend upon every year.

The Charitable Unitrust. Under this trust the annual payment to you must be a fixed percentage of the market value of a trust's assets as determined each year or, alternatively, the lesser of 5 percent of such value or the trust's income. You can see that there are no guarantees of the specific amount you will receive. Your payments will depend upon the changing values of the trust property or income from year to year. This can have both positive and negative consequences to your income.

The Charitable Pool. This way you give the money or property to a public charity to be placed in a pool or common fund. The charity pays your share of the pool's income to you annually. Here again, the annual payment to you is not determined and will probably vary each year.

As you can see, these types of arrangements are particularly valuable to the older person with appreciated property. If he tried to diversify his holdings he would have to pay capital gains taxes and so lose part of his capital through tax erosion. Under these arrangements he exchanges his property for a guaranteed income without any tax on the appreciation of the property. In addition, he gets a charitable deduction of up to 30 percent of his adjusted gross income. The amount of the charitable gift is determined by calculating his income interest and subtracting that from the value of the property itself.

Many institutions (particularly universities) are offering attractive arrangements of this kind today. They work for the mutual benefit of both parties.

Private Foundations

The philanthropy of the Rockefellers, the Fords, and the Gateses has made the "foundation" a household word. But the use of foundations is not limited to multimillionaires. They can be a valuable estate planning tool for people whose estates are not huge, but nonetheless substantial. They are used to obtain the benefits of income tax deductions and also to build up funds to meet specific charitable obligations or purposes.

A private foundation is your own personal charity—a tax-exempt trust or corporation that you create. In order to qualify for this exemption, it must be created and operated for charitable, religious, scientific, literary, or educational purposes. The creator and his family can control the organization as trustees, but the activities of the foundation must be directed toward its charitable purposes if its tax-exempt status is to be maintained.

Ms. Community Leader is called upon to donate large sums annually to a number of charities. She finds that sometimes the sum expected from her exceeds her charitable deduction for the year. At times she isn't in a position to meet these obligations. It's easy enough in a good year, difficult in a lean one.

To solve her problem, she sets up her own foundation, either endowing it with a certain amount of property or annually contributing amounts up to 30 percent of her adjusted gross income, the maximum deduction she will be allowed (20 percent if she donates appreciated capital gain property). She diverts income from herself and realizes further tax savings from her deductions. The foundation's income is received income-tax-free, but does incur a 2 percent excise tax on investment income. However, a minimum percentage (approximately 5 percent) must be paid out each year for the charitable purposes for which the foundation was created; otherwise the foundation will be subject to penalty. Ms. Leader can select the charitable recipients of the fund and determine the amount and time of payments, but must assure recipients are tax-exempt organizations. She gets her charitable deduction, however, when she makes her contribution to the foundation, not when it makes distributions to charities.

Charitable foundations, we shall see, can be particularly useful for estate tax purposes when the major asset is a closely held corporation. For a businessperson, it can be even more than a means of satisfying his charitable obligations and saving taxes. It can help his business now and for future generations.

Phineas Phlump is the president and sole stockholder of Phlump Pump, Inc., a leading manufacturer of bicycle pumps. Phineas makes sizable charitable contributions each year. He wants to get something more out of it than a charitable deduction. He wants to use it to help his business, especially since he is grooming his two children to become active in the company. He creates the Phlump Foundation and makes his contributions to it. (Note: The gifts cannot be interests in or stock in his business.) He makes his two adult children members of the board of trustees. The foundation's funds are used to promote cycling through scientific research, scholarships to worthy cyclists, rest homes for retired ones, and bicycle museums. These charitable gifts bearing the Phlump name have three by-products—free advertising, the buildup of goodwill among the cycling part of the consumer market, and the continuation of his values and interest in cycling into the next generation of the family.

If the cost and administrative functions of a private foundation are not justified for smaller estates, consider supporting charitable organizations or community foundations with donor-directed funds.

CHARITY AFTER DEATH: HELPING TO CONSERVE THE ESTATE

Unlike the income tax deduction, there is no limitation on the amount of the estate tax deduction. The full amount of any property passing to a qualified charity is tax-free.

Thus the estate tax charitable deduction enables a planner to satisfy his charitable instincts tax-free at his death, but it can serve other purposes as well. The tax savings realized through use of the deduction can mean greater security for the family.

USING A CHARITABLE TRUST: THE CHARITABLE REMAINDER TRUST

Security for a noncharitable beneficiary can be provided through a charitable remainder trust. You can create a trust to pay the income to someone for life, leaving the remainder to charity. However, the charitable tax deduction (the present value of the charity's remainder interest in a charitable remainder trust) must be 10 percent of the value of the assets contributed to the trust. This limits the payout rate that can be used to generate income based on the value of the trust and on your age. The younger you are, with more actuarial years to receive income from the trust, the lower the maximum payout allowed. The maximum payout is limited to 50 percent of the value of the trust when it is established, even if the donor is over age 80. The minimum payout rate is 5 percent. This limits the percentage of payout from such a trust that could be paid to younger donors.

It follows then (depending upon the applicable federal rate at the time) that an 80-year-old person might be allowed a payout rate as high as 50 percent; a 45-year-old might have a maximum payout rate of 9 percent; a 30-year-old as low as the minimum 5 percent. If the percentage for payouts falls below 5 percent, there is no further benefit allowed. Yet, under the right circumstances, charitable remainder trusts can preserve the income-generating value of an asset for an heir, give the donor a tax deduction and allow their charitable intent to be fulfilled.

Ms. Testatrix, a widow, age 80, has an estate of $2,000,000. She wants to leave it in some manner to provide first for the support of her only child, an unmarried woman of 60, and to leave the rest to her favorite charity. If she leaves it all to her daughter, who she knows will eventually leave it to the same charity, there will be estate taxes of about $225,000 (in 2004). The net bequest will then be $1,775,000. At a 7 percent return, her daughter will receive a taxable income of $124,250.

Instead she establishes a plan to leave her $2,000,000 estate in trust with an annuity payable to her daughter for her life and the principal passing to the charity at the daughter's death. The charitable deduction for the value of the remainder interest left to charity wipes out the estate tax. The entire $2,000,000 will be left for the trust. If Ms. Testatrix dies when her daughter is age 60, her payout (depending upon the applicable federal rate at the time) might be around 10 percent. For our example, let's say she opts for a 7 percent payout and receives an income of $140,000. Thus the daughter will receive $15,750 a year more income, and the charity will have $225,000 more principal with a resulting larger remainder amount upon the daughter's death.

Of course, Ms. Testatrix could have opted to receive the income from such a trust herself to boost her own retirement income. Many have done this as a way of avoiding capital gains tax on appreciated assets such as stock, real estate, an interest in a business, artwork, etc. The asset, once owned by the charitable remainder trust, can be sold for full fair-market value with no capital gains tax reducing its sale proceeds. This is because a charitable beneficiary is named for the trust. The full proceeds can be invested to provide better diversification and unlock the full income-producing potential of an appreciated asset. If Ms. Testatrix had done this, she could have selected to be paid the same *fixed* annuity income from the trust of $140,000, or 7 percent of $2,000,000, (or at her age a much higher payout rate up to 50 percent), or she could have selected her 7 percent payout to be *based on the value of the trust's portfolio as determined each year.* With a good investment manager working for her, this could mean a rising income in good years. She would still be removing the $2,000,000 from her taxable estate, and would receive an income tax deduction she could spread over the next five years if necessary.

Wealth Replacement: Suppose our widow did this for herself, but did not want to disinherit her daughter. If she is healthy, she could purchase a life insurance policy on herself for $2,000,000 and have it owned by an irrevocable trust (described in Chapter 14). That way her daughter will inherit the full $2,000,000, both income and estate tax free.

Mind you, if this had been a younger widow with a daughter, of, say, age 25, this approach would not have worked at all.

THE CHARITABLE LEAD TRUST

Sometimes it may be better to split the trust in the opposite way: income to charity, remainder to family. This would be so when estate taxes will be great and the family or beneficiary does not have a current need for income.

Let us say Mr. Testator wants to leave his entire $2,000,000 estate to his only child, a son who has already reached the top income tax bracket. Not only does his son not need the income from his inheritance, but if he received it, 35 percent of it would go out in income taxes. So Mr. Testator creates a lead trust in his will, under which an annuity will be paid to charity for a stated number of years or until his son reaches a specific age, perhaps 65, and then the principal goes to his son. Mr. Testator's estate taxes will be reduced by the value of the gift of the annuity interest to charity, leaving a larger amount of principal to eventually pass to his son at about the time he may retire and have a lower income.

Such a technique works especially well for very large estates where grandparents want to maximize gifts to grandchildren and have assets that pay income they do not need. The limit on gifts that will skip a generation is $1 million per grandparent, as we have seen in Chapter 14 (temporarily increasing to as high as $3.5 million in 2009, then reverting to around $1 million in 2011). By using the trust that pays income to a charity for a period of years, and then having the remainder go to a grandchild, the gift could potentially be much more than $1 million.

Take the case of Mr. Patriarch, a vigorous 78-year-old who has an estate of $6 million. He admires his granddaughter's early interest in investing and the returns she achieves on her small but well-constructed portfolio. He wishes to make a gift of his considerable stock portfolio to her, but knows it exceeds by a few hundred thousand dollars his generation-skipping gift limit of $1 million. Because he has invested well, he feels sure that the value of the portfolio will increase by quite a lot over his lifetime.

Here are his choices: He can wait until his death to pass on the stock, but estate taxes and generation-skipping taxes could erode his gift. Besides, given his good health, by the time he dies the generation-skipping limit may have gone back to pre-EGTRRA 2001 limits of around $1 million. He can make a gift of the portfolio to his granddaughter in the near future, but his gift could exceed his $1 million limit. Or he could create a lead trust, and have an annuity income of a fixed percentage of the portfolio's value paid to his favorite business school each year for the next ten years (perhaps a percentage equal to the dividends he typically receives). During that time, if all goes as he predicts, the value of the stocks will increase considerably.

After checking the numbers with his attorney, he determines that the value of this annuity payout to the school will reduce the value of his gift to his granddaughter so much that he will freeze his gift at a sum just under his $1 million limit. Now regardless of the appreciation in the stocks' future value, his gift will have been calculated for estate tax purposes at under $1 million. He is excited about his plan, and has visions of collaborating with his granddaughter to hone her portfolio management skills to assure the future growth of his investments—growth that will not be included in his taxable estate—growth that will go to her! The business school is thrilled by the addition to its scholarship funds for the next ten years.

Planning Note: Under EGTRRA 2001, our Mr. Patriarch could run the numbers with his attorney and determine much larger amounts for his lead trust that he could allocate to the higher generation-skipping tax exemptions; $1.5 million in 2004–5, $2 million in 2006–8, $3.5 million in 2009.

THE CHARITABLE FOUNDATION AND THE FAMILY BUSINESS

The person who has created a foundation during his life has a recipient for his charitable bequests. After his death, his family can continue to control its operation. The foundation can be of particular importance in an estate plan where the major asset is the family business. We think of the Ford family, where Henry Ford faced such enormous estate taxes that a choice had to be made between selling most of the Ford stock to raise the money needed to pay the tax, or making a substantial contribution in order to reduce the taxes to an amount that could be paid out of other assets of the estate. Ford common stock was reclassified into voting common and nonvoting. The nonvoting common went to the Ford Foundation. Control of the corporation remained in the hands of the Ford family, in this case by the retention of the voting stock.

The role of the family foundation in estate planning is useful for perpetuating family values and creating philanthropic leadership opportunities for the business owner and his family. It can be used to remove a portion of the family business value from the taxable estate, but less so than in the past. If large percentages of stock are transferred to the family foundation, chances are that much of it will have to be sold by the foundation within a five-year period. As such it is important to consider who the buyer may be, and where the funds will be derived.

These days, this technique has become much more complicated than in the time of the founding Fords. There are strict rules about who the other stock owners can be and complicated percentage limitations on the stock holding a foundation may have in a business. These rules may require the foundation to either partially or fully divest itself of these stock holdings during periods ranging from five to ten years (if an extension is granted). Since this is another of the planning techniques that has become not only very technical, but also one with onerous tax consequences (two-tier excise taxes on excess business holdings of 5 percent and 200 percent), this should be undertaken only with very skilled counsel.

CHARITABLE GIFTS THROUGH INSURANCE

Gifts of insurance can be made in a number of ways.

1. Give away an insurance policy and get an income tax deduction for its value—approximately the cash value of the policy.
2. Name a charity as irrevocable beneficiary. You receive an income tax deduction for your premium payments.
3. Give more than you would otherwise be able to afford by making your favorite charity the beneficiary of a large insurance policy.

   A man age 45 wants to make a very large gift to a charity he has headed for many years—something impressive and lasting, like a new building. His estate will just be sufficient to take care of his family after his death and now he can't spare more than $10,000 a year out of his capital. Ten thousand dollars a year doesn't seem like much, but he can use it to build a fund of $500,000 by means of insurance. His net premium for the first year is $7,294, but in his 35 percent tax bracket, his actual net cost is only $4,741. Over a period of ten years, his after-tax premium cost will be $47,411—which buys him a charitable gift worth a half million dollars at his death. In addition, he may be able to use dividends to limit payments in future years.

4.   Provide a guaranteed income for a member of your family. You name a charity as irrevocable beneficiary of life insurance, and it agrees to pay an annuity or income to your daughter out of the proceeds of insurance. You get an income tax deduction for your annual premiums to the extent they are attributable to the remainder of the proceeds, which the charity will keep.

5.   Wealth replacement using life insurance. You donate appreciated property to charity in trust, take the tax deduction, let the charity have the gain, and still transfer the economic value of the property to your family. Let's say you have some highly appreciated stock that is not yielding high current dividends, and you'd really like your children to receive the value of the stock at your death. You contribute the stock to a charitable remainder trust as described above. The stock can then be sold and its full value invested for greater diversification and higher yields. An income from the principal is paid to you for your lifetime or a specified period. You then create another trust that purchases life insurance on your life with death proceeds equal to the value of the donated stock. Premiums for this policy are paid out of some of the income you receive from the charitable remainder trust. The children are the beneficiaries of the insurance trust and so will receive the life insurance proceeds (for the value of your donated stock). Both the charity and your children receive a tax-free benefit at your death. You receive a substantial charitable deduction against taxable income in the year given. And the income generated by the trust pays for you to replace the donated asset for your family.

CHARITY: WHICH WAY?

Which is the best way of making your charitable gifts? That, of course, is up to you as the individual planner. Indeed, as we have pointed out, the whole matter of charitable giving, during your life or at death, is one in which many motives, desires, and needs interact; some philanthropic, some personal, and some financial. One type of charitable gift is better than another only insofar as it fits in with and improves both the estate and the personal plan of each individual.

CHAPTER 19

What to Do with Your Business: The Sole Proprietorship, the Family Enterprise, the Part Ownership

Mr. Independent owns his own business. He draws a salary of $125,000. By coincidence, this is just about the same amount as his brother-in-law, Mr. Executive, earns. He is the vice president of a small manufacturing company.

Equals in income, are they equals in their ability to provide security for themselves and their families?

Independent would tell you that he is better off. After all, if his business continues to prosper, he will have an estate worth at least $1,250,000, the present value of his company.

Executive, on the other hand, has assets—stocks, bonds, savings, and insurance—that total about $600,000. Not much of an estate in Independent's eyes.

But Independent is only looking at Executive's surface estate. If he were to probe further, he would find that Executive is worth much more than $600,000. He has neglected to consider that the most important part of Executive's estate lies in his employee benefits. Under the corporation's pension and profit-sharing plans, his beneficiaries will receive at least $40,000 a year after he dies. This, together with the income that can be expected from his other assets, will provide his family a yearly income of $70,000; just about the same as Independent expects his family to receive from his $1,250,000 estate.

At this point Independent alters his judgment and in his mind raises Executive to an equal position with himself.

But his judgment is still superficial. Again he has neglected to consider an important aspect—the relative stability of the two estate potentials. Executive's fringe benefits on retirement and at death are guaranteed and his investments are diversified. Barring unlikely events, a minimum of $70,000 a year for his family is a sure thing.

In Independent's case, however, the amount of income is predicated on a theoretical assumption—that the business could be sold at its present operating value of $1,250,000 when he dies, or if continued, would bring in a predictable amount of income for his family.

This is theory only. In fact, no one knows exactly what the business will be worth at his death. Between now and then its value can decrease or increase substantially. Even assuming its value were $1,250,000 the moment before his death, what would it be worth the moment after? The loss of the key person can have a serious impact on a business, greatly affecting its market value or its value as a going concern.

Even if the business could be continued, a replacement for Independent would have to be found. This could mean that a large part of the profits that Independent had been drawing in salary would be paid out in wages, leaving little income for the family. As an alternative, the business could be put up for sale, but then there would have to be a buyer ready, willing, and able to pay its true value. There is often a scarcity of such people. It might come down to a matter of choosing the lesser of two evils.

Where will the money come from to pay the taxes, administration expenses, and debts in Independent's estate? He doesn't have much cash, nor does the business. Will it cause a forced sale or liquidation of his business?

Whichever alternative is selected, continuation or sale, Independent's family could find itself with an annual income of less than $70,000. It could be more, of course, too. The point is that Independent's position as of now is uncertain.

Any Independent, whether he is a sole proprietor, the head of a family enterprise, or a part owner, must have a special estate planning objective—the preservation of his business or its value for his beneficiaries.

As a rule, his business is his major asset, perhaps the only asset of real value. Thus his family's security will depend largely or even entirely on whether he is successful in achieving this objective.

Before embarking on an examination of the ways available for meeting this objective, let's see who these independents are and point up the major problems of each.

THE SOLE PROPRIETOR

He is the person who owns all or virtually all of his business. If someone else has an interest in it, it is only nominal. The business may or may not be incorporated, and it may be a small shop with a few employees or a large company employing a hundred or more people. No matter what its size, the business depends for its success on the skill, acumen, and ability of its owner. The sole proprietor is usually faced with two problems. When he dies, there is no one to take over and so the business will have to be sold. If it is put up for sale it may be difficult for his estate to find a ready market for the business.

THE HEAD OF THE FAMILY ENTERPRISE

He is an owner, too, but members of his immediate family own interests and actively participate in the business. This situation normally calls for continuation of the business for the benefit of the family since he usually has, within the family, the people to take over the management and they are interested in continuing it.

His problem is how to prepare them for their future responsibilities and how to assure them a harmonious working arrangement.

Often, too, there will be beneficiaries who are not in the business. His estate plan must be arranged so that it will not discriminate against the nonparticipating members of the family, either by some method of having them share in the profits of the business, or by providing their inheritance out of other assets of his estate.

A further problem he must deal with is that of assuring liquidity for the payment of taxes and expenses without impairing the working capital of the business.

THE PART OWNER

He is a partner or a stockholder in a closely held corporation, or perhaps a member of a limited liability company. His partners, fellow members or stockholders may be relatives, such as brothers or cousins, or colleagues, or a combination of both. In all probability the business will continue after his death, but his family may or may not retain its interest in it. If they are going to keep it, then his problem is to assure that they will receive a sufficient income from it. This is particularly important if their interest is a minority one. If their interest is to be sold, he must make arrangements to assure that it will be purchased at a fair price and that cash will be available to carry out the arrangement.

Although the problems of these three independents differ, there are three possible solutions available to each of them: continuation of the business for the benefit of the family; sale at death; sale or gift of all or part of the business interest during life.

CONTINUATION FOR THE FAMILY

A person may be bent on preserving a thriving enterprise for the benefit of his family, but before he goes about making arrangements to carry this out he must ask himself this important question: Is my business worthwhile continuing?

This isn't a rhetorical question. What may be a worthwhile enterprise for him may not be worthwhile for his family after his death. The particular industry or the particular business may be subject to periodic slumps. By its nature, the business may depend for its success on his personal leadership, talents and instincts. Continuation may mean taking too great a risk with his family's security.

A further consideration is the future of the business. This requires weighing the effects of possible changes in the market, technology, competition, expiration of patents or licenses, and potential for growth or decline.

Assuming the business is sound and its future looks good, the next important question is whether it will produce the necessary family security in terms of sufficient income. It may do a good job of supporting the family while its head is alive, but that fact in and of itself isn't a guarantee as to future performance.

Take the case of Ms. Entrepreneur, a woman with a corporation worth $400,000. Its annual net profit is very small, and every second or third year it has a small loss. However, it pays her a salary of $60,000 a year, so from her point of view it is a worthwhile enterprise. Now, if, at her death, the family were to sell the business and realize its full value (ignoring taxes and other expenses), the maximum income it could expect to receive from investment of the proceeds at 6 percent after taxes would be $24,000. On the face of it, it would seem to be wiser to continue operation of the business than to dispose of it. But if continuation requires hiring one or two people to replace the owner, or increasing salaries for employees, there might be little profit left over for the family. Unless it can produce the necessary profit, the business is not worth continuing.

If a business is sound, however, its future expectations good, and it can be expected to produce sufficient profit to support the family, the planner must next turn her attention to a vital question: Who is going to run the business?

MANAGEMENT AND THE FAMILY ENTERPRISE

The person with a family enterprise probably has her future management within the business itself. To assure that it will continue to operate successfully, she must see that the person or persons she selects to succeed her are properly trained to take over the responsibilities that will eventually fall to them. It may be of value to pass along some of this responsibility before her death, not only as part of the training but also to see how the arrangement will work out.

We know of one businessman who learned a bitter, important lesson in that way. His son, whom he envisioned as his eventual successor, had started by working in the office of his business, a manufacturing corporation. One day he decided that it was time for his son to learn something about the production side of the company and so he put him in charge of a particular project in the factory.

Unfortunately, or perhaps fortunately, his timing was bad. His son's assumption of responsibility coincided with a business trip the father had to make. When he returned to the plant a week later, he found it in turmoil. Three of his best employees had quit. The head of the union local was waiting to see him. Production was at a complete standstill. His son had somehow managed to alienate almost everyone in the plant, regardless of whether they were connected with his particular job or not. Management was obviously not his forte. Today he is employed elsewhere and one of his brothers-in-law is slated for the top job.

When some of the family do not participate in the business another problem is created. On one hand, is it wise to give these "nonpartici-pants" interests in a business over which they have no control? Should a widow, for example, have to depend for her security on a business that is run by sons of a prior marriage?

On the other hand, is it fair to those in the business who are con-tributing their time and energy to the success of the enterprise to let a nonparticipator have a voice in the operation? Should a father with two daughters and a son give them equal interests, when it is the son who will have all the problems of running the business and the daughters who will have the controlling shares?

Arrangements can and should be worked out in such situations, not only in the interest of fairness to the family members, but for the sake of the business itself. In the case of a widow whose stepsons run the busi-ness, her share of her husband's estate should come from his other assets. If these are not sufficient, additional insurance might be obtained to make up the difference. Another way of providing for her security is through use of a salary continuation agreement between the owner and the corporation, or a pension or profit-sharing arrangement that will be payable to her at his death.

The father with two daughters and a son could make similar arrange-ments. Or if this were not feasible, he could divide his business equally among them, but permit the corporation or the son to buy out the inter-ests of his sisters. The purchase could be made in installments. The father could also purchase life insurance to provide his daughters with estate and income tax-free cash equal to their fair share of the estate and leave the entire business to his son.

Another method he could use is the reclassification of the corporate stock into preferred and common, the preferred to go to the daughters and the common to the son. This would give the son full voting power and, in addition, any future increase in the value of the business that log-ically should go to him as the fruits of his labor. It would assure the daughters of an income from the dividends on the preferred. Further, in order to ensure their security, these dividend rights could be made cumu-lative with the right to convert to common if, for any reason, dividends on the preferred weren't paid for a specified period of time. Thus the daughters would be able to share in the control of the corporation if the expected income was not forthcoming.

Whichever arrangement the head of a family business selects, it should be one that will assure adequate protection for the nonparticipating members and give the participating members some degree of freedom from outside control. At the same time it must provide for efficient and harmonious continuation of the enterprise, as well as harmony in the family.

Management and the Part Owner

Continuation of a part owner's interest by his family after his death might seem to present no problems. This is so in many cases. Certain businesses can easily be continued with the former owner's family sharing in its profits. This is true where capital and not services is the major income-producing factor. A partnership, a corporation or a limited liability company whose assets consisted of real estate would be a case in point.

But when the business depends in large part upon the personal services of its owners, the surviving partners may not be willing to share the profits of their labor with the surviving family. Happy working relationships do not necessarily extend beyond the grave. Consider, for example, this case.

Joe, Jim, and John are equal stockholders in a corporation in which they are all active employees. They receive substantial salaries but rarely declare dividends.

Joe dies. His widow inherits his stock, which is worth about $500,000. But what income does she realize from it? Her husband received a salary; she gets none. No dividends are paid. She wants to sell the stock but there are usually no buyers for a minority interest in a closely held corporation—except, of course, Jim and John. They want to buy her out, but not right now. Why not wait a bit, they reason. Let the widow go hungry for a while and then buy up her shares at bargain-basement prices.

The result is a family lockout instead of a family continuation. Jim and John were the villains, but Joe had the basic responsibility; he should have made arrangements to assure that his widow would receive at least a minimum of income from the business. If he wanted her to be able to keep the stock in the corporation, he, too, could have set up a salary continuation agreement, perhaps funded with sufficient life insurance, or a pension arrangement that would ensure that she wouldn't go hungry and be squeezed out.

More commonly, troubles of the same sort occur when there are really no villains at all, but only certain unfortunate tendencies of human nature. Three brothers own a business. One dies. The remaining two vow solemnly to take care of his widow—and they mean it. Sometime later the business hits a lean period that lasts for a long time. Little by little the brothers' resolution and devotion wear off until finally they ask themselves, not how long can we take care of her, but rather, how can we get her out of the business?

If you can see such situations arising in your business, then now is the time to establish a formal agreement for salary continuation for your surviving family, or a buyout. Such agreements are usually funded with sufficient life insurance to assure that neither your family nor the business is left in a financially vulnerable position.

Management and the Sole Owner

What happens when the planner wants to continue his business for the benefit of the family but there is no one to take over the management? Obviously, he must create his own successor management.

This is the time when parents should look at their children with a dispassionate eye. Tradition, sentiment, and ego all say that a son or daughter should step into a father's shoes. But history tells a different story. Not only are there inefficient sons and daughters, or wayward children, there are also artist children or professional children; scientist daughters or social worker sons—none of whom has either the bent or the desire to take over his or her father's business.

If your child is one of these, it is better to accept the situation gracefully and make other arrangements for the management of your business.

Creating successor management means bringing in one or more executives and training them for the job. It also means providing them with incentives to ensure their continued, long-term loyalty.

What kind of incentive? Bonuses, profit sharing, pension plans, long-term care policies paid up by age 65 that are normally offered by the large corporations are possible. The best form of incentive in this situation, however, is probably some form of ownership interest—a stake in the business. If the business is unincorporated this means eventually taking the potential successor in as a partner. It may be better to incorporate so as to obtain more flexibility in working out a suitable arrangement.

With a corporation form of business, key personnel can be given shares of stock as bonuses or in the form of profit sharing. The potential successors might be given an opportunity to purchase shares at a reduced price or over a period of time under advantageous financing arrangements. Another possible way of providing incentive would be by giving them options to purchase stock at a fixed price on the death of the owner.

Yet the incentive plan should not be so great that it jeopardizes the security of the family. The arrangement should be such that an adequate income is assured for the family and/or control remains within its hands. To assure this protection for the family, it may be necessary to change the capital structure of the corporation. For example, the stock might be reclassified into voting common and nonvoting common. The family would receive all the voting common and the successor management part or all of the nonvoting. The family retains complete control but the key people are given incentive because they share in the company's future growth and earnings by virtue of their stock holdings.

Another method that might be used is reclassification into preferred and common, with the family owning the preferred stock and successor management the common stock. Under this arrangement most of the value of the business is put into the preferred and it has preference as to dividends and assets on liquidation. Successor management can afford to buy the common since its value is low. Its incentive will be great since its stock will reap the full benefits of all future increases in the value of the business.

These are not the only ways of rearranging capital structure to protect the family while providing incentive for outsiders. There are many possibilities, and various features may be added to provide further security. For example, the owner could have an insured salary continuation agreement. Then the members of the family are not only stockholders of the corporation but also creditors, a more desirable status.

If the owner wants his family to be bought out by the other stockholders at an agreed upon price, he needs to be sure that an up-to-date buy-sell agreement is in place with updated business valuations. This can be backed by enough life insurance to pay the family the value of the deceased owner's share of the business. The family gets the financial security the owner wanted for them; the other stockholders have immediate tax-free cash without placing a burden on the business.

ECONOMIC CUSHIONS

If the business is to be continued, whether its management is in the hands of the family or outsiders, the family needs an economic cushion.

In a well-planned estate, its security should not rest solely on the fortunes of the business. There should be assets outside the business to provide this reserve. Unfortunately for the average businessperson, most of his estate is his business. How does he create other forms of economic security? He uses the usual methods of estate building: life insurance, disability insurance, outside investments, funded pension and profit-sharing plans protected further by long-term care coverage.

The business as well as the family needs a cushion—this in the form of extra liquidity. On the death of its head, a sole proprietorship or family enterprise may encounter some rough going for a while. There may be a decrease in business because of the loss of personal contacts or because customers wait to see whether the company will continue or liquidate. Credit may be temporarily withdrawn. Extra cash will help to tide the business over this uncertain period. The corporation can obtain this needed liquidity by insuring the life of its key person, and possibly setting up a sinking fund for this purpose.

LIQUIDITY AND TAXES

Often a more important reason for providing liquidity is the need to pay estate taxes and administration expenses. It may be possible to pay these out of other estate assets, but unless they are ample (and they rarely are in this type of estate), it is wiser to take the cash out of the business and leave the family as large a reserve as possible. There are two ways of paying the taxes out of the business.

1. *Redemption of Stock.* Ordinarily, cash or other property paid by a corporation to its stockholders out of its earnings and profits is treated as a dividend to the stockholders. One of the exceptions to this rule is a distribution by a corporation in redemption of stock to pay estate taxes. This is popularly known as a "Section 303 redemption." If the value of the decedent's stock exceeds 35 percent of the value of his adjusted gross taxable estate, the stock can be redeemed without it being considered a dividend, to the extent that the amount received does not exceed the taxes, funeral costs, and administration expenses. If the redemption price is higher than the tax basis for the stock, some taxable gains will be realized.

   In other words, the estate can take money out of the surplus of the corporation with little income tax liability. This is one of the few ways of getting money out of corporate surplus without having it treated as income. Unfortunately, one has to go to the extreme of dying to achieve this tax savings.

In closely held corporations one should be careful in planning a Section 303 redemption. This is a highly technical matter and cannot be adequately dealt with here. Let it suffice to say that expert tax advice is always required in planning a stock redemption to avoid adverse tax results.

2.   *Installment Method.* Estate taxes must usually be paid within nine months after the death of the estate owner. The tax laws, however, permit an executor to pay the portion of the federal tax attributable to the value of a closely held business over a period of fifteen years, provided that the value of the business exceeds 35 percent of the value of the adjusted gross estate. To qualify for this type of payment a business can be a sole proprietorship, a partnership, or a corporation. To meet the over 35 percent requirement, business entities can be aggregated if, in each, the decedent's capital interest or voting power is at least 20 percent or if there are fifteen or fewer partners or stockholders.

During the first five years the estate need only pay interest on the deferred taxes. The tax with the interest can then be paid in up to ten annual installments. In addition, the tax on the first $1 million of such business property has a special low interest rate of 2 percent.

The installment method allows an estate to pay the estate tax over a period of time, and perhaps to do it out of earnings of the business without impairing its capital. Remember, though, that it only applies to the part of the tax that is attributable to the value of the business interest. The balance of the tax must still be paid within nine months. There is another problem to consider in using this method of payment. Since an executor is personally liable for estate taxes, by paying in installments he is extending the period of his liability. If the business should fail or estate assets decline in value, he might have to pay the balance of the taxes out of his own pocket. However, the tax law allows the discharge of executors from such personal liability if certain requirements are met.

ESTATE TAX EXCLUSION FOR "QUALIFIED FAMILY-OWNED BUSINESSES"

During the years 2004–10, increases in the unified credit equivalent for estate taxes (under the provisions of EGTRRA 2001) have caused the qualified family-owned business deduction to be repealed. If the estate tax is reinstated as scheduled in 2011, the special deduction for qualified family-owned businesses will be reinstated as described below.

The Taxpayer Relief Act of 1997 allows an estate tax exclusion of up to $1,300,000 for interests in qualifying family-owned businesses. Since this dollar amount would include the restored general estate tax exclusion of $1,000,000, the $1,300,000 amount will only provide relief from estate tax on an additional $300,000. Take an example of a business worth $2 million in the year 2011. If the owner dies that year his gross estate is reduced by $1,300,000:

- $300,000 special exclusion for the qualified family-owned business.
- $1,000,000 general applicable estate exemption.

Nonetheless, additional tax relief always sounds good, but this provision has complex tests for participation by family members during a ten-year period prior to the owner's death. The business may be acquired only by a "qualified heir," which includes certain unrelated but long-time employees. To add to this complexity, there is a ten-year period during which the following disqualifying events can occur:

- Heirs cease to "materially participate" in the business or farm.
- The business or farm is sold to outsiders.
- The business is no longer located in the U.S.
- Heirs cease to be U.S. citizens.

While this increased exemption from estate taxes can provide savings when passing a business or farm to family members and/or long-time employees, careful planning prior to death is needed. You should have your current will or trust reviewed to be sure the provisions for transferring your business or farm meet the very complex requirements, or whether other methods of paying or reducing estate taxes can be employed.

CONTINUATION AND YOUR WILL OR
LIVING TRUST

The last, but by no means the least, thing that must be done to carry out a plan of continuing your business is the granting of authorization in your will or living trust. In the absence of a specific authorization to do so in the will or living trust, the executors or trustees may be required to sell or liquidate, or risk personal liability for failing to do so. The executors and trustees should therefore be given the broadest powers to carry out the plan of continuation.

SALE AT DEATH

If the business is to be sold and its full value realized by the family, there must be a market for the business. There may be willing buyers for it today, but this is no assurance that the same will hold true at the time of the owner's death. Moreover, the death of the owner or key person tends to reduce the price offer. Buyers are always in a better bargaining position when the estate or family is *forced* to sell.

Then, too, there is an interim period between the death and sale during which profits may drop, making the business a less attractive investment. If a ready buyer cannot be found, the estate may be forced to liquidate the business and realize substantially less on the sale of the assets than the true value of the enterprise as a going business.

The conclusion is obvious. If you plan to have your business interest sold at your death, it is better to make the arrangements for that sale while you are alive than to leave it to chance.

The best market may be found within the business itself—your partners, fellow stockholders, key personnel, the corporation's pension plan, or possibly a family foundation.

1. *Partnership Agreement.* A partnership agreement should make provision for having the surviving partners buy the estate's interest. The scale can be worked out to permit installment payments over a number of years, or it can be financed by each partner owning insurance on the lives of the others.
2. *Buy-Sell Agreement.* If the business is incorporated, you can have an

agreement requiring the other stockholders or the corporation to buy or redeem your stock after you die. Some agreements obligate only the estate to sell or the stockholders to buy, while others make it mandatory on both sides. In most cases the planner should be sure that under his agreement the purchase and sale are mandatory unless he has valid reasons for wanting his estate to have flexibility.

Such agreements can be financed by the stockholders insuring each other if they are the potential purchasers, or by the corporation insuring its stockholders if the agreement calls for redemption. The price to be paid is set forth in the agreement. It may be a fixed amount, which should be adjusted periodically to reflect increases or decreases in value, or it can be based upon a formula involving net worth and goodwill.

3. *Key Personnel.* The person who has no partners or fellow stockholders to buy out his interest must create his own market. He can do this perhaps through his key personnel. Financing the sale may be difficult, but installments, venture capital life insurance on the owner owned by the key person, and other methods can be worked out.

4. *Employee Stock Ownership Plans.* These are also possible purchasers. These plans already own large shares of the businesses that created them. If the employees' trust is not in a position to finance such a purchase, it can carry insurance on the owner's life to provide the necessary funds.

LIFETIME TRANSFERS: SALES AND GIFTS

Like any other asset, a business may be sold or given away, in whole or in part, during the owner's lifetime in order to carry out his estate plan. The decision to make a business transfer a lifetime one might be motivated by any one of a number of reasons: inability to arrange for a profitable after-death sale; desire to benefit or provide incentive and mentoring for family members or successor management; need to diversify investments; need for liquidity; and, of course, the classic motive for lifetime transfer— removing the subsequent growth on a substantial asset from the taxable estate.

Lifetime sale has its economic disadvantages as well as its advantages. On the one hand, a living owner can probably get a better price than the executor of his estate. On the other hand, the gain realized on the sale is subject to taxes and so reduces the planner's capital during his lifetime.

Planning Note: With respect to family-owned businesses, special planning is required. There are several issues in the tax code regarding intrafamily gifts and sales of business interests where other family members are owners. Not addressing these issues properly can have very adverse, unintended effects.

Family Attribution: Under the family attribution rules, a business owner wanting to sell all his stock in the business to the corporation could be in for a surprise when he discovers that he is still considered owner of corporation stock owned by his children. Under the family attribution rules, he would be considered the owner of any stock that his parents, grandchildren, children or spouse own—directly or indirectly. The sale of his stock would then be treated as a dividend and not a capital transaction.

Lifetime Gifts for Estate Freezes: A business owner may want to make gifts of interests in his business during his lifetime in order to transfer future growth in value to other family members. How these gifts are valued for gift tax purposes depends on how well he navigates through very specific requirements. Lets say he *recapitalizes* the business stock into preferred stock, which he retains, and nonvoting common stock, which he gives to his two children. His goal is to "freeze" the value of his retained stock, lower the value of his gift of nonvoting common stock, and transfer all future growth to the stock owned by his children.

In order to accomplish this, the corporation *must be required* to pay his retained preferred stock annual dividends at a fixed rate. His retained stock is then *frozen* at roughly the present value of future payments. That value is then subtracted from the value of the total stock to determine the value of the gifted shares.

Needless to say, it is critical to have very skilled legal and tax advice when doing intrafamily transfers or sales of family-owned businesses.

There are a number of methods of lifetime transfer. Not all of them are affected by the estate freeze rules. Which of them you select will depend to a large extent on your objectives. Those that *are* affected include the following: recapitalizations, family limited partnerships, buy-sell agreements, personal and family holding companies, grantor retained interest trusts (see Chapter 14) and remainder interest transactions.

To avoid estate freeze issues, the business owner could use instead such things as: installment sales, private annuities, deferred compensation and irrevocable life insurance trusts.

Sale for a Lump Sum

This is the simplest method. The problem may be that a potential buyer doesn't have the available funds. An employee stock ownership plan or your family foundation may be able to pay a lump sum. A competitor or other interested buyer may be able to arrange for financing or venture capital.

Installment Sale

Under this arrangement the seller usually, but not always, gets a down payment. The balance is paid to him over a period of years. This is a common practice when the sale is made to a member of the family or key personnel. The buyer, by being allowed to spread out his payments over a period of time, is able to finance it, at least in part, out of the earnings of the business. The seller can spread the taxation of his gain over several years. The seller should, however, be sure the buyer has the ability to run the business and retain or increase its profitability, so the installments are paid.

Sale Plus Contract

For the owner who really doesn't want to retire, this can be a good solution. The sale is tied in with an employment contract retaining the owner as manager or consultant at a specified salary. When there is such an employment arrangement, the sales price of the business might be contingent on future earnings. For example, the sales arrangement might involve a lump sum or installment payments combined with a percentage of the profits for the next five or ten years. This *can* be advantageous to buyer and seller.

Exchange of Stock

Large companies interested in acquiring businesses generally offer their own stock in exchange. The stock received by the seller is usually listed and therefore readily marketable.

This arrangement is highly recommended for owners who will realize large gains on an outright sale. On the exchange of stock there is no tax payable. The tax is payable only when you sell the new stock. One way to reduce the tax impact is to sell the new stock gradually over a period of years. A charitable remainder trust could also be used to sell the stock, owe no tax on the sale, establish a diversified portfolio, receive an income that would spread taxation over many years or a lifetime, *and* benefit a charity. (See Chapter 18.) The value of the donated stock can then be replaced by his purchasing a life insurance policy on himself and his wife that is owned by an irrevocable trust. His children and grandchildren can be the beneficiaries of that trust.

Private Annuity

This arrangement (the sale of your business in exchange for an agreement by the buyer to pay you an annuity) has its tax advantages, as we know. It is especially well suited to the sale of a business since annuity payments, like installment payments, can be financed out of the profits of the business.

Private annuities carry some risk, however. The buyer could default in his obligation to make payments. That's why these are customarily limited to arrangements between members of the family.

Family Limited Partnership

One estate planning technique for family-owned or closely held businesses that can have multiple advantages is the family limited partnership. Properly structured, it can impact some basic components of the business: control, income and ownership proportions, and discounts on transferred limited partnership interests—even future appreciation under very carefully planned techniques.

In a family limited partnership parents can maintain control over the business and continue to receive some of the income. By gifting minority limited partnership interests to children through the partnership and restricting the transferability of the shares, significant discounts of 20–35 percent on the value of those shares may be achieved. If the partnership is structured very carefully, the parents may also be able to pass on the future appreciation of gifted shares in the company to the children.

Let's take the example of Mr. and Mrs. Businessowner, age 60. They started a manufacturing company many years ago that is now worth $3,700,000. They have three children who will someday operate the business, and wish to transfer it to them cost-effectively during their lifetimes. However, Mr. and Mrs. Businessowner wish to maintain control over the day-to-day operations, and continue to receive income. Their at-

torney recommends a family limited partnership, which is set up as follows: first, the limited partnership entity is created. The entire business is
placed within the partnership. Mr. and Mrs. Businessowner (or their living trust) retain 1 percent ownership and are the general partners. In this
role they maintain control of the business and can receive management
fees or other income. The other 99 percent partnership interest is deemed
to be a limited partnership interest and is placed in their living trust. The
transferability of this interest is restricted.

The parents now begin gifting minority limited partnership interest
to their three children, planning to use interests worth just $600,000 of
both their estate tax exemptions. (The interests could have been gifted
to an irrevocable trust for the benefit of the children as well.) Mr. and
Mrs. B, as general partners, will distribute income proportionately to the
limited partners. However, as general partners they can make cash distributions on a discretionary basis as the needs of the business dictate.

Because the interests gifted are minority interests and have limited
transferability, they are discounted (we'll use 30 percent here). At this discount rate the $1,200,000 of interests can be grossed up to $1,714,286—
a notable increase in the gift! If, over the next five years, they gift additional
$10,000 interests grossed up by the 30 percent discount to $14,286 to
each child, they will have transferred a total of $1,928,572. This is now
52 percent of the business distributed among the three children. The con-
sequence is that Mr. and Mrs. B now own only 48 percent (a minority
partnership interest). At their deaths their holdings will thereby be discounted for purposes of determining the size of the taxable estate. By creating the family limited partnership, Mr. and Mrs. B have maintained
effective control of the business during their lifetimes while achieving
substantial estate and gift savings. However, as mentioned earlier, they
will need very skilled legal and tax advice to structure this transfer technique to achieve the shifting of future growth to their children.

GOING PUBLIC

As many owners of small corporations have discovered, it can be worthwhile to go public. The usual method is for the owner to sell only part of
his interest while retaining enough to keep control. In this way he is able
to convert some of his closely held interests into cash and can diversify his
investments. At the same time he has created a market which can be used
for future sale of his remaining stock, either during his life or at his death.

How to Value Your Business

The determination of the worth of a business is vital to many aspects of estate planning. If your business is the major part of your estate, you can scarcely begin your plan of transfer without coming to grips with this problem.

You must know the value of your business in order to calculate your estate taxes. The failure to make these estimates can frustrate the formulation of a satisfactory estate plan.

The valuation of a business is also important in another aspect of estate planning—lifetime transfers and gift taxes. The planner who is making gifts to his children or other members of his family must place a value on any business interests he gives in order to determine whether they come within his annual exclusion and unified credit and, if not, the amount of gift taxes that will be payable.

Valuation has income tax ramifications as well. If an employee is given stock or an interest in the business, it is considered compensation and therefore income to him. The value of what has been given to him must be established. If a businessperson makes a charitable gift of, for example, shares of stock to his foundation, its value must be determined in order to calculate his income tax deduction.

How to Determine Value

For tax purposes the fair market value of a business interest is the net amount a willing buyer would pay to a willing seller. When dealing with publicly traded securities, we have a ready reference—market quotations. With stock of a closely held corporation or an interest in an unincorporated business, determining valuation can be a difficult matter.

For estate tax purposes, if a business or business interest is sold within a reasonable time after death, the sale price will usually establish the value—provided it is an arm's-length transaction. The price paid, for example, on a sale by an estate to the children of a deceased owner would be subject to very close scrutiny. If it was obviously not reasonable, it might not carry any weight as evidence of true value.

A partnership agreement or stockholders' agreement or an option to purchase, which fixes the sale price beforehand, determines the value for estate tax purposes. The price set in the agreement or option will be taken as the value (even though it is less than actual value) provided the estate is obligated to sell. For example, Corporation X is owned by two stockholders. They enter into an agreement that provides (1) that if either wishes to dispose of his stock, he must first offer it to the other at a price of $1,000 per share; and (2) at the death of either, the survivor has the right to purchase the shares at the same price. One of them dies. Although a share might be actually worth $1,500 the estate's obligation to sell the stock makes its value for tax purposes the price set in the agreement.

Other Methods

In the absence of actual sales or buy-sell agreements, other methods to determine value must be used. Unfortunately, there is no pat formula or set of rules for valuing a business. The Internal Revenue Service does offer certain "factors" stating that these are not "all-inclusive" but that they are "fundamental and require careful analysis in each case."

- "The nature of the business and the history of the enterprise from its inception." This means looking at its past record to determine potential stability.
- "The economic outlook in general and the condition and outlook of the specific industry in particular."
- "The book value of the stock and the financial condition of the business." In spite of the fact that the book value is almost always considered in dealing with valuations, a planner shouldn't rely on it. Since book value rarely reflects actual value, it isn't often accepted by the Internal Revenue Service.
- "The earning capacity of the company." Potential future income is a major factor in the value of most businesses, and past earnings are used as an indication of future performance. Due weight is given to any trend toward increasing or decreasing net income.
- "The dividend-paying capacity." This means more than just the dividends that were actually paid in the past. It means what could have been paid after retention of a reasonable amount of profits in the company. In a family corporation this factor is given less weight. Here profits can be taken out in the form of salaries and a dividend-paying policy may be determined by the needs and tax brackets of the family.
- "Whether or not the enterprise has goodwill or other intangible value." There is no general definition of goodwill and no set formula for its valuation. The Internal Revenue Service generally

values goodwill by capitalizing the excess of net earnings over and above a fair return on the net tangible assets. In actual figures how would this work out? A company has a net worth of $500,000, and makes a profit of $50,000. Using 6 percent as the norm, a reasonable return would have been $30,000. But since they have earned $20,000 more than this, the amount is attributed to goodwill.

- "Sales of the stock and the size of the block of stock to be valued." First of all, to be a test of value, sales must be arm's-length transactions. Forced sales or distress sales or small, isolated sales will not be relied upon to determine actual value. If the stock represents a controlling interest, its value may be greater than its per share value. On the other hand, if it is a minority interest it might be less.

- "The market price of stocks of corporations engaged in the same or a similar line of business having their stocks actively traded in a free and open market." The companies must truly be comparable in order to make a valid comparison. This includes comparable capital structures as well as market and business trends.

Although there are these various factors to be given consideration, certain ones carry more weight than others. Earnings will be a more important factor for a company that sells products or services. However, for an investment or holding company, such as a real estate corporation, the value of its underlying assets is of greatest importance.

A great deal of emphasis is put on capitalization of earnings and, at times, capitalization of dividends. One of the most difficult aspects, however, is the determination of the capitalization rate to be used. There is no formula, even within the same industry. In addition, it varies from time to time depending on economic conditions.

To repeat: in the absence of a buy-sell agreement or actual sale, there is no way to be sure of what the ultimate valuation of a business will be for tax purposes. Certainly, the businessperson himself can't determine it. He needs the help of his accountant and attorney. He might be well advised to get expert appraisals by someone specializing in business valuation.

If possible, you should try to establish the value now—during your life—rather than leave it for your executor to argue it out with the tax authorities. This can be done by making taxable gifts and filing gift tax returns, or by making charitable donations and claiming income tax deductions. It might involve litigation, but because valuation is so difficult and each side is bound to have conflicting appraisals, the usual result is a compromise. While the valuation of one purpose is not necessarily binding on the government, it is some evidence and carries weight for the future.

KEEP IT WORKABLE

Your business transfer plan should not be treated differently from the rest of your estate plan. Like it, it must be periodically reviewed. Changes of circumstances, whether personal or economic, can turn a good arrangement into an unworkable one. Be sure it doesn't happen to yours.

CHAPTER 20

CHOOSING YOUR ESTATE

MANAGERS

While we're alive, we are the ones who provide for our families, ensure their security, and make plans for their future. We wish we could do the same thing after our deaths. We want a form of immortality.

If that wish is not attainable, something close to it is. In the people whom we select to manage our estates, to take care of the needs of our families, we beget an immortality of a sort. Competent representatives can be found to act in our names and use our stated intent to do what we would wish to be done.

The word that defines these people is "fiduciary." It refers to the executor, the trustee, the guardian of a minor's person and property. Technically and actually, the fiduciary is a person who has assumed the responsibility or duty of acting for the benefit of another person with whom he stands in a relationship of confidence and trust.

Confidence and trust it indeed is—or should be. Choosing a fiduciary is not a mere formality; no legal fiction is involved here. Few people realize the responsibilities they are assigning when they select their fiduciaries, and so leave the choice until the last minute. Then the tendency is to choose someone who is a friend or relation without any thought as to whether he, she, or they possess the necessary abilities, let alone the willingness to do the job.

Let us take just one of the fiduciary roles—guardianship. Guardianship of the person of a minor implies one set of qualities—the ability (and the desire) to give children love and affection, and to raise them according to the values and principles held by their parents. Guardianship of property implies another set—the ability to handle their financial affairs, to invest and use their money wisely, to conserve their capital. Skill in financial affairs is the requirement here.

Sometimes these two sets of abilities are combined in one person, but more often they are not. Yet how many people, in making a will, consider this? A couple make a devoted aunt the guardian of their children's property *and* person. They think they have done the right thing.

But suppose the aunt knows nothing about financial matters? Wouldn't it have been wiser to separate the guardianship functions, appointing her the guardian of the persons of the children, and another guardian of their property? This would relieve her of an unwanted burden as well as ensuring the financial security of the children.

The function of a fiduciary, then, is often a double one: it may involve both personal and impersonal responsibilities; it demands both sense and sensibility. That is why it is often necessary to have multiple fiduciaries, and why their selection is a serious matter that calls for careful consideration and the balancing of many requirements. It is just as important to the small estate as it is to the large one—if the amount of money involved is not substantial, that does not mean that the need for sound management is lessened; it may indeed be that much greater.

THE EXECUTOR

The source of the executor's function is twofold: the law and the will. Under the law, someone must collect the assets of the estate; protect the property against loss or harm; assert any claims against third parties that the deceased or the estate may have; value and inventory the property; liquidate assets; pay all debts and expenses; prepare and file estate and income tax returns. These duties end when the beneficiaries are accounted to and the property is distributed.

The person who does these things is the executor. If you die without a will or if the people you designated as your executors refuse to take the job, or resign or die, or cease to act for any reason, the law steps in, and the court appoints someone to do the job of the executor. He is called an administrator.

As testator you have the right to impose additional responsibilities and duties on your executor. You can leave it up to him, for example, to select certain beneficiaries, to choose charities, or perhaps to distribute personal effects among relatives. He might also be given powers of investment—broader or more limited than the law accords him.

The executor (or administrator) has a time-consuming and important function. He will need the services of a lawyer and possibly also of an investment counselor. But even so, it is he who is responsible for the decisions made, the steps taken. If he acts recklessly or imprudently, or oversteps his authority, then he will be held responsible and is personally liable for any consequent losses.

THE TRUSTEE

The trustee receives, and is responsible for, the administration, investment, and distribution of trust property. He collects the income, pays the trust expenses, distributes the income and/or the principal in accordance with the directions of the trust instrument or will.

The executor's job is over in a few years at the most but the trustee will probably have to act over a long period of time. An estate might require trustees for as long as seventy-five years. The financial security of not one but several generations may be involved. The trustee's investment duties may require repeated investments with periodic reviews of holdings and appraisals. Over the years he will have to make accountings to the beneficiaries, and he will have to file income tax returns for the trust every year.

Beyond this the trustee usually has to work personally with the beneficiaries. He may be required to continuously exercise his own discretion as to the distribution of the trust monies; deciding between one beneficiary and another, setting rival claims. He may have the duty to sprinkle income among a group of beneficiaries to keep himself informed of their needs and resources. And, especially, the trustee must be able to assess, reappraise, and deal with all the changes and cycles that inevitably occur in the economic world over a period of time.

All this means that a trustee must be a *person* of experience and mature judgment—or an *organization* that is capable of handling these many duties. Don't forget that the trustee—as well as other fiduciaries—need not be an individual. It can also be a corporation—a bank or a trust company. Corporate trustees can provide the expertise and continuity of administration that may be appropriate for trusts of prolonged duration, multiple provisions and/or multiple beneficiaries. They can also serve a cotrustee role with a person you have appointed, and could be named as a successor trustee should the person you appointed have resigned or died.

Like the executor, the trustee is responsible for the administration of the trust property and thus can be subject to personal liability or corporate liability for any losses due to their reckless or imprudent exercise of authority.

THE GUARDIAN

As we know, guardianships are of two types: personal and property. The duty of the guardian of the person is, of course, to assume the responsibilities of personal care that the deceased parents had. The personal guardian may be—and usually is—a member of the family. But it could also be a trusted friend.

The guardian of the property, as the name implies, handles only property. He makes investments, collects income, pays expenses, and uses or applies the income or the principal for the benefit of his ward. His duties last until his minor is of age. Then he submits his account and turns the property over to his former charge.

The law limits the authority of a property guardian, however. He is bound to seek and follow the directions of the court. He is limited in his ability to exercise discretion. Because of this it is far better to leave property to a minor in trust under the care of a trustee who is provided with all the powers for carrying out the objectives of the estate owner.

But this doesn't mean that the guardian of the property should be completely eliminated. Even if you leave everything in trust you should designate one, so that there will be someone to take care of property that the child now owns or may later acquire from other sources.

CHOOSING YOUR FIDUCIARIES: HOW MANY?

As a testator you have a choice in your selection of fiduciaries. You can have one person perform all the functions, acting simultaneously and continuously as executor, trustee, and guardian. Conversely, you may appoint several people for each of the jobs. Or you may choose a corporate fiduciary—a bank or trust company. Which is best depends on the size and character of your estate, the needs of your beneficiaries, and your own feelings as to who will be able to carry out your objectives most effectively.

Cofiduciaries: A Special Problem

When two or more people are given the responsibility for one function, whether it is as guardians, trustees, or executors, they are cofiduciaries.

There are often excellent reasons for appointing cofiduciaries. You may want to use the special talent or experience of one person, but feel that he isn't qualified to take on the entire job. For instance, a person might want a business friend to take on the job of managing his estate investments, but at the same time want someone else who is closer to his family take on the responsibilities of evaluating their needs. His solution is to have his friend act as cotrustee with his spouse or another relative. Sometimes cofiduciaries are appointed for reasons of family harmony. A planner, for instance, might want one of his brothers to be his executor, but doesn't want to offend his second brother. So he names them jointly.

The life of a cofiduciary does not always run smoothly, however, and a planner should be aware of this. If he's going to appoint cofiduciaries, he should try as far as is humanly possible to make sure that they are people who will be able to work together. Disagreement or dissension is serious; it can result in court proceedings, with a consequent waste of time and money.

Some planners have tried to solve this problem beforehand by appointing odd numbers of people as cofiduciaries, and specifying in their wills that the majority rules. But committees are burdensome things: too often they complicate rather than simplify estate administration.

Successor Fiduciaries

If you appoint an individual or individuals, you must be sure also to appoint successor or substitute fiduciaries as well. The person you select might die, become incapacitated, resign, or simply refuse to serve. If you haven't nominated a substitute in your will or trust instrument, the appointment of one is left up to the court. You can also take care of this contingency by giving a fiduciary or one of your beneficiaries the authority to name a successor. If you have a corporate fiduciary, however, there is usually no reason to name a successor. A bank or trust company is immortal and can be expected to last for the duration of its assigned responsibility. However, you may want to provide for the replacement of a corporate fiduciary, in case problems arise.

CHOOSING YOUR FIDUCIARIES: WHO?

This is, of course, the key question, for upon your selection of the proper people or groups depends, in large measure, the future of your estate.

There are only a few restrictions on your choice. Some states do not allow nonresidents to be appointed. Others allow them to qualify only if they are blood relatives. In some states corporations cannot serve unless they are qualified to do business in that state. And, of course, the court will not permit the appointment of someone obviously not qualified to serve, such as a minor, an incompetent, or a felon.

The main problem in fiduciary selection is whether to select individuals or corporations, or possibly a combination of both. Let's see some of the ramifications involved in each case.

The Individual Fiduciary

First, some general qualifications. Whoever you select should be a responsible, mature person. Beyond this, he should have some experience in business and financial matters. That doesn't mean that he has to be a specialist, just that he has the information and judgment to know how and know where he can find specialized advice when he needs it, plus the ability to evaluate this advice when he receives it.

He should be someone whose opinion and judgment, whether in business or personal affairs, you value and respect. In addition, he should know your family, and know your goals and aims for them. It's just as important that your family, too, have confidence and respect for him. In a sense your fiduciary is taking over as head of the family. This is a big job, and unless there is mutual confidence all around, there is likely to be trouble.

We remember one case of a frustrated executor who was trying to work out an investment portfolio which, in conjunction with the widow's own investments, would be well balanced and produce the most after-tax income for her. The widow, who happened to be his sister-in-law, refused to give him any information concerning her personal affairs. We tried to help by explaining to her that his purpose was not to pry into her business but to help her. Her answer: She understood why he wanted the information and appreciated his efforts in her behalf. It wasn't that she didn't trust him; it was his wife she didn't trust. Who knew what information he might pass on to her?

This was the result of bad planning on the part of the estate owner. Perhaps the brother-in-law should not have been selected to do the job. There is, after all, no point in selecting someone who—for whatever reason—will not be able to elicit full cooperation from your beneficiaries.

Leaving the personal question aside, there are also some practical considerations. The individual selected should not be too old and he should be in good health. As planner you should make sure, too, that he has the time and the willingness to carry out his duties.

Family Members as Fiduciaries

Most people turn to their own family for fiduciaries. This is usually both proper and just. Naturally you want those closest to you to carry on after you. But when you come to decide which member of your family to select, reason and not sentiment should rule.

One's husband or wife is usually the first choice as executor or trustee of a living trust, but what happens when it comes to choosing an alternate if there is no spouse surviving? Too often the planner wants to do "the right thing" and lets wisdom and judgment go to the winds. Thus he names all four of his children as executors or in some way gives responsibility to the whole family. This rarely works out. There's bound to be trouble. Better to make a decision and a selection now based on your own assessment of the individual qualifications of your family's members.

It goes without saying that the individual selected, no matter what his specialty, should be a person of integrity. Instances of malfeasance are rare, but they can happen. Fiduciaries can be bonded, of course, but this is expensive—and, more important, it is, or should be, unnecessary. If you are so unsure of a person that you think he should be bonded, then choose someone else. Or, if you cannot find anyone whose integrity you know you can rely on, then you would certainly be better off with a corporate fiduciary.

The Corporate Fiduciary

The usefulness of the corporate fiduciary is becoming more and more recognized. We believe that in many types of estates a corporation is preferable to an individual. When the estate is sizable or complicated, an institutional fiduciary is usually a wise choice. Handling an estate of this type is quite a burden for an individual—often too much so. In addition, it takes experience and know-how that few individuals can be expected to have. How can one person be investment counselor, tax expert, accountant, and administrator at the same time?

The bank or trust company contains all these elements. It offers a packaged service that is often cheaper and more efficient in the long run. Take for instance the corporate trust officer. Not only is he a person with background and training in his specialty; he also has at hand, when he needs them, the experience and background and training of the entire bank staff.

A corporation provides full-time management; it is financially responsible; it is experienced.

And it has continuity. This is a great plus. We have mentioned the fact that a trust can last through several generations. No one person can handle such a trust. But a bank or trust company will be able to.

Corporate fiduciaries do tend to be more conservative in their investments than most individual investors. This is a factor you should take into consideration. Depending on your aims and desires, it may or may not be a point in their favor. Remember, however, that you can direct your fiduciaries to follow any particular program of investment you think advisable. In other words, the inherent conservative tendency of the corporate fiduciary is not really a stumbling block to a more imaginative and aggressive investment program, if that is what you want.

Corporations are more impersonal in their administration. Again, this is advantageous or disadvantageous depending upon the circumstances. A bank or trust company can't give an intimate, personal touch to its administration, but sometimes its very impersonality prevents pressures and strains that might otherwise occur if a family member is made a fiduciary. It usually can deal more effectively with the "problem" beneficiary. It is more difficult to harass or pressure a corporate fiduciary. It is impossible to call a bank at midnight and complain that you can't live on the income of a trust.

Compromises are always possible, too. The person who wants both the impersonal, experienced management of a corporation and the personal touch of an individual can appoint both of them, either formally as cofiduciaries or under a more informal (but clearly spelled out) arrangement. The bank is made the executor or trustee, and an individual is given certain powers over the distribution of income and principal, but not over investment or administration. A variety of collaboration arrangements is possible.

If your decision is to use a corporate fiduciary, be sure to consult with them beforehand. They can help you to set up your estate transfer program in the most efficient way possible; they can review your will and your trust arrangements with your lawyer to make sure that both are properly organized for good administration.

You should be aware that corporations, just like individuals, may decline an appointment. This is most likely to happen if the estate or trust is not set up to be easily administered, or if the estate is a small one and commissions aren't adequate to compensate them for the work involved. A trust company, for instance, would probably decline to serve as a trustee of a $100,000 to $200,000 trust fund unless it will receive the minimum commission it specifies.

FIDUCIARY POWERS

Beyond those provided by law, what sort of powers should a planner give his fiduciary?

Investment

Unless you specifically empower him with additional authority, a fiduciary's investment freedom is limited by law. In some states he can invest only in property that is specified by law, known as "legals" or "legal lists." In other states his scope of investments is limited by what is called a "standard of prudence," i.e., measured by how prudent people of intelligence and discretion would act in managing their own affairs.

Under your will or in the trust instrument, however, you can do pretty much as you please: either making the investment power a broad one, or limiting it to specific kinds of investments. On the whole we favor giving wide powers for a number of reasons. First of all, if you have carefully chosen your fiduciaries, you should have sufficient confidence in them to rely on their judgment.

Further, a live investor obviously is a better judge of the changing economic needs of the estate than a dead one. As the past decades have proved, few can guess with real accuracy the swing of an economic cycle; what was a sound investment twenty-five years ago may no longer be. Many an estate has diminished because the testator has not foreseen this possibility and has not armed his executor or trustee with the power to switch, change, reinvest, etc., according to his own discretion. The principle that the dead hand of the testator should not rule the living is especially applicable to investment powers.

Just as you may make the investment power flexible, so also with the people you confer it on. The power can be limited to one of the cofiduciaries or it can even be given to a beneficiary or a third person.

Property Retention

It is usually wise to give a fiduciary the power to *retain* property in the estate. This power is important when the estate has a variety of investments, some of which do not fall within the usual permissible investment categories. Unless the fiduciary has the right to retain them, they must be sold, sometimes to the detriment of the estate.

Suppose an estate was probated that consisted almost entirely of high-grade corporate stocks worth, say $800,000. The portfolio was well-founded, the dividend return was high, and each individual stock represented a good investment. The will, however, did not give the executor or the trust any authority to keep the property and was silent on investments. Suppose further, in the absence of specific authorization, a particular state did not allow a fiduciary to invest just in common or preferred stock. Therefore the executor would have to liquidate some of these securities and invest in "legals" that may provide a smaller income return.

Business Disposal

A businessperson should always specifically empower his fiduciaries to continue his business or to enter into new partnership arrangements. Otherwise sale or liquidation is required with the possibility of losses being incurred.

Real Estate

Broad powers are particularly important here since the authority granted by law can be especially limited with respect to real estate dealings in many states. A fiduciary might be able to sell a million dollars' worth of securities but would not be allowed to dispose of a $10,000 piece of real estate without judicial approval. By all means, give your fiduciary the power to deal with real estate, including the right to mortgage and lease, as well as to sell.

Borrowing and Lending

Unless he is given the authority, the fiduciary may not be able to borrow or lend. If the estate needs cash to pay taxes but the executor is unable or doesn't want to liquidate assets, this restriction can be onerous. Sometimes beneficiaries may need cash funds at a time when distribution cannot be made. All this makes the borrowing and lending power an important one.

Tax Savings

Give your fiduciary the right to exercise options, file joint returns with your spouse, the consent to prior gifts. This will allow him to take advantage of many possible tax savings.

COMMISSIONS: FIDUCIARY COMPENSATION

All fiduciaries are entitled to compensation for their services. It is fixed by statute or determined by the court.

State laws on commissions vary greatly. In some states, depending on the size of the estate or trust, each fiduciary gets a full commission. In other states there is one commission that is divided among the fiduciaries, usually according to the service rendered. If a fiduciary performs special services, such as managing a business or real estate, he may be entitled to a "management commission" that is in addition to his regular fee.

Suppose the estate uses an attorney who is also a fiduciary. He has a double function, but in most states he cannot receive both commissions and attorney fees. In these states you will probably be saving money if you make an attorney a fiduciary. Even if you live in a state where an attorney is entitled to commissions as well as attorney's fees it may still be best to use him. His experience and knowledge and the confidence you and your beneficiaries have in him make the cost worthwhile. Remember, too, that your executor and often your trustee will need legal services, so the alternate cost will be no greater. Moreover, many attorneys who act as executors or trustees waive their commissions and take only legal fees.

If you wish, you can enter into an agreement to fix your fiduciaries' commissions, either by agreement during your life or by the terms of your will. Members of the family, for example, will often serve as fiduciaries without compensation. When there is a prior agreement on commissions, this takes precedence over the statute or court-fixed commissions.

FINALLY

The people who administer your estate are just as important as its assets. Be sure that you select them with *at least* the same care that you use in selecting your investments.

A LAST WORD ON

ESTATE PLANNING:

DON'T DO IT ALL YOURSELF

With a book like this to use as a reference and with guides and charts to aid him, could an intelligent person do his own estate planning? Are estate creation and transfer a matter of technique, like boat building, which the knowledgeable amateur can master?

The idea is alluring but dangerous. For this is precisely what estate planning is *not*. It does not demand the mastery of a *single* area of knowledge but of *many*. It is by nature made up of many parts and requires the use of many skills which, while interrelated, are yet quite different. It deals with such subjects as the laws of trusts, taxation, corporations, wills, personal and real property, and many others. It involves a knowledge of economics and financial dealings, of the ways people make their livings, and then their fortunes. It must take into account not only material things, but also the delicate and involved problems of personal and family relationships. It is, in a sense, as broad and complicated as life itself. It has a philosophy of its own evolved over the years and is based on the experience of countless numbers of people.

What must you know to plan an estate? Much more than is in this book. What is contained here are only general principles and broad statements. To cite all the exceptions to these would take volumes. As a matter of fact, there is a great body of legal literature on each aspect of any one of these chapters. It is beyond the capacity of any individual to absorb all this knowledge. And even if he could, there is always the difference between knowledge and skilled action. Assuming the possibility of acquiring the former, putting it into practice is another matter. This takes experience, something that no do-it-yourselfer can readily come by.

Let us cite three do-it-yourself estate plans and their unfortunate outcomes.

The first one concerns wills and how they are drawn. A man had one prepared by his lawyer that gave the bulk of his property to his wife. A few years later his wife died, and eventually the man remarried. He realized that he needed another will, but saw no need to consult a lawyer. He used the old will as a guide and drew a new one, substituting the name of his second wife for his first. He executed the will in his own handwriting and therefore did not bother to have witnesses; these were only necessary, he thought, when the will was typed or written by someone else.

If he had lived in any one of a number of states other than where he did, New York, he would have been on safe ground. What he did not know was that the principle that a handwritten will does not need witnesses does not hold true in New York. Only if he had made the will while in service as a soldier or sailor would it have been valid.

The result: when he died, the will came to probate and was declared invalid. The laws of intestacy prevailed and his property was not distributed the way he wanted.

The second do-it-yourself plan concerns insurance. A widower had made the proceeds of a $200,000 term life insurance policy payable to his estate. This was to make sure that there would be sufficient cash available to meet expenses at the time of his death. He knew there would be estate taxes of about $70,000 due on this when he died but thought this was inevitable. The fact is that it wasn't; had he transferred the policy to his children, they would have received the $200,000 free of estate or income taxes. The proceeds could then have been paid to the estate to meet its liquidity needs. Alternatively, he could have transferred the policy to a trust which could have purchased property from the estate with the proceeds, with the same results.

The third concerns that most important of all estate tax savings tools, the marital deduction. This last do-it-yourselfer thought he had qualified the proceeds of a life insurance policy for it. He had made sure that his wife had the power to withdraw the principal.

But his particular beneficiary provisions for this insurance policy had certain technical requirements for withdrawals: they could only be made on certain dates, a limited number of times a year, and in specified minimum amounts. This is not an unusual provision in many policies. The Internal Revenue Service, however, claimed that because the widow did not have the right to withdraw the proceeds according to the language of the statute "in all events," a marital deduction could not be taken. The court upheld its contention. As a result a substantial additional tax had to be unnecessarily paid.

The annals of estate planning abound with similar stories. The point is clear. No matter what the size of your estate, you will need advisers and helpers to assist you in its planning. If the estate is small, perhaps there need be only two, the lawyer and the insurance underwriter. If it is larger, then a team of experts is required.

THE ATTORNEY

He is the captain of your team. As such it is his function to analyze the existing situation, to make recommendations for improvements and changes, to carry out a program of gifts and sales, and to perform such services as the reorganization of corporations and the drawing up of stockholder and partnership agreements. He plans and draws wills, sets up trusts, and gives tax advice.

Beyond this the lawyer brings to his job a special type of expertise without which the entire estate plan would flounder—language. By this we do not mean grace of style or expression, but the use of language to convey precise meaning. Like any discipline, the law has developed its own language over the years because of the need to express a particular meaning or shade of meaning that is not accurately communicated by the use of ordinary words. Take the simple word *residence*, for instance. A person may have several residences, but only one of them can be what is commonly known as his legal one. Which one? A great deal may depend upon how this word is construed. Many thousands of dollars in taxes or perhaps the way an estate may be distributed could be involved. The lawyer solves this semantic quandry by using the word *domicile*, which in its law meaning signifies the place of residence which a person intends as his official and legal one.

This technical usage of language comes into play with the execution of the numerous documents that are required for estate transfer. Once a person dies and the transfer process goes into motion, these papers are all that remain to express what his intentions were. To make these as precise, as clear, as truly reflective of the estate planner's intentions as possible is the attorney's all-important function, one that only he can perform.

The attorney should also be of aid in helping you to go through a dry run of your estate plan. By all means, ask him to prepare a hypothetical administration of your estate to show mathematically just what the taxes, costs, and eventual distribution will be. He is the person who will help you figure out exactly how the plan will operate once put into action.

Just as the estate planner cannot do his job of planning by himself, neither can the attorney perform his function in isolation. He must coordinate many elements and so will need to call continuously on the aid and advice of other specialists on the team.

THE ACCOUNTANT

As the one who annually audits a person's financial affairs and prepares income tax reports on the basis of his analysis, the accountant is perhaps closer to the changing financial condition of your estate than anyone else. When a business is involved, he has intimate knowledge of its operations. When property is involved, he is continuously aware of its changing value. All of this knowledge comes about because of his concern with your continuing financial health through good tax planning and the proper preparations of your income tax returns. He is the team member who functions as the keeper of your records, alerting the others to new circumstances and fresh requirements. Often he is the adviser who has the greatest continuity and familiarity with your financial affairs over a long period of time. He can be an invaluable member of the estate planning team, helping to assure that all the tax planning fits together in a synergistic fashion.

THE LIFE INSURANCE UNDERWRITER

His role has changed and deepened as modern estate planning has become more complex and as life insurance has come to play a more important part in it.

The old-fashioned way of buying life insurance—from a friend or relative who needs the commission—won't do for the serious estate planner. He needs to seek out a professional life insurance person with a background and experience in estate analysis, one who can operate on equal terms of expertise with the other members of the team. He is your authority on insurance. He knows the different forms of life insurance to be used, and he presents tax-effective ways it can be paid for and the methods by which the proceeds can be most effectively employed. He coordinates the life insurance estate with the general estate. Twenty-five years ago such an individual was hard to find. Today there are many such professionals. It is up to you as the planner to make sure that you find one and not to fall back on the favor-to-a-friend approach.

The insurance person is out to sell insurance. Strangely enough, this makes him of special use to the estate planner. He must analyze estates to find how and where life insurance needs can be met, applying the right tool to a job that needs to be done. As a solicitor (which the lawyer cannot be), the insurance broker is, in fact, the person who most often initiates the idea of an estate planning effort. His role is that of a point person to see that this effort is not only begun but carried out to a conclusion so that the life insurance program he presents is truly integrated into your overall plan.

An insurance person who is skilled in the underwriting process can also play a critical role if something in your health history makes you difficult to insure. His expertise in conducting this process discreetly and knowing how to present your application and negotiate for the best possible outcome can have enormous impact on the cost and likelihood of your being properly insured.

Be sure that your insurance underwriter gives you an audit of all your life insurance policies, showing the types, the amounts, the premium payments and their dates, the cash values, the ownerships, the beneficiary arrangements, and the modes of settlement and options. This audit should then be given to the attorney. Without it he cannot fit the life insurance plan into the overall estate picture.

THE BANK OR TRUST OFFICER

Your attorney will call on the bank or trust officer frequently because of his special background: he has experience in the actual operation of estates. He knows how property can be conserved, how a business can be run when the owner has died. He is an authority on investment and the marketability of securities and property.

He is also the person who, in all likelihood, will be the one who takes over most of the job of handling the estate after you have died. Therefore it's important to get his advice on exactly what powers he will need to do his job well and on the various administrative problems that may arise. He should work with the attorney in drawing up the plan or the documents which will form the basis for the administration.

We have spoken before of the special function of the trustee—of the demands, both personal and financial, that will be made on him. If you want him to be able to act in your place, you must take him into your confidence now, while you are alive and making all these plans. He needs to know—not generally, but specifically—your aims and objectives for each member of your family. If there are special problems, let him know about them. Forewarned is forearmed.

THE INVESTMENT ADVISOR

His function is obvious. He reviews the present holdings of the estate and plans the future investments. His particular contribution is the balancing of the long-term and short-term needs of an individual during his life. His advice on diversification of securities holdings will be of special value. He can also play a vital role in providing continuity for a surviving spouse who may not have been the one with an understanding of investments.

THE ESTATE PLANNING TEAM

We call this group of advisers an estate-planning team, and we use the word *team* in its real sense—a group that meets regularly, acts in concert, and consults with each of its members, who include *you*.

Unfortunately, this rarely happens. Most estate plans are not reviewed frequently enough and are not prepared collectively. This is a mistake—and a costly one. When sizable estates are involved, it is absolutely necessary to preserve this team principle. Each adviser should be aware of your goals. In fact, the advisers can help you expand your thinking to include possibilities and issues you may not have thought of on your own. They should work collaboratively, combining and coordinating their skills and efforts to create a plan in which every part works in concert with the others. It is up to you as the estate planner to see that this is carried out. You must take the initiative in seeing that your team is a working one.

Nor can you leave everything up to the team. If that were true, there would be no need for books such as this one, no reason why a person should inform himself of the basic ideas and concepts of estate planning. In actuality, the more the planner knows about the subject, the better the plan will be. If he cannot and should not act as an expert, he must nevertheless be a knowing amateur.

Any lawyer can tell you that a knowledgeable client is a pearl of great price. It is difficult, almost impossible, to advise a person on how to plan his finances, his savings, his investments, his insurance, and all the multitude of things that make up his estate unless the client himself has a good general grasp of the principles involving creation and transfer of this estate.

In the long run the expert is a technician, and only that. He is not a seer, not a prophet. He cannot plan your estate for you if he has no idea of what your objectives are—if he does not know how and why and where you want to distribute your property.

There are decisions you must make. But how can you make them unless you are aware of the number and extent of possibilities and choices open to you? Or, in other words, unless you are knowledgeable.

APPENDIX

For tax years beginning in 2004

	Single Taxpayers	Married Taxpayers Filing Jointly
10%	$1–7,150	$1–$14,300
15%	$7,151–$29,050	$14,301–$58,100
25%	$29,051–$70,350	$58,101–$117,250
28%	$70,351–$146,750	$117,251–$178,650
33%	$146,751–$319,100	$178,651–$319,100
35%	Over $319,100	Over $319,100
	Heads of Household	Married Filing Separately
10%	$1–10,200	$1–$7,150
15%	$10,201–$38,900	$7,151–$29,050

	Heads of Household	Married Filing Separately
25%	$38,901–$100,500	$29,051–$58,625
28%	$100,501–$162,700	$58,626–$89,325
33%	$162,701–$319,100	$89,326–$159,550
35%	Over $319,100	Over $159,550

Trusts and Estates

15%	$1–$1,950
25%	$1,951–$4,600
28%	$4,601–$7,000
33%	$7,001–$9,550
35%	Over $9,550

UNIFIED ESTATE AND GIFT TAX RATES

Rate Schedule

If the amount with respect to which the tentative tax to be computed is:	The tentative tax is:
Not over $10,000	18 percent of such amount.
Over $10,000 but not over $20,000	$1,800, plus 20 percent of the excess of such amount over $10,000.
Over $20,000 but not over $40,000	$3,800, plus 22 percent of the excess of such amount over $20,000.
Over $40,000 but not over $60,000	$8,200, plus 24 percent of the excess of such amount over $40,000.
Over $60,000 but not over $80,000	$13,000, plus 26 percent of the excess of such amount over $60,000.
Over $80,000 but not over $100,000	$18,200, plus 28 percent of the excess of such amount over $80,000.
Over $100,000 but not over $150,000	$23,800, plus 30 percent of the excess of such amount over $100,000.

If the amount with respect to
which the tentative tax to be
computed is: **The tentative tax is:**

Over $150,000 but not over $250,000 ....$38,800, plus 32 percent of the excess
                                        of such amount over $150,000.

Over $250,000 but not over $500,000 ....$70,800, plus 34 percent of the excess
                                        of such amount over $250,000.

Over $500,000 but not over $750,000 ....$155,800, plus 37 percent of the excess
                                        of such amount over $500,000.

Over $750,000 but not over $248,300, plus 39 percent of the excess
$1,000,000 ....of such amount over $750,000.

Over $1,000,000 but not over $345,800, plus 41 percent of the
$1,250,000 ....excess of such amount over
                                        $1,000,000.

Over $1,250,000 but not over $448,300, plus 43 percent of the
$1,500,000 ....excess of such amount over
                                        $1,250,000.

Over $1,500,000 but not over $555,800, plus 45 percent of the
$2,000,000 ....excess of such amount over
                                        $1,500,000.

Over $2,000,000.....................................$780,800, plus 48 percent of the excess
                                        of such amount over $2,000,000.

UNIFIED CREDIT INCREASES—FOR ESTATE TAX

Year	Unified Credit	Equivalent Exclusions
2004–5	$555,800	$1,500,000
2006–8	$780,800	$2,000,000
2009	$1,455,800	$3,500,000
2010	Estate Tax Repealed	
2011	$345,800	$1,000,000

UNIFIED CREDIT INCREASES—FOR GIFT TAX

Year	Unified Credit	Equivalent Exclusions
2002–9	$345,800	$1,000,000
2010	$330,800	$1,000,000
2011	$345,800	$1,000,000

As amended by EGTRRA 2001

THE UNIFIED TAX CREDIT

An estate tax return is required only if the decedent's cumulative taxable gifts and the value of the decedent's adjusted gross estate exceed the amount of exemption for estate tax ($1,500,000 in 2004–5). To determine the size of the adjusted gross estate you do the following:

1.) First **add together the value of everything the deceased owned** (regardless of its location) and the value of partial ownership they had in any assets. Let's say the total value is $4,800,000.

Income in Respect of a Decedent: You should also include the value of income to which they were entitled, but had not yet received, such as commissions due for services rendered by the decedent before death; their share of partnership income; receivables not yet paid; dividends declared, but not received before death; distributions from a retirement account payout such as an IRA, a 403(b) plan and the like. They are referred to as *income in respect of a decedent (IRD).* They receive no step-up in basis *and* are subject to income tax. This imposition of both estate and income taxes is relieved to some degree by receiving a deduction for the amount of estate tax paid on the IRD. For our example, we'll say the IRD total is $200,000. We then have a gross estate of $5,000,000.

2.) Next **subtract all debts and estate expenses** (such as administrative costs, funeral costs). We'll say these total $300,000 in mortgage debt, $20,000 in funeral expenses and administrative costs of $200,000. That leaves a taxable estate of $4,480,000.

3.) **Add back any post-1976 taxable gifts made during the deceased's lifetime.** We'll say these totaled $150,000.

4.) You then **calculate the tentative estate tax due on this sum**, $4,630,000. In 2004–5 this would be $780,800 on the first $2,000,000 and 48 percent on the remaining $2,680,000 (an amount of $1,262,400); a total tentative tax of $2,043,200.

5.) **Subtract the gift tax due on post-1976 gifts,** in this case $38,800. This leaves a tax of $2,004,400.

6.) From this gross estate tax you now **subtract the Unified Credit,** which in 2004–5 is $555,800 leaving an estate tax of $1,448,600. At this point you would **apply any other credits available** (for foreign death taxes, or tax on prior transfers), including state death tax credit (though as part of the repeal of estate taxes under EGTRRA 2001, after 2004 the credit is repealed and replaced with a *deduction* for state death taxes).

7.) Lastly, you would **add any tax due for generation-skipping transfers** that were being made.

LIFE EXPECTANCY TABLES

EXPECTATION OF LIFE IN YEARS

Age	Total	White		Black	
		Male	Female	Male	Female
0–1	77.2	75.0	80.2	68.6	75.5
1–2	76.7	74.5	79.6	68.6	75.4
2–3	75.7	73.5	78.7	67.7	74.5
3–4	74.8	72.6	77.7	66.7	73.5
4–5	73.8	71.6	76.7	65.8	72.5
5–6	72.8	70.6	75.7	64.8	71.5
6–7	71.8	69.6	74.7	63.8	70.6
7–8	70.8	68.6	73.7	62.8	69.6
8–9	69.8	67.6	72.7	61.8	68.6
9–10	68.8	66.6	71.7	60.8	67.6
10–11	67.9	65.6	70.8	59.8	66.6
11–12	66.9	64.7	69.8	58.9	65.6
12–13	65.9	63.7	68.8	57.9	64.6
13–14	64.9	62.7	67.8	56.9	63.6
14–15	63.9	61.7	66.8	55.9	62.6
15–16	62.9	60.7	65.8	54.9	61.7
16–17	61.9	59.7	64.8	54.0	60.7
17–18	61.0	58.8	63.8	53.0	59.7
18–19	60.0	57.8	62.9	52.1	58.7
19–20	59.1	56.9	61.9	51.2	57.8

EXPECTATION OF LIFE IN YEARS

Age	Total	White		Black	
		Male	Female	Male	Female
20–21	58.1	56.0	60.9	50.3	56.8
21–22	57.2	55.0	60.0	49.4	55.8
22–23	56.2	54.1	59.0	48.5	54.9
23–24	55.3	53.2	58.0	47.6	53.9
24–25	54.3	52.2	57.0	46.7	52.9
25–26	53.4	51.3	56.1	45.8	52.0
26–27	52.4	50.4	55.1	45.0	51.0
27–28	51.5	49.4	54.1	44.1	50.1
28–29	50.5	48.5	53.1	43.2	49.1
29–30	49.6	47.6	52.2	42.3	48.2
30–31	48.6	46.6	51.2	41.4	47.2
31–32	47.7	45.7	50.2	40.5	46.3
32–33	46.7	44.7	49.2	39.6	45.3
33–34	45.8	43.8	48.3	38.7	44.4
34–35	44.8	42.9	47.3	37.8	43.5
35–36	43.9	41.9	46.3	36.9	42.5
36–37	43.0	41.0	45.4	36.0	41.6
37–38	42.0	40.1	44.4	35.1	40.7
38–39	41.1	39.1	43.5	34.3	39.8
39–40	40.2	38.2	42.5	33.4	38.9
40–41	39.2	37.3	41.6	32.5	38.0
41–42	38.3	36.4	40.6	31.7	37.1
42–43	37.4	35.5	39.7	30.8	36.2
43–44	36.5	34.6	38.7	30.0	35.3
44–45	35.6	33.7	37.8	29.2	34.4
45–46	34.7	32.8	36.9	28.4	33.6
46–47	33.8	31.9	36.0	27.5	32.7
47–48	32.9	31.0	35.0	26.8	31.8
48–49	32.0	30.2	34.1	26.0	31.0
49–50	31.1	29.3	33.2	25.2	30.2
50–51	30.3	28.4	32.3	24.4	29.3
51–52	29.4	27.6	31.4	23.7	28.5
52–53	28.5	26.7	30.5	23.0	27.7
53–54	27.7	25.9	29.6	22.2	26.9
54–55	26.8	25.0	28.7	21.5	26.1
55–56	26.0	24.2	27.8	20.8	25.3
56–57	25.1	23.4	26.9	20.1	24.5
57–58	24.3	22.6	26.1	19.4	23.7
58–59	23.5	21.8	25.2	18.7	23.0
59–60	22.7	21.0	24.4	18.1	22.2
60–61	21.9	20.2	23.5	17.5	21.5
61–62	21.1	19.4	22.7	16.8	20.7

EXPECTATION OF LIFE IN YEARS

Age	Total	White		Black	
		Male	Female	Male	Female
62–63	20.3	18.7	21.9	16.2	20.0
63–64	19.6	18.0	21.1	15.6	19.3
64–65	18.8	17.2	20.3	15.0	18.6
65–66	18.1	16.5	19.5	14.4	17.9
66–67	17.4	15.8	18.7	13.8	17.2
67–68	16.7	15.1	17.9	13.3	16.6
68–69	16.0	14.5	17.2	12.7	15.9
69–70	15.3	13.8	16.5	12.2	15.3
70–71	14.6	13.2	15.7	11.7	14.7
71–72	14.0	12.5	15.0	11.2	14.1
72–73	13.3	11.9	14.3	10.7	13.5
73–74	12.7	11.3	13.6	10.2	12.9
74–75	12.1	10.8	13.0	9.8	12.3
75–76	11.5	10.2	12.3	9.3	11.7
76–77	10.9	9.7	11.7	8.9	11.2
77–78	10.3	9.1	11.0	8.5	10.7
78–79	9.8	8.6	10.4	8.1	10.2
79–80	9.3	8.2	9.8	7.7	9.7
80–81	8.8	7.7	9.3	7.3	9.2
81–82	8.3	7.2	8.7	7.0	8.7
82–83	7.8	6.8	8.2	6.7	8.3
83–84	7.3	6.4	7.7	6.3	7.8
84–85	6.9	6.0	7.2	6.0	7.4
85–86	6.5	5.6	6.7	5.7	7.0
86–87	6.1	5.3	6.3	5.5	6.6
87–88	5.8	5.0	5.9	5.2	6.3
88–89	5.4	4.7	5.5	5.0	5.9
89–90	5.1	4.4	5.2	4.7	5.6
90–91	4.8	4.1	4.8	4.5	5.3
91–92	4.5	3.8	4.5	4.3	5.0
92–93	4.3	3.6	4.2	4.1	4.7
93–94	4.0	3.4	3.9	3.9	4.5
94–95	3.8	3.2	3.7	3.7	4.2
95–96	3.6	3.0	3.4	3.6	4.0
96–97	3.4	2.8	3.2	3.4	3.8
97–98	3.2	2.7	3.0	3.3	3.6
98–99	3.0	2.5	2.8	3.1	3.4
99–100	2.8	2.4	2.6	3.0	3.2
100 years and over	2.7	2.3	2.5	2.9	3.0

Source: National Center for Health Statistics, Vital Statistics of the United States, 2001

Compound Interest Table

The magic of compound interest on regular savings in the creation and building of an estate is indicated by the following table. It shows the amount to which $1.00, invested at the beginning of each year, will accumulate, in the number of years and at the interest rates indicated.

YRS	7.00% Annual Rate	8.00% Annual Rate	9.00% Annual Rate	10.00% Annual Rate
1	$1.000	1.000	1.000	1.000
2	2.070	2.080	2.090	2.100
3	3.214	3.246	3.278	3.310
4	4.439	4.506	4.573	4.641
5	5.750	5.866	5.984	6.105
6	7.153	7.335	7.523	7.715
7	8.654	8.922	9.200	9.487
8	10.259	10.636	11.028	11.435
9	11.977	12.487	13.021	13.579
10	13.816	14.486	15.192	15.937
11	15.783	16.645	17.560	18.531
12	17.888	18.977	20.140	21.384
13	20.140	21.495	22.953	24.522
14	22.550	24.214	26.019	27.974
15	25.129	27.152	29.360	31.772
16	27.888	30.324	33.003	35.949
17	30.840	33.750	36.973	40.544
18	33.999	37.450	41.301	45.599
19	37.378	41.446	46.018	51.159
20	40.995	45.761	51.160	57.274
21	44.865	50.422	56.764	64.002
22	49.005	55.456	62.873	71.402
23	53.436	60.893	69.531	79.543
24	58.176	66.764	76.789	88.497
25	63.249	73.105	84.700	98.347
26	68.676	79.954	93.323	109.181
27	74.483	87.350	102.723	121.099
28	80.697	95.338	112.968	134.209
29	87.346	103.965	124.135	148.630
30	94.460	113.283	136.307	164.494
31	102.073	123.345	149.575	181.943
32	110.218	134.213	164.036	201.137
33	118.933	145.950	179.800	222.251

YRS	7.00% Annual Rate	8.00% Annual Rate	9.00% Annual Rate	10.00% Annual Rate
34	128.258	158.626	196.982	245.476
35	138.236	172.316	215.710	271.024
36	148.913	187.102	236.124	299.126
37	160.337	203.070	258.375	330.039
38	172.561	220.315	282.629	364.043
39	185.640	238.941	309.066	401.447
40	199.635	259.056	337.882	442.592

Example: If you invest $1,000 a year at 9 percent, compounded annually, your total investment will be worth $51,160 in twenty years; $136,307 in thirty years; $337,882 in forty years.

ESTATE PLANNING WORKSHEETS

MY ADVISORS ARE

	Name	Address
Attorney:		
Accountant:		
Life Insurance:		
General Insurance:		
Financial Planner:		
Investments:		
Bank Officer:		
Other:		

My Records and Documents Are Kept At

	Name	Address
Wills and Trusts: Securities: Insurance Policies: Receivables: Mortgages and Deeds: Business Interests: Safety Deposit Box: Other: 1. 2. 3.		

Property Record

Properly filled out and kept up to date, this section will provide you with a continuous record of your family's property. Be sure to differentiate between that held seperately by the husband or the wife, or jointly by both. A simple code beside each listing, such as h for husband, w for wife, and j for jointly held will make the ownership clear.

CASH

On hand		Amount
On deposit Bank	Interest Rate	
1.		
2.		
3.		
4.		

SECURITIES

Number of Shares	Company	Cost	Value	Income

BONDS

Company	Cost	Value	Income	Due Date

RECEIVABLES

Debtor	Address	Amount	Income	Due Date

MUTUAL FUNDS, SYNDICATES, REALTY TRUSTS, ETC.

Name	Cost	Value	Income

REAL ESTATE

	Property 1	Property 2	Property 3
Type			
Location			
Title			
Cost			
Value			
Mortgage			
Upkeep			
Income			

MORTGAGES RECEIVABLE

Mortgages	Address	Amount	Income	Due Date

PATENTS AND ROYALTIES

Description	Value	Income

PERSONAL PROPERTY

Description	Cost	Value

BUSINESS INTERESTS

	Business 1	Business 2	Business 3
Name of Business			
Form of Doing Business			
Fiscal Year Ends			
Parties to Business and Participating Shares			
If a family business, intended successor(s)			

	Business 1	Business 2	Business 3
Book Value			
Estimated Estate Tax Value			
Is there an agreement to sell at disability? at retirement? at death?			
If so, has cash been provided?			
Are the partners insured? In what amount?			
If interest is not to be sold at death 1. Who will receive it? 2. Who will take over management? 3. What incentives should be arranged?			

EMPLOYMENT BENEFITS

	Company	Amounts Vested, Contributed, or Deferred	Estimated Income or Lump-sum Payments	Death Benefit
Pension Plan Profit-sharing Plan Thrift Plan Deferred Compensation Salary Continuation Health, Accident, etc. Self-employed Retirement Fund Other				

GOVERNMENT BENEFITS

	Description	Social Security or Registration No.	Retirement Benefit	Death Benefit
Social Security Veteran's Pension Veteran's Death Benefits Disability Benefits Other				

HEALTH, ACCIDENT, MEDICAL-SURGICAL-HOSPITALIZATION INSURANCE

Company or Source	Description	Benefits	Policy Number	Issued	Expires

FIRE, LIABILITY, OTHER INSURANCE

Company	Description	Amount	Policy Number	Issued	Expires

LIFE INSURANCE

Company	Face Amount	Type*	Policy Number	Date of Issue	Cash Value	Owned by	Beneficiary
On Husband's Life							
On Wife's Life							

*Such as 5-year term, ordinary life, endowment, etc.

OTHER PROPERTIES OR INCOME SOURCES

Description	Cost	Value	Income

NOTES OR ACCOUNTS PAYABLE*

Amount	Creditor	When Due	Interest Payable	Remarks

*Include in this schedule all amounts owed on notes and accounts payable, mortgages, income taxes, etc.

TRUSTS

Grantor	Revocable or Irrevocable	Principal	Income	Termination Date	Life Beneficiaries	Remainder Beneficiaries

ANTICIPATED INHERITANCES

				If Inheritance Will Be in Trust		
Source	Age	Estimated Principal	Estimated Income	Termination Date	Life Beneficiaries	Remainder Beneficiaries
Father						
Mother						
Others						
1.						
2.						
3.						

ESTATE ANALYSIS SCHEDULES

These schedules will help you to analyze your estate and show you to what extent it can provide security for your family. They will supply you with (1) a summary of your family's property inventory, (2) how much cash will be needed at your death to pay your estate's taxes and expenses, (3) the source of the cash and what property will have to be sold to raise it, (4) what property and other sources of income will be left to your family, and (5) how much annual income your family can expect to have in the event of your disability, retirement, or death.

INSTRUCTIONS

Schedule A—INVENTORY VALUATION

The first step is to make an inventory of your family's property. This inventory can be taken from the property record entries on pages 376–385.

Enter the present market value of each asset in the appropriate columns. If the husband owns the property, enter it in column one. If the wife owns it, enter it in column four. If it is jointly owned enter one-half of the value of the property in each of columns two and three. Enter the total value of each type of asset in column five. Total all columns at the bottom.

Schedule B—COMPUTATION OF ESTATE COSTS AND TAXES

1. Add together the values of each asset in Schedule A, columns one and two, and enter them in column one of Schedule B. Total the entries at the bottom of column one to arrive at your "Gross Estate Valuation."

2. Transfer that figure to the top of the schedule in column three, opposite the words "Gross Estate Valuation."

3. For your deductions, enter in column two the amounts you estimate as estate expenses, such as mortgages, loans, funeral expenses, income or other taxes due, and 7½ percent of all property that will pass under your will for administration costs. Total your deductions and enter them in column three. Subtract them from the Gross Estate Valuation above. Enter the net figure as your "Adjusted Gross Estate" in column four.

4. If you plan to use a marital deduction, total up the value of the property that will qualify for the deduction (see page 280) and en-

ter the amount opposite the words "Marital Deduction" in column three. You should also make an alternate calculation without a marital deduction for your estate plan, in the event your spouse dies before you. The amount to be entered would be "0."

5. Next, enter the value of charitable contributions opposite the appropriate heading in column three.

6. Total the last two items in column three, enter the total in column four, and subtract it from "Adjusted Gross Estate." Enter the net figure as your "Net Taxable Estate" in column four.

7. By using the U.S. Estate Tax Table in the Appendix, you can calculate the federal estate taxes that will be payable. There will, in most cases, be a state inheritance or an estate tax to pay as well.

Schedule C—ESTATE CASH REQUIREMENTS

This schedule will show how much cash your executor will need to pay off the estate costs. It also shows how much your estate will shrink as it passes to your beneficiaries.

1. Fill in the first three items from the figures you developed in Schedule B.

2. Enter the total amount of cash bequests in your will.

3. An addition of these items will show the "Total Cash Needed."

Schedule D—LIQUIDATION AND AFTER-DEATH INCOME SCHEDULE

Col. 1—Enter each type of property and after-death income source.

Col. 2—Enter the value of each item that will have to be liquidated to supply the cash needed to pay off the estate cash requirements. The total at the bottom of this column should be equal to the "Total Cash Needed" in Schedule C.

Col. 3—Deduct column two from column one.

Col. 4—Enter spouse's property and jointly held property from Schedule A.

Col. 5—Add columns three and four.

Col. 6—Estimate income from items in column five. If in doubt, use an overall return of 4 percent on income-producing property.

Schedule E—ESTIMATED INCOME SCHEDULE

Col. 1—Enter items from Schedule A, column five.

Col. 2—Enter estimated present income from items in column one, as well as income from present employment.

Col. 3—Enter the estimated income you will receive from all sources in case you are disabled *now* and the length of time you will receive each item of income.

Col. 4—Enter the estimated income you will receive from all sources when you retire and the length of time you will receive each item of income.

Col. 5—Enter the items of income listed in Schedule D, column six, and the length of time your family will receive them after your death.

The totals at the bottom of Schedule E will show the all-important estimates of what income your family will have if you become disabled, or retire, or die.

Schedule A
INVENTORY VALUATION

Inventory	(1) Husband's	(2) Jointly Owned Husband	(3) Jointly Owned Wife	(4) Wife's	(5) Total
Type of Property					
Personally Owned?					
Cash					
Securities					
Stocks					
Bonds					
Receivables:					
Notes and Mortgages					
Real Estate:					
Income Producing					
Non-income Producing					
Business Interests					
Family Limited Partnership					
Mutual Funds					
Investment Syndicates and Trusts					
Trusts, Patents, and Royalties					
Oil, Cattle, Timber, etc.					
Residence					

Inventory	(1) Husband's	(2) Jointly Owned Husband	(3) Jointly Owned Wife	(4) Wife's	(5) Total
Personal Property					
Other Property					
Employment Benefits:					
Pension Plan					
Profit-sharing Plan					
Rollover IRA					
401(k), 403(b) plan					
Deferred Compensation					
Salary Continuation					
Stock Options					
Self-employed Retirement Plan					
Other Sources					

Government Benefits
Social Security
Veteran's Benefits

Life Insurance and Annuities?
Personal Life Insurance
Group Life Insurance
Pension Life Insurance
Annuities, Personal or Qualified Plans

Other Sources
Present Employment

TOTAL

Schedule B

COMPUTATION OF ESTATE COSTS AND TAXES

(Assuming husband predeceases wife)

Inventory	(1) Estate Tax Valuation*	Computation of Estate Costs and Taxes	(2)	(3)	(4)
Type of Property					
Personally Owned:		*Gross Estate Valuations*			
Cash		*Deduct:*			
Securities:					
Stocks		Debts and Expenses			
Bonds		Debts			
Receivables:		Funeral and Last Illness			
Notes and Mortgages		Income or Other Taxes Due			
Real Estate:		Administration Costs			
Income Producing		Deduct Total			
Non-income Producing		*Adjusted Gross Estate*			
Business Interests					
Mutual Funds		*Deduct:*			
Investment Syndicates and Trusts		Marital Deduction			
Trusts, Patents, and Royalties		Charitable Contributions			
Oil, Cattle, Timber, etc.		Deduct Total			

Residence
Personal Property
Other Property

Employment Benefits:
Pension Plan
Profit-sharing Plan
Thrift Plan
Deferred Compensation
Salary Continuation
Stock Options
Self-employed Retirement Plan
Other Sources

Life Insurance and Annuities:
Personal Life Insurance
Group Life Insurance
Pension Life Insurance
Annuities: Personal
or Qualified Plans

Other Sources

TOTAL GROSS ESTATE

NET TAXABLE ESTATE
U.S. ESTATE TAX (tentative)
Less: UNIFIED CREDIT
U.S. ESTATE TAX

(state death tax credits not dealt with)
*To help you figure the estate tax valuations for Schedule B you should carefully read Chapter 12. This is especially so for certain items of your inventory.
• *Business Interests:* see Chapter 19.
• *Trust Interests:* see Chapter 14.
• *Life Insurance:* see Chapter 3.

Schedule C

ESTATE CASH REQUIREMENTS SCHEDULE

Total Debts and Expenses, as above

Charitable Contributions, as above

Estate Taxes, as above

Cash Bequests, as per Will
TOTAL CASH NEEDED

Schedule D
LIQUIDATION AND INCOME SCHEDULE
(After death of husband)

Inventory Type of Property and Income Source:	(1) Valuation	(2) Property Sold to Meet Estate Costs	(3) Balance Available to Family	(4) Other Family Property	(5) Total Property Available to Family	(6) Estimated Income to Family
Personally Owned:						
Cash						
Securities:						
Stocks						
Bonds						
Receivables:						
Notes and Mortgages						
Real Estate:						
Income Producing						
Non-income Producing						
Business Interests						
Family Limited Partnership						
Mutual Funds						
Investment Syndicates and Trusts						
Trusts, Patents, and Royalties						
Oil, Cattle, Timber, etc.						
Residence						

Personal Property
Other Property

Employment Benefits
Pension Plan
Rollover IRA
Profit-sharing Plan
401(k), 403(b) plan
Deferred Compensation
Salary Continuation
Stock Options
Self-employed Retirement Plan
Other Sources

Government Benefits:
Social Security
Veteran's Benefits

Life Insurance and Annuities:
Personal Life Insurance
Group Life Insurance
Pension Life Insurance
Annuities: Personal or Qualified Plans

Other Sources:

TOTAL

Schedule E
ESTIMATED INCOME SCHEDULE

| Inventory

Type of Property and Income Source:	(1) Total Value	(2) Present Income	(3) Disability		(4) Retirement		(5) Death	
			Income	Period	Income	Period	Income	Period
Personally Owned:								
Cash								
Securities:								
Stocks								
Bonds								
Receivables								
Notes and Mortgages								
Real Estate:								
Income Producing								
Non-Income Producing								
Business Interests								
Family Limited Partnership								
Mutual Funds								
Investment Syndicates and Trusts								
Trusts, Patents, and Royalties								
Oil, Cattle, Timber, etc.								
Residence								
Personal Property								

Other Property

Employment Benefits
Pension Plan
Profit-sharing Plan
Rollover IRA
401(k), 403(b) Plan
Deferred Compensation
Salary Continuation
Stock Options
Self-employed Retirement Plan
Other Sources

Life Insurance and Annuities:
Personal Life Insurance
Group Life Insurance
Pension Life Insurance
Annuities: Personal or Qualified Plans

Other Sources:

TOTAL

ESTATE FINANCIAL PLANNING SURVEY

For the estate planner, investment acumen lies not as much in the ability to select a certain "right" security as in the ability to create a long-term, well-balanced investment program that will produce the capital needed to carry out estate planning objectives. How you as an investor-planner accomplish this and how well you accomplish it is a highly individual matter. There are a number of factors to consider that will help you gain a clearer idea of what you must accomplish and why. Below is a list of such factors. Your responses to them will begin to give you an idea of what your individual investment objectives should be.

1. How many years do you have in which to reach your intermediate or long-range financial goals? _____

2. How many college-bound children do you have? _____ How many years from now do you need to have funds for the education of each child? _____

3. At what age do you hope to retire? _____ How much time do you have before you need to draw income from investments? _____

4. How much income do you expect you will need at the time of your retirement? $_____

5. Will you need capital to start a business after early retirement? ____ How much do you think you will need? $_____

6. What is the degree of risk you are willing to take in growth-oriented investments (emotionally and financially) on a scale of 1–10, low to high? _____ How much risk are you willing to take to achieve capital appreciation that will be required to reach your financial goals on a scale of 1–10? _____

7. What is the amount of capital you have available to initiate your

plan? $_____ How much ($_____) and when can you put in additional capital? _____

8. How experienced are you as an investor? _____ How much advice or management do you require?_____ _____

9. What tax advantages are available to you?_____ _____ _____ _____

Using this list of questions and your responses as a starting point, make a list of your goals for building your estate. Having your goals clearly in mind is the first and most critical key to setting up a balanced investment program.

A PROGRESSION OF INVESTMENT STRATEGIES FOR ESTATE PLANNING

Earlier you were asked to consider a series of factors that help to establish your investment goals for planning your estate. Not everyone presents the same profile, and the variations of needs and aspirations are vast. Here are some guidelines that should be of use to you in focusing on both short- and long-term investment strategy:

1. Most people's first major outlay of capital is basic—buying a house.
2. Purchase life insurance for yourself and your spouse both as an investment and to provide for early loss of the other's income and support for the family in the event of early death.
3. Purchase disability insurance to replace your income in the event of a prolonged illness or recovery from an accident. If you have group coverage, consider buying an individually-owned policy to supplement it, so your income is replaced as much as possible.

4. Establish a liquid emergency fund to cover at least three to six months of household expenses.

5. Save capital sufficient to meet the minimum entry requirements for your desired investments.

6. Select an investment in which the risk factor meets your comfort level (see section below on "Degrees of Safety") and that is geared strictly for increasing your capital. (See also the section below entitled "Making Investment Decisions.")

7. Establish and implement a plan to build capital for college education for your children. Such investments or tax strategies could include:

   - *Zero Coupon Bonds.* These bonds let you know the exact amount you will have at maturity and are useful for building toward the predicted sums you will need. They have long-term maturity that can coincide with the projected time children will be entering college.

   - *Whole Life Insurance from a Mutual Insurance Company.* This is insurance with the potential for cash accumulation on a tax-deferred basis. At a certain time, you can borrow a portion of the cash value tax-free, pay interest and still maintain a death benefit (minus the loan).

   - *Variable Life Insurance.* This is insurance with an investment component. Premium dollars beyond immediate costs of the insurance itself can grow in tax-deferred mutual fund sub accounts. The policy owner directs which sub accounts will be used. As cash value grows over time, you can take out a given amount of the money, pay interest, and leave the rest to maintain the insurance policy.

   - *Section 529 Qualified Tuition Programs.* These federally authorized programs are sponsored privately or by individual states and allow taxpayers to do either of the following: 1) Enter into a prepaid educational arrangement with a private college or university whereby you buy certificates or tuition credits for a specified would-be student beneficiary; or 2) contribute within specified limits to an educational savings account where after-tax contributions may be invested in a diversified portfolio and grow tax-free, then be withdrawn tax-free if funds are used for what are called *qualified higher education expenses.* These expenses include tuition, fees, room and board, books, equipment, supplies, and special needs services when attending a postsecondary and/or graduate school. Contributions are considered completed gifts, so annual exclusions can be used ($11,000 in 2004). Five years' worth of gifts can be compiled into a contribution, allowing $55,000 per person or $110,000 per couple without using any of the unified credit, but further gifts cannot be made until the end of that five years without using the unified credit. Multiple contributors are allowed, but there are overall limits on the total from all sources. There are programs that allow maximum contributions for a beneficiary as high as $250,000 (considered to be the cost of five years of higher education at some of the more costly schools).

- *Coverdell Education Savings Account (originally the Education IRA)*. For children under age 18, maximum annual non-deductible contributions of only $2,000 per beneficiary can be made as a total from all contributors. Earnings accumulate tax-free and, together with the principal, are not taxable gifts if used for qualified education expenses. These include elementary and secondary tuition, expenses for a special needs beneficiary, and postsecondary education expenses for the designated child (tuition, certain room-and-board costs, books, supplies, equipment, even uniforms). If funds are used by the beneficiary for other purposes, they are taxed to the beneficiary. A bank must be the account's custodian or trustee. The beneficiary of a Coverdell Educations Savings Account may be changed to another family member with no income tax consequences if they are under age 30, or have special needs. This special IRA is not available if modified adjusted gross income exceeds $220,000 (married, filing jointly) or $110,000 (single parent).
- *Hope Scholarship*. A higher education tax credit is available at a maximum of $1,500 per student for the first two years of postsecondary education for couples filing jointly whose modified adjusted gross income does not exceed $105,000, or singles not exceeding $52,000 (2004, indexed for inflation). Students must be enrolled for at least a half-time program.
- *Lifetime Learning Credit*. A credit against taxes on an annual tax return can be taken for 20 percent of up to $10,000 of qualified education expenses (i.e., a $2,000 tax credit per

year). Qualifying expenses are not limited to the first two years of postsecondary education, and the student need not be enrolled at least half-time. This applies to married taxpayers filing jointly with adjusted gross income over $105,000, or single over $52,000 (2004, indexed for inflation).

- *Bonds with a Fixed Return.* These bonds allow you to work on the basis of projected earnings needed. In this way you can determine the amount to invest at a certain time, or over a period of time.
- *Financial Aid.* Your assets, your income, your planned contributions to college costs, and your child's assets and income are all part of a federal formula used for determining eligibility for financial aid. Since greater weight is given to assets owned by the child, plan not to make large gifts directly to a child seeking financial aid.

8. Once the children finish school, you can concentrate on retirement funds and begin to build capital beyond your pension plan with growth-oriented investments that allow you optimum appreciation of your capital (commensurate with your risk/comfort level). Often one's peak earning years occur at about this time of life. For instance, someone with a successful career who works his way up to a substantial income reaches peak income during the last 20 percent of his working life. During this time, you should be able to accumulate large sums of money, especially if you plan ahead and avoid the temptation to raise your standard of living beyond your ability to continue saving and investing. Most people really focus on building funds for their retirement out of these peak earnings when they are between the ages of 50 and 60.

9. Any time that your capital has appreciated to a sufficient level, you can begin to diversify your portfolio with a variety of investments with which you feel comfortable. The goal at this point is to generally build your estate for family use and for your retirement. The priorities you place on growth versus income, however, may shift in emphasis as you approach and then begin your retirement.

ESTABLISHING A BALANCED PORTFOLIO

Estate planning can be confusing given the variety of investments available, fluctuations in the economy, the markets, world affairs and changes in your own needs as time goes on. The classic investment portfolio can, however, be laid out in simple categories that will assist you in structuring the plan that suits and adjusts to your evolving needs.

A model portfolio is diversified so that no one type of investment and no one sector of the economy is the sole focus. The basic investment categories are: cash, growth, fixed income return. Because you are trying to build the value of your portfolio, the emphasis should be on capital appreciation. The actual percentages of funds in any of the three categories may change from time to time depending upon the state of the economy, market dynamics, and the period of your life.

For example, the larger amount should probably be in the growth category (ownership of shares in such things as stocks, growth-oriented mutual funds, etc.). The amount you have in cash, such as a money market account, fixed income investments, bonds, CDs, annuities, etc., will vary depending upon the economy and whether you need income more than appreciation. It may also depend upon the liquidity needed to shift to investments that have greater flexibility in changing economic conditions. If the economy is volatile and you are in doubt about what will happen, cash placed in a money market fund, certificates of deposit, treasury bills, or savings accounts (low yield but safe and liquid) is probably your best bet until economic and market factors become clearer. During a time of growth in the economy you may want to place larger amounts in growth investments, such as stocks and mutual funds. Yet trying to guess the best time for one emphasis over another can leave you out of phase; selling low out of fear; buying in too high on market enthusiasm that may have peaked. Being diversified, with a balance of asset types suited to your investment timeline and tolerance for risk, is more likely to help you sustain an investment program that meets your needs.

A SIMPLE RULE OF THUMB

To simplify the matter, the proportions of cash, growth, and fixed income investments should vary over your lifetime, and should be monitored by you and your investment counselor. Your changing goals for greater appreciation or greater income will tip the balance one way or another, but a rule of thumb after you have built your solid base of capital and perhaps the security of a home might be something like the following:

GROWING ECONOMY			HIGH INTEREST RATES		
CASH	GROWTH	FIXED INCOME	CASH	GROWTH	FIXED INCOME
10%	70%	20%	20%	50%	30%

RETIREMENT YEARS		
CASH	GROWTH	FIXED INCOME
20%	20%	60%

These are not by any means hard-and-fast percentages, but are meant to illustrate a point about shifting times and advancing years.

STRUCTURING YOUR INVESTMENTS

Having established the long-term goals for building your estate, you then need to have a strategy for operating in the world of investing. To begin with, your strategy will depend upon your financial status—that is, how much capital you have available for investment, whether you have purchased a home, and if you have established liquid funds for emergencies for at least six months.

Below are five levels of estate building at varying points in life and financial worth. Finding where you fit will help you to determine some strategies to follow.

Level 1: Zero capital. Ready to save. Need to establish a regular program of saving to build capital for initial investments.

Level 2: May have purchased a home. May have set aside liquid funds for emergencies. Put together a small additional nest egg of, say, $4,000 or $5,000, and are ready to make an initial investment.

Level 3: Have surplus capital ($10,000+). Have several conservative investments that are performing well on a steady basis. Ready for higher capital appreciation and growth (therefore ready for a higher level of risk).

Level 4: Ready to shift to more conservative investments that provide fixed income while maintaining those that provide appreciation and growth.

Level 5: Receiving income from your investments. Beginning to live off investments with fixed returns. Want to preserve capital.

Once you know your needs and have considered your priorities among the three segments of your portfolio (cash, growth, fixed income), you are ready to select investments on the basis of how well they meet your current financial status and goals.

MAKING INVESTMENT DECISIONS

Keeping an objective perspective is crucial for successful investing. Your level of understanding of the bottom line of investment can really make the difference between low performance or loss of your money, and achieving high performance and gain. In this experienced advisors can help you. You must know that in building your estate the only way to truly increase your wealth is to obtain a significant *real* return on your money. The real return is the rate at which you increase the value of your invested capital after taking into consideration the factors of inflation, taxes, and investment and management costs. Low-risk, conservative investments are important for psychological and financial reasons, when safety is the key element in your planning. If you decide to stay with such investments for safety reasons, you should be aware that you have made an informed choice, knowing that you paid a price for that safety— namely, low return and perhaps a real loss on your investment. As an example, if you are receiving 3 percent interest on your savings account, your net after a 28 percent tax would be 2.16 percent. With inflation typically more than 2.16 percent, you have obviously lost the difference in real value. On the other hand, if your investment earns a return or profit that is in excess of the inflation rate, you have increased the real value of your assets accordingly.

Common stocks and stock mutual funds have, on average, provided a greater margin of profit than most other investments. Stocks and mutual funds investing in stocks are obviously the media of investment that are most likely to increase the value of your estate. It is uncertain, however, that the general rise in market values will continue at the same rate as in the past. It is possible that changed economic and market conditions will cause values to plummet as much as one-third or more, as occurred in 1952, 1973, and 1987, and starting in the spring of 2000, with the consequent loss of your hard-earned money. If you have the stamina to stay with your investments, experience has shown that the market will *usually* attain its former value, or possibly increase in value. An exception to this may be the market downturn in 2000, when stocks were so severely overvalued. Even then, reviewing your portfolio, rebalancing to retain your original diversification model by taking profits from sectors of your port-folio that are yielding extreme returns and spreading profits back over your other asset classes, helps to mitigate the proportion of loss that is experienced. However, in the short term and in a fluctuating market, the critical factor is to remain objective. Becoming emotionally wedded to an investment is the pitfall. If a security shows consistently poor perfor-mance, or is growing in value way out of proportion to its earnings, you must be willing to reevaluate how much if any of it you will keep. Know-ing your own timing, having a plan, maintaining objectivity and facts about your investments are the essential elements. This is where the ob-jective analysis of the merits of your investment program by a profes-sional advisor or manager can be of crucial value to you. Such a fee-based advisor has no interest other than the success of your investment strate-gies. Your success will further his own potential for success.

DEGREES OF SAFETY

To determine which categories of investment are suitable for building low-risk investments, consult the following lists.

Low-Risk/Low-Return Investments
- A home (if desired)
- Life insurance
- Annuities
- Bank certificates of deposit
- Money market accounts
- Treasury bills, bonds, and notes
- 401(k) plans
- U.S. savings bonds
- Municipal bonds (grade A or better)

Once you have built a foundation of secure, low-risk/low-return invest-ments, you can begin to consider ways of achieving greater capital ap-preciation. Investments that allow you to achieve this can still involve only minimum to moderate risk. They include the following types of investments:

Moderate Risk/Moderate Return Investments
- Blue chip stocks
- Preferred stocks

- Mutual funds (well established/well diversified)
- Corporate bonds
- Real estate trusts
- Real estate partnerships

After you have begun to achieve your moderate capital appreciation goals and have built a comfortable margin of fairly reliable growth, you can then assess the amount of discretionary income you have for some of the more speculative types of investments that offer high rewards. These speculatives are not for everyone. Your tolerance for risk is a factor to consider before venturing into such aggressive investments, and the funds used for them must be dispensable, since there is always the possibility of losing them. These, then, are the high-risk/high-return investments. They are capital gains–oriented, but tend to be volatile and may reflect sudden swings in the market.

High-Risk/High-Return Investments
- Specialized mutual funds (concentrate on one industry group only—e.g., a fund with stocks *only* in companies involved in high-technology manufacturing)
- Stocks of newer companies, emerging foreign companies, emerging industries
- Commodities (metals, currencies, agricultural products, oil)
- Futures contracts
- Options
- Warrants

DIVERSIFICATION

As stated earlier, it is important to keep your investments diversified so that no one economic factor has a disproportionate effect on your estate. You must seek to achieve diversification not only in the relationship of each investment to the others, but also in the relationship to the rest of your assets and your sources of income.

DEGREES OF LIQUIDITY

Another factor to consider in building a portfolio is the degree of liquidity available in your various investments. Being able to liquidate easily allows you to handle emergencies, take advantage of sudden investment opportunities, and at the time of death allows for greater ease in handling estate taxes, expenses, and debts. The list below shows samples of degrees of liquidity from greatest to least.

- Cash/checking account
- Passbook savings account
- Money market account
- Treasury bills: ninety days, six months, one year
- Treasury notes (one to five years)
- Treasury bonds (five-plus years)
- Stocks (always liquid, but at the risk of being in a loss position at the time you wish to sell)
- Mutual funds
- Real estate (considered to be the least liquid investment)

INFLATION HEDGE

As previously mentioned, you need to consider how well a particular investment will preserve your capital against inflation. It is just as important to protect the purchasing power of your capital as it is to protect yourself against the possible loss of capital. In any inflationary period, it won't do to just maintain the number of your dollars. If that is all you do, you will suffer an economic loss. Here again, the whole question of diversification enters the picture. A portfolio that is invested entirely in a savings account or other low-interest investments is no protection against inflation. Only a portfolio based on a variety of investments—some with fixed returns and some with potential for capital appreciation—will do that.

GROWTH

What is growth potential? It is the inherent ability of the investment not just to protect against inflation, but to actually appreciate the capital beyond a normal inflationary increase. Generally speaking, these investments are found in the industries that have great growth potential. Growth areas in the economy shift over the years. In the early part of the century it was the railroad and the steel industry. In recent years it has been automobiles and chemicals, then electronics, then high technologies and overseas manufacturing.

INCOME

What is the expected income return on the investment? It is expected future income production as well as current income. Is the income guaranteed? Will the income return be available in bad times as well as in good times? Is it fixed? Will the rate of return move up and down with general money rates so as to reflect the state of the economy and the probable changing costs of living?

MARKETABILITY

What is the marketability of the investment? Is this a security that you can readily sell? Or will buyers perhaps be hard to find? There are many securities that are not readily marketable, but still make worthwhile investments. Obviously, however, your investment portfolio should not be weighted with these. Liquidity is extremely important to many aspects of estate planning.

TAX-DEFERRED INVESTMENTS

Portions of your portfolio should allow for long-range planning. Here you need to be concerned with issues of immediate liquidity or fluctuating markets. These are the investments you enter into for the sake of planning for retirement and for college education expenses for your children. Some allow you to defer payment of taxes on both the principal you invest and on earnings; others on just the earnings made from the investment itself. These include deferred fixed and variable annuities, and qualified retirement plans, IRAs, Section 529 plans, Coverdell Educations Savings Accounts and cash value life insurance of various types.

TAX-ADVANTAGED INVESTMENTS

There are certain types of investments that allow you substantial tax advantages. These are:

1. *Tax-free municipal bonds.* Earnings are not subject to tax at the federal level or in the issuing town and state.
2. *Cash value life insurance.* Taxes on the buildup of the cash value are deferred. Withdrawals up to the amount of premium you withdraw are tax-free. Further cash can then be borrowed on a tax-free basis, say, to supplement retirement income.

3. *Deferred fixed or variable annuities.* Taxes are deferred on earnings until withdrawn. A 10 percent penalty also applies to withdrawals prior to age 59½.

4. *Individual Retirement Accounts (IRAs).* Taxes on earned income that is contributed plus earnings are tax-deferred until withdrawn at retirement. Withdrawals prior to age 59½ also incur a 10 percent penalty. However, this tax advantage is available only to individuals not covered by a company plan or whose income is less than $50,000 a year (2005 and thereafter) (or $70,000 a year if filing jointly in 2005, $75,000 in 2006, $80,000 in 2007 and thereafter).

5. *Qualified Retirement Plans.* Percentages of earned income can be deferred as contributions to qualified employer-sponsored or self-employed retirement plans. Taxes on contributions and underlying investment returns are deferred until withdrawn for retirement income. A 10 percent penalty is also applied to withdrawals prior to age 59½.

6. *Limited Partnerships with Federal Tax Credits.* Investors are given federally allocated tax credits over a period of years for investing in limited partnerships that build low-income housing

7. *Real Property.* Interest on principal and second-residence mortgages and taxes may be deducted. Interest, taxes, and depreciation may be deducted on commercial properties.

8. *Oil, cattle, timber, and certain other natural resources.* Depletion allowances are deductible.

INVESTMENT CHECKLIST

This checklist provides an overview of the gamut of investments generally available. They are grouped according to the investment characteristics that make them appropriate for varying programs and objectives: cash, growth and fixed income return.

CASH

There are many reasons for keeping funds in cash or cash equivalents. They are a saving medium; they are available for unforeseen family needs; they are a reservoir of which uninvested amounts are kept for later investment; they are generally free of risk and as such a source of psychological and financial security.

Investment	Source	What It Is	Use	Risk	Advantages	Disadvantages	Minimum Entry
Money Market Deposit Account.	Banks, savings & loans, brokerage firms.	Funds invested in short-term instruments: CD's, U.S. T-bills, government securities, short-term municipal bonds.	Preservation of capital, liquidity and highest possible interest income given these objectives.	Low.	Rates not subject to federal regulation. Banks set their own. Insured by federal agency up to $100,000. No withdrawal penalties.	Monthly fees, limited check writing, minimum balances required.	$1,000–$2,500
Savings Account.	Banks, savings & loans, credit unions.	Passbook account wherein money deposited earns interest.	Earns interest income.	Low.	Insured by federal agency up to $100,000. Yield is guaranteed. Can use balance as collateral.	Interest rates are low. In some cases minimum balances required.	$5–$100

GROWTH

The purpose of placing funds in equity-type investments is to achieve greater growth potential for your capital. Such investments carry various degrees of risk that generally correspond to their potential for reward. They can be short- or long-term investments, depending upon the amount of time you hold the investment to maximize your return. As of 1986 the new tax laws no longer offer any advantage to long-term versus short-term capital gains. As a result, you are now free to move into and out of equity positions at the times most advantageous for you to obtain the greatest profit.

Investment	Source	What It Is	Use	Risk	Advantage	Disadvantage	Minimum Entry
Annuity.	Life insurance companies, employer's 401(k) programs	Investments made by insurance companies that guarantee a fixed return with no risk of capital for a fixed duration.	Retirement income; building of retirement funds within a 401(k) plan. Tax deferral.	Low.	Very secure. Guaranteed minimum interest rate allows for higher fluctuating rate. Usually can borrow the cash value at low interest rates.	Low returns.	Varies
Common Stock.	Brokerage firms; in a few cases employees can purchase their company's stock directly from their company.	A security that represents a stated amount of ownership in a company.	Dividend income and/or appreciation in value.	Medium to high.	Carries the potential for a high rate of return.	Carries risk of market fluctuations on a daily basis. Not insured by federal government.	$1,000

Investment	Source	What It Is	Use	Risk	Advantages	Disadvantages	Minimum Entry
Convertible stock.	Brokerage firms.	Preferred stock or a bond, or a debenture that may be exchanged by holder for common stock—generally of the same company.	Income and/or appreciation.	Medium.	Carries safety of preferred stocks and bonds along with potential for capital appreciation of common stock.	Yields are lower than similar quality nonconvertibles. They sell at premiums to conversion value of the common stock purchased.	$5,000
401 (k) plans.	Various Employers.	Tax-deferred investment plans. You regularly contribute portions of pre-tax salary dollars to a variety of investment options.	Appreciation, tax deferral.	Low.	High yield growth of savings on tax-deferred income. Provides growth of retirement funds. Diversified, professionally managed.	Not liquid until retirement. 10% penalty on early withdrawals. Annual deferrals.	No minimum
Individual Retirement Account (IRA).	Banks, mutual fund companies, brokerage	Tax-advantaged retirement accounts for indi-	Retirement income.	Varies.	If you qualify, contribution of up to $2,000 a	Subject to penalty of 10% if withdrawn before	$250

	firms, credit unions, insurance companies.	viduals not covered by company plans or whose income is under $25,000, or under $40,000 if filing jointly.			year is fully tax deductible. Growth of account is tax-free until withdrawn.		age of 59½.
Master Limited Partnerships.	Investment brokerage firms.	Group ownership of specific diversified properties (real estate, oil, gas). Can buy and sell like stock, or hold until properties are sold.	Appreciation, tax advantage.	Low to high.	Liquidity—can buy & sell as desired. Reasonable yield. 50–60% tax-exempt. Potential for appreciation.	Subject to fluctuation in real estate market—you could be tempted to sell out at low point before property reaches projected appreciated value.	$800–$1,500

Investment	Source	What It Is	Use	Risk	Advantages	Disadvantages	Minimum Entry
Mutual Fund.	Brokerage firms, mutual fund companies, insurance companies.	An investment trust. Your money is pooled with that of other investors. Professional managers invest this pool of funds in specified assets in the U.S. or overseas.	Income and/or appreciation.	Varies.	Management by professionals. Risk reduced by diversification. Wide selection of specialized funds within a family of funds. Can switch from one to another within a family. Low minimums.	Not insured by federal government. Yield influenced by fluctuation in stock market and interest rates.	$1,000
Real Estate Investment Trusts (REITs).	Brokerage firms.	A trust or corporation that invests in or finances real estate (shopping centers, office buildings, apartments, etc.). Sold as securites.	Appreciation, income.	Medium.	Allows for participation in real estate with little money.	Dependent upon inflation—value fluctuates with real estate and stock market.	$2,000

	Where to Buy	What It Is	Objective	Risk	Advantages	Disadvantages	Minimum Investment
Real Estate as Your Residence.	Real estate brokers, individual owners, banks.	A house, condominium, or apartment in a cooperative.	Appreciation, tax advantage.	Average.	While providing residence, allows for tax write-off or loan interest, appreciation potential, and collateral for other loans.	Value can depreciate; not liquid; ongoing maintenance costs.	Varies.
Real Estate Limited Partnerships/Public Partnerships.	Investment brokerage firms.	A group ownership of diversified properties (office buildings, apartment complexes, shopping centers). Can buy units of the package offered during a specified period.	Appreciation, tax advantage.	Low to high.	Can invest in real estate for little capital. Diversified properties—not dependent upon any one property. Professional management.	Not very liquid. Dependent upon inflation. Subject to fluctuation in real estate market.	$3,000–$5,000

Investment	Source	What It Is	Use	Risk	Advantages	Disadvantages	Minimum Entry
Real Estate Limited Partnerships/ Private Partnerships.	Investment and brokerage firms.	Group ownership of a specific property of any size and kind. Can buy units of the package offered during a specific period.	Appreciation, tax advantage.	Low to high.	Chance to invest in major property with fewer partners (higher percentage of ownership). Professionally managed.	Not diversified. Subject to specific fluctuation in real estate market. Not liquid. Dependent upon regional inflation.	$3,000–$5,000
Variable Annuity.	Life insurance companies, 401(k) programs, 403(b) programs.	A policy with investment options, including stock mutual funds, stock/bond fund, money market or interest accounts.	Building funds for retirement, tax deferred.	Low.	Conservator professional management	Subject to 10% tax penalty if funds are withdrawn prior to age 59½.	$500 per year

FIXED INCOME RETURN

The purpose of fixed income investments is to provide for reliable sources of predictable income from your capital. Such investments generally allow for the investment of earnings when growth is still a goal. Once you want or need to live off your investments, however, fixed income-providing investments should occupy a higher proportion of your portfolio.

Investment	Source	What It Is	Use	Risk	Advantages	Disadvantages	Minimum Entry
Certificates of Deposit.	Banks, savings & loans, credit unions, brokerage firms.	A set sum of money left in a bank for a set period earns agreed-upon interest rate. Deposit plus interest paid at end of period.	Interest income.	Low.	Insured by federal government for up to $100,000; interest rates competitive	Penalties for early withdrawal.	$500
Commercial Paper.	Brokerage firms, corporations, bank holding companies.	Short-term unsecured notes offered by large corporations.	Interest income.	Varies.	Yields are competitive. Backed by the credit of the borrowing company.	More risk than a CD. No secondary market. Not covered by collateral of the issuing company.	$25,000
Corporate Bond.	Brokerage firms.	Debt obligation of corporation for your loan of the bond price.	Income.	Medium.	Assured return over long period of time with high quality available through bond ratings.	Could be called in before maturity and paid off only to that date.	$5,000

Plan	Where to Get	Purpose	Advantage	Fees	Contribution	Restrictions	Minimum
Keogh Plan.	Banks, brokerage firms, credit unions, mutual fund companies, insurance companies.	Retirement plan for self-employed.	Tax deferral retirement income.	Varies.	May contribute 25% or $41,000 (whichever is less) each year tax-deductible. Funds grow tax-free until withdrawn.	Subject to 10% penalty and taxes if withdrawn before age 59½. If a defined benefit plan, cannot receive full benefits until age 65.	$250
Simplified Employees Pension Plan (SEP IRA)	Banks, brokerage firms, credit unions, mutual fund companies, insurance companies.	Retirement plan for businesses of 25 employees or less; & self-employed.	Tax deferral to build retirement funds.	Varies depending upon investments used.	May contribute 25% or $41,000 (whichever is less) each year tax-deductible (20% if self-employed). Funds grow tax-free until withdrawn.	Subject to 10% penalty & income taxes if withdrawn before age 59½.	Depends upon investment. Generally $250.

Investment	Source	What It Is	Use	Risk	Advantages	Disadvantages	Minimum Entry
Mortgage-Backed Securities.	Securities dealers, brokerage firms, issuing institutions.	Shares of ownership in pools of mortgages that are backed by federal, state or local governments (Ginnie Maes, Fannie Maes, etc.)	Interest income, retirement income.	Low.	High yields. Liquidity, backed by government agencies. Pays regular prorated monthly income.	Subject to fluctuations in interest rates. As mortgages are paid off, payments diminish and eventually cease.	$1,000 (in a mutual fund) or $25,000
Treasury Notes.	Banks, federal reserve banks, brokerage firms, U.S. Treasury.	U.S. Treasury securities with medium term maturity (not less than 1 year, not more than 10).	Interest income.	None.	Interest paid is exempt from state and local taxes. Backed by the U.S. government. May be traded like corporate securities.	Same as T-bills	$1,000 (4 plus years) $5,000 (less than 4 years)

Investment	Where to Buy	Description	Objective	Risk	Advantages	Disadvantages	Minimum
U.S. Savings Bonds. Series EE.	Banks, savings and loans, federal reserve banks, U.S. Treasury.	Debt obligation of U.S. Treasury for amount of bond. Designed for small investors.	Interest income.	None.	Exempt from state and local taxes. May defer federal tax. Principal and interest guaranteed. If held to maturity, the interest is exempt from income taxes, if proceeds are used for qualified educational expenses.	Usually lower interest rate than available with other fixed income investments.	$25
Zero Coupon Bonds.	Banks, brokerage firms.	Discounted from face value with zero annual interest paid out. Capital appreciation is realized at maturity.	Appreciation.	Medium.	Low expense initially. Balloon payment to you at maturity. Good for long-term planning since you know the exact amount you will receive.	Lower yield than regular bonds. Have to pay annual taxes (as if you had received interest).	$1,000

Investment	Source	What It Is	Use	Risk	Advantages	Disadvantages	Minimum Entry
Inflation-Indexed Bonds, Series I Bonds	Banks, brokerage firms	Sold at face value. Pay fixed, taxable interest for 30 years, *plus* semiannually adjusted inflation rate tied to Consumer Price Index. Have a 30-yr. life. Redeemable any time after 12 months.	Rates adjust to inflation.	Medium	Proceeds tax-free if used for qualified higher education expenses. All other proceeds not taxable until redeemed. Taxed at federal rates.	Less attractive adjustment to payout rates during low inflation. Three month interest penalty if redeemed within first 5 years.	$50–$10,000

Checklist
Family Objectives and Needs Estate
Planning Questions

Estate planning begins with an appraisal of yourself and your family. What, exactly, do you want to accomplish during your life? What are your chances of realizing these aims? Will these aims meet the needs of your family? What are those needs now and in the future, while you are alive, after you are dead, when you retire, if you become disabled: for yourself, your spouse, your children, your parents, your grandchildren, charities you wish to benefit?

Here, for your guidance, is a checklist that can help you. It has none of the answers—those you must evolve yourself. It should start you thinking; provide the framework on which you can build your estate plan—the determination of your objectives.

All the questions in this checklist are dealt with in the main book. Use the book as a guide and aid. It contains much of the information you will need to formulate your own personal estate planning objectives.

Family Income and Requirements

   A. During My Working Life
      1. How much income do I have, and from what sources?
        a. Employment or business.
        b. Investments.
        c. Other sources.
        d. What will my income probably be in five, ten, fifteen, or twenty years?
      2. How much are my living costs?
        a. Household expenses.
       b. Rent or home-ownership expenses.
        c. Business incidentals, i.e., commuting, lunches, entertainment, etc.
        d. Taxes.
        e. Miscellaneous—interest, medical, auto, etc.
        f. What will my family's outlay probably be in five, ten, fifteen, twenty years?

B. In the Event I Become Disabled, Retire, or Die
1. *If I become disabled now*
   a. How much income will I need?
   b. How much income will I have? From employment or from business?
   c. How much income will I have from investments or other sources?
   d. How much income will I have from my disability insurance, social security, veteran's benefits?
   e. How much more disability insurance do I need to make up a probable income deficit? How can I pay for it?
   f. What would the differences be if I became disabled five, ten, fifteen, twenty years from now?
2. *If I retire*
   a. Will I have to retire?
   b. How much income will I need if I retire?
   c. How much income will I have? From employment or from business?
   d. How much income will I have from my investments or other sources?
   e. How much income will I have from annuities and social security?
   f. What am I equipped to do after my retirement? What training should I have?
   g. What business can I start now to prepare for my retirement years?
   h. Shall I live in the same place or shall I move to one of the retirement states? What advantages are there, if any, in these states from income, health, and tax-shelter points of view?
3. *If I die now*
   a. What will my estate consist of and how much will it be worth?
   b. What will the estate costs amount to?
      (1) Debts and obligations.
      (2) Administration expenses.
      (3) Estate and inheritance taxes.
   c. What specific assets of my estate will have to be paid out or sold to meet these estate costs?
   d. How much will be left for the support of my family?

e. How much income will my family need and for how long?
    (1) For my spouse.
    (2) For my children.
    (3) For children's education.
    (4) For parents.

f. How much income will be available and in what form and for how long?

g. Will some part of principal have to be paid out to support my family and, if so, how long will it last?

h. How much income will be available to my family five, ten, fifteen, twenty years after my death?

i. What would the differences be if I died five, ten, fifteen, twenty years from now?

ESTATE CREATION OBJECTIVES

A. Residence
1. Where should I live on the basis of my income, my family's needs, and occupational convenience?
2. Should I rent or own?
3. Would a move increase my standard of living, and what would be the consequent costs?
4. Would the additional costs, if any, interfere with my long-term estate creation objectives?

B. Savings
1. How much am I setting aside to create an estate?
    a. Cushion savings account. How much should I have to meet a three- to six-month loss of income?
    b. Investment savings account.
    c. Life insurance investment.
    d. Other investments.
    e. Do I have a systematic, enforced savings program?
    f. How much can I save in five, ten, fifteen, twenty years? How much would it be worth at 4%, compounded?

C. Personal Insurance
1. How much insurance do I need to make up my family's income deficit?
2. How much can I invest each year in insurance? Am I using tax-sheltered methods of financing the premiums?

3. Are the policies owned and payable so as to minimize taxes and maximize use of the proceeds?
4. Who are the beneficiaries: the estate, spouse, children, parents, charity; a trust in behalf of spouse, children, parents, charity; the trustees under my will?
5. Are the death payments to be made in a lump sum or according to what option? In what installments and during what period?
6. Has my insurance been integrated with my will and the rest of my estate?
7. When did I see my insurance underwriter last? Has he given me a complete written audit and analysis of my insurance portfolio?

D. Employment

What opportunities do I have for creating or increasing my estate through my employment or business?

1. *The Employed Executive*
   a. Pension, profit sharing, stock options, thrift plans.
   b. Group life, disability, medical and surgical and split-dollar insurance.
   c. Deferred compensation, salary continuation, bonuses, and deferred bonuses.
   d. How can I bargain for position, salary, capital gains returns, or any fringe benefits not now available to me?

2. *The Professional*
   a. Fringe benefits from unincorporated associations, professional corporations, corporation owning professional building, etc.
   b. Self-employed retirement act, tax-exempt organization annuities, forfeitable plans.
   c. Can I take part of the deal instead of a fee?
   d. If I have partners, have arrangements been made to cover the sale of a partner's interest at the disability, retirement, or death of a partner?

3. *The Business Owner*
   a. Am I using the best forms of doing business—individual ownership, partnership, or corporate forms—in order to obtain maximum tax advantages?
   b. Can I obtain corporate fringe benefits as a stockholder-executive (see Employed Executive)?

    c.   Should I use Subchapter-S treatment?

    d.   Should I sell the business or an interest in it, reorganize stock, merge, etc., to obtain capital gains advantages?

    e.   Have I arranged proper disposition of my business or shares in case of sale of an interest, or the disability, retirement, or death of a partner?

E. Investments

   1. Have I looked at my investment portfolio critically?

   2. How much cash value do I have in my insurance policies?

   3. Have I established a proper ratio between my fixed return and equity investments?

   4. Should I have tax-free bonds?

   5. Am I getting the most mileage from capital gains treatment?

   6. Am I looking at my investment program on the basis of long-term objectives?

   7. Have I looked into the feasibility of an outside or a second business?

   8. Have I examined the possibilities for real estate investment: undeveloped land, income-producing property, syndicates, investment trusts, corporations, etc.?

ESTATE TRANSFER AND CONSERVATION OBJECTIVES

A. My Family

Have I assessed the character, abilities, and needs of my family and each of its members?

   1. *My Spouse*

    a.   Is my spouse my primary beneficiary?

    b.   What is his or her life expectancy? How long will my spouse need support?

    c.   Does my spouse have the ability to manage and invest property?

    d.   How can I prepare my spouse during my life for the management and investment of property?

    e.   If property were left to my spouse outright, could he or she maintain it intact for their own use by resisting the demands made by children and relatives?

    f.   Should property be left to my spouse outright or in trust?

   2. *My Children*

    a.   What is the educational status of each child?

    b. Have I supplied sufficient funds to assure that each child can complete his education?

    c. Does one child require special consideration because of disability or handicap or, on the other hand, because of special educational requirements?

    d. Should boys be treated differently from girls?

    e. If they are adults, have they had experience in the management and investment of property?

    f. Are they stable and reliable?

    g. Should property be left to them outright or in trust? If in trust, should distribution of principal from the trust be made to them when they reach certain ages, or for certain types of events, or should it be kept in trust for life?

B. Conservation

    1. *Taxation*

        a. Am I using available tax-shelter opportunities to reduce the combined total family income tax during my life and after my death?

            (1) Would lifetime gifts of income-producing property to members of my family or to trusts in their behalf spread income and take advantage of lower tax brackets?

            (2) Am I using multiple trusts, living and testamentary, to receive the proceeds of my estate, such as insurance policies, qualified retirement plans, deferred compensation, etc., so as to reduce my family's combined income tax after my death?

        b. Am I using available tax-shelter opportunities to reduce estate and inheritance taxes?

            (1) Do I know how much the estate taxes and administration costs on my estate will be? Have I had my attorney do a hypothetical administration (dry run) of my estate to determine these costs?

            (2) Are the transfer patterns of the estates of both my wife and myself integrated so as to incur minimum transfer taxes and administration expenses in both?

            (3) Should I make lifetime transfers of property in order to reduce the size of my taxable estate?

            (4) Am I using the maximum marital deduction? Should I?

(5) Will there be double taxation on some part of my property, both in my estate and in my spouse's estate?

(6) Should I save estate taxes on my spouse's estate if he or she survives me, by setting up a "wasting" marital deduction trust in my will?

(7) Should I use the charitable deduction to reduce estate taxes?

2. *Liquidity*

    a. Have I calculated the amount of cash that will be needed to pay estate taxes, expenses, and debts?

    b. Will there be sufficient liquid assets, life insurance to pay for these items?

    c. If not, what steps shall I take to provide the necessary cash?

        (1) Shall I rearrange my investments to make them more liquid?

        (2) Do I need more life insurance?

        (3) Can I get money out of the surplus of my business through a tax-free redemption of stock?

    d. Will my estate have to be paid within nine months or within ten years of my death?

3. *Management*

    a. When was the last time I discussed my estate and my objectives with an attorney, accountant, life insurance advisor, trust or bank officer, and investment counselor?

    b. Have we carried out the plans we made?

    c. Have I ever had a conference of all my advisors to work out an integrated, overall estate plan?

    d. Should my investments be managed by a trust or an investment management organization?

    e. Have I arranged for efficient management of my estate after my death?

        (1) Have I appointed executors and trustees who have both a personal interest in my family's welfare and the experience to do an efficient job of investment and management?

        (2) Have I considered the use of a corporate fiduciary?

        (3) Should members of my family be named as executors and trustees? If so, who?

        (4) Should the investment duties and the discretion to

distribute income and principal be placed in the hands of different fiduciaries?

(5) Does the guardian I have named for my minor children have skill and experience in financial matters?

(6) Have I arranged for substitute or successor fiduciaries?

(7) Have I given my executors and trustees broad powers to handle any changing requirements of my estate and my family? If I have a business, do they have the power to continue it?

C. Charitable Contributions

1. Do I have charitable objectives?

2. Should I make charitable contributions during my life or at my death? Or both?

3. Would a charitable foundation help me achieve charitable, family, and business objectives?

4. Would life insurance further my charitable objectives?

5. How can I obtain maximum income and estate tax benefits in my charitable program? Can I have the advantages of both?

D. Business Interests

1. Shall my business interests be continued or sold at my death or retirement?

2. If they are to be continued, who will continue their management? What training does successor management need? What incentives must be offered? Will there be sufficient cash and working capital available to the business? Will the family's income be assured?

3. If they are to be sold, who will buy them? Is there a buy-sell or stock-redemption arrangement? Are the funds available to finance such an arrangement? Are there key people in the business who can purchase an interest? Should the transfer be made now, through an outright sale or by a public issue of stock?

E. My Will

(All the following questions apply equally to spouse's will.)

- When was my will executed?
- When was it last reviewed by me? By my attorney?
- Have any changes occurred in my business or family situation which would require changes in the will provisions?
- Have I made an inventory of property that will pass under my will?

- Have I made an inventory of property that will pass at my death outside of my will?
- Have I integrated the transference of both of these types of property with my will so that my objectives will be achieved?
- Does my will use available opportunities to reduce my estate taxes and administrative expenses?
- Does my will use available opportunities to reduce income taxes for my beneficiaries after my death?
- Does my will take advantage of the maximum marital deduction?
- If my spouse has property of his or her own, should I use the maximum marital deduction?
- Does my will provide for distribution of my property, either outright or in trust, in such a way as to meet the specific needs of each of my beneficiaries?
- Does my will have a common disaster clause?
- Have I provided a guardian for minor children?
- Have I exercised any powers of appointment that I may have? Do I want to?
- Have I provided that adopted children or descendants shall inherit in the same way as natural-born ones?
- Have I provided that estate and inheritance taxes shall be paid out of the residuary estate and shall not be apportioned among any beneficiaries? Do I want to?

OUTLINE OF MY WILL

My will was executed on (date)

My will was prepared by (attorney)

It provides the following distribution of my property:

A. Specific Bequests

1. Personal property to:

   Name   Property Description

2. Money Bequests to:

   Name   Amount

3. Charitable Bequests to:

   Name   Amount

    4. Business Interests or Other Property to:
       Name   Property Description

B. Residence and Real Estate Devised to:
       Name   Property Description

C. Distribution of the Rest
    1. To My Spouse
        a. If outright, how much and what property?
        b. If in trust, how much and what property?
           (1) If one trust, what are the provisions dealing with the distribution of income and principal during her life and after her death?
           (2) If there is a second trust for her, describe its income and principal distributions during her life and after her death.
    2. To My Children
        a. If outright, how much and what property goes to each?
        b. If in trust, how much and what property is set up in trust for each?
        Describe its income and principal distributions during each beneficiary's life and after his death.
    3. To Others
        a. Describe how much and what property each will get, and the way it will be distributed (outright or in trust).

I have appointed the following fiduciaries:

Executors

Successor Executors

Trustees

Successor Trustees

Guardians of Minor Children

Successor Guardians

INDEX

A.M. Best Company, 203
Accountants, functions of, 363
Accumulation phase, 138, 139
Accumulation trusts, 253–254
Actuarial tables, 33
Adjusted basis of asset, 122–123
Alternate minimum tax (AMT), 85
American Medical Association (AMA), 174
Annual gift exclusion, 42, 215, 217–220, 285–286
Annuitization (payout) phase, 139
Asset management programs, 148
Attorneys, functions of, 362–363

Bequests, 304
Bill and Melinda Gates Foundation, 309
Bonuses, 82–83, 96
Breakpoints, 137
Brokerage houses, 146–147
Brokers, 147, 163
Business ownership, 326–347
  economic cushions, 334–335

family enterprise, 328–334, 337
going public, 343
lifetime transfers, 339–343
part ownership, 329, 332–333
sole proprietorship, 108, 328, 333–334
taxation and, 335–337
valuation of business, 344–347
Buy-sell agreement, 338–339, 346
Bypass (credit shelter) trusts, 243, 245

Cafeteria plans, 68
Capital gains tax, 26, 229, 231–232
  basis of, 122–124
Cash-and-carry bonuses, 82
Cash value of life insurance, 30–34, 36, 39, 42, 67, 145, 185
Cattle, 135
C corporation, 102, 108, 109, 188
Certificates of deposit, 126, 299
Charitable annuity trusts, 316–317
Charitable giving, 209, 281–282, 309–325
  defined, 311

Charitable giving (*cont.*)
  gifts in kind, 313–314
  lifetime giving, 312–319
  present gifts of future interests,
    315–317
  private foundations, 309, 317–319,
    322–323
  through insurance, 323–324
  timing of, 312
  trusts, 316–317, 319–322
Charitable lead trusts, 321–322
Charitable pools, 317
Charitable remainder trusts, 319–321, 342
Charitable unitrusts, 317
Closed end investment companies (*see*
  Unit investment trusts)
Cofiduciaries, 352
Collateral assignment plans, 94, 95
College tuition
  Section 529 plans (qualified tuition
    programs) and, 142–144, 234, 254
  tax-favored ways of funding, 144–145
Commercial annuity contracts, 138–139
Commercial banks, 127
Common stock, 133–134
Compensation, 45–46 (*see also* Employee
  benefit package)
  of fiduciaries, 358–359
Compound interest table, 374–375
Condominiums, 155–156
Constructive receipt problem, 83
Constructive sales, 126
Consumer debt, growth of, 8
Consumer Price Index, 214, 218
Contingent deferred sales charge, 137
Contingent insurance trust, 259
Convertible preferred stock, 133
Cooperative apartments, 154–155
Corporate bonds, 131
Corporate fiduciaries, 351, 355–356
Corporate scandals, 64, 82
Cost of living, 9–10
Coverdell Education Savings Accounts, 144
Cradle to grave careers, 46
Credit unions, 127
Cromwell, William Nelson, 311
Curtesy, 302

Debenture bonds, 131
Default
  causes of, 14
  defined, 13–14
Deferred bonuses, 83
Deferred compensation plans, 12,
  90–95, 177
Deferred fixed annuities, 138
Deferred variable annuities, 139
Defined benefit plans, 53–56, 103, 113
Defined contribution plans, 103, 113
Determination, estate planning and, 17,
  20, 23
Devises, 304
Disability, 16, 151, 164–173
  G.I. insurance, 168
  group disability income insurance,
    69–70, 172
  group health insurance, 169
  group long term disability plans,
    169–170
  individual insurance, 171–172
  pension plans, 170
  profit-sharing plans, 170
  self-employment retirement plans, 170
  sickness disability, 167
  Social Security disability benefits, 167
  veterans' benefits, 167–168
  workers' compensation, 166–167
Disability waiver, 36, 37
Disinherit, freedom to, 303
Distributable estate, 292–298
Diversification, of investments, 120,
  134–135, 138, 407
Double indemnity rider, 36
Double jobs, 8
Double taxation, 108–112
Dower, 302
Dulles, John Foster, 311
Durable power of attorney, 242, 285

Economic Growth and Tax Relief
  Reconciliation Act (EGTRRA) of
  2001, 71, 77, 209, 214–216, 246,
  248, 322, 337
Economic Recovery Tax Act of 1981,
  214, 280

Employee benefit package, 46–78, 296, 297
  defined benefit pension plans, 53–56
  employee stock ownership plans (ESOPs), 64–65, 339
  401(k) plans, 50, 51, 56–58
  401(k) safe harbor plans, 61–62
  403(b) plans, 58–59
  group disability income insurance, 69–70
  group life insurance, 66–67
  group medical, health, and accident insurance, 67–69
  IRAs (*see* IRAs [individual retirement accounts])
  nonqualified deferred compensation, 65–66
  profit sharing, 48–53
  Section 457 plans, 58, 59–60
  SIMPLE IRAs, 62–63
  SIMPLE 401(k) plans, 61, 62
  simplified pension plans (SEP), 63–64
  thrift savings plans, 60–61
Employee stock ownership plans (ESOPs), 64–65, 339
Endorsement plans, 94, 95
Endowment insurance, 180, 255
Energy costs, 9
Equity REITs, 161
Estate conservation and transference, 207–212
  beneficiaries, 210–211, 300–303
  businesses (*see* Business ownership)
  charitable giving (*see* Charitable giving)
  erosion, problem of, 208–209
  estate managers (*see* Estate management)
  gift tax (*see* Gift tax)
  lifetime giving and (*see* Lifetime giving)
  objectives, 209–212, 429–433
  trial run, 291–308
  trusts (*see* Trusts)
  wills (*see* Wills)
Estate creation (*see* Estate planning)
Estate management, 209, 348–359

  cofiduciaries, 352
  compensation of fiduciaries, 358–359
  corporate fiduciaries, 351, 355–356
  executors, 349–350
  family members as fiduciaries, 354
  guardians, 351
  individual fiduciaries, 353–354
  powers of fiduciaries, 356–358
  successor fiduciaries, 352–353
  trustees, 350–351
Estate planning (*see also* Estate conservation and transference; Estate management)
  ability and, 23
  checklist, 425–429
  classic, 12
  default and, 13–14
  defined, 15, 209
  determination and, 17, 20, 23
  disability and (*see* Disability)
  do-it-yourself, 360–362
  estate analysis schedules, 386–397
  fringe benefits and (*see* Fringe benefits)
  getting started, 15–22
  intergenerational planning and, 235–237
  investments (*see* Investments)
  life insurance and (*see* Life insurance)
  long-term care (*see* Long-term care)
  objectives of, 15–19, 398–399, 427–429
  occupations and (*see* Business ownership; Employee benefit package; Fringe benefits; Self-employment)
  opportunity and, 23
  professional help, 362–366
  retirement and (*see* Retirement)
  taxes and (*see* Estate tax; Gift tax; Taxation)
  time and, 23
  worksheets, 21, 22, 165–166, 174, 212, 282, 298, 375–385
Estate tax, 12, 26, 35, 209, 275–290
  adjusted basis of asset, 123
  business ownership and, 335–337
  charitable deduction, 281–282

Estate tax (*cont.*)
  in different states, 181
  do-it-yourself plans, 361
  expenses and debts, 279–280
  gross estate, 276–279, 283
  irrevocable trusts and, 247–249,
      254–256
  joint ownership of property and, 222
  last-minute deathbed strategies,
      286–287
  life insurance and, 41–42
  lifetime giving and, 228–229
  marital deduction, 207–208, 280–281,
      283–284, 287–289, 361–362
  state, 276
  step-up basis rule, 124, 126
  stock options and, 88
  tax planning, 282–290
  unified system, 213, 214–216, 243,
      282–285, 368–371
  wasting trust arrangement, 287–288
Estate transference (*see* Estate
      conservation and transference)
Executive fringe benefits (*see* Fringe
      benefits)
Executor/executrix, 271
  functions of, 349–350

Family attribution rules, 340
Family education, 211
Family enterprise, 328–334, 337
Family limited partnerships, 285, 342–343
Family members, as fiduciaries, 354
Fannie Maes, 162
Federal Deposit Insurance Corporation
      (FDIC), 126
Federal Reserve Bank, 127
Federal Savings and Loan Insurance
      Corporation (FSLIC), 126
Feudal laws, 302, 303
Fiduciaries (*see* Estate management)
Fifth dividend option, 39
Financial aid, 145
Financial security
  dilemma of, 9–12
  examples of, 4–7
  statistics of, 7–9

Fitch IBCA, Duff & Phelps, Inc., 203
Fixed amount option, 37
Fixed period option, 37
Flexible-spending plans, 68
Ford family, 322–323
Foundation charitable giving, 309,
      317–319, 322–323
401(k) plans, 50, 51, 56–58, 77, 106, 128
401(k) safe harbor plans, 61–62
403(b) plans, 58–59, 105
412(i) plans, 55
Freddie Macs, 162
Freedom of disposition, 301–303
Fringe benefits, 12, 13, 46–47, 79–98
      (*see also* Employee benefit package)
  bonuses, 82–83, 96
  deferred compensation plans, 90–95
  goals of executive and, 80–81
  key person life insurance, 26, 92–93
  long-term care insurance, 97–98
  phantom stock, 90
  restricted endorsement benefit
      arrangements, 96–97
  restricted sale stock plans, 89–90
  split dollar life insurance, 93–95
  stock options, 83–88
  stock warrants, 88–89
Futures contracts, 125

G.I. insurance, 168
Gates, Bill, 309
Gates, Melinda, 309
General obligation municipal bonds, 129
Generation-skipping transfers, 235,
      245–249, 279
George, Henry, 150
Gifts in kind, 313–314
Gift splitting, 218, 220
Gift tax, 123, 209, 213–223 (*see also*
      Lifetime giving)
  annual exclusion, 42, 215, 217–220,
      285–286
  application of, 217
  filing, 219
  gift splitting, 218, 220
  joint ownership of property and,
      221–222

pre-1977, 214, 219
state, 223
unified system and, 213, 214–216, 368–370
value of gift, 217
Ginny Maes, 162
Golden handcuff executive benefits, 46, 66
Grantor Retained Annuity Trusts (GRATs), 251
Grantor Retained Unitrusts (GRUTs), 252
Gross estate, 276–279, 283
Group disability income insurance, 69–70, 172
Group health insurance, 67–69, 169
Group life insurance, 66–67
Group long term disability plans, 169–170
Growth, of investments, 120, 408, 412
Guardianship of children, 264, 267, 349, 351

Hazlitt, William, 14
Health insurance, 67–69, 169 (*see also* Disability; Long-term care)
Health Insurance Portability and Accountability Act (HIPAA) of 1996, 190
Health Spending Accounts (HSAs), 68–69
High deductible health plans, 68
Home equity loans, 39
Home health care, 194–196
Home ownership (*see* Real estate)
Hope Scholarship Credits, 143, 144
HR10 plans (*see* Keogh plans)

Immediate annuities, 139–140, 178–179, 186
Improved real estate, 157
Incentive stock options (ISOs), 85–86
Incentive trusts, 261
Incidents of ownership, 41
Income tax, 12, 209, 276, 289
charitable giving and, 312–313
in different states, 181

investments and, 122
irrevocable trusts and, 247, 254–256
life insurance and, 41
lifetime giving and, 228
private (family) annuities and, 232–233
tables, 367–368
Indemnification, 24–25
Independent businesspersons (*see* Self-employment)
Individual disability insurance, 171–172
Individual retirement accounts (*see* IRAs)
Inflation, 9, 139
gift and estate taxes and, 214, 218
hedge, 120–121, 408
long-term care and, 197
pensions and, 54–55
Inheritance tax (*see* Estate tax)
Installment sales, 231–232
Insurability protection rider, 36–37
Insurance (*see* Disability; Life insurance; Long-term care)
Interest, 8
compound interest table, 374–375
taxation and, 122
Interest option, 37, 38
Internal Revenue Code, Section 162 of, 96
Intestacy, laws of, 264–269, 274
Investment advisors, 148
functions of, 364–365
Investments, 117–149, 180 (*see also* College tuition)
advice and assistance, 145–149
asset management programs, 148
balanced portfolio, 403–410
brokerage houses, 146–147
brokers, 147
checklist of, 410–424
commercial annuity contracts, 138–139
corporate bonds, 131
diversification of, 120, 134–135, 138, 403, 407
estate planning principles of, 119–121
guidelines for, 399–402
for high tax brackets, 135–136
investment advisors, 148, 364–365
market letters and security reports, 146

investments (*cont.*)
  municipal bonds, 129–130
  mutual funds, 136–138, 140–142
  objectives of, 117–118
  online trading, 147–148
  payroll savings plans, 127–129
  real estate (*see* Real estate)
  safety of, 120, 406–407
  savings accounts, 126–127
  Section 529 plans (qualified tuition
    programs), 142–144, 234, 254
  stocks, 132–135
  surplus capital as basis for, 118–119
  taxation and, 121–126, 409–410
  trust departments, 148–149
  types of, 126–140
  unit investment trusts, 136
Investor risk profile questionnaires,
  141
Investor's Business Daily, 140
IRAs (individual retirement accounts),
  50–51, 70–78
  beneficiary accounts, 74–75
  early withdrawal penalties, 72–73
  multiple, 74
  rollover, 53, 58, 59, 64, 77–76, 178
  ROTH, 75–76
  SEP, 73, 74, 77
  SIMPLE, 62–63, 73–75, 77, 115
  spousal, 72
  traditional, 71–72, 75–77
Irrevocable trusts, 247–253
  life insurance, 26, 254–256

Jobs and Growth Tax Relief
    Reconciliation Act (JGTRRA) of
    2003, 108, 124, 134, 231
Job security, 3, 5
Jobs (*see* Business ownership; Employee
    benefit package; Fringe benefits;
    Self-employment)
Joint and survivor annuity payout
    option, 179
Joint ownership of property
  taxation and, 221–222
  wills and, 295
Joint wills, 273–274

Keogh plans, 103–105, 113–114
Kerr, Robert S., 207
Key person life insurance policy, 26,
    92–93
Kiddie tax rules, 125
Kintner, Arthur R., 101, 102

Life expectancy, 20, 29, 33, 34, 164,
    183, 226
  tables, 371–373
Life income option, 37
Life insurance, 16, 23–44, 151
  beneficiaries, 297
  cash value, 30–34, 36, 39, 42, 67,
    145, 185
  charitable gifts through, 323–324
  defined benefit pension plans and,
    55–56
  determining amount of, 43–44
  dividends, 38–39
  do-it-yourself plans, 361
  estate tax and, 41–42
  functions of underwriters, 363–364
  as funding device, 24, 25–26
  funding through profit-sharing plan,
    52
  group, 66–67
  income tax and, 41
  indemnification and, 24–25
  as investment, 24, 27–28
  key person policy, 26, 92–93
  life settlements, 185
  modes of settlement and options,
    37–38
  premiums, 39–41
  riders, 35–37
  split dollar, 93–95
  trusts, 38, 254–258
  types of, 28–35
  uses of, 24–28
  viatical settlements, 185
  waiver of premium, 172
Lifetime giving, 209, 213–216,
    224–237, 283 (*see also* Trusts)
  charitable giving, 312–319
  economic side of, 227–229
  generation-skipping transfers, 235

gifts to minors, 233–234
intergenerational planning and, 234–237
personal side of, 224–227
types of gifts, 229–233
Lifetime Learning Credits, 143, 144
Lifetime transfers of business, 339–343
Limited liabilities companies (LLCs), 102, 108
Limited liabilities partnerships (LLPs), 102
Limited payment life insurance, 33
Lincoln, Abraham, 274
Living trusts (*see* Trusts)
Long-term care, 13, 182–204
    definition of need and type of care, 192–193
    eligibility for benefits, 199
    as executive benefit, 97–98, 188
    insurance coverage of costs of care, 187–189
    insurance quotes, 201–203
    Medicaid and, 186–187, 190
    need for insurance, 183
    Non-Tax or Tax-Qualified Policies, 191–192
    paying for, 184–186
    payment of benefits, 200
    policy benefits, 194–200
    types of policies, 193–194
Lump sum payout, 37

Marital deduction, 207–208, 280–281, 283–284, 287–289, 361–362
Marketability, of investments, 120, 409
Market discount bonds, 125
Market letters and security reports, 146
Master limited partnerships, 162
Materialism, 10
Median family income, rise in, 8, 9
Medicaid, 186–187, 190, 193
Medicare, 183
Medicare Prescription & Modernization Act of 2003, 68
Medicare Supplemental policy (Medigap), 183, 186
Microsoft, 309

Modified endowment contract, 32, 34
Money market accounts, 126
Moody's Investor Service, Inc., 146, 203
Moral obligation or agency municipal bonds, 129
Mortgage-backed securities, 162
Mortgage debt, 8
Mortgage insurance, 25
Mortgage REITs, 161
Municipal bonds, 129–130
Mutual funds, 136–138
    selection of, 140–142
Mutual savings banks, 127
Mutual wills, 273–274

National Association of Insurance Commissioners, 204
National Association of Real Estate Investment Trusts (NAREIT), 161
National Association of Securities Dealers, 146
National Service Life Insurance policies, 168
New York Stock Exchange, 146
Nonqualified annuities, 138
Nonqualified deferred compensation, 65–66
Nonqualified stock options, 86–87
Normal Retirement Age (NRA), 176
Nursing home care, 194, 195

Occupations (*see* Business ownership; Employee benefit package; Fringe benefits; Self-employment)
Oil and gas wells, 135
Online trading, 147–148
Open end investment companies (*see* Mutual funds)
Ordinary whole life insurance, 30–31, 33

Paid-up life insurance, 33
Participating preferred stock, 133
Partnership agreement, 338
Partnerships, 108, 158
Part ownership of business, 329, 332–333

Passbook savings, 126
Payroll savings plans, 127–129
Pension maximization, 54
Pension plans, 12, 52, 177
    defined benefit, 53–56
    disability income provisions, 170
Period certain annuity payout option, 179
Phantom stock, 90
Pouring over, 258, 307
Powers of appointment, 249–250, 258, 278, 283, 297–298
Preferred stock, 132–133
Premium-only plans, 68
Present gifts of future interests, 315–317
Private (family) annuities, 232–233, 342
Probate estate, 293, 294, 296
Procrastination, 18
Professionals (*see* Self-employment)
Profit sharing, 12, 48–53, 77
    disability income provisions, 170
Pure deferred compensation plans, 91

Qualified annuities, 138
Qualified dividend income, 124
Qualified Personal Residence Trusts (QPRTs), 252–253
Qualified profit sharing plans, 48–49, 52
Qualified Terminable Interest Property Trusts (QTIPs), 244–245, 281

Real estate, 16, 150–163
    brokers, 163
    condominiums, 155–156
    cooperative apartments, 154–155
    corporations, 159–160
    improved, 157
    individual home ownership, 153–154
    liquidity problem, 151, 160
    master limited partnerships, 162
    mortgage-backed securities, 162
    ownership versus rental, 152
    partnerships, 158
    Real Estate Investment Trust (REITs), 160–161
    syndicates, 158–159
    unimproved, 156–157

Real Estate Investment Trust (REITs), 160–161
Residence, change of, 180–181
Residue, 304
Restricted bonuses, 83
Restricted endorsement benefit arrangements, 96–97
Restricted sale stock plans, 89–90
Retirement, 173–181
    annuity, 33–34
    change of residence, 180–181
    financial planning, 174
    income policy, 34
    personal investments, 180
    personal planning, 173–174
    sources of income, 175–180
Revenue municipal bonds, 129
Revenue Reconciliation Act of 1993, 125
Reverse mortgages, 184–185
Revocable life insurance trusts, 256–258
Revocable living trusts, 241–244, 263
Rollover IRAs, 53, 58, 59, 64, 77–76, 178
ROTH IRAs, 75–76

Safe deposit boxes, 295
Safety, of investments, 120, 406–407
Salary continuation plans, 91
Sarbanes-Oxley Act of 2002, 94–95
Savings accounts, 12, 16, 126–127, 151
Savings and loan accounts, 126
Savings and loan associations, 127
S corporation, 102, 108, 110, 111
Second-to-die (survivor) life insurance, 35
Section 125 Cafeteria Plan, 68
Section 303 redemption, 335–336
Section 457 plans, 58, 59–60, 77
Section 529 plans (qualified tuition programs), 142–144, 234, 254
Sector mutual funds, 141–142
Security (*see* Financial security)
Self-employed Individuals Tax Retirement Act of 1962 (Keogh Act), 103
Self-employment, 99–116
    avenues to security, 101–107

Keogh plans, 103–105, 113–114
retirement plans, 170, 178
SIMPLE IRAs, 115
Simplified Employee Pension Plan
(SEP), 114–115
taking a piece of the deal, 106–107
taxes, 64
tax-exempt institutions, 105–106
SEP IRAs, 73, 74, 77
Series E and EE bonds, 128–129, 145,
234
Series H and HH bonds, 128–129
Series I bonds, 128–129
*Shopper's Guide to Long-Term Care
Insurance, A* (National Association
of Insurance Commissioners), 204
Short against the box transaction, 125–126
Sickness disability, 167
SIMPLE 401(k) plans, 61, 62
SIMPLE (Savings Incentive Match Plan
for Employees) IRAs, 62–63,
73–75, 77, 115
Simplified Employee Pension Plans
(SEP), 63–64, 114–115
Single Premium Immediate Annuity,
139–140
Single premium life insurance, 34–35
Small Business Job Protection Act of
1996, 110
Social Security, 175–177
disability benefits, 167
Sole proprietorship, 108, 328, 333–334
Spendthrift clause, 37
Spendthrift trusts, 260
Split-dollar financing, 40–41
Split dollar life insurance, 93–95
Sprinkling trusts, 261, 289
Standard & Poor's, 146, 203
Step-up basis rule, 124, 126
Stock bonuses, 82–83
Stock options, 83–88
Stocks, 132–135, 295
Stock warrants, 88–89
Straddles, 125
Subchapter S corporations, 108,
110–111, 116
Succession tax (*see* Estate tax)

Successor fiduciaries, 352–353
Supplemental Executive Retirement
Programs (SERPs), 94
Surplus capital, as basis for investments,
118–119
Surrender charge, 138
Syndicates, real estate, 158–159

Taxation, 11–13
bonds and, 129–132
bonuses and, 82–83
business ownership and, 335–337
capital gains, 26, 122–124, 229,
231–232
charitable giving and, 310–322
college tuition plans, 144–145
deferred compensation plans and, 91,
92, 95–96
distributable estate and, 293
double taxation, 108–112
estate tax (*see* Estate tax)
401(k) plans and, 57
403(b) plans and, 58
gift tax (*see* Gift tax)
income tax (*see* Income tax)
investments and, 121–126, 409–410
IRAs and, 51, 72, 74–78
Keogh plans and, 103, 104
kiddie tax rules, 125
payroll savings plans and, 128
pension plans and, 54
phantom stock and, 90
profit-sharing plans and, 48–52
real estate and, 153–154, 157
restricted sale stock plans and, 89
split dollar life insurance and, 94
stock options and, 85–87
stock warrants and, 88–89
unincorporated associations and,
101–102
valuation of business and, 344–347
wills and, 264, 269
Tax Equity and Fiscal Responsibility Act
of 1982, 100
Tax-exempt institutions, 105–106
Taxpayer Relief Act of 1997, 143, 219, 337
Tax Reform Act of 1976, 135, 213, 245

Tax Reform Act of 1986, 234, 245
Term life insurance, 28–30, 66–67
Testamentary trusts, 240, 245, 257,
    305–307
Thrift savings plans, 60–61
Throwback rule, 253–254
Timber, 135–136
Timeline, of investments, 120
Traditional IRAs, 71–72, 75–77
Transfer for value rule, 41
Trustees, functions of, 350–351
Trust officers, functions of, 364–365
Trusts, 209, 232–235, 238–262,
    280–281, 295, 297
  accumulation, 253–254
  charitable, 316–317, 319–322
  generation-skipping transfers,
    245–249
  Grantor Retained Annuity Trusts
    (GRATs), 251
  with grantor retained interests, 250–253
  Grantor Retained Unitrusts (GRUTs),
    252
  incentive, 261
  irrevocable, 247–253
  life insurance, 38, 254–258
  pouring over, 258, 307
  protection of beneficiaries, 259–261
  Qualified Personal Residence Trusts
    (QPRTs), 252–253
  Qualified Terminable Interest Property
    Trusts (QTIPs), 244–245, 281
  revocable living trust agreement,
    241–244
  smaller estates and, 258–259
  spendthrift, 260
  sprinkling, 261, 289
  state laws and, 241
  testamentary, 240, 245, 257, 305–307

Unified tax credit, 213, 214–216, 243,
    282–285, 368–371

Uniform Transfer to Minors Acts,
    144–145, 218, 234
Unimproved real estate, 156–157
Unincorporated associations, 101–102
United States government life insurance
    policies, 168
United States government securities
    (Treasury bills, notes, and bonds),
    128–131, 222, 295, 299
Unit investment trusts, 136
Universal life insurance, 32–33
Unlimited marital deduction, 42
Unqualified profit sharing plans, 48, 49

Valuation of business, 344–347
Variable universal life insurance, 32–33
Veterans Administration, 168
Veterans' benefits, 167–168

Waiver of premium riders, 36, 37, 197
Wash sales, 125
Wasting trust arrangement, 287–288
Weiss Research, Inc., 203
Whole life insurance, 30, 179
  with supplemental term life, 35
Wills, 263–274
  administration expenses, 267, 270
  beneficiaries, choice of, 269–270
  distributable estate, 292–298
  do-it-yourself, 361
  establishing liquidity, 298–299
  freedom of disposition, 301–303
  intestacy, laws of, 264–269, 274
  joint and mutual, 273–274
  joint property and, 272–273
  sample, 433–434
  up-to-date, 207–208
  women and, 271–272
Workers' compensation, 166–167
Worksheets, estate planning, 21, 22,
    165–166, 174, 212, 282, 298,
    375–385